JOHN DONNE AND THE
NEW PHILOSOPHY

JOHN DONNE AND THE

NEW PHILOSOPHY

By CHARLES MONROE COFFIN

ASSOCIATE PROFESSOR OF ENGLISH
KENYON COLLEGE

THE HUMANITIES PRESS
New York 1958

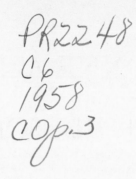
First Published 1937
Copyright 1958 by
THE HUMANITIES PRESS, Inc.

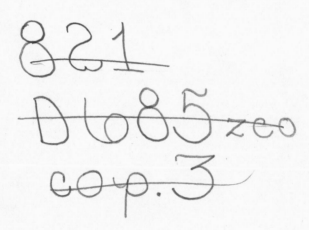
Printed in U.S.A. by
NOBLE OFFSET PRINTERS, INC.
NEW YORK 3, N. Y.

TO MY FATHER AND MOTHER

CHARLES JEROME AND MARGARET COFFIN

PREFACE

THIS work, though undertaken as an "academic exercise," marks the fulfillment of a long-standing desire to record my reaction to a poet with whose peculiar charm I was infected many years ago when I first heard the *Songs and Sonets* most fortunately read by an old teacher and friend, the late Clarence E. Andrews of Ohio State University. That my interest in Donne should have turned to the subject of his response to the "new philosophy" was dictated mainly by two facts: (1) among the numerous and worthy studies of Donne appearing in late years there was none that did more than lightly touch the subject; (2) in the exploration of Donne's familiarity with the new science, a phase of the Renaissance productive of so much significance both for Donne and for ourselves, I believed there would be found a satisfactory explanation of the compelling interest he has had for the twentieth century. In developing the subject I have tried always to subordinate the treatment of sources and of historical influences to what I considered my primary purpose, the analysis of the poetic imagination. I regret that Professor Marjorie Nicolson's brilliant essays on astronomy and literature in the seventeenth century appeared too late for me to make use of them.

Though only the author's name appears on the title page, the making of this book has required the labor of many hands, and at this time I have the gratifying pleasure of sincerely thanking those who have helped me to bring my work to completion. First, I wish to acknowledge with thanks my obligation to the Columbia University Press for its valuable criticism of my manuscript and for the care it has exercised in printing the book. To Columbia University I am deeply indebted for honoring me with a University Fellowship in 1930–31 and with the William Bayard Cutting Travelling Fellowship in 1933–34. In order for me to take advantage of these honors and the opportunities they afforded, President William Foster Peirce and the Trustees of Kenyon College, together with my colleagues in the Department of English, have given their gracious coöperation. Of my colleagues, I am especially indebted to Professor William Peters Reeves whose friendly encouragement and ripe scholarship have been an inspiration and whose valuable library has more than once come to my assistance. For the kind attention and competent service of the following libraries I am deeply grateful: The British Museum, the Bodleian, the University Library, Cambridge, Dr. Williams's Library, the Columbia University Library, the Harvard University Library, the Union Theological Seminary Library, the New York Public Library, the Ohio State University Library, and the library of Kenyon College. To those who have been closely associated with the conception and the writing of this book, I take very great pleasure in expressing my gratitude, particularly to Professors Frank Allen Patterson, Jefferson Butler Fletcher, and Harry Morgan Ayres of the Faculty of English of Columbia University. They have carefully read the manuscript and have generously shared with me their experience and scholarship in the way of inestimably valuable criticism. Of these, Professor Patterson as teacher, adviser, and friend has placed me in so great a debt that I can only hope that this work may prove of such merit as to make some part of the large recompense which is his due. I am happy to have this opportunity to express my great appreciation for the painstaking and excellent work done by Mrs. George Butler Shaffer in typing the manuscript for the printer. It remains for me to speak of my wife, the constant companion of my labor, who by her intelligent help and unselfish devotion has laid claim to so great a share of gratitude that "all measure, and all language, I should passe," were I to attempt to name its value.

Let me add that I care to keep but one thing solely unto myself— the book's imperfections.

CHARLES MONROE COFFIN

Kenyon College
Gambier, Ohio
December 10, 1936

CONTENTS

I

POETRY AND SCIENCE

BECAUSE the literary scholar does not live apart from his fellowmen, it is to be expected that his work will reflect the influence of the prevailing culture of the age in which he lives. Thus, in the nineteenth century he began the practice of a method of inquiry and criticism which acknowledged its indebtedness to the ways of thinking that had come to characterize the advancing scientific movement. More recently, however, the influence of science has passed beyond the formal methods of literary research to affect its subject matter. The scholar, sensitive to the increasingly intimate effects of science—whether for better or for worse—upon our common lives, our habits of thought and modes of expression, has discovered the existence of a great province of unexplored history—the contribution of scientific learning to both the form and the matter of much of the world's literature. In response to this new interest there have appeared such studies as Professor Curry's book on Chaucer and the medieval sciences,[1] Professor Gilbert's account of Milton's acquaintance with astronomy and geography,[2] Cumberland Clark's *Shakespeare and Science* (1913), and parts of Professor Lowes's fascinating analysis of the "shaping power" which directed the composition of *The Ancient Mariner* and *Kubla Khan*.[3] It is true that in an earlier generation Masson, in his *Life of John Milton,* included an exposition of the poet's knowledge of the sciences, followed shortly by Orchard's more specialized study,[4] and that Edward Dowden essayed to set out the relation of literature and science;[5] but these are definitely the products of a time not yet ripe for the fullest appreciation of the part that scientific learning may play in the formation of the poetic imagination.

[1] W. C. Curry, *Chaucer and the Mediaeval Sciences* (Oxford, 1926).

[2] Allan H. Gilbert, *A Geographical Dictionary of Milton,* "Cornell Studies in English," Vol. IV (New Haven, 1919); "Milton's Text Book of Astronomy," *Publications of the Modern Language Association,* XXXVIII (1923), 297-307; "The Outside Shell of Milton's World," *Studies in Philology,* XX (1923), 444-47.

[3] John Livingston Lowes, *The Road to Xanadu* (Boston and New York, 1927).

[4] Thomas N. Orchard, *The Astronomy of Paradise Lost* (London, 1896). This work was revised in 1913 under the title *Milton's Astronomy of Paradise Lost.*

[5] "The Scientific Movement in Literature," *Studies in Literature, 1789-1877* (5th ed.; London, 1889), pp. 85-121.

Not every writer invites criticism by the student whose interests
are focused upon the subject of the interrelations of art and science;
but among those whose works particularly call for analysis on the principle of this relation is John Donne. Donne's interest in scientific
learning, both of the Middle Ages and of the Renaissance, has long
been known. In 1899 Edmund Gosse called attention to the poet's
familiarity with some of the important scientific writings of the Renaissance, but went no further into the matter than to attribute falsely a
quotation in *Ignatius his Conclave* to Kepler's *Dissertatio cum Nuncio
Sidereo*,[6] and to make the generalization that "whatever was new and
strong and mysterious had an instant welcome from the intellect of
Donne." [7]

After Gosse and the editorial work of his contemporaries Charles
Eliot Norton [8] and E. K. Chambers [9] interest in Donne became temporarily dormant. When it awakened again, primarily under the stimulus
of Professor Grierson's edition of the *Poems* in 1912,[10] it awakened
with a scholarly zeal and enthusiasm that have seldom attended the
revival of any poet. From that time the interest has continued to the
present hour. Whether this popularity should cause apprehension for
Donne's future need hardly raise in us the fears that seem to beset
T. S. Eliot's critical mind.[11] Neither can we be greatly disturbed by
the veritable canonization Donne has been accorded by a group of
ardent worshippers nor by the fact that the title of one of the latest
books in his honor, *A Garland for John Donne*, suggests a tribute

[6] *The Life and Letters of John Donne* (New York, 1899), I, 257. Gosse is here
guilty of two errors: (1) he ascribes Donne's quotation from Kepler's *De Stella in
Cygno* (1606) to Kepler's *Dissertatio cum Nuncio Sidereo* (1610), which he dates
1611; (2) he states that "if the reader pushes on to the last few pages of *Ignatius
his Conclave* he will be rewarded . . . by nothing less than a quotation from the
Sidereus Nuncius [of Galileo] itself." Mrs. Evelyn M. Simpson corrected the first
error in her book, *A Study of the Prose Works of John Donne* (Oxford, 1924),
p. 180. The quotation from Galileo's *Sidereus Nuncius*, with which the reader is to
be "rewarded," does not exist; in fact, Gosse makes no attempt to point it out.

[7] *Ibid.*, p. 258.

[8] *The Poems of John Donne; from the text of the edition of 1633 revised by
James Russell Lowell . . . with a preface, an introduction, and notes by Charles
Eliot Norton* (New York, The Grolier Club, 1895).

[9] *The Poems of John Donne* (London, 1896). "The Muses' Library."

[10] *The Poems of John Donne, edited from the old editions and numerous manuscripts with introductions & commentary by Herbert J. C. Grierson* (Oxford, 1912).
This text is hereafter referred to as *Grierson*.

[11] In "Donne in Our Time," *A Garland for John Donne*, ed. Theodore Spencer
(Cambridge, Mass., 1931), Mr. Eliot writes: ". . . I know that by 1926, when I
gave some lectures on Donne, the subject was already popular, almost topical; and
I know that by 1931 the subject has been so fully treated that there appears to me
to be no possible justification of turning my lectures into a book."—p. 4.

rather to the dead than to the "re-inanimated" dust of a tercentenary idol.[12] The thing of importance is that in our own generation we have established Donne as a great English worthy. What the future may do with him lies with it, not with ourselves. In any event, we shall have left for posterity a fuller record of the poet's life and art than any earlier time thought fit to provide.

Though it is unnecessary here to enumerate the critical books and articles that have been written on Donne since 1912, it is necessary to call attention to the fact that Donne's knowledge of science and his indebtedness to that learning have not been fully treated. Professor Grierson appreciated the significance of the subject thoroughly enough to remark that "no other poet of the seventeenth century known to me shows the same sensitiveness to the consequences of the new discoveries of traveller, astronomer, physiologist and physician as Donne."[13] But standing between the critic and Donne's sensitivity to both the old and the new science of his day was the more obvious bulk of his great theological learning; thus, the first conception of Donne emerging from the recent scholarship was that of the poet and preacher whose mind and imagination were shaped largely by medieval scholasticism. At least, this is the impression that one gets from Miss Mary Paton Ramsay's book, Les Doctrines médiévales chez Donne (1917), in which even when writing the chapter "Des 'Sciences,'" she does not take advantage of the names of Galileo, Kepler, and William Gilbert to confirm by way of easy contrast her thesis that l'attitude de Donne envers les sciences est médiévale.[14] Mrs. Evelyn M. Simpson in A Study of the Prose Works of John Donne (1924), gives a more discriminating account of Donne's thought and its constituent elements; but in making too much of Miss Ramsay's shadowy mysticism she fails to emphasize sufficiently what she clearly saw, that as a result of the influence upon Donne of the beginnings of modern science, "the break-up of a whole system of thought, is reflected in his pages."[15]

Gradually Donne the man of his own time has been produced, as

[12] See note 11, above. Particularly distinguished, however, are the essays by Mrs. Evelyn M. Simpson, "Donne's 'Paradoxes and Problems,'" pp. 21-49, and by Mr. John Sparrow, "The Date of Donne's Travels," pp. 121-51.

[13] Grierson, II, 189.

[14] Ibid., p. 336.

[15] Ibid., pp. 56-57. A very valuable chapter in the history of Donne's thought, which should be considered in connection with Miss Ramsay's and Mrs. Simpson's books, is Professor Louis I. Bredvold's, "The Religious Thought of Donne in Relation to Medieval and Later Traditions," in Studies in Shakespeare, Milton, and Donne, "University of Michigan Publications, Language and Literature," I (New York and London, 1925), 190-232.

the result not of scholarly caprice but of the accumulating knowledge about him and of the closer reading of his works. Nor is it an unwarranted enthusiasm that has effected this result. Rather we have discovered in Donne something answering to the needs of the present mind. We may dismiss the idea that he is read because he perplexes "the minds of the fair sex with the speculations of philosophy," [16] or compels by the force of his scholastic quiddities. He represents the effort of the late Renaissance mind to make an adjustment to its world of changing values without sacrificing its regard for the equal claims of emotion and reason. His works sincerely express a great human experience compounded of passion and deep thinking. This experience embraces the diversities of love that can play with the "tangles of Neaera's hair" as well as "touch infinity at points," and learning that includes as easy an acquaintance with the doctrines of the Thomists and the Scotists as with the geography of the "new-found-land" and the satellites of Jupiter. Though made up of many parts, this experience is regarded by an eye that sees all the parts as interdependent and related—absorbed into the paradoxical unity of life. Thus, in considering any one of its elements, we must necessarily be aware of all; but for the purposes of clarity and emphasis we may legitimately focus our attention upon that particular one which our scientific age has given us eyes to look at. Furthermore, by working inward from the many points on the circumference of his imagination at which Donne's scientific learning touched, we may get nearer the true center of his personality so that we can appreciate the response he made to all life. "Science," it is true, "is only one of the things which colour the glass through which the writer looks at life"; [17] yet, it alone will suffice to color the vision of the whole, and what is said of science, may be said of any other great learning or experience. It is imperative to realize that Donne does not look at life through any one glass at a time; his personality is prism-like, breaking up into a spectral pattern and diffusing over all else that he thinks and feels the light that flows into him from any one great experience of mind or body.

Before proceeding specifically to Donne it is desirable to give some attention to the way in which science may affect poetry. Admittedly, the ends and methods of science and poetry are different. Though both seek truth, scientific truth and poetical truth, as Aristotle early pointed

[16] John Dryden, "A Discourse concerning the Original and Progress of Satire," in *Essays of John Dryden*, ed. W. P. Ker (Oxford, 1926), II, 19.

[17] John Middleton Murry, "Literature and Science," in *Pencillings, Little Essays in Literature* (London, 1923), p. 61.

out, are not identical.[18] "Poetry is not a metrical version of the facts of medicine, physics, or history." [19] For the man of science truth is a description of the physical world in quantitative terms; for the poet it remains something as baffling as the question put by a jesting Pilate, or as indefinable as Conrad's "strange and melancholy illusion, evolved half-consciously like all our illusions, which I suspect only to be visions of remote unattainable truth, seen dimly," [20] yet something that the poet most certainly regards as real. Again, in method the difference between science and poetry is just as obvious. Through careful observation and experiment attended by critical measurement and comparison the scientist arrives at generalizations, which after patient testing may be handed over to us as laws. The poet, though he may observe the world about him, does not apply the yardstick; he rather looks within himself and without and translates what he sees into the music of words, the verbal patterns of imagined reality. The scientist boasts of his detachment and objectivity toward all matter; the poet, though he may pretend to be as disinterested as Joyce's artist, remaining "like the God of the creation . . . within or behind or beyond or above his handiwork, invisible, refined out of existence, indifferent, paring his fingernails," [21] has, nevertheless, beguiled us with an illusion of objectivity. In brief, both poetry and science are ways of life and attitudes toward the universe; but whereas science can only describe the forms of existing things, poetry attempts to say something about the very nature of reality.

Different, however, as science and poetry are, the wise man acknowledges the validity of both. Nor can the vulgar opinions that science destroys the wonder and beauty of life and that poetry fosters a kind of magic inimical to scientific truth obliterate the fact that science has contributed richly to poetry. On Helicon, with her sisters of the sacred well, dwelt Urania, the guardian of all knowledge of astronomy, the most important science of antiquity. Her inspiration lifted the poet's theme above the affairs of men and the facts of earth to embrace the greater world of the wheeling stars and the solar sphere. He who will follow the course of the poetic imagination throughout the centuries will find upon both the master and the novice in the poet's craft the impress of scientific learning. It is to be seen in Lucretius, wandering

[18] *Theory of Poetry and Fine Art with a Critical Text and a Translation of The Poetics by S. H. Butcher* (London, 1895), p. 207.
[19] *Ibid.*, p. 207.
[20] *Lord Jim*, "The Modern Library" (New York, 1931), p. 323.
[21] *A Portrait of the Artist as a Young Man*, "The Modern Library" (New York, 1928), p. 252.

"afield" touching "with sweet honey of the Muse" his conception of the atomic universe, drawn

> From regions where the Muses never yet
> Have garlanded the temples of a man.[22]

It is to be seen in Chaucer's knowledge of the stars and tides and in his portrait of the "doctour" bulging with the lore of "Old Ypocras," "Galien," and "Avicen," and other worthies of the pantheon of ancient medicine; [23] in Marlowe's colloquy of Faustus and Mephistopheles in which the former is "answered" on the secrets of the celestial world; [24] and in Addison's translation of "Newtonian law" into a hymn of praise to the divine Creator.[25] More recent times have revealed it in Tennyson's fear that "the stars . . . blindly run"; [26] in Thomas Hardy's stubborn exposure of the veneer of optimism laid upon the Victorian mind by a shallow conception of evolutionary theory; and, it may be added, it is implicit in the background of the imagination that conceived *The Wasteland*.

Though it is evident that science may contribute something to poetry, the conditions of the contribution call for definition. There is a common ground existing between poetry and science; and that ground is not in some promised land of make-believe or theory lying beyond our reach. It is rather in the world of fact itself. Here the word "fact" is understood to cover all things as concrete as stars, and trees, and butterflies; as intangible as atoms, electricity, and the invisible process of the chemistry of growth; and as elusive as those manifestations in matter of the abstract properties of instinct, thought, and feeling. In short, all nature is the province of science as well as of art, and in so far as the face of nature is constantly being changed under the scrutiny of the man of science, the materials of the poet are being kneaded into new shapes for his imagination to work upon.

It is true that the poet need not go to the scientist for his description of nature, that he may follow the promptings of his own sentient being and depend upon his own imagination entirely, even if he is led to ambiguity and to open contradiction of physical fact in the larger benefits of truth that is felt on the pulse rather than seen with the eye.

---

[22] *Of the Nature of Things*, trans. William Ellery Leonard, "Everyman's Library" (1922), I, 35, ll. 33-34.

[23] "Prologue" to *The Canterbury Tales*, ed. W. W. Skeat, ll. 411-44. On Chaucer's astrological and astronomical learning, see Curry, *op. cit.*, especially pp. 91-194.

[24] *The Tragical History of Doctor Faustus*, sc. vi.

[25] [*Divine Ode*], 1712.

[26] *In Memoriam*, III, 5.

It is a dull and stubborn mind that delights in pointing out that the miracle of Satan's flight from hell to earth violates the law of gravitation, that a paradox so bewildering as "Before Abraham was, I am" is a senseless contradiction of chronology; or that would find fault with the poet for writing

> The hornéd Moon, with one bright star
> Within the nether tip,

even had not Professor Lowes made clear that Coleridge knew what he was about.[27] There is no place in the poetic mind for savage literalness any more than there is a place in science for a suspicion of the validity of mathematical symbolism.

Again, in moments of exalted independence when the poet's mind is lighted with a quick intuitive gleam, he may even complain that science with its deliberate and patient method—slow and tedious compared to the immediacy of his own apprehension—seems but to throw a veil over the face of nature. Thus Shakespeare complains:

> Study is like the heaven's glorious sun,
>   That will not be deep-search'd with saucy looks;
> Small have continual plodders ever won,
>   Save base authority from others' books.
> These earthly godfathers of heaven's lights,
>   That give a name to every fixed star,
> Have no more profit of their shining nights
>   Than those that walk and wot not what they are.[28]

Justly enough the poet may frown upon the scientist who ironically abuses his power like the lecturer in the Kensington Museum who announced that "the object of his lecture would be entirely accomplished if he could convince his hearers that there was no such thing as a flower." [29] Nor will the poet be attracted by the insipid response of the woman who heard the lecture and thought that it was altogether charming and delightful to learn that flowers do not exist. It is not, however, with the fictitious warfare of science and art, waged by pseudo-scientists and sentimentalists, that we are presently concerned. Nor are we interested in salving the wounded consciences of either by pouring on the balm of reconciliation.

As the world of human experience and natural fact is the common meeting ground of both, it is to be expected that poetry may be affected

[27] *Op. cit.*, pp. 41, 179-85, 476, 477, 509, 510, 511.
[28] *Love's Labour's Lost*, I, i, 84-91.
[29] John Ruskin, *Fors Clavigera* (1871), Letter 5, paragraphs iv-vii.

by science. Above, it has been noted that as the poet's physical world is enlarged by the efforts of science, so is the material on which his imagination may exercise itself replenished and increased and his language enriched with new words and new images. There is no assurance that the fruits gathered by the poet may not be so ill-digested as to result in a sickly art. One recalls the couplets of Erasmus Darwin, telling how,

> . . . insect Loves arise on cobweb wings,
> Aim their light shafts, and point their little stings,[30]

or how,

> Soon shall thy arm, UNCONQUER'D STEAM! afar
> Drag the slow barge, or drive the rapid car.[31]

But one recalls also the glories of Shelley's earth spinning beneath its pyramid of night, Donne's "naturall world" of "quotidian things, and equidistant hence," and Chapman's reflections on the moving earth.[32]

How generously the poet has acknowledged the contribution of science in anticipation of future indebtedness is doubly emphasized by the testimony of William Wordsworth, coming as it does when least to be expected, in a time of revolt against the first century of modern science, at the end of an era in which little more than a veil of sentimentalism protected poetry against complete surrender to the influence of an "age of reason." In the *Preface to the Second Edition . . . of Lyrical Ballads,* 1800, Wordsworth wrote:

If the labours of Men of science should ever create any material revolution, direct or indirect, in our condition, and in the impressions which we habitually receive, the Poet will sleep then no more than at present; he will be ready to follow the steps of the Man of science, not only in those general indirect effects, but he will be at his side, *carrying sensation into the midst of the objects of the science itself.* [Italics mine.] The remotest discoveries of the Chemist, the Botanist, or Mineralogist, will be as proper objects of the Poet's art as any upon which it can be employed, if the time should ever come when these things shall be familiar to us, and the relations under which they are contemplated by the followers of these respective sciences shall be manifestly and palpably material to us as enjoying and suffering beings.[33]

[30] *The Loves of the Plants* (1789), I, 37-38.
[31] *The Economy of Vegetation* (1791), I, 289-91.
[32] *Bussy d'Ambois,* V, ii, 161 ff., in *The Plays and Poems of George Chapman,* ed. Thomas Marc Parrott (London, 1910), I, 62.
[33] In *The Poems of Wordsworth,* ed. Thomas Hutchinson (London, 1926), p. 939. Cf. Milton's third *Prolusion,* "Against the Scholastic Philosophy," wherein he urges his fellow students "to make at this time a tour as it were with your eyes about the whole earth as represented on the map and view the places trodden by ancient heroes,

This is not merely the poet's tribute to science; it is a statement bringing us nearer to a comprehension of the attitude that both the poet and the man of science have toward the world of fact of which we have been speaking. The poet will be at the side of the man of science, "carrying sensation into the midst of the objects of the science itself." The depth to which this goes toward the heart of the matter is disclosed in a statement made earlier in the *Preface* in which the ends of both science and poetry are set out in significant contrast:

The knowledge both of the Poet and the Man of science is pleasure; but the knowledge of the one cleaves to us as a necessary part of our existence, our natural and unalienable inheritance; the other is a personal and individual acquisition, slow to come to us, and by no habitual and direct smypathy connecting us with our fellow-beings. The Man of science seeks truth as a remote and unknown benefactor; he cherishes and loves it in his solitude: The Poet, singing a song in which all human beings join with him, rejoices in the presence of truth as our visible friend and hourly companion. *Poetry is the breath and finer spirit of all knowledge; it is the impassioned expression which is in the countenance of all Science.*[34] [Italics mine.]

At last we have a statement of what the poet can do with the scientific fact. But *what* has he really done? He comes, not with a yardstick, a chronometer, or test tube, but with a "thumb of gold" to feel the fact, and pronounce upon its value. Value, it is, that the poet bestows upon the objects of science; or better, it is the poet who sets forth these objects in such a way as to make us aware of the rich quality latent within them. But how, we may rightly inquire, is this done? By what power does the blood of kings the "multitudinous seas incarnadine"? How is the pulse quickened by the feel of "the Winds come to me from the fields of sleep"? How does man in death merge into the silence of

---

and to travel through the regions made famous by wars, by triumphs, and even by the tales of illustrious poets . . . to investigate and to observe the natures of all living creatures; from these to plunge the mind into the secret essences of stones and plants. Do not hesitate, my hearers," he continues, "to fly even up to the skies, there to behold those multiform aspects of the clouds, the massy power of the snow, and the source of those tears of early morn; next to peer into the caskets of the hail and to survey the arsenals of the thunderbolts. Nor let what Jupiter or Nature veils from you be concealed when a baleful comet ofttimes threatens a conflagration from heaven; nor let the most minute little stars be hidden from you, however many there may be scattered and straving between the two poles. Yea, follow as companion the wandering sun, and subject time itself to a reckoning and demand the order of its everlasting journey. Nay, let not your mind suffer itself to be hemmed in and bounded by the same limits as the earth, but let it wander also outside the boundaries of the world."— *The Student's Milton*, ed. Frank Allen Patterson (New York, 1933), p. 1106.

[34] *Ibid.*, p. 938.

. . . earth's diurnal course
With rocks, and stones, and trees?

In such revelations as these we know instinctively that value *does* accrue to the concrete fact, that here is to be found the "infinite variety of vivid values achieved by an organism in its proper environment," [35] and that the poet has etched the ineffable expression which plays upon the countenance of nature.

To understand just what has happened—if we may presume to understand such things—we must have some notion of what "value" is. Vague as this word may be, or however suspect its meaning when loosely employed to suggest the goodness or badness of things rather than their worth, we may assume that for the sensitive man it carries a legitimate meaning. For him it is the quality of concrete fact that is elicited by the exercise of the selective imagination upon this fact. It is the "radiance" in the sunset "felt by the artist when the esthetic image is first conceived in his imagination." "The mind in that mysterious instant Shelley likened beautifully to a fading coal." [36] It is like the wind which bloweth where it listeth, and whence it comes or whither it goes no one knows; yet, it is not because of nor in spite of the poet's knowledge of the motion of the earth, the laws of perspective, or the chemistry of the atmosphere.

Alone, unrelated, an isolated unity, if such can be thought of, though thoroughly understood as the bundle of atoms that it is, the fact is negative and without value. Unless eaten, bread remains but a baked lump of leavened dough; unless associated with the concept in the mathematician's mind, the mysterious x or y has no more the quality of a symbol than any other mark made with the crayon upon the board; and unless correlated with other sounds in a particular way that can be represented by characters written upon a score, the musical note is but the product of a definite number of vibrating currents of air. Thus, the fact requires that it be associated with something else if it is to have the property of value, whether this something else be the arbitrarily fixed medium of exchange, the postulated concept, or whether it be the trepidations of a human heart, to which the song of the nightingale becomes the symbol of the transitory loveliness of earth. Thus, in the process of evaluating facts, the fact, itself, for the artist seems to pass out of existence as a fact and to become pure symbol, the visible form of an illusion through which is mediated some

[35] Alfred North Whitehead, *Science and the Modern World* (New York, 1926), p. 286.

[36] James Joyce, *op. cit.,* p. 250.

reality—the expression, however evanescent, which is in the countenance of all measurable things. How the imagination works upon the
fact to draw out this particular quality is nicely summarized by Professor Whitehead during the course of his argument for the cultivation
of the "aesthetic apprehension." He writes:

Thus "art" . . . is any selection by which the concrete facts are so arranged
as to elicit attention to particular values which are realisable by them. For
example, the mere disposing of the human body and the eyesight so as to
get a good view of a sunset is a simple form of artistic selection. The habit
of art is the habit of enjoying vivid values.[37]

The poet, like all other artists, gives evidence of possessing an acute
appreciation of this "habit"; his creations exhibit in a high degree what
the same writer earlier describes as "concrete fact with a high light
thrown on what is relevant to its preciousness." [38] Comprehended under
this relevancy is the value of which we have been speaking, the property which a thing has or which is given to the thing by the poet of
exciting the maximum response in the whole thinking and feeling
being. It may go by such other names as artistic truth, or pleasure, or
beauty, but whatever name is given to the quality, it is to be identified
as that truth about a thing which derives from consideration of all
that is relevant to it. Of this, the scientist as scientist dare not speak;
it quite eludes quantitative description, for it does not exist in the
object itself. It is something new, the creation of the imagination that
conceives the object related significantly to its environment of form,
color, sound, thought, and emotion.

That the concrete fact which the poet endows with value is necessarily an "object of science" is, of course, absurd. Independent of
science, the poet may reach into the depths of life, touch swiftly the
chameleon-like appearance of its surface, or be gone into the airy nothingness of Xanadu and faëry. The softness of thistledown, the acrid
pungency of cider oozing from the press, the magic of a graceful attitude, or the strange irony of a child's laughter heard amidst the sordid-
ness of dirty streets—these but suggest the great area of experience which
the poet may explore with his unaided senses. But he may venture further
still with the help of the instruments of science which extend the vision,
to recover worlds from the vast confines of space, to behold the swarm-
ing minutiae of microscopic life by which we are environed, and to
enlarge the sensitivity of the ear to catch the tiny horns blowing from
an elfland of atomic silence—in short, to apprehend the great unseen
and unheard phenomena of earth and sky.

[37] *Op. cit.*, p. 287.   [38] *Ibid.*, p. 286.

Moreover, if the poet would extend his imagination to consider the place of man in the whole universe, he must needs accept the work of the man of science, for it is upon the accumulation of the labors of the scientist that a picture of the cosmic situation is based. This world picture is the organized system of facts which exhibits the fundamental relationships existing amidst the confusion of the multifarious aspects of the physical universe. It emerges as the product of patient search carried on by experimentation, analysis, and correlation for the common denominator in all observable matter which is the unifying principle running through all things. Thus, science no less than art, though for different ends, is directed toward the establishment of relationships. As Francis Bacon put it, "there is no proceeding in invention of knowledge but by similitude." [39]

Because of disagreements among scientists and philosophers and the increase of knowledge, the world picture is not a static thing, but something always in the process of being revised. The rate of revision is directly proportionate to the amount of scientific activity in any age. Thus, before the Renaissance the world pattern remained for centuries without substantial change; present-day scientific developments, however, would seem almost to make the above generalization about the scientist's search for order in the external world obsolete and naïve, for he seems to be in revolt against his historical position. At least, some are led to conclude that "such orderliness as we appear to find in the external world" is but the result of "our own passion for pigeonholes," and that "it is quite doubtful whether there are such things as laws of nature." "Every day some new physicist publishes a new volume to conceal from himself and others the fact that in his scientific capacity he has plunged the world into unreason and unreality." And further disturbance to the equanimity with which we have been inclined to accept "Newtonian order and solidity" comes in the statement of one distinguished mathematician that "the most fundamental of my intellectual beliefs" is that any notion of orderliness, coherence, or unity in the world "is rubbish" because "modern science considered as a metaphysic" presents no evidence justifying the belief in such an illusion. [40]

In studying the contribution of science to poetry it does not matter whether the world picture is a composition of orderliness, coherence, and unity, or the revelation of a universe where

[39] *Valerius Terminus*, in *Works*, ed. Spedding, Ellis, and Heath, VI (Boston, 1863), 29.
[40] Bertrand Russell, *The Scientific Outlook* (New York, 1931), pp. 95, 96, 97.

> . . . *Chaos* Umpire sits,
> And by decision more imbroiles the fray
> By which he Reigns.

In fact, as our problem concerns primarily the relation of science to poetry in the works of Donne, it is well to recognize at once that Donne was presented with a version of the world picture more chaotic than orderly. Bertrand Russell's dreary "rubbish" of the present day has the faint smell about it of some "old unhappy far-off thing" when we recall how intensely Donne appreciated

What fragmentary rubbidge this world is [41]

after the new philosophy had appeared, to destroy the unity of a system as staid and honored as our own recent law-abiding universe.

Whatever be the world picture as it comes from the hand of science, it is a lifeless thing of measured fact and formulae—a skeleton awaiting the "prophecy" of the poet to quicken the dead bones into the animated pattern of life. Under his influence it becomes the framework of human destiny; it comes to embrace the creation of the world, the beginning of life, and ranges widely over man's birth, his intercourse with his fellowmen and the world of nature about him, and even ventures upon death and the aspiration for immortality. Science does not justify this leap of the imagination; but the poet seeks no justification, for the wonder of the spectacle revealed to him makes it inevitable that his "roving eye" should pass easily from earth to heaven, that he should find within this spectacle intimations of its association with divinity. The high light of the poet's imagination thrown upon the concrete fact to disclose "what is relevant to its preciousness" is diffused in radiance over all the concrete facts or objects of science with which it is associated in the mind. But it is at this point that the great circle of the poetical imagination touches religion or, more truthfully, moves into that realm wherein is revealed the essentially religious quality of all poetry, into the realm of the metaphysical, which the man of science cannot enter, for "so doth the sense discover natural things, but darken and shut up divine." [42] According to Bertrand Russell, the "value of science as metaphysic belongs in another sphere. It belongs," he continues, "with religion and art and love, with the pursuit of the beatific vision, with the Promethean madness that leads the greatest men to strive to become gods." [43] It is definitely a value that is not scientific.

[41] *The second Anniversary*, Grierson, I, 253, l. 82.
[42] Bacon, *op. cit.*, VI, 29.
[43] *Op. cit.*, p. 98.

In making use of the scientist's world picture, a poet like Dante or Lucretius may figure forth the whole of human destiny in terms of an already accepted world scheme; or one like Milton may erect upon the framework of a tottering philosophical and scientific system an epic structure justifying the ways of God to man. On the other hand, if like Donne, the poet is apparently uninterested in giving an orderly presentation of the cosmic situation and probably unable to irradiate with his imagination the whole of the universal scheme, yet ever aware that in the very nature of things there is present the paradoxical and seemingly contradictory suggestion of the physical and the spiritual, the material and the ideal, the manifestation of both the real and the unreal, in short, if the poet is metaphysical (not one who makes poetry of a system of metaphysics), he may discover that through the association of concrete human experience with the concepts of science he is capable of suggesting just this metaphysical value of things.

The term "metaphysical" needs further definition. Here, when used to describe a poet like Donne, it means a predisposition of the poet to regard the individual fact or experience as participating in the universal. This is an attitude that takes its rise from the unified personality, which, while realizing the contradiction involved in its position, nevertheless, refuses to relax hold on the idea that the very nature of things in essence is an interpenetration of mind and matter. When cast into its most general and comprehensive terms, the metaphysical problem with which the poet is concerned, as stated above in other words, is the relation of the Many to the One. Under this relationship may be subsumed all those perplexities of the human mind such as how the spirit functions through the flesh which at the same time seems to burden its activity, how love nourished on the fragile fare of human bodies may take on the aspect of divinity, or how death seems to confound the instinct for immortality.

When the poet attempts expression of the metaphysical problem, he inevitably falls into paradox and incongruity and into the use of imagery suggesting the fundamental conflict involved in the problem itself. Yet the clash of apparently contradictory terms like the sharp stroke of steel on flint produces the momentary spark by which reality is illuminated. As an illustration of how this metaphysical quality may inhere in poetry Donne's well-known *A Valediction: of weeping* [44] may be chosen:

[44] Grierson, I, 38-39.

Let me powre forth
My teares before thy face, whil'st I stay here,
For thy face coines them, and thy stampe they beare,
And by this Mintage they are something worth,
For thus they bee
Pregnant of thee;
Fruits of much griefe they are, emblemes of more,
When a teare falls, that thou falst which it bore,
So thou and I are nothing then, when on a divers shore.

On a round ball
A workeman that hath copies by, can lay
An Europe, Afrique, and an Asia,
And quickly make that, which was nothing, *All*,
So doth each teare,
Which thee doth weare,
A globe, yea world by that impression grow,
Till thy teares mixt with mine doe overflow
This world, by waters sent from thee, my heaven dissolved so.

O more then Moone,
Draw not up seas to drowne me in thy spheare,
Weepe me not dead, in thine armes, but forbeare
To teach the sea, what it may doe too soone;
Let not the winde
Example finde,
To doe me more harme, then it purposeth;
Since thou and I sigh one anothers breath,
Who e'r sighes most, is cruellest, and hasts the others death.

In this poem Donne considers the paradoxical problem of how love, the very life tonic of the soul, can under the duress of grief threaten to annihilate the lovers on whom it has laid hold. The detailed means by which the poet exhibits this paradox in all its poignancy need not be described, but there should be noted its evolution through a series of discordant figures nicely graduated from the concrete and familiar to the general and cosmic, by which at once the poet's emotion is intensified subjectively and universalized. First, is presented the "mintage" of the raw emotional metal of the lover's tears into the coin of "something worth" by the "impression" of his sweetheart's face. Like money spent and gone irrecoverably, his falling tears are emblematic of the increasing poverty of the soul subjected to the destroying influence of grief. Next, these tears, marked by the same impression, "grow" from nothingness to all, as the blank surface of a sphere is transformed into a world by the cosmographer—only to be too, like the world, threatened by universal inundation,

. . . by waters sent from thee, my heaven dissolved so.

Finally, the intimation of general annihilation is confirmed by the analogy of tears to the great processes of nature effected by the moon and by the winds, as disclosed in the last stanza.

In the second and third stanzas of the *Valediction* may be observed the way the "objects of science" help the poet to realize the metaphysical quality which characterizes the poem. Through the association of the particular fact or experience with which the poet is concerned with the "scientific" fact there adheres to the former something of the quality implied by the latter, particularly that significance possessed by the scientific term by virtue of its relation to the larger order of things of which it is but a specific part. Moreover, in so far as the order of things to which it belongs is associated in the poet's mind with a still greater set of principles, universal in their influence and importance, even including the divine, so do the particular objects of science help to extend the meaning of the poet's experience to suggest the intermingling of the concrete and the abstract, the real and the spiritual, which is the mark of the metaphysical. Thus, by associating the lover's particular experience significantly with the cosmographer's art, the poet is able to analyze his emotion in scientific terms which are swiftly extended in his imagination to include a reflection upon the creation of the world, its vastness, and its dissolution by some heaven-sent flood—a thought provoking the recognition of a parallel to the drama being played in his own heart, wherein love elemented of grief threatens to destroy the beloved through excess of itself. Here love is made by the poet to reveal the fullness of its strange power both to create and to destroy. In "each teare, which thee doth weare" may be studied the paradoxical manifestation of the kinship it has with the changing and the changeless. As the light and giver of life, love, like the creator, moves upon the void of tears and quickly makes "that which was nothing, *All*"—but an All enveloped like the earth in the destiny of impermanence and mortality through the very fact that it is subject to the divine powers which made it. The recollection of the part heaven plays in the destiny of the world at once makes the poet aware of the higher powers to which his own little experience must answer. As the earth may easily be "dissolved" by the floods of heaven, so the seas, more vast than earth, may be drowned in the sphere of the moon to which they are daily drawn, or may be subdued even by the mysterious and unseen forces of the winds. So love, divine passion that it is, manifesting itself in the flesh, through grief which it inevitably suffers when its free expression is threatened, may destroy the lover. Donne does not resolve this paradox; he only states it and analyzes it. To resolve it would be to pretend to understand why that which seems divine is overshadowed by mortality; why the mutable and fragile may sometimes touch the unfathomable permanence of the spirit.

The symbolic quality of the scientific term drawn into the poet's figure should be noted. If the term is the product of a deduction from sense experience rather than a description of sense experience itself, such as, for instance, a figure based on the conception of the moon's influence upon the tides, the motion of the planets, or the poles of the celestial globe, it partakes of the quality of both sense and mind and appears in the poem as a symbol of some reality rather than a direct impression of reality itself. Consequently, the figure, on one level touching the concrete and on another the abstract, reinforces the poet's power to suggest just that perplexing association of felt experience (sense) and abstract reality which is his end.

The matter of science will be particularly useful to the metaphysical poet in the ways suggested above if it so happens that to this matter as it assumes the form of a world picture is attached by philosopher and theologian a definite metaphysical and spiritual value. The Ptolemaic-Aristotelian cosmology, once "Christianized" by Aquinas and brought into harmony with the Platonism of the Middle Ages, while respecting the difference between matter and spirit, presented the world as a great organization of interlocking parts. This system, wrought on the anvil of Aristotelian dialectic into a grand unity of inanimate nature, man, and God, nevertheless did not fail to appreciate the complexity of the whole and the profoundly paradoxical nature of things. As the whole may be inferred from the part, or if the part is linked in the mind to the whole, the association in a poetic figure—either congruous or incongruous—of the part with a concrete fact or human experience will communicate to the particular situation being treated by the poet the metaphysical value attributed to the whole. An illustration of the way in which a situation takes on the metaphysical value through the association in a poetic figure of an experience with a particular doctrine drawn from the medieval system is conveniently provided by the following passage from Donne's *The Extasie:*

> But O alas, so long, so farre
> Our bodies why doe wee forbeare?
> They are ours, though they are not wee, Wee are
> The intelligences, they the spheare.[45]

Here, Donne is striving to make clear the interdependence of body and soul in order to establish the idea that the complete unity of two lovers, though their souls already enjoy a oneness, is not realized until their bodies also are joined. In casting about for means to reach this end he has come upon a solution of the relation of body and soul in the above analogy of their relation to that of the sphere and its intelligence.

Under the influence of the "new philosophy" the medieval science and metaphysics began in Donne's time to suffer disintegration and decay. Their usefulness to the poet, however, as a source of language and idea, as shown by the above quotation, was not destroyed. The remarkable effectiveness with which Milton employed roughly the framework of the Ptolemaic conception of the world more than a hundred years after the Copernican "revolution" began is likewise evidence of how scientifically archaic conceptions may retain a vitality for art. This is true not because art is reactionary and science "progressive" but because there is value to the poet in the symbolic function of the facts and concepts of science independent of their literal value as descriptions of the physical world. Consequently, it is necessary for the critic to guard against the fallacy of assuming that because the poet employs the materials of some particular school of thought, he is necessarily a disciple of that school. The surface confusion apparent in Donne's facile use of imagery derived from Neoplatonism, the scholastic philosophy, Ptolemaic and Copernican astronomy, and Paracelsian and Hippocratean medicine, ought to be evidence enough that the poet's mind is not grooved to any one way of thinking. For the moment he may be Aristotelian or Copernican, as it may be; but if he is regarded consistently, it will be found that he is neither, for his purpose is not to expound a system of philosophy but to express some value that a particular experience holds for himself. Any means that leads to this end he may employ.

Again, if the poet, like Donne, happens to live in an age when the traditional scientific system is breaking down under the influence of a newly conceived description of the physical world, especial importance is attached to the contribution that science makes to his art. If he is sensitive to both the new and the old, the materials drawn from the

[45] *Ibid.,* I, 53, ll. 49-54.

former, not yet fully established, and those drawn from the latter, stripped of much of their historical connotation, are nevertheless not without their value if use is made of them as symbols. In this symbolic function they are both valid means of conferring the metaphysical quality described above upon the objects with which they are associated. Moreover, the very uncertainty surrounding the matter of the conflicting systems communicates to the elements drawn upon by the poet a sharper and more vivid sense of the paradoxical nature of the metaphysical problem.

More important than this, however, is the metaphysical problem presented by the conflict itself. The Ptolemaic-Aristotelian scheme offered a thoroughly rational synthesis of the diverse elements comprising the spheres of both material and spiritual reality. Though different levels of existence were recognized (the natural, the human, and the divine), these levels were regarded as forming a universal hierarchy, according to their respective values, graduated upward from inanimate nature to God and knit together by the influence imposed by the higher upon the lower, an influence running through all the world, described by a doctrine of form and matter which holds that "every creature, animate or inanimate, owes its existence to the actualization of less determinate matter by its supervening but inseparable form." [46] The new science, on the other hand, by applying reason critically to an acute observation of the stubborn facts of nature, arrived at conclusions well known to be inconsistent with the traditional system. The result was that reason as a way of reaching truth obviously fell under suspicion, particularly as a valid tool for the exploration of the supersensuous world. In the scholastic system, though faith is indeed above reason, it is not contrary to reason; and it was held that reason directed upon its proper objects would lead toward faith, at least would confirm the conception of the character and existence of the objects of faith. By no means could the new world be so certain of the interdependence of the two.

In anticipation of what must needs receive careful treatment further on, it is sufficient at present to make the generalization that the world heretofore regarded as a rational whole was broken down into two worlds, one of matter and the other of spirit. The former became the realm of science wherein reason and the "light of nature" operate to discover truth; the latter is the sphere of religion which reason is powerless to illuminate. Thus, the light of faith, fueled by the "word and oracles of God" [47] became the true guide of the soul. According

[46] A. Boyce Gibson, *The Philosophy of Descartes* (London, 1932), p. 7.
[47] Bacon, *Of the Advancement of Learning, in Works,* IX (Boston, 1864), 347.

to Bacon physics had become corrupted by metaphysics, superstition, and reason basking in the perversities of dialectic; and the purity of religion tainted by the "unwholesome mixture of things human and divine" from which proceed heresies and fantastical philosophy.[48] How fully the "great split" characterized the new thought is evidenced further by the way Bacon departed from Aristotle to safeguard science as well as religion by considering the subject of metaphysics as a branch of natural science rather than a study of the knowledge of ultimate reality—an inquiry "at present lying beyond the range of scientific investigation." Outside the pale of human reason is left the realm of inspired divinity for the treatment of which neither the reason nor the "stars of philosophy which have hitherto so nobly shone upon us, any longer supply their light." "According to just limitations," however, reason may be of use in religion; but, unfortunately, an account of *The Legitimate Use of Human Reason in Divine Subjects* is "among the things deficient" in our knowledge. How this deficiency could be removed he suggests but does not elaborate; but even if removed, reason could not go beyond the observation of these "just limitations" where it is necessary to follow the exhortation that it is "very meet . . . therefore that we be sober-minded, and give to faith that only which is faith's."

Thus, the poet eager for the learning that will help to illuminate the paradox enveloping all experience discovers himself in a world witnessing the decay of an old way of thinking and the struggle of a new way to establish itself. In this new world truth seems to assume a twofold aspect, one to be comprehended by reason, the other by faith. In short, it is a sundered universe anticipating a complete dualism of mind and matter such as Descartes elaborated. Yet, persisting through the vicissitudes and mutations of science and theology is his belief that in some way these sundered parts do touch one another. For him, value accrues to the physical through its associations with the divine just as the supernatural is mediated to him through the physical. He may seem to say, "we are bound to . . . believe His word though we find a reluctation in our reason," or "the more discordant therefore and incredible the Divine mystery is, the more honour is shown to God in believing it, and the nobler is the victory of faith." But actually this kind of temporizing with the miracle of the nature of things is not native to the true poetic imagination. He believes in the divine neither in spite of reason nor because of it; the fascination the world of sense

---

[48] *Novum Organum*, in *Works*, VIII (Boston, 1863), 94. For the following quotations from Bacon see *Of the Advancement of Learning* and *Novum Organum*, *passim*.

holds for him is not the result of a purely philosophical regard for it as the moving image of eternity. His faith abides in a deep conviction. Though he may be unable to say why that which he believes is true, he can find no reason why it is not true. For the expression of this inherently contradictory quality in his experience theology may come to his aid and science may come to his aid; in fact, as pointed out, science may even increase the sensitivity of his perceptions, for more closely than any other learning it concerns itself with the world which he inhabits. But should science present nature to him as a "dull affair, soundless, scentless, colourless . . . the hurrying of material, endlessly, meaninglessly," which many are helpless to deny as the "most concrete rendering of fact," [49] the value-giving faculty of the poet may carry even into this world the sensation of that puzzling richness and strangeness born of the mingling of the world of nature and the world of spirit which haunts Donne's definition of divinity as something all compacted of "love and wonder."

[49] Whitehead, *op. cit.*, pp. 80-82.

II

EARLY EDUCATIONAL INFLUENCES

THE study of how Donne's thought and art were affected by scientific learning may justifiably, for the sake of clarity and penetration, be limited in certain definite ways. First we shall consider the influence of astronomy only, because its influence goes deeper with Donne than that of any other science.[1] Moreover, in so far as astronomy in its many aspects touches cosmic problems more frequently than any other science of the Renaissance and is thus inextricably bound up with religion and philosophy, a study of its influence provides scope for a more penetrating analysis of the poet's imagination. In the second place we shall emphasize its effects upon that particular period of Donne's life when he was most actively engaged in reading the books of astronomers and mathematicians. It is then that the metaphysical quality which he is inclined to associate with experience is most strongly suggested by his scientific studies and effectively mediated through the language of science. Significantly, this period of Donne's life coincides with a time of epoch-making importance for the "new philosophy" of the Renaissance. Although this period cannot be defined precisely, it may be limited to those years between the composition of *The Progresse of the Soule,* in 1601,[2] and the time when Donne took holy orders, in 1615. These, likewise, are the years of greatest *Sturm und Drang* for Donne, the years of his greatest restlessness and of his most ardent study of the authors who were helping to remake the world.

In advance of an examination of Donne's indebtedness to the new scientific learning, it is necessary to have some clear-cut notion of what the old science, or the old philosophy, was like, and of how it came about that he should have burdened his mind with the complications of a revolutionary doctrine. As the educational process which ac-

[1] A tabulation of Donne's numerous allusions to many kinds of science contains a far greater number of references to medicine than to astronomy. In affecting his attitude toward the great philosophical problems presented by his age, his study of astronomy, however, is of much greater importance than his study of medicine. Donne's knowledge of medicine is a subject that should be investigated; to date, Miss Ramsay is the only person to have attempted it. Her treatment (wherein she rightly gives consideration to alchemy and astrology also) does little more than open the possibilities of the subject. *Op. cit.,* pp. 269-80.

[2] Grierson, I, 293-316. This fragmentary poem is dated by Donne, "16. *Augusti* 1601."

quainted him with the traditional ways of thinking appears also to have presented to him a set of conditions to which he was temperamentally indisposed, one may get a better understanding of the fundamental conflict in Donne between the old and the new—including, naturally, his shift from the Roman position to the Anglican—by taking into account the progress of his formal education prior to his admission to Thavies Inn in 1591.[3]

Meager as the specific source materials are for the study of Donne's early education—provided mainly by Walton's *Life*, published nine years after the poet's death, and by a few autobiographical statements to be found in Donne's works—an understanding of the conditions and institutions instrumental in his education may help us to set forth a more ample account. The subject naturally involves a study of the influence exerted upon him by the Jesuits, by Oxford University, and by Cambridge University.

Donne, as is well known, was born into a devout Roman Catholic family, the maternal side of which, including the Mores, the Rastells and the Heywoods, not only kept the old faith but produced men who endured death and persecution in its behalf. The oft-cited passage in the "Preface" to *Pseudo-Martyr*, declaring that "no family, (which is not of farre larger extent, and greater branches,) hath endured and suffered more in their persons and fortunes, for obeying the Teachers of Romane Doctrine, then it hath done," [4] reveals adequately the environment of Catholic loyalty in which the young Donne grew up. The Heywoods, the immediate family of Donne's mother, had fallen, meanwhile, under the influence of the Jesuits to such an extent that Mrs. Donne's own brother, Jasper Heywood, after being obliged to resign his fellowship at Oxford and to "retire to the Continent, returned to England as the head of the Jesuit mission." [5] A record of the activities of this man, leading to his imprisonment and expatriation may be found in the writings of Gosse, Miss Ramsay, and Mrs. Simpson. It is the first of these authors who conjures up the ghost of Jasper Heywood to utter upon beholding his precocious nephew the words

---

[3] After this date Donne's education was largely in his own hands. In 1594 he fell heir to his share of his father's fortune, and he was thus allowed further freedom to release his energies in the ways in which they were inclinded to flow. For an account of Donne's admission to Thavies Inn see John Sparrow, "The Date of Donne's Travels," in *A Garland for John Donne*, pp. 131-32. Mr. Sparrow's essay greatly illuminates many of the chronological problems connected with Donne's early life. See also, I. A. Shapiro, "John Donne and Lincoln's Inn," *The Times Literary Supplement*, 1930, pp. 833, 861.

[4] *An Advertisement to the Reader*, sig. ¶.

[5] Simpson, *op. cit.*, p. 15.

reported by Walton, "That this age hath brought forth another Picus Mirandula."

As Donne seems to imply that his earliest teachers were members of his own family,[6] it follows that they were not only Roman Catholics, "advised to instil into him particular Principles of the *Romish Church*," but Jesuits, or persons of strong Jesuit sympathies, who presumably would have taken it upon themselves to indoctrinate their sensitive pupil with their own ways of thinking. Miss Ramsay, recognizing the importance of this fact, has given in some detail an account of the influence of the Jesuits upon education in the late sixteenth century; but unfortunately she confines her conclusions as to their influence upon Donne to a few general remarks.

How far Donne progressed under his Jesuit tutors it is impossible to say. Gosse conjectures in a rather characteristic way that it is not improbable that as a child he was sent abroad to Malines or Louvain where his grandfather had taken up his residence.[7] If this conjecture could be confirmed, it would serve to account more definitely for the marks of scholastic influence upon Donne, and perhaps, too, for his later antagonism to the whole Jesuit system. It is certain, however, that by the time Donne went to Oxford at the age of eleven, he had been thoroughly catechized by his teachers and had come to appreciate something of the rigor of their discipline.

Broad as the educational program is as laid down by the *Ratio Studiorum* of the Society of Jesus [8] and commendable as the teachers

[6] Though not absolutely convincing, the following statement from *Pseudo-Martyr* concerning his early teachers strongly suggests that some of those persons in charge of his childhood education were members of his own family, and others very intimate associates of his family. He describes them as "persons who by nature had a power and superiority ouer my will, and others who by their learning and good life, seem'd to me iustly to claime an interest for the guiding, and rectifying of mine vnderstanding. . . ."—sig. B₂ § 4.

[7] *Op. cit.*, I, 12-13. Miss Ramsay seems to agree with this idea. *Op. cit.*, p. 40.

[8] Defined by Père Joseph Brucker as the "plan des études," which is "le code des régles communes aux establissements enseignants de la Compagnie." Of its history, he goes on to say: "Il a été rédigé d'abord sous forme provisoire, en 1584-85; puis examiné, remainé à plusieurs reprises, enfin mis à l'essai dans les provinces. Après quoi, le P. Aquaviva, en 1599, promulgua le texte qui, avec quelques modifications, est resté en usage jusqu'à nos jours. . . . le plan existait déja dans la quatrième partie des Constitutions de S. Ignace."—*La Compagnie de Jésus* (Paris, 1919), p. 442.

For a specific account of the nature and scope of the educational program of the Society in Donne's time, see *Ratio studiorum et institutiones scholasticae societatis Jesu . . . a* G. M. Pachtler S. J., in "Monumenta Germaniae paedagogica," herausgegeben von Karl Kehrbach, Band I and V (Berlin, 1886, 1887), Tomus I 'Constitutionum S. J.' (1541 ad annum 1599), cap. v, "De doctrina cui scholastici Societatis studere debent," and cap. xiv, "De libris, qui praelegendi sunt."

are for their thoroughness, both the curriculum and the pedagogical methods of the Society have as their underlying purpose, and naturally so, the advancement of the Roman Church and the papacy. In effecting the primary purpose of the Order at a time when the Church had suffered externally from the disintegrating influence of the Reformation and internally from the decay of the schools of the later Middle Ages, it became necessary, if the work of the Counter Reformation was to succeed, to appeal to authority with a renewed and intensified vigor. Consequently, the *Summa Theologica* of St. Thomas Aquinas was invoked as the stabilizing and regulating influence which was to condition all theological thinking.[9] Moreover, as the *Summa* of the "angelic doctor" had incorporated the physical system of Aristotle, and had adapted it to medieval ecclesiasticism in all matters pertaining to natural philosophy, or science, Aristotle was to be regarded as the final authority: *In Logica, et Philosophia Naturali et Morali, et Metaphysica doctrina Aristotelis sequenda est.*[10] The antiquated Aristotelian system of natural philosophy thus authorized by the Constitution and Decretals of the Order had provided the authentic description of the natural world since the thirteenth century, when the revered physical works of the master were discovered or rather reclaimed from their early medieval oblivion.

It is not surprising, then, that despite the constructive end it was intended to serve, this authoritarian attitude was unfavorable to the development of any unorthodox scientific doctrine. In fact, the professors of the Society of Jesus, as a recent Jesuit historian of the Society, Père Joseph Brucker, remarks, *n'ont pas pris une part exceptionelle à l'avancement des sciences modernes.* He reasonably explains *il faut considérer que les plus capables ont eu rarement des loisirs pour les recherches de science pure, après les tâches journalières et obligatoires avant tout, de l'enseignement et du ministère.* Père Brucker would not, however, overlook the fact that scientific study has not been neglected by the Jesuits. If their activities in this direction were not ahead, they were always *du moins au pas du progrès de l'époque,* and when members of the Society have given evidence of particular talents for the study of natural science, *ils n'y ont pas été étouffés.* But that in Donne's time the achievements of the Jesuits in science were not particularly remarkable is ironically supported by Père Brucker's list of eminent scientists of the Society from Clavius

[9] See *Decretum* XLI (Congregationum generalis, 1573), "Regulae pro delectu opinionum pro theologis," *ibid.,* pp. 79-80.

[10] *Ibid.,* p. 58, § 3.

(1555–1612) to Paul Guilden (1597–1643),[11] wherein not one truly significant name appears unless one allows Clavius, concerning whom Delambre agrees with Vieta's judgment that he was *un bon professeur qui pouvait exposer avec clarté les inventions des autres et qui était à peu près hors d'état de rien inventer lui-même.*[12]

Thus, from the very outset of his career, and it is possible to speak of the childhood training of a genius as a part of his career, Donne, a sensitive and inquiring child, was subjected to a discipline which, regardless of its theoretical value, allowed little room for the exercise of the originality with which he was naturally endowed. The elements of spirituality to which the progress of his entire life give testimony, of a love of experience of the senses, and of an ardent attachment to things of the mind, were at the beginning poured into a mold whose shape they were ill constituted to assume. Indeed, Donne's adolescent and mature years appear as an effort to reshape his life according to its most congenial pattern. What Donne might have become had he been allowed to enjoy the almost ideal growth that the young Milton enjoyed under the encouragement of a generous and sympathetic father is idle speculation; that his first approach to an understanding of the truth was made under conditions that did not permit him to work out matters entirely for himself nor allow the exercise of his own favorite habit of doubting "wisely," of which he speaks in *Satyre III,* cannot easily be denied.

Of what Donne's early training in the years before he entered the university contributed to his understanding of natural philosophy there is no way of making a close estimate. Probably they contributed nothing at all; but if he was introduced to the study of science, it was to the stock-in-trade of the Middle Ages, the account of the system of the world given by Aristotle in *De Coelo,* in *De Mundo,* and in the *Meteorologica,* or the substance of these works as adapted to the use of his Jesuit tutors by some acceptable commentator. The significant deduction to be drawn with certainty is that whatever he did learn was expounded to him by men who accepted a system which taught that truth—spiritual and physical—was necessarily the arbitrary pronouncement of authority.

Nor was the second phase of his educational experience destined, it would seem, to contribute more wisely than the first to the cultivation of a mind which, though avid for learning, had almost as great disdain for the value of books as did Descartes. If Donne was to discover the truth of things, it must be largely through an examination

[11] *Op. cit.,* pp. 487-88.   [12] *Histoire de l'astronomie moderne* (Paris, 1821), II, 47.

of himself in a free association with rich and varied experience, not through the exploration of other men's thoughts, as we shall see later. If his Jesuit instruction stimulated his interest in many kinds of learning, it likewise hemmed in the free spirit with a *sequendum est*, a condition implying that an Aquinas or an Aristotle must be the final judge, not John Donne or Almighty God. When in 1584 Donne went to Oxford with his brother, who was one year his junior, he was, if the records of the university are to be trusted, to enter upon a course of training important as a legacy of past learning, but able to do very little toward firing the enthusiasm of a spirit essentially akin to the Renaissance.

At Oxford Donne entered Hart Hall, which, under Philip Rondell, principal for half a cenutry after 1549, had assumed a fresh importance as a "refuge for adherents of the old religion." [13] Thus, residence at Hart Hall in the late sixteenth century meant for Donne little more than an extension of his early training. In addition to the Roman Catholic atmosphere enveloping this particular bit of Oxford, there must be taken into consideration a curriculum of study hardly less medieval than any that could have been devised by his previous tutors.

The course of study to be followed by a student and the pedagogical method in use when Donne arrived at Oxford were, in the main, still dictated by the Statutes of Edward VI, as revised, however, toward a greater conservatism by Elizabeth in 1564–65. Under the Edwardian Statutes for one proceeding to the bachelor's degree the materials of study were distributed as follows: first year, mathematics; second year, dialectic; third year, philosophy. "Three years more, including philosophy, astronomy, perspective and Greek qualified him for the Master's rank." At once one discovers a rather free revision and recasting of the old trivium and quadrivium of the medieval schools. Music, however, is not mentioned at all; the old stress on grammar—Latin— has been relaxed; and in advanced study, Greek enjoys a place of worthy recognition. In Elizabeth's more conservative program music was added to the curriculum for the baccalaureate degree; grammar and rhetoric were reintroduced; philosophy was omitted entirely; and the time given to arithmetic reduced in favor of dialectic which was extended to five terms. Furthermore, in the requirements for the master's degree Greek no longer had a place; philosophy, which had been withdrawn from the undergraduate curriculum, was restored here.

[13] Sir Charles Edward Mallet, *History of the University of Oxford* (London, 1924 ff.), II, 297. Cf. Anthony Wood, *Athenae Oxonienses* (London, 1813), I, 479-80; Sidney Graves Hamilton, *Hertford College* (London, 1903), pp. 20-21.

Thus, more specifically, in the three departments of philosophy, natural philosophy, moral philosophy, and metaphysics, together with geometry and astronomy, were constituted the requirements for the advanced degree. Of the authors recommended for use it is significant for our purpose to note those containing some knowledge of natural philosophy, astronomy, and related subjects. To the works of Aristotle were added the writings of Pliny and of Plato. Strabo as well as Ptolemy was counted among the authorities on mathematics. The only change effected in this direction by the Nova Statuta of Elizabeth was to allow certain alternatives: *Arithmeticam vel Boetii vel Tunstalli vel Gemmephrisii.* "Vitellio's Perspective may be allowed in Place of Euclid." [14]

Little as the Elizabethan Statutes modified the corpus of sixteenth-century learning in England, when considered as a whole they did effect a change which certainly must have exerted its influence upon all entering the university after they were instituted. For Donne, in particular, it meant prolonging the study of dialectic and suspending temporarily all formal study of the sciences, except arithmetic.[15]

Moreover, the atmosphere in which this learning was imbibed was that of strict authoritarianism. The two arms of the pedagogical system, the "lecture," "supposed to give the scholar matter for the exercises he had to perform," and the "disputation," "supposed to teach him the form in which he would be required to put his matter," [16] were wielded over the students with a rigor bound to provoke disfavor. In fact, students began to "cut" the lectures; and as they came to share less and less in the sacrosanct regard for Aristotle's dialectic, attendance at the disputations grew so slack that it was necessary in 1607 for the university to pass decrees to "reinforce it." [17]

Although no list of *quaestiones*, as the subjects for disputation were called, for scholars preparing for the bachelor's degree, seems to have been found, one may learn from the record of Elizabeth's progress to Oxford in 1566 some of the subjects with which the advanced students entertained the Queen.[18] For instance, on Tuesday, September 3,

[14] For the above discussion, see Mallet, *op. cit., passim.*
[15] Donne's writings are richly influenced by his knowledge of mathematics. For the Renaissance, the "Books of the Mathematics" included such diverse related subjects as "Arithmetic, Geometry, Musick, Astronomy, Astrology, Dialling, Measuring of Land and Timber, Gaging vessels, Navigation, and Architecture." See William London's *Catalogue of Vendible Books* (1658), cited by Foster Watson, *The Beginning of the Teaching of Modern Subjects in England* (London, 1909), p. 279.
[16] Andrew Clark, *Register of the University of Oxford,* II (Oxford, 1887), i, 8.
[17] *Ibid.,* p. 13. Cf. pp. 9-13.
[18] See *Of the Acts Done at Oxford, when the Queen's Majesty was There; so Collected and Noted by Nicholas Robinson [Lawrence Humphrey], at Oxford; now being Bishop of Bangor,* ed. Charles Plummer (Oxford, 1887).

the Royal Party assembled in Great St. Mary's, where *sedes erant hoc tempore apparatae, ad Cantábrig. Theatri similitudinem, ubi facultatem omnium Disputationes publicae fierent,* to hear debated the questions *An inferiora regantur a superioribus?* and *An Luna sit causa fluxus et refluxus?* [19] The first proposition was greeted with enthusiasm by many, and it is interesting to note that the affirmative was stanchly supported by a "Mr. Campion" [20] on whom the crown of martyrdom was to be set fifteen years later by the Roman Church, a victim of one of the cruelest ironies that crossed Elizabeth's reign.

The disputations continued through the sixteenth century, on into the seventeenth, and survived even in the nineteenth century as vestigial remains of medievalism, but as the Renaissance advanced in England this method of learning gradually lost favor.[21] Nevertheless, when Donne was in Hart Hall the logic of Aristotle, according to which the disputation was framed, still determined the character of the method whereby knowledge was wont to be dispensed. Even though we may agree with Petrarch in thinking that because Aristotle was a man he was liable to err,[22] we are inclined to prefer the value of his vast library of learning to the effect of a pedantic application of his dialectic. The appeal to abstract conceptions away from the "stubborn facts" of experience was inevitably to become an obstruction to the enrichment of knowledge of the physical world and an astringent to the soul bent upon realizing the freshness and invigoration of a personal spiritual experience. It was against this dialectical method that the humanists bent their efforts; it was through their activities that "the spirit of revolt against 'Aristotelianism' was intensified." [23] That the method of seeking the truth through disputation had degenerated to a level of pedantic futility against which the "spirit of revolt" was justified, is evidenced by the bold satire of Rabelais, and later by Bacon's thoroughgoing reproach.[24] And, at Oxford, more than fifty years before Donne entered, Juan Luis Vives had protested in his *Liber in pseudo-dialecticos* against the authority of Aristotle: "who would tolerate the painter who occupied all his life in preparing his

[19] *Ibid.,* pp. 181-82.
[20] ". . . ex Collegio D. Joannis, ubi totidiem verbis et 4 versibus has quaestiones repetisset, adjunxit rationes quasdam suae defensionis, idque non longa oratione."— *Ibid.,* p. 181.
[21] Clark, *op. cit.,* p. 22 and n. 3, p. 23.
[22] See James Bass Mullinger, *A History of the University of Cambridge* (Cambridge, 1884), I, 386.
[23] Watson, *op. cit.,* p. 213.
[24] See *The Second Book of Rabelais, Treating of the Heroic Deeds and Sayings of the Good Pantagruel,* especially v, vi, vii, and viii. See *Dr. Rawley's Life of Bacon, Works,* I (Boston, 1864), 37.

brushes and colours? Logic is a most respectable art, but what are we
to think of this cursed babel which has corrupted every branch of
knowledge?" [25] Yet, despite Vives, the "pseudo-dialectic" persisted
at Oxford, and while Donne was there, received the tribute of a
triweekly disputation at which the moderators made a speech " 'in
praise of Aristotle and true logic,' and gave each person who had
that day completed his disputation *pro forma* a copy of the Logic of
Aristotle and put around his neck *simplex caputium*, a plain hood of
black stuff." [26]

Donne did not remain at Oxford to take a degree, because, as
Walton says, he acceded to the "advice from his friends, who being
for their Religion of the Romish perswasion, were *conscionably* averse
to some parts of the Oath that is alwaies tendered at those times [of
supplicating for the degree]." In a measure, he had escaped the influence of the Jesuits by going to the university; but the environment
which greeted him still fostered the methods of the schoolmen, and
whether or not he knew it, silently fed the fires of inward dissatisfaction which were to break out once he was ready to speak for himself.

In 1586 Donne is reputed to have gone to Cambridge. The evidence
for his migration, though not authenticated by official university documents, is, nevertheless, generally accepted today.[27] That Donne left
Oxford, or declined to take a degree there because he did not care to
subscribe to the oath, is certain enough; and why he took up residence
in the sister university is a matter to cause no great perplexity. The
practice of quitting one university for another was not without precedent.
Donne was still hardly more than a child (in 1586 he was only four-
teen), and being eager for knowledge, doubtless he was, as Winstanley
picturesquely phrases it, "translated" to Cambridge "like a laborious
bee, desirous to gather from more flowers than one," where, the historian adds, "he much improved his studies." [28]

That Donne's removal from Oxford to Cambridge was considerably
more of a "translation" than is implied by the mere journey of less

[25] In Watson, *op. cit.*, pp. 212-13.
[26] Clark, *op. cit.*, p. 22.
[27] The evidence that Donne attended Cambridge is Walton's well known statement:
"About the fourteenth year of his age, he was transplanted from *Oxford* to *Cambridge;*
where, that he might receive nourishment from both Soils, he staied till his seventeenth
year." The case for Donne's residence at Cambridge as it stands today is well summarized by Sparrow, *op. cit.*, pp. 134-38. Sparrow thinks that Walton exaggerated the
length of Donne's residence at the sister university.
[28] Quoted by Gosse, *op. cit.*, I, 15.

than a hundred miles separating the two universities is borne out by the greatly different histories of the two institutions in the second half of the sixteenth century. The passage of time is very apt to becloud our conception of the places occupied by England's two great universities in the later Renaissance to such an extent that we mingle their names in the same breath without discrimination. This was the age of the Reformation, and Reformation England was clearly mirrored in the life of Oxford and of Cambridge. The former, following a more reactionary course, from even before the time of Queen Mary when it profited abundantly by the royal patronage, held the Roman doctrines in higher favor than the latter, which was developing into the very stronghold of the Protestant party.

Thus, from the annals of Cambridge drops out the issue between Catholic and Protestant, and the pages are filled instead with the fortunes of the conflict raging between the national Church and the dissenters. Puritan sympathies, strong as they were, were not allowed, however, to expand without restraint, and the chief restraining hand was that of the astute and determined Master of Trinity, Joseph Whitgift, Regius Professor of Divinity, and finally Archbishop of Canterbury. Though Whitgift by no means escaped opposition, he succeeded through rigorous discipline and shrewd administration in bringing the university substantially into the fold of "orthodoxy," with the result that Cambridge rose in national esteem as the fountainhead of Anglicanism and the accepted training camp of its clergy. The achievements of Whitgift were largely the product of his own insight and the fearless sincerity of his convictions; by virtue of the former he encouraged the statutory reforms of 1570 which virtually subjected the university to the State and made it the stronghold of ecclesiasticism; [29] by the latter he had the courage to deprive Thomas Cartwright, the Puritan leader, of his fellowship, and thus hold in check the spread of dissidence and heresy.

At Oxford the story was different, for, as the Reformation advanced, and as Mullinger says, as "Catholicism had been compelled to hide its head, not only in the Universities but throughout the realm, the Puritan section at Oxford were rewarded by a success proportionate to the less resolute and effectual resistance which the orthodox party were able to offer." [30] As a result, Oxford suffered a general demoralization

[29] W. W. Rouse Ball, *A History of Mathematics at Cambridge* (Cambridge, 1889), p. 245.

[30] *Op. cit.*, II, 283.

that greatly injured both her reputation for good learning and her national prestige. Evidence of this decline is to be found in contemporary reports of those who knew something about the university. Whitgift reporting on his official visitation to Oxford in 1589 inveighs against "the general neglect of public lectures,—the insufficient endowment of the professorial body,—the lack of proper guidance of the younger students in the prosecution of their studies—the practice of admitting unfit persons to degrees without any regard to the statutory requirements with respect to acts and exercises and terms of residence . . . and finally, the contempt for discipline exhibited by the great body of scholars." [31] A very different observer, Giordano Bruno, who visited Oxford in 1582–84, "avers that the pedantry of its schools, their ignorance and arrogance, conjoined with the rudeness of their demeanour, would have tried the patience of Job." [32] And of the year Donne left Oxford for Cambridge, Anthony Wood remarks pessimistically "that the face of the University was so much altered that there was but little to be seen of the Church of England, according to the principles and positions upon which it had been reformed." [33]

If Donne had been at Oxford at an unpropitious time, at Cambridge he was to find himself in an atmosphere both stimulating and new. The attention of Elizabeth and her ministers had for some time been diverted from the Puritans by the attempts of the Roman Catholics to reassert their influence. As a result, the polemical strife which had for so long absorbed the minds of both student and professor suffered a temporary lapse before it broke out again in 1588 upon the publication of the first of the Martin Marprelate tracts. During this temporary abatement Cambridge experienced a moment of respite from the distraction of controversy, when good learning and literature could begin to flourish and a scholar might hope to "improve his studies."

Stimulating as the new environment promised to be, it did not hold out a welcome hand to Roman Catholics; and presumably Donne was still a Catholic when he took up residence at Cambridge. At Oxford, Hart Hall was recognized as an institution favorably inclined toward Romanism; and because it had no chapel in Donne's time, a modest amount of discretion saved its members from the charge of observing papist practices. Two years later at Cambridge Donne found no similar refuge. If we are to believe the testimony of the *Douay Diaries* for the time, which report "a constant accession of students from Oxford and Cambridge, seeking liberty of conscience or freedom for their

[31] *Ibid.,* pp. 283-84.   [32] Quoted, *ibid.,* p. 284.   [33] Quoted, *ibid.,* p. 283.

persons in voluntary or forced exile,"[34] we may gather that a close watch was kept on all Catholic students. Thus, with the Anglican party securely entrenched at Cambridge against the Catholics, it is not likely that any Catholic could have escaped detection if cause for suspicion had been aroused. Concerning Donne, we may conclude that his presence at Cambridge gave no cause for suspicion. Either he conducted himself so sensibly as to be above reproach, or he no longer felt so heavily constrained by the bonds of his family Church as to find Anglicanism entirely uncongenial. It is not improbable that already in Donne was developing that dissatisfaction with his Roman background which in the course of years was to impose upon him the necessity of "surveying all Divinity" before accepting the position of the Church of England.

Though the aggressive spirit of Cambridge Puritanism had been subdued by Whitgift (who resigned his post in 1577 to accept the See of Worcester), it by no means had been destroyed. The air was charged with the potential fire of dissent. This could not have failed to impress the young Donne. Here, he found himself not necessarily involved, but, nevertheless, a fascinated spectator of a great religious epic. Authority, which had nourished him thus far, was not only tacitly questioned but openly challenged. Though the challengers were not of the Catholic faith, Donne could share their dislike for arbitrarily enforced authority. Amidst such complications Donne may have found himself kindling to the reasoned calm of the *via media;* but it is likely that at first he was stirred with a profound contempt for all factions and moved to the firm conviction that true religion was not to be confined within the doctrines of Geneva, Rome, or London.

If the Reformation had become enshrined at Cambridge more securely than at Oxford, so, too, had a more liberal conception of the matter of education. In so far as the Statutes of Elizabeth, 1570, applying alike to both universities, emphasized the study of dialectic at the expense of mathematics (which had been encouraged by the Edwardian Statutes), this statement does not hold; but as in real prac-

[34] *Ibid.,* p. 281. Cf. the letter of Dr. Allen (Dr. William Allen, fellow of Oriel College, who in 1568 opened a house at Douay for the reception of English students) to the Cardinal Protector, dated from Rheims, Sept. 12, 1583: "Though the heretics forbid anyone to come to us under pain of death, and use the greatest diligence, especially in the universities, to prevent us from obtaining men of choicer wit, still since the first of March this year, that is during six months, eighty students have come hither from the English Universities and public schools; so that in these months we have hardly ever been fewer at Rheims than 200, etc."—Introduction to the *Douay Diaries,* p. lxxi, quoted *ibid.,* n. 3.

tice the statutes were not diligently observed, particular forces for the dissipation of the old order were allowed to manifest themselves. Already, some years before Donne went to Cambridge, Francis Bacon had indicated his dissatisfaction when he condemned the dominant influence of Aristotle at the university as being "only strong for disputations and contention." [35] By Donne's time, however, the reputation of the Aristotelian dialectic was threatened by something more specific than the disaffection of an occasional student. Though doubtless Aristotle was still honored and accepted in conservative circles as the master of logic, in 1584 he was confronted by an effective rival.

Twenty years earlier there had been voiced at the College of Navarre (in Paris) one of those heresies which, though absurdly indiscreet, deserve for their very audacity and freshness eternal respect. At the College of Navarre, Pierre Rami, or Peter Ramus, sustained for a whole day against all comers his master's thesis that *Quaecumque ab Aristotele dicta essent, commentitia esse.*[36] Once the challenge had been dropped, the new conception of logic by which it was supported spread widely through the learned world, and in the course of time got a strong foothold at Cambridge. By 1584 the *Dialecta* in which was expounded the Ramist doctrine had so far ingratiated itself at Cambridge that there issued from the University Press a "modest duodecimo volume" of the work, which was "probably in the possession of every Cambridge scholar who laid claim to anything beyond the most conventional acquaintance of the subject of which it treated." [37]

At this time we are not interested in any probable influence of Ramus upon Donne; that he knew Ramus is certain from the allusion to him along with those other *haeretici,* Lullius, Gemma, Sebundus, Empiricus, Trithemius, Agrippa, and Erasmus.[38] At present we wish only to call attention to the significant fact that at Cambridge Donne would have found himself in an environment responding acutely to the growing pace of religious dissent and an environment in which some of his fellows could exultantly attack the sanctity of Aristotle to whom his earlier university had been "ever blindly loyal." [39]

[35] Dr. Rawley's *Life of Bacon, op. cit.,* p. 37.

[36] Henry Osborn Taylor, *Thought and Expression in the Sixteenth Century* (2d ed., revised; New York, 1930), I, 376. See pp. 376-83 for account of Ramus and his work.

[37] Mullinger, *op. cit.,* II, 406. Mullinger cites Temple's dedication to the Cambridge edition of the *Dialecta* (1584), as evidence that the Ramistic logic had already spread throughout Europe and had "numerous adherents in the chief universities." He adds, that before the close of the century, "it was taught and defended from nearly all the Protestant chairs of philosophy."—pp. 409-10.

[38] *Catalogus Librorum,* ed. Evelyn Mary Simpson (London, 1930), p. 28.

[39] Mullinger, *op. cit.,* II, 410.

From the history of Cambridge during these years we gather that little attention was paid to the study of the natural sciences or natural philosophy. Theology was still the queen of the curriculum and logic her handmaiden. If some industrious bachelor pushed ahead to explore a more fertile plain of culture, it was to read in the "traditional ethics, physics, or metaphysics of the time" in the manner recorded by one student: "From logicke, I proceeded to ethicks, physicks, and metaphysicks (consulting the schoolmen on such points) according to the methods of philosophy then in fashion in that university." [40] The provisions of the Elizabethan Statutes regarding the courses of study naturally applied at Cambridge as well as at Oxford; and, as indicated above, for undergraduates the only study which might be considered as a science by the Statutes of 1649, that is, mathematics, had been replaced by dialectic and grammar. It is pointed out that though the mathematics professor continued to deliver lectures, "there is no evidence that the attendance of students was in any way compulsory, and those who did attend appear to have been either sophisters or bachelors of arts." [41] Donne would have been eligible to attend these lectures; but that they could have added much to his stature is doubtful, for only the rudiments of arithmetic according to Tonstall and Cardan were expounded, and the course in geometry was confined to the definitions and axioms, and a few propositions drawn from the first book of Euclid. Closely related to mathematics, astronomy, the other subject of the quadrivium with which we are concerned, was treated in an equally unsatisfactory way. The celestial system of Ptolemy, from the Σύνταξις was expounded, and for the related subjects cosmography and geography, the *Timaeus* of Plato, and Strabo and Pliny, respectively, were supposed to provide the necessary knowledge. Walton reports that Donne at Cambridge "changed" his studies considerably, and it is in this qualification that one finds reason to assume that his eagerness for all kinds of learning together with his catholic taste prompted him to sample as many offerings of the curriculum as time and convenience permitted.

This brief account of the orthodox status of the study of natural philosophy at Cambridge does not, however, represent the whole truth about the study of science any more than would an account of Aristotle unchallenged by Ramus be faithful to the history of sixteenth-century logic. Though theological controversy wore down the energies of many of the Cambridge minds of the sixteenth century, there are

---

[40] Hearne, Langtoft, *Preface,* p. cxix, quoted, *ibid.,* p. 414, n. 3.
[41] *Ibid.,* p. 402.

on the register of the university the names of a goodly number of brilliant scholars who not only impressed their own age with their independence and originality but also contributed richly to the future history of learning. These are the men who comprise the beginning of the great tradition of scientific study at Cambridge. The intellectual environment into which Donne was thrown reflected something more than the mind of Reformation England; out of the atmosphere of Cambridge proceeded the first champions of the new science of the Renaissance. Among those before Donne's time were Robert Recorde and John Dee, both Copernicans; the former was the author of the first arithmetic and the first geometry books in English,[42] and the latter, the first translator of Euclid into English.[43] Contemporary with Dee were Thomas Blundeville and Thomas Digges. Blundeville was a great popularizer of scientific learning, whose oft-printed *Exercises* and *Theoriques*, appearing first in 1594 and 1602, respectively, were certainly known to all readers who pretended to an interest in geography and astronomy. Digges, the son of the eminent mathematician, Leonard Digges, was the first Englishman to translate Copernicus and to prepare a map of the heavens according to the new system.[44] Closer to Donne's own generation were Edward Wright, Fellow of Caius and at one time mathematical tutor to Prince Henry, and Henry Briggs, who was made Fellow of St. John's in 1588, while Donne was still at the university. After distinguishing himself at Gresham College, Briggs became the first Savilian Professor of Geometry at Oxford at the dawn of a happier day for the study of the sciences at that university.

[42] *The Grounde of Artes, Teachying the Worke a. Practise of Arithmetike* (1542). (The *Short-Title Catalogue* notes 14 editions of this work between 1542 and 1640.) *The Pathway to Knowledg, Containing the First Principles of Geometrie* (1551).

[43] *The Elements of Geometrie of the Most Auncient Philosopher Evclide of Megara. Faithfully (now first) translated into the Englishe toung by H. Billingsley, Citizen of London. Whereunto are annexed certaine Scholies, annotations, and Inventions, of the best Mathematiciens, both of time past, and in our own age. With a very fruitful Preface made by M. I. Dee, specifying the chiefe Mathematicall Scièces, what they are, and whereunto commodious* (London, 1570). Although this first English translation of Euclid is attributed to H. Billingsley, it is thought that Dee himself made the translation in whole or in part. See A. De Morgan, "Notices of English Mathematical and Astronomical Writers between the Norman Conquest and the year, 1600," *Companion to the Almanac* (1837), p. 38. Also, David Eugene Smith, *History of Mathematics* (Boston, n. d.), I, 323-24.

[44] The importance of the work of Thomas Digges was brought to my attention in the winter of 1933 by Dr. Sanford V. Larkey, who in the following spring (April, 1934), brought out in collaboration with Francis R. Johnson, the valuable monograph on Digges: *Thomas Digges, the Copernican System, and the Idea of the Infinity of the Universe in 1576*, "Huntington Library Bulletin, No. 5."

This list of names, which might be extended further, is not a roll call of the dead; it is a list of honorable and distinguished men whose minds were kindled by the Renaissance to enrich the tradition of medieval science and even to depart from that tradition in behalf of the advancement of human learning. Nor is it mere coincidence that they were nurtured by a university whose atmosphere had been the breath of the chief reformers of the Church and the most enthusiastic champions of a logic that looked away from Aristotle. If this rendering of the conditions of Cambridge in the sixteenth century be accepted, it is certain that Donne's experience there was no arid repetition of his earlier lessons. Regardless of what he studied, he could not have been blind to the sunrise of a new day, promising freshness and vitality to the human soul.

III

THE OLD ORDER

THE glorious freedom from philosophical speculation and from the necessity of setting one's own thinking against the intellectual background of one's age—even though its influence may be absorbed—is a privilege shared, perhaps, only by those who do not think at all and by those whose very genius delivers God directly into their understanding and makes of experience steadily and sensitively perceived the ultimate criterion and source of all natural and divine knowledge. Of the latter is Shakespeare, who without obligation to any system or creed can mirror most faithfully the world which he inhabits, because his glass is clear, unmarred by those speculations and entangling alliances of thought which refract and distort the image of reality. He may borrow at will from the learned books of his day without committing himself, and he may glean for his "word hoard" a multitude of figures from the language of science and philosophy to serve him in making his translation of experience into the music of love or of death—of the miracle of life itself.

On the other hand, a poet like Donne, with a quiveringly sensitive imagination, susceptible to the stimulation of both learning and physical experience, educated by the Jesuits, and in the universities where "disputation" was the accepted mode of improving the mind, could not escape the necessity of relating his thought to some world scheme, that is, of making life and the world scheme fit together in some way. Moreover, as he discovered, the world scheme enjoyed no settled and sure definition, but was a complex of warring traditions, all meeting within himself to make difficult a frank and direct acceptance of human experience.

In order to grasp the significance for Donne of his studies in philosophy and science, between which there was theoretically no breach in the time of the Renaissance, we must look particularly at the conception of the world system that emerged from his formal studies. The important books studied in the schools containing scientific material have already been noted: Aristotle, Ptolemy, the *Timaeus* of Plato, Pliny, Strabo, and in mathematics, Euclid, with perhaps Tonstall and Cardan for arithmetic. With the exception of Tonstall, Donne at one time or another mentioned all of these authors; but even if he had not,

circumference the sphere of the *Primum Mobile,* beyond which lay the pure empyrean, heaven itself, the realm of God, the first mover and the unmoved creator.[4] Surveying this ingenious contrivance from outer circumference to center, one passes through the *Primum Mobile* to the sphere of the firmament wherein the fixed stars have their places, and on through the spheres of the planets [5] to the elementary world with its spheres of fire, air, water, and earth.[6]

The whole scheme is compact, orderly, and picturesque, suggesting a toy, or one of those cleverly carved baubles of ivory made up of many balls within one another, rather than a description of the cosmos itself. [Nevertheless, artful and mechanical as it may seem to us, it was the accepted conception of the greater world, a revelation of the handiwork of the great artist, and the book wherein with the help of the interpreter might be read the story of all important things—of God and creation, of matter, and of the rôle played by the soul and body of man on the cosmic stage.] To repeat the story would be to write the history of medieval theology and philosophy; consequently, only a statement of the most important ideas directly associated with and developed from this conception of the physical system can be given here.

To begin with the stuff of which the world is made, the matter of the universe is found to be of two kinds, celestial and elemental. The celestial matter, or the fifth element, of which the heavens are composed—all of the universe above the sphere of fire—is pure and

---

place of the' one that had been sufficient for Ptolemy in representing the motion of the eighth heaven (of the fixed stars). See Delambre, *Histoire de l'astronomie du moyen âge* (Paris, 1819), p. 264. Allan Gilbert in his study of "Milton's Textbook of Astronomy," cites the testimony of Jacobus Martinus, a further commentator on Sacrobosco, that by 1608 recent observers had discovered as many as four motions in the eighth heaven. *PMLA, XXXVIII,* 1923, p. 298. The additional spheres necessary to explain these various motions had come to be known as the "crystalline heavens." In England, as early as 1556, Robert Recorde, viewing the growing complexity of the old world scheme, undertook an explanation which he was obliged to conclude by saying that the addition of more spheres is considered unnecessary and awkward by "most wise men in that arte," namely, astronomy.—*The Castle of Knowledge,* fols. 276 ff.

[4] See Aquinas, *In quatuor libros Aristotelis de coelo, et mundo commentaria* (Venice, 1562), fol. 106.

[5] Aquinas gives the number and order of the planets as follows: Saturn, Jupiter, Mars, Sun, Venus, Mercury, Moon. This is the Ptolemaic arrangement, which Aquinas accepts as against that of Aristotle, wherein the sun is immediately above the moon, and the places of Venus and Mercury reversed.—*Ibid.,* fol. 228.

[6] See Aristotle, *De Coelo* iv. v. in *op. cit.,* I, 622-23; *De Generatione* ii. i., *ibid.,* pp. 662-63.

incorruptible.[7] Being pure and incorruptible, it enjoys the form proper to such matter, that of the sphere, the figure of perfection itself. In this element, both in the highest heaven of God himself and in the heavens of the stars and planets, there is no change. Though the heavens are not subject to change, they do enjoy motion, for motion is one of the qualities of matter. It is necessary to potentiality and to actuality, the very principles of being with which matter is endowed; and through motion the eternal process of the potential realizing itself is effected. As the heavens are divine, without beginning or end, to them belongs the motion becoming to divinity, that of the circle, the motion proper also to their spherical form.

Thus, the *Primum Mobile*, on the periphery of this ingenious universe, moves under the immediate compulsion of God, and in turn imparts motion, though less rapid than its own, to all the world below it. The stars and planets move in their great circles, conformable to the motion of the particular spheres to which they are attracted. Having observed the heavenly bodies, the astronomers were able to calculate their order, their distances, and the speed of their spheres. But, here again, the calculations were a curious mixture of the facts and the metaphysical implications of the "facts." The degree of purity possessed by anything is relative to its proximity to God. Consequently, of all the heavenly spheres which have bodies, the firmament of the fixed stars, being farthest removed from the center, is most pure and contains many bodies, whereas the lower spheres have but one each. Moreover, as the rate of speed of the spheres is proportionate to their distance from the *Primum Mobile* and the center, respectively, the firmament of the fixed stars whirls faster than the spheres below it. They are not, however, to be considered more corruptible and less pure than the firmament just because they are farther removed from the divine source. All are celestial, and therefore all are pure; things removed from God who is pure actuality are only less fully actualized according to the degree of their removal. In compensation for their

---

[7] By the analysis of the kinds of motion and the bodies to which these motions are natural, Aristotle proves the existence of a fifth body or element. There are three motions: motion toward, away from, and about. As the first two are natural to the four elements, and the third not natural to any of them, there must be a fifth body to which circular motion is natural. This body is the pure, incorruptible heavens, which move circularly.—*De Coelo* i. ii., *ibid.*, pp. 552-54. Cf. Clavius on the "proprietates aetherae regionis," *op. cit.*, pp. 39-40. He speaks of a "corpus alterius cuiusdam immixtae naturae a quatuor elementis valde remotae, unde ut a quatuor elementis distingueretur. Quinta essentia est appellata."—p. 40. For a full account of other matter in this and the paragraphs immediately succeeding, see *De Coelo* ii. caps. iii. iv. viii. x. xii. and *Physica* vii. cap. i. in *op. cit.*, Vol. I.

distance and comparative simplicity the lower spheres enjoy diversity and complexity of motion.

Below the celestial world is the realm of elemental matter, composed with respect to their descending values of the spheres of the four elements, fire, air, water, and earth, the latter, least perfect of all, lying stationary at the sluggish center. If they are displaced accidentally from their respective spheres, they at once manifest their native inclination to return. Thus, fire mounts upward; air, less confined, also moves upward, though not so rapidly; and heavy objects fall that they may return to the earth. These elements are the realization of nature's fundamental potentialities, the radical essences of matter, the hot, the cold, the wet, and the dry, from which

. . . all . . . in thir pregnant causes mixt [8]

emerge the animate and inanimate orders of terrestrial things.

The myriad forms of earthly things, though constituted of the elements, are nevertheless distinct and individual entities, endowed separately with an essence which is the thing itself, although it may not superficially reveal itself to the sense. Only through the intellect, which being capable of the power of abstraction takes up the data delivered to it by the sense, is this essence to be apprehended. Thus, behind the veil of exterior qualities lies the essence, the universal in things, and the quality which is actually intelligible. An object is hot because it has within it the quality of heat; an object is smooth or rough because it possesses the quality of smoothness or roughness, qualities which are things in themselves, not determined, but determinable.[9]

The problem of essence more than any other problem provoked the battle between the new and the old philosophy, because as long as the intelligence rested in the belief that particular qualities determine the nature of things, it was quite impossible to reduce the facts of nature to quantitative measurement. It was on this point that Galileo, complaining against the medieval disposition to regard Aristotle's doctrine that "all knowledge begins with the senses," as interpreted above, revealed the inadequacy of sense experience and affirmed a distinction between the primary and secondary qualities of things.[10]

Apart from this question, to which attention will be drawn later on,

[8] *Paradise Lost*, II, l. 913. Cf. Aristotle, *De Generatione* ii. caps. i. ii. iii. in *op. cit.*, I, 663-66. Cf. Clavius, *op. cit.*, pp. 30 ff.

[9] For a recent interpretation of the Aristotelian and medieval conceptions of the doctrine of essence, see Gibson, *op. cit.*, pp. 7-8, 13-14, 77-78.

[10] See Edwin Arthur Burtt, *The Metaphysical Foundations of Modern Physical Science* (New York, 1927), pp. 73-80.

it is necessary to observe that the terrestrial world of the medieval system enjoyed no certain harmony and order. Unlike the heavens with their spheres uniformly moving according to the pattern of perfect motion, the world is subject to change, uncertainty, and corruptibility. The problem of how such a world came into being and how it is sustained, implying as it does, a consideration of the nature of God, cannot be reckoned with in a simple manner. The details, subject to the disputation of the schools, are frequently at variance. There does emerge, however, a skeleton of ideas which may serve as a working basis for the treatment of Donne's indebtedness to and departure from this system of thought.

Throughout the universe as has been described there is in operation the principle of cause.[11] For Aristotle, on whom the metaphysical implications of the system ultimately rest, cause is conceived as "form" and stands in relation to matter as the pattern stands in relation to the material. It is the very essence of phenomena, the determining quality, and in the process of action fundamental in all being, it is the actuality into which potentiality is always being converted. This process of the realization of the essence of phenomena is elaborated by Aristotle in relation to the doctrine of the four causes, or the four forms, an elaboration which need not be described here. The important thing to be noted is the idea that matter is wrought upon by a cause, an action resulting in "bringing into actuality what was somehow potentially contained in the matter on which the agent (the efficient cause) works." Thus, for Aristotle, creation (for this process of the realization of the actual from the potential may loosely be termed "creation") is an eternal process. Being and motion, its principal quality, are eternal; and, as the doctrine of causes presupposes always something for the cause to work upon, there follows the account of the creation summed up in the phrase *ex nihilo nihil fit.* But Christianity could not accept this unscriptural account with literalness. Consequently, to save the text it argued that all creation took place from nothing, that is, creation proceeded *ex nihilo,* and to preserve the conception of God's omnipotence, declared that it took place in time, not from eternity.

God, the pure actuality, is the first cause and the "unmoved mover"; to the *Primum Mobile* He imparts motion which in turn is transmitted to the entire universal system:

The Supreme Being (Actuality) imparted movement to the universe by moving the First Heaven; the movement, however, emanated from the first

[11] For discussion immediately following, see art. "Aristotle," *Catholic Encyclopaedia* (New York, 1907), I, 713-18.

IV

THE DEEPENING YEARS

IN THE first of Galileo's dialogues on the *Two Great Systems of the World*, Salviatus, the spokesman of the new philosophy, remarks:

But to give Simplicius yet fuller satisfaction, and to reclaim him, if possible, from his error, *I affirm, that we have in our age new accidents and observations*, and such, that I question not in the least, but if Aristotle were now alive, they would make him change his opinion; which may be easily collected from the manner of his discoursing.

The conversation has turned to the question of the inalterability of the heavens, and Salviatus would attempt to persuade the Peripatetics of their error by pointing out how far they violate the spirit of their master. But Aristotle was dead, as the reply of Simplicius, his apostle, revealed, for he declined the compliment that Salviatus honestly bestowed upon the father of the sciences, stubbornly preferring to hold to the cherished and timeworn notion that,

Aristotle deduceth his principal Argument a priori, shewing the necessity of the inalterability of Heaven by natural, manifest and clear principles; and then stablisheth the same a posteriori, by sense, and the traditions of the ancients.[1]

In this brief expostulation and reply is indicated the radical difference between the old world and the new world that was emerging—between the mind that determined all knowledge by what had already been said and thought and the mind that was willing to forsake the comforts of an unchanging heaven in the faith that knowledge might be increased. If science is thought of as "the process of making knowledge," [2] the faith of Galileo amounts to a belief in the idea of intellectual progress, but for him and for all the Renaissance it is an idea bright with the freshness of hope, not yet become tarnished by the sentimental optimism of a later age. The development of such an idea demanded an active participation in life itself, a critical attitude toward the knowledge of the past, and a direction of the imagination upon the discovery of new things. It is significant that the years

[1] In Thomas Salusbury, *Mathematical Collections and Translations* (London, 1661), I, 37.
[2] Charles Singer, *From Magic to Science* (London, 1928), p. 60.

of Donne's early maturity witnessed the singular assertion of these demands.

The date in Donne's life when the solvent of the new philosophy—the way of thinking demanded by the "new accidents and observations"—was first poured upon his conception of the old cosmology cannot be set with any exactness. In this, however, we are no more in the dark than in our efforts to resolve other perplexing matters concerning his life. We know when he was married, but we know, too, that in the same year his bitterest expression of contempt for woman came from his pen.[3] The notion that Anne More's coming into his life made witty sallies against the sex impossible is but a fiction to be enjoyed by those who believe in the alchemical power of marriage. It is known when Donne took holy orders, but when he made up his mind to follow this course is a matter still perplexing to the critics, and certainly the secular coloring of many of Donne's activities up to the very time of his ordination does nothing to lessen the perplexity.[4] If the chronological outlines bounding such major events of Donne's mental and spiritual life are obscure, it is not surprising to recognize a similar condition when we come to deal with his introduction to the influence of the new philosophy. Time and the shadow of incidental circumstance too readily consume the moment when ideas are born and a new day dawns for the spirit. But few can recall the time when Homer was first opened or when the Pacific, hitherto unseen, lay vast, below some peak in Darien. Moreover, there may be no moment of revelation, no experience marking the turning point. Gradually we are wont to become aware of things; and for Donne, the awakening into the new world was a movement as gradual as it was inevitable. Sooner or later his studies were to acquaint him with the new philosophy; circumstances were preparing him for its reception, and at the same time giving to the new philosophy a form in which it could be received.

One of the first conceptions of Donne that comes to the reader is that of the poet in the early satire, imprisoned in his library amidst "jolly Statesmen," "giddie fantastique Poëts," and "gathering Chroniclers" who share the "constant company" of

. . . Gods conduits, grave Divines; and . . .
Natures Secretary, the Philosopher.[5]

[3] Donne was married to Anne More in 1601, "three weeks before Christmas" (Gosse, *op. cit.*, I, 98), and *The Progresse of the Soule*, in which he releases some of his bitterest statements against women, is dated by himself, "16. *Augusti* 1601."

[4] See Gosse, *op. cit.*, ch. x, "Last Years as a Layman," II, 3-54.

[5] *Satyre I*, Grierson, I, 145, ll. 5-6. The date of *Satyre I* is somewhere around 1594. See Grierson, II, 100-3.

Already his strong taste for learning is clearly manifest. The easy familiarity with which he notes these sources of inspiration gives anticipation of the intellectual quality flavoring all his work. But of particular importance to us are the "grave Divines," and "Natures Secretary." [6] It is they who confirm the poet's interest at this time in the materials from which was formulated the old theological-philosophical system of the universe described above. Deeply scored as the products of Donne's early poetical career are by the influence of this system wherein natural philosophy or science and divinity enjoyed a mutual dependency, there is no obvious attempt made to use this learning in a systematic way. In short, Donne gives no evidence of being a disciple of any school of thinking. Among these works there is to be found no long poem like the *Nosce Teipsum* of Sir John Davies, translating philosophy into fluent verse, and none like *The Purple Island* of Phineas Fletcher, so ambitiously adapting a great store of natural learning to the elaboration of the theme that a study of the self,

> . . . like an Index briefly should impart
> The summe of all.[7]

In so far as the historical-philosophical system does affect Donne's early poems, it is, then, not as a formal guide to life but as a body of learning coerced into the service of a more particular and more personal end. This end, broadly speaking, is the fulfillment of an ambition for self-expression through a concentration upon authentic human experience in the face of circumstances and conventions tending always to thwart this realization. Consequently, throughout the work of these years there may be seen the operation of both a destructive and a constructive principle: the former acting to eliminate the taboos, artificialities, and affectations of the day which beset the free conduct of mind and body; the latter burrowing beneath these artificialities into the matrix of mental and emotional life to reveal the springs of genuine experience. To the accomplishment of this end in its double aspect, his philosophical learning lent its aid.

This learning serves in a paradoxical way as one of the causes of Donne's rebellious spirit and provides him with a medium through which this spirit can imaginatively be expressed. In so far as the old philosophy presented an accumulation of dogma and fixed concepts,

---

[6] Undoubtedly Aristotle.
[7] *The Purple Island*, canto i, stanza 43, in *The Poetical Works of Giles Fletcher and Phineas Fletcher*, ed. F. S. Boas (Cambridge, 1909), II, 21.

expressed with finality, it nourished Donne's stubborn unconventionalism, not because the system itself was necessarily suspect, but because its matter and the logical method sustaining it represented a kind of authoritarianism that made a personal search for the truth invalid. Thus, Donne strikes at the very root of its authority when he cynically reminds his mistress how thinking may be subordinated to the arbitrary ends of the will through the manipulation of the syllogism:

> Vaine lunatique, against these scapes I could
> Dispute, and conquer, if I would,
> Which I abstaine to doe,
> For by to morrow, I may thinke so too. [That is, that woman
> "Can have no way but falsehood to be true."] [8]

The strain of skepticism running through Donne could at times find support in the method of the schools. Because of the irony seeming to surround all certainties, he was inclined to "perplex security with doubt"; [9] but he could turn his skill to flattery,

> But thou which lov'st to bee
> Subtile to plague thy selfe, wilt say,
> Alas, if thou must goe, what's that to mee? [10]

in order to lay bare the irony of trusting in such subtleties, aware all the time of the movements of his own mind and of the fundamental weakness of the "wrangling schooles" of the late Middle Ages which presumed to uphold an intellectual tradition by applying a specious kind of rationalism to such flimsy questions as "what fire shall burne this world," [11] or their ingenuity to the invention of "new tenements in hell." [12] In fact, it is back to the schoolmen that the poet turns his "doubtfulnesse," his predilection for equivocation, in The Will wherein he "disproportions" his gifts to express his elegant contempt for their usefulness. [13]

In the early poems, Donne's heretical nature most strikingly exercises itself upon the theme of love. Discretion is named "that which love worst endures"; a shallow Platonism is ridiculed; ugliness is held up for compliment; Venus is made to swear "by Loves sweetest Part, Variety"; the affectation and polite deception practiced by men of

[8] Womans constancy, Grierson, I, 9, ll. 14-17.
[9] To the Countesse of Bedford. On New-yeares day, ibid., p. 200, l. 38.
[10] The Blossome, ibid., p. 60, ll. 17-19.
[11] A Feaver, ibid., p. 21, ll. 13-14.
[12] Satyre II, ibid., p. 151, l. 36.
[13] The Will, ibid., pp. 56-58.

letters are scorned as "heresy" against human nature; and the poet himself longs

> . . . to talke with some old lovers ghost,
> Who dyed before the god of Love was borne,

in order to learn the ancient secrets of love unconfined by "custom" and the pedantic "laws" in which passionless men have trapped it.

This "rebell and Atheist" who turns exultantly from the killing restraint of "late law" and custom which "shadow" and "disguise" genuine affection, to a glorification of primitive naturalism, finds the old philosophy at times a convenient vehicle for the communication of his moods. For instance, in the doctrine that angelic intermediaries between the human and divine intelligence reside in the heavenly spheres, Donne discovers a way to suggest his impatience with spiritualized affection and the essentially earth-bound nature of his passion:

> Search every spheare
> And firmament, our *Cupid* is not there:
> He's an infernal god and under ground,
> With *Pluto* dwells, where gold and fire abound:
> Men to such Gods, their sacrificing Coles
> Did not in Altars lay, but pits and holes.
> Although we see Celestial bodies move
> Above the earth, the earth we Till and love:
> So we her ayres contemplate, words and heart,
> And virtues; but we love the Centrique part.[14]

Again, in his usual manner of noting some subtle point at which his thought and the image material are tangent to one another, he forces upon the image regardless of logical meaning or traditional connotation, an interpretation that will exactly convey the significance of his thought, as when the uniform motions of the heavenly bodies are invoked to justify the principle of relativity in love and his own propensity for inconstancy:

> The heavens rejoyce in motion, why should I
> Abjure my so much lov'd variety,
> And not with many youth and love divide? [15]

In *The Sunne Rising*, elaborating a traditional theme in a traditional *aubade* pattern, figures drawn with a critical eye from the old astronomy communicate an originality to the lines excluded by the slavish invocation of the sun in the orthodox *aubade*. "Busie old foole, unruly

[14] *Elegie XVIII. Loves Progress, ibid.*, p. 117, ll. 27-36.
[15] *Elegie XVII. Variety, ibid.*, p. 113, ll. 1-3.

Sunne"—the opening address, at once indicates the poet's boisterous indifference to the conventional form and anticipates the free treatment that follows wherein the accustomed complaining tones give way to a disregard completely reversing the usual supplication to make the sun submissive to the lover's whims:

> Thy beames, so reverend, and strong
> Why shouldst thou thinke?
> I could eclipse and cloud them with a winke,
> But that I would not lose her sight so long.[16]

Here is the attitude of the humanist, not as it finds expression in the revival of antique poetic forms, but as it avows the priority of man as a living personality, not an abstract idea. To emphasize this point of view Donne makes dramatic use of the mystical union of true lovers—a conception that in so far as it affirms the depth and fineness of love does not require the support of poetic convention. Of particular importance here is the fact that Donne's escape from convention is greatly aided by imposing upon the necessary sun imagery drawn from a literary tradition, a personal interpretation based directly upon his scientific learning. Thus, not only does the familiar and impertinent address, cited above, contradict the manner of the formal *aubade*, but it also dissipates through defiant questions the respect paid by astronomer and poet alike to the greatest of the heavenly bodies. The completeness of Donne's defiance becomes apparent when a momentary reflection upon the sun's true motion,

> Must to thy motions lovers seasons run? [17]

tells him that it is but the action of a "pedantique wretch" marking off into "the rags of time," with stupid regularity, the "houres, dayes, moneths," irrelevant to the eternity of his love which "no season knowes, nor clyme." [18]

If the old philosophy could be called into use by the "rebell and Atheist" to exorcise the repressing influence of tradition, it also could be retained to strengthen the treatment of a higher theme. This theme, broadly sensed, is love as a great moving and constructive force—and, particularly regarded, is the analysis of the poet's own conception of love and the realization of self-fulfillment through love. It is here, despite the subtlety of Donne's expression, that the fundamentally human level of his interest is revealed. Though his concern is with himself, the terms into which the individual motivation and response are analyzed—ranging through all the activities of flesh and spirit—

[16] *The Sunne Rising, ibid.,* p. 11, ll. 11-14.   [17] *Ibid.,* l. 4.   [18] *Ibid.,* ll. 5, 10, 9.

are thoroughly consonant with general human truth. Man, for Donne, becomes a paradoxical combination of sense and spirit; though seemingly anchored to this world, he has faculties by which he reaches outward and upward to the divine. In the frank acknowledgment of this duality within unity he recognizes the deepest mystery of life and finds its most dramatic manifestation in love. In this experience the claims of neither flesh nor spirit are slighted. True, some poems, for example *Loves Progress* (*Elegy XVIII*) and *The Indifferent*, evidence the poet's personality operating on a level of pure naturalism; furthermore, in no poem does he try to transcend the world of sense as Spenser does in *An Hymn of Heavenlie Beautie*. Yet, he is always trying to get to some truth about man larger than that contained either in pure sensualism or in pure Platonism—a truth acknowledging that in the unified expression of both body and soul is the self fulfilled.

Through the aid of philosophy, in the manner described above, he is able to endow his poetry with that metaphysical quality implied by an attempt to analyze the intercourse of matter and spirit. In practice it means the projection of the poet's emotion upon a framework of intellectual imagery. The working out of this practice may be observed in many of the early love poems, but the actual use made of the scientific elements of the old philosophy is found to be greatly restricted. An instance may be found, however, in *A Feaver*, a dramatization of the poet's agony at the thought of his mistress's death in which the concept of the incorruptibility of the heavens is skillfully used to reveal the eternal aspect of beauty worn by the flesh:

> And yet she cannot wast by this,
> Nor long beare this torturing wrong,
> For much corruption needfull is
> To fuell such a feaver long.
> These burning fits but meteors bee,
> Whose matter in thee is soone spent.
> Thy beauty,'and all parts, which are thee,
> Are unchangeable firmament.[19]

The doctrines of the perfection of unity, of the influence of the heavenly bodies upon human destiny, of the resident intelligences of the spheres, of the disposition of man into the four elements, of the three souls (of reason, growth, and sense)—all contribute to the analysis of the complexity of love as an emotion of the flesh and a theme involving the relationship of souls and the intercourse of the human with the divine. But the climax of Donne's utilization of the

[19] *Ibid.*, p. 21, ll. 17-24.

materials of the old philosophy unquestionably is *The Extasie,* a poem standing near the zenith of his whole poetical career. Since the way this learning is mingled with his own emotionalism to give to the poem its peculiarly intense metaphysical quality has already been referred to and will be touched upon later, present elaboration may be forborne. Even though, as indicated, Donne in these early poems makes less use of the purely physical matter of the old philosophy than of the metaphysical, the familiarity with the one logically would argue a familiarity with the other were there no evidence at all that he was acquainted with the old science. But even this meager use of scientific matter becomes significant in itself when one notices how rapidly the images drawn from this source multiply after the stimulating influence of the new philosophy begins to make itself felt.

The conclusion, significant for our purpose, that may be drawn from a survey of Donne's early poems, is that his indebtedness to the old philosophy—regardless of the phase that is given particular consideration—does not amount to the adoption of its doctrines as a systematic interpretation of experience. Even in the more sustained efforts like *The Extasie* and *The Progresse of the Soule* in which obligation is laid definitely upon particular modes of thought, the poet's emotion and thought are not evoked from, but rather realized through, the philosophical patterns used. The first of these poems is more intensely human than ingeniously philosophical; and the second is not an expression of the poet's avowal of the Pythagorean doctrine of the transmigration of souls. Vague and hidden as its meaning is, we know that it is concerned with bitterness and with contempt for

Great Destiny the Commissary of God,[20]

that preserves the "deathlesse soule" with ironical indifference to the dignity of its habitation.

The freedom to treat the themes presented in his poems in his own way, unrestrained by the compulsion to follow any system of thought, does not in itself, however, affirm Donne's distrust of the old philosophy. One cannot infer from the evidence given that were he to think philosophically he would find the old order of things inadequate. Conceivably it might still be the precious refuge of the mind interested in such refuges; it might still be thought to bind heaven and earth together in a pretty cosmic unity; but in these early years the poet is hardly interested in a search for some philosophical abode for the soul, nor a way of escape from experiences still fascinating.

[20] *Ibid.,* p. 296, l. 31.

Nevertheless, his early writings do emphasize one thing—if Donne is to pursue his wonted course he must necessarily destroy the house in which some day his soul might seek its rest. His contempt for authority, his paradoxical trifling with the sacred motions of the sun, the exposure of his whole being to the full gales of experience and doctrine, and the subordination of all to the prior claims of the human self, could, except in the most stubbornly reactionary mind, lead only to the dissipation of all confidence in the traditional philosophy. Thus, though his mind may know it not, there are at work in the nerves and in the pulse forces of life capable of conditioning his modes of thought once they are set in the critical environment that will provide the test. Nor was the testing day far off for Donne.

By a bundle of circumstances—the repercussion of the influence of early years; the vicissitudes of personal fortune; and powerful aspects of the treacherously vague "climate of the age"—a sober aspect of character present in Donne from the beginning was re-emphasized to bring about in the decade following the turn of the century a significant alteration in his attitude toward the world. In his youth this serious turn of mind colored the theme of love with a gloomy fatalism, and an awareness of the transitory nature of temporal things:

> Alas, true joyes at best are *dreame* enough;
> Though you stay here you passe too fast away:
> For even at first lifes *Taper* is a snuffe.[21]

It emerged in his mockery of the ignobilities of man; but in no way did it assert itself more clearly than in the expression of a fundamentally religious temperament.

> With God, and with the Muses I conferre,[22]

he wrote, designating the two main sources of his inspiration, and confessing how his personality inclined toward the cardinal points of heaven and earth. The "muse" betokens his earthly mistress; religion is his heavenly mistress: "our Mistresse faire Religion," [23] is the object of his courtship as well as the unnamed Julias and Lauras of the *Songs and Sonets*. And for Donne, significantly, religion early in life is identified with truth.[24]

But in Donne's maturing years, coincident with the close of the

---

[21] *Elegie X. The Dreame, ibid.,* p. 95, ll. 22-24. Grierson dates this poem sometime between 1593 and 1598. See II, 62.

[22] *Satyre I, ibid.,* p. 147, l. 48.

[23] *Satyre III, ibid.,* p. 154, l. 5.

[24] Cf. "my Mistresse Truth," *Satyre IIII, ibid.,* p. 164, l. 163.

century and with the decline of the exuberance of Elizabethan England,
this reflective strain ripened—as reflection is wont to do—into a
melancholy that clung to him through the rest of his life, save when
its shadow faded before the warmth of love or friendship or was dissolved by such moments of illumination as flood *The second Anniversary*, or mark the happier periods of his priesthood. In these years
the note of inescapable destiny is heard more frequently; scorn, no
longer tempered by "kinde pitty," becomes embittered by a world
bankrupt of virtue:

> O Age of rusty iron! Some better wit
> Call it some worse name, if ought equall it;
> The iron Age *that* was, when justice was sold; now
> Injustice is sold dearer farre.[25]

And from the general picture of human depravity, to receive his most
acrid thrust, he singles out woman, the epitome of all frail things,
whose vows

> . . . are writ in water,
> And blowne away with winde.[26]

But more devastating to the stability of his mind is the growing sense
of the uselessness of a search for truth in experience and of the
vanity of human learning.[27] As his reflective nature asserts itself most
powerfully, Donne retires deeper and deeper into his own consciousness, into those "soft still walks" to "languish, prest with Melancholy," [28] where he is left to create from the emptiness of doubt and
disillusionment some conception of life not unworthy of the contemplations of a poet who still retains faith in the belief that the end of
life lies in the complete fulfillment of the sensitive human self. Since
it is with these years of transition that we are particularly concerned,
a somewhat detailed analysis of their significance for Donne will
not be amiss.

In 1596 or 1597, in a letter to some gentleman—a friend of Sir
Henry Wotton—whose acquaintance Donne wished to make, he declared that

Knowledg is as a tast wᶜʰ doth rather stir vpp appetite thē satisfy itt: and yᵗ
therefore I do infinitly desire to increase itt by oʳ acquaintance.[29]

[25] *Satyre V, ibid.*, p. 169, ll. 35-38.
[26] *Elegie XV. The Expostulation, ibid.*, p. 108, ll. 10-11.
[27] Cf. *To Mr. Rowland Woodward, ibid.*, pp. 185-86 [1604–05]. Donne speaks of
his "retirednesse," regrets that his muse dallied with his "love-song weeds" and
"Satyrique thornes," and concludes, "There is no Vertue, but Religion."
[28] *To Mr. T. W., ibid.*, p. 206, ll. 2, 7.
[29] Printed by Mrs. Simpson, *op. cit.*, p. 307.

This avidness for both learning and experience, regardless of its consequences, had dominated Donne's early life. But both, as is to be seen, were carrying him along the way to difficulty; the one was whetting his already sharpened wit, and the other was providing him with the circumstances of life whereby his increasingly responsive mind might be pricked. In short, the irony of knowing deeply and feeling acutely was overtaking his enthusiastic career. Thus, shortly after the above letter, he wrote to his friend Wotton lamenting that the times were changing from bad to worse and wondering why "then should wee much desire lyfe or her delights since we see much ill & feare more," inasmuch as the Court into which he had recently been translated as secretary to Sir Thomas Egerton had become a place where "to be in fashion is to be dishonest since poverty is dispised & hapines envyed? since vertue is not only not worne as a compleat royall garment but not as a color or a skarfe: no man desiring now to cover his vice wth her shew." [30] Donne ends the letter with a sentence of advice:

I canot therefore honestly pswade you to abandon ye Country bycause if my fortunes fitted it I should pswade y^o to stay there by my exsample. yet I desyre much sometyme to see you here & to haue y^o a litle trip though not fall nor stumble att ambition or other distractions. least I seing an honest man happy should begin for y^r sake to loue the world againe wch I would be loath to do. [31]

Moreover, to the realization of how difficult it is for an "honest man" to be happy in a world into which his own desires and inclinations have thrust him, there was added a series of personal reverses that helped to constitute a genuine crisis in his life.

The gloomy fate of Essex struck Donne to the quick. Here was brought home to him with a sickening reality the fickleness of fortune and the gross indifference of a world consumed in its own pleasures to the hero of the moment past. How soon the yesterdays are forgotten!

[The court is] full of iollyty & revells & playes and as merry as if it were not sick . . . my lo: of Essex & his trayne are no more mist here then the Aungells wch were cast downe from heaven nor (for anything I see) likelyer to retourne. he withers still in his sickness & plods on to his end in the same place where y^o left us. [32]

Essex, though in "disgrace with fortune and men's eyes" remains for

---

[30] *Ibid.*, p. 293. Mrs. Simpson says the letter "probably belongs to the period 1599–1600."—p. 294.

[31] *Ibid.*, p. 294.

[32] *Ibid.*, p. 292. In a letter probably addressed to Wotton in 1600.

his friend the gallant spirit who understands not his age out of the "naturall weaknes of innocency." [33] It was he who gave promise of new life to the declining years of Elizabeth, and tone and color to those "my Lord of *Essex* dayes" which a decade later Donne has his sullen citizen look back upon as the good old times.[34]

Another circumstance of great significance to Donne occurring in these years was his marriage. The account of his romantic conquest of Anne More with its subsequent complication is too well known by now to require repetition. Loss of position, imprisonment, the embarrassing entanglement of good friends, and the humiliation inflicted upon both husband and wife by an enraged peer—all served to shadow Donne's life with sobriety and to bring into a closer focus upon himself those thoughts and feelings which had hitherto been diffused over a wider area of experience.

Already, however, this introspective turn had seriously asserted itself. Marriage, entailing the difficulties related above, could only intensify it. In the letter cited earlier, written before Donne had married Anne More, the effects of an eagerness for experience and knowledge upon a sensitive mind are clearly presented. Experience had confirmed his native mistrust of human nature; learning had revealed the vanity of human knowledge. The combination made him suspicious of both sense and reason and encouraged his natural inclination toward gloomy meditation upon himself. In other men—in Wotton particularly—learning might strengthen virtue to fend off the evils besetting the life of the honest man at court, a life from which Donne himself would gladly have fled had he known but where to run—"so am I in this warfare enforced to fight it out bycause I know not whether to rū." [35]

Donne's wit and brilliance had won for him his appointment at court, and he undoubtedly believed at one time that the honest use of his talents would secure advancement. That he learned otherwise may be inferred from another letter possibly written to the same friend in the same year as the one previously mentioned.[36] His own studiousness and his "love of learning," he thinks, are not destined to aid in the fulfillment of his ambitions and do not hold out for him any bright promise of fashioning an armor of virtue (such as he had declared to be the product of Wotton's learning) to resist the disintegrating

[33] *Ibid.*, p. 292.
[34] *Elegie XIV. A Tale of a Citizen and His Wife*, Grierson, I, 107, ll. 39-41.
[35] Simpson, *op cit.*, p. 294.
[36] *Ibid.*, pp. 294-96.

forces at work upon his life. Such an armor, he knew, must be forged within himself.

To know how to liue by the booke is a pedantery, & to do it is a bondage. . . . And he that will liue by pᵣcept shalbe long wᵗʰout yᵉ habite of honesty: as he that would every day gather one or two feathers might become brawne wᵗʰ hard lying before he make a feather bed of his gettings.

Thus, disillusioned, he has given up his "voyaging" "in other mens works," his "swallowing," "devouring," and "pursuing" of authors, trusting rather in his native ability to assume the full responsibility for his own salvation, for, as he confesses,

I find borne in my self knowledg or apᵣhension enough for (wᵗʰout forfeiture or impeachment of modesty) I think I am bond to god thankfully to acknowledg it) to consyder him & my self . . . I find it true that after long reading I can only tell yᵒ how many leaves I haue read. I do therfore more willingly blow & keep awake yᵗ smale coole wᶜʰ god hath pleased to kindle in mee then farr off to gather a faggott of greene sticks wᶜʰ consume wᵗʰout flame or heat in a black smoother.

It is at once apparent how far Donne had traveled in the seven years between 1593 and 1600, from the day when his love of study warred with his lust for adventure, and he sadly left the comfort of "these few bookes": "Gods conduits, grave Divines"; "the Philosopher"; "jolly Statesmen"; the chroniclers; and the "giddie fantastique Poëts of each land"; to "follow headlong" the "wild uncertaine" motley humorist of the first satire.[37] Though in apparent revolt against all learning, he was a rebel who found that the best weapons of attack and defense were those used by the enemy. To consider for a moment that Donne was about to beat a romantic retreat from the city to the country, which he loathed, or to immure himself in some bookless cloister, is to mistake his very nature. The letter in which this denouncement appears was written as a diversion from reading Dante and reflecting upon the wisdom of Seneca.[38] What was happening to Donne is exactly what is apt to happen to any sensitive person, as his allusion to the fate of Pope Celestine clearly explains.[39] In books are mirrored

[37] Grierson, I, 145, ll. 1 ff.

[38] Simpson, op. cit., p. 296.

[39] Pope Celestine V, according to Mrs. Simpson's note, "was persuaded by Cardinal Gaetano that it was against his soul's health to retain the Papacy, and solemnly resigned his office, Gaetano being elected to succeed him as Boniface VIII." Mrs. Simpson also records the fact that though Dante does not mention Celestine by name, "according to the early commentators, particularly Boccaccio, he referred to Celestine in Canto iii. 59, 60 of the Inferno."—Ibid., p. 296, n. 1. Donne's comment upon Celestine, following upon the witty remark that Dante was a "man pert enough to bee beloved & to much

the movements of our own minds; and for Donne the tale of Gaetano's treachery and deceit revealed the vanity of his own aspirations and the futility of resisting the guile of the jealous courtier who would profit at the expense of innocence.

From the above concrete material the following generalizations may be drawn. In a unified personality such as Donne possessed, the love of experience and the love of learning, evidenced as the activities of the body and the mind, the sense and the reason, in search of some medium through which expression can be complete and satisfying, come to rest upon the self as this medium. It is both the experiencing subject and the proper object of knowledge. This development does not, however, necessitate the denial of the stimulating quality of the external world nor of books, but rather signifies the establishment of an awareness that it is only as they (physical experience and the objects of study) contribute to the fuller comprehension of the self that they remain significant stimuli; otherwise, the one runs to libertine indulgence which is cloying to the senses and the other to sheer pedantry; both turn out to be the source of disappointment and illusion. Thus, the practiced senses turn inward with the penetrating mind bent upon discovering the basis for that fulfillment withheld by the external world and by the thoughts gleaned from an ardent study of other men's books. This statement greatly simplifies a very complex condition. It does not describe the paradoxical confusion of the facts— nor can description aspire to that clarity, for Donne's life is not a periodic oscillation between the activities of sense and reason with now one dominant and now the other. Always both are operating, and

---

to bee beeleeved," indicates how thoroughly the Italian poet had aroused him to a realization of his own present state. Donne remarks, "it angred me that Celestine a pope far fro the manners of other popes y^t he left even there seat should by ye court of Dants witt bee attacked & by him throwne into his purgatory. & it angred me as much. y^t in ye life of a pope he should spy no greater fault, then y^t in ye affectation of a cowardly securyty he slipt frō ye great burthen layd vpon him. alas? what would Dant haue him do? thus wee find the story related: he that thought himself next in succession by a trunke thorough a wall whispered in Celestines eare counsell to remoue ye papacy: why should not Dant be content to thinke that Celestine tooke this for as imediate a salutaciō & discourse of ye holy ghost as Abrahim did the cōmandment of killing his sonn? if he will needs punish retyrednes thus what hell can his witt devise for ambitiō?"—*Ibid.*, p. 296. The account undeniably betrays to us that Donne is not at ease in Elizabeth's court. The cunning Gaetano, the rival of Celestine, the type of the ambitious courtier, is too much to Donne's disliking to be a welcome pattern of conduct. And how thoroughly and ironically is the innocent Celestine punished for his retirement! Donne is not planning a similar withdrawal, but experience and learning have taught him the shams and vanities of a life in which he had hoped to find happiness and fulfillment of his ambitions.

always their action is reciprocal. What we find existing around 1600 is the effect of just such an action, and that effect is, as stated above, a strengthening of the practice of looking closely within himself, a practice that, once directed upon the witty analysis of the vacillating moods of the lover, is to be pursued into the deeper shadows of the consciousness and bent upon the more somber themes of spiritual experience wherein the mind becomes entangled in problems of greater and more cosmic dimensions. The claims of the speculative intellect begin to assert themselves; and these claims are not to be measured by the yardstick of any authority, but solely by the standards of value discovered within the self.

When the faculties of sense and reason are so concentrated upon the self, they combine to enable the imagination to affirm the nature of truth itself. In his youth Donne had a vision of such truth afar off when he wrote:

> On a huge hill
> Cragged, and steep, Truth stands, and hee that will
> Reach her, about must, and about must goe;
> And what the hills suddennes resists, winne so;
> Yet strive so, that before age, deaths twilight,
> Thy Soule rest, for none can worke in that night.[40]

Too seldom was the vision realized for Donne. But when his voice was lifted to utter the "things invisible to mortal sight," it reported no mystical vision, nor coldly rational deduction but expressed the affirmation of the creative imagination—an axiom born within the self and confirmed by the general human voice.

Thus, he was already set upon an effort to adjust his mind toward a more serious consideration of life, when the accumulation of unhappy circumstances—the tragic fate of his master Essex, disappointment with the life at court, and a marriage that brought imprisonment and poverty—joined with this effort, not only to hasten, but also to compel this consideration. How far the facts of life, the biographical elements, enter to color the dozen years following 1600 would be difficult to determine with exactness. Certainly their importance cannot be underestimated. *Biathanatos*, in 1608, assuredly reflects the influence of the depressing and hopeless state of Donne's fortunes in the Mitcham years. The influence may be studied particularly in his letters of this period. To suggest, however, that the work of the early years of the new century was based entirely upon personal experience is to fail to understand the nature of the spiritual struggle in which Donne's

[40] *Satyre III*, Grierson, I, 157, ll. 79-84.

hypersensitive faculties were engaged. The climax of this struggle was reached by 1611 and 1612 in the *Anniversaries*. As we come to learn, Donne was not waging a twofold battle: on the one side against the gloomy consequences of poverty and family cares, on the other side against the philosophical confusion attendant upon the break-up of the medieval world. Donne was not so naïve as to enjoy the ability to regiment his life in this way. For him physical fact and thought impinged upon one another, acknowledged no boundaries, and mingled with one another in the imagination to arouse whatever powers of creation he possessed.

Thus, in a condition of heightened susceptibility to the motions of both his heart and mind, Donne entered upon the most critical period of his life. Nor is it without singular importance, as stated earlier, that this period corresponds with the period in the history of the new philosophy that ushered in a series of brilliant triumphs which ultimately led to its general acceptance. For Donne this meant that within himself the old order and the new would be brought into sharpest opposition. The difficulty that followed might have been avoided had he turned to the former—by no means yet in disrepute—where it was reasonable that he should find the "metaphysical support" which he sought and seemed to need. But the very conditions that produced this crisis made so easy a retreat an impossible solution. These conditions had sensitized his whole personality to respond to the waves of influence pouring in upon him from the surrounding atmosphere. The old world and the new must meet. To his Aristotelian inheritance he had added a sufficient knowledge of the Copernican philosophy to reinforce profoundly his original and intensely personal way of regarding life.

V

THE RISE OF THE NEW PHILOSOPHY

IN ONE of his Table Talks, Luther bluntly declared that "The fool will upset the whole science of astronomy." [1] The "fool" referred to was none other than Copernicus; and ironically—even unwittingly, apart from the deprecation—Luther had spoken the truth of him. The thing that this modest Polish ecclesiastic had done was through long years of patient calculating carried on in the privacy of his retreat at Frauenburg to develop a theory of the universe in which he affirmed that the earth moved. Then, with reluctance he yielded to the persuasions of his friends to publish the results of his long studies. Under the direction of his pupil, Rheticus, the work was done, and a copy of *De revolutionibus orbium coelestium* forwarded to the author from the printer at Nuremberg. It reached Frauenburg on May 24, 1543— the day of Copernicus's death. Such is the unexciting record of the man who shattered the underpinnings of the old world scheme; and because, as Luther went on to say, "Holy Scripture shows, it was the sun and not the earth which Joshua ordered to stand still," [2] Copernicus might be called a "fool" by the divines—though he himself was a canon of the Church—and his theory be relegated to the discard of nonsense and absurdity.

That the earth moved was the primary doctrine of the new philosophy, if the word "doctrine" may be permitted to describe what is now accepted as a physical fact. In reality, the new philosophy was not a body of doctrine at all, but an accumulation of facts about nature and the development of a critical and objective method of observing the phenomena of the physical universe. Though today we regard the facts of science as the product of the use of such a method, the theory of Copernicus did not result exclusively from the employment of experimental technique or the observation of physical data. It was the method in the hands of such men as Galileo and Kepler that brought to light the facts necessary to confirm the validity of the theory set forth in *De Revolutionibus*. Consequently, in order to understand just how the new philosophy got under way it is necessary to consider briefly the reasons why Copernicus was persuaded to search

[1] Quoted by Dreyer, *op. cit.*, p. 352. [2] *Ibid.*, p. 352.

for a new description of the universe, the method by which he arrived at his conclusions, and the circumstances surrounding their early history.

In the "dedication" of his book to Pope Paul III Copernicus tells us what first induced him to seek for a new theory of the heavenly bodies: "The Mathematicians do not agree among themselves," on the problem of the motions of the spheres.[3] In fact, the centuries since Ptolemy's time had invited complication and accretion so that the comparatively simple construction of the master had been

> With Centric and Eccentric scrib'ld o're,
> Cycle and Epicycle, Orb in Orb:[4]

until cumbersomeness alone threatened it with disaster. But dissatisfaction with the old would have accomplished nothing. Consequently, Copernicus set about, as he relates, to read the writings of all the ancient philosophers that he could get hold of in order to find out where in the course of the history of the theory of the universe the error —for error he thought there must be—had slipped in to confuse the scheme. Nor were his researches without their reward, for, if we are to accept his own word for it, he found in antiquity not the cause of error, but a theory of the universe, long neglected, in which motion had been ascribed to the earth. This idea was sufficient to turn his own mind to the development of a system of the universe with a moving earth as its basic principle.[5]

The ancients, however, who had put the earth to work were not of much help. They gave to the earth but a single rotary motion among the planets; whereas, the phenomena which greeted Copernicus's eye seemed far too complex "to be saved" so easily. Nevertheless, at the outset Copernicus agreed with his predecessors that the world is spherical—the most perfect of all figures—and that the heavenly bodies

[3] "Itaque nolo Sanctitatem tuam latere, me nihil aliud movisse, ad cogitandum de alia ratione subducendorum motuum sphaerarum mundi, quam quod intellexi, Mathematicos sibiipsis non constare in illis perquirendis." "Ad sanctissimum dominum Paulum III. pontificem maximum," in *Nicolai Copernici Torinensis, astronomia instavrata, libris sex comprehensa, qui de revolutionibus orbium coelestium inscribuntur. Nunc demum post 75 ab obitu authoris annum integritati suae restituta, notisque illustrata, opera & studio D. Nicolai Mvlerii medicinae ac matheseos professoris ordinarij in nova academia quae est Groningae* (Amsterdam, 1617), sig. (ₓ*ₓ) 2 recto. Because of its less archaic typography, I shall quote from the above edition of De Revolutionibus, rather than from the first edition of 1543 published at Nuremberg (apud Jo. Petreium), with the title, *De revolutionibus orbium coelestium, libri vi.*

[4] *Paradise Lost*, VIII, ll. 83-84.

[5] *De Revolutionibus*, "Praefatio," sig. (ₓ*ₓ) 2 verso, and (ₓ*ₓ) 3 recto. Copernicus cites the testimony of Cicero that "Nicetam sensisse terram moveri," and gives the Greek text of Plutarch [the pseudo-Plutarch], concerning the opinions of Philolaus, Heraclides, and Ecphantus.

move in uniform and circular courses, or, what is more important, that they describe a composition of circular motions.[6] The earth, too, he held to be spherical.[7] With these matters settled in a way not adverse to tradition, Copernicus proceeded to release his revolutionary doctrine by cautiously disillusioning the reader of his book concerning the old system.[8] Whereas the old scheme was a rationalization from sense experience, Copernicus, in the manner of a true scientist, pointed out that by submitting this experience to critical examination, results quite different from those traditionally accepted might be realized. For example, if we assume that the earth travels with a uniform motion from west to east, the rising and setting of the stars, the moon, and the sun, may as reasonably and as satisfactorily be accounted for as they were when a similar motion was ascribed to the sun. There would be in the universe "an apparent motion of everything outside it [the earth] in the opposite direction" from which it was assumed to move.[9] Again, if it is assumed that the earth is removed from its central position in the old plan and allowed to move, all of the irregularities of the heavenly motions observed by the orthodox astronomers would clearly be understood to have arisen from the fact that these motions had hitherto been referred, uncritically, to the position of the earth rather than to some center outside its sphere.[10]

Having entered this wedge into the security of the old system, Copernicus went on to give his interpretation of the universe in the bold terms required by the principle that he had laid down. The earth was removed from the center and sent on its way among the moving spheres. Though he had found precedent in antiquity for taking this step, in the description of the motion ascribed to the earth, he was without any traditional support. In order to save the phenomena presented in the old system—a thing that he was anxious to do—he found it neces-

[6] See cap. i, "Quod mundus sit sphaericus," and cap. iv, "Quod motus corporum coelestium sit aequalia ac circularis, perpetuus, vel ex circularibus compositus," *ibid.,* I, 1, 6-7.

[7] See cap. ii, "Quod terra quoque sphaerica sit," *ibid.,* I, 2.

[8] See cap. v, "An terrae competat motus circularis, & de loco ejus," *ibid.,* I, 7-9. Copernicus, while drawing support from the tradition of "Heraclides & Ecphantus Pythagorici, ac Nicetas Syracusanus," whose opinion it was that "in medio mundi terram volventes," does not refrain from concluding: "Quo assumpto sequitur & alia, nec minor de loco terrae dubitatio, quamvis jam ob omnibus fere receptum creditumque sit, medium mundi esse terram," which anticipates the exposition that is to follow. *Ibid.,* p. 8.

[9] Quoted by Dreyer, *op. cit.,* p. 322. Cf. *De Revolutionibus,* I, v, 8.

[10] "Si igitur motus aliquis terrae deputetur, ipse in universis quae extrinsecus sunt, idem apparebit, sed ad partem oppositam, tanquam praetereuntibus, qualis est revolutio cotidiana in primis, etc."—*De Revolutionibus,* I, v, 8.

sary to place the sun in the center of the universe,[11] and, most heretical of all his ideas, to give the earth not one motion, but three motions. He held that, first, there is the diurnal rotation; second, the orbital motion, in which the earth, like the other planets, participates in the great progress round the sun; and last, there is the "motion of declination" (*declinationis motus*) [12] designed to account for the fact that the axis of the earth "notwithstanding the annual motion, always points to the same spot on the celestial sphere." [13]

Without pausing here to consider the implications of shifting the point of reference in the universe from man to the sun and to the fixed stars or to consider the redistribution of the planets entailed by the theory, let us briefly take note of the reasons offered by Copernicus to justify his radical departure from antiquity and of the method whereby it was effected. It will be recalled that he essayed some new interpretation of the world because he had found the old grown unwieldy and confused, weighed down with its burden of deferents, epicycles, eccentrics, and equants. Inevitably, then, his work was to reduce complication to simplicity, or at least, to a lesser complexity, to give to his system economy, where only prodigality was present. Moreover, the principle of simplicity had been one of the governing dicta of both ancient and medieval science. As Professor Burtt reports, the old observers had "recorded the substance of their observations . . . in the form of proverbial axioms which had become currently accepted bits of man's conception of the world," such as "that falling bodies moved perpendicularly towards the earth, that light travelled in straight lines, that projectiles did not vary from the direction in which they were impelled," which "had given rise to such common proverbs as *Natura semper agit per vias brevissimas; Natura nihil facit frustra; Natura neque redundat in superfluis, neque deficit in necessariis.*" [14]

That Copernicus was aware of the scientist's obligation to the principle of simplicity and that he had provided a more commodious arrangement of things are evidenced by his praise of his own system as one representable *paucioribus et multo convenientioribus rebus.* What was this particular economy of which Copernicus boasted? How was the complexity reduced? Briefly, it amounted to the resolution into

[11] On the place of the sun in the Pythagorean system, see Sir Thomas Heath, *Aristarchus of Samos* (Oxford, 1913), p. 99.

[12] See cap. xi, "De triplici motu telluris demonstratio," *De Revolutionibus,* I, 24.

[13] Dreyer, *op. cit.,* p. 328.

[14] Burtt, *op. cit.,* pp. 26-27. Cf. "sed naturae sagacitas magis sequenda est, quae sicut maxime cavit superfluum quiddam, vel inutile produxisse."—*De Revolutionibus,* I, x, 20.

fewer motions the many motions which the "orb in orb" arrangement of Ptolemy had necessitated. As the result was not determined by observing that actually there were fewer motions but by recognizing that the apparent motions of the heavenly bodies could be represented by a simpler scheme, the operation was entirely a matter of geometrical procedure. Thus, such an operation is symbolic and succeeds in being convincing in so far as it represents or seems to represent the observed facts in a manner that is more thoroughly than the old scheme in accord with the principle that nature always acts in the most commodious ways.

In describing "exactly the way in which Copernicus thought out the new astronomy" Professor Burtt gives a simple illustration of the kind of "mathematical reduction of Ptolemy's highly complex geometry of the planets" that Copernicus made. Without here resorting to Burtt's graphic illustration we may take for granted its primary implication, that whereas Ptolemy, taking the earth as the point of reference, would have had to use a system of three circles to represent the motions of a chosen heavenly body in relation to the earth and the sun, Copernicus, by shifting the point of reference to the sun around which the earth and the heavenly body were made to revolve, could explain all the phenomena by a system of but two circles.

Moreover, as tradition provided the suggestion of the earth's motion, it likewise gave Copernicus authority to use the geometrical method of demonstrating the soundness of the theory. Down to the Renaissance geometry was by far the most important of the mathematical sciences. In fact, in the late sixteenth century and the early seventeenth, contemporaneous with the development of new approaches to the study of mathematics, pure geometry under the influence of Kepler and other new astronomers was enthusiastically revived.[15]

For geometry nature is a system of limited spatial relations that can be represented graphically in definitely visible figures. From antiquity this science of "magnitudes," as John Dee speaks of it in his Preface to the first English translation of Euclid,[16] was closely allied to arithmetic, or the science of "numbers," so that problems which now would be solved without thought of geometry were earlier dealt with by translating the situation they presented into visibly extended images. Thus, Euclid himself found the method of geometry the most effective way of dealing with the clumsy system of numeration practiced in his

[15] W. W. Rouse Ball, *A Short Account of the History of Mathematics* (3d ed.; London, 1901), p. 262.
[16] Sig. a iii. See above, p. 38 n. 43.

day.[17] Throughout the *Elements* he was accustomed to represent numbers by lines, that is, to treat geometrically quantities which could have been handled numerically—algebraically, had the algebraic method been developed in his time.[18] Again, Plato could turn to mathematics to illustrate his ideas, as when, for example, in the *Meno* he demonstrates the meaning of his doctrine of reminiscence by use of an illustration that could be presented geometrically. How firm a hold the geometrical tradition had on the mathematical minds of the Renaissance is clearly evidenced in the work of Tartaglia, Pacioli, and Cardan, who, though interested in the development of algebra, continued to use the method of geometrical construction to solve equations.[19]

For the history of mathematics this treatment of metrical situations geometrically meant that as problems became more difficult, capable of involving frequent transformations, that is, permitting of the "reduction of complex to simple terms, without any change of value," it became necessary to devise ways of reducing the involved geometrical representations to simpler figures. This means that mathematical processes take into account a principle of relativity, or a conception of how a set of conditions may be expressed in different ways, with the most economical way always to be preferred and always to be sought. An appreciation of this principle is fundamental in the comprehension of the operations performed by Copernicus, for it explains the paradox that the physical truth of any matter subject to geometrical representation exists independent of the point of reference assumed by the mathematician to effect the most satisfactory demonstration. In brief, the demonstration symbolizes rather than describes the phenomena. Actually, then, either the Copernican or the Ptolemaic system might be accepted as true, for the diagrammatic or figurative representation of the motions of the heavens in both systems is, in the end, purely relative to the point of reference assumed as the focus of the operations.

Though the question of the physical truth of the Copernican uni-

[17] See Ball, *op. cit.*, p. 60.

[18] Aristotle's views of space, on the other hand, are predominantly metrical. "He thinks of extension first and foremost as a 'quantity' of something, in fact, as bulk, not as a complex of relations of situations. Cubic capacity, not direction is the capital thing with him. . . . This is an unfortunate prejudice, for though it is quite possible to construct a body of geometry without introducing metrical considerations, it is quite impossible to construct a geometry on a purely metrical basis."—A. E. Taylor, *A Commentary on Plato's Timaeus* (Oxford, 1928), p, 674. Cf. Ball, *op. cit.*, pp. 60, 61, 62. On p. 60 Ball demonstrates Euclid's way of solving equations by geometry.

[19] Burtt, *op. cit.*, pp. 30, 31, 32. Burtt calls attention to a typical problem which Pacioli can do "only by an elaborate geometrical construction, using algebra merely to help him find the lengths of the various lines required," pp. 31-32.

verse thus might be raised, the question of the mathematical truth of the new system could not exist, for by virtue of the very object of mathematical operations, namely, the most economical representation of a given set of conditions, it had prior claims. As De Morgan remarks,

No geometer could fail to be a mathematical Copernican. . . . Accordingly, from the moment when the work of Copernicus appeared, the beauty of the explanation was fully acknowledged . . . the highest terms of praise are found in the writings of those who were most opposed to the physical truth.[20]

To win this commendation Copernicus had done no more than shift the point of reference of his operations from the earth to the sun and present in simpler imagery than had previously been used the traditional phenomena, without altering their value. He had revolutionized man's conception of the universe and at the same time, as he put it, "saved the appearances."

The application of geometrical method to astronomy is of profound significance in so far as it permits of the implication that the universe as a whole is fundamentally mathematical in structure. Such a conclusion follows inevitably from the old geometer's conception of space, or extension, not as ideal or theoretical space as the moderns conceive it, but real space. Naturally enough, then, astronomy seemed more like geometry than any other mathematical science. Not yet equipped with his telescope, the astronomer could not investigate the heavens closely; as a result, the physical nature of the celestial world remained for him almost a mystery. With their great circles and luminous orbs, suggesting little more than brilliantly fixed or moving points, the heavens appeared to be like a great geometrical figure, a chart in which the Creator, employing the concepts of lines and points and surfaces, exhibited himself symbolically. The study of these "images" extended in space thus becomes essentially a geometrical process—the very "geometry of the heavens." [21] Nor was the importance of this conception lessened when Copernicus carried the earth up into the heavens to become a part of the great geometrical pattern.

[20] A. De Morgan, "The Progress of the Doctrine of the Earth's Motion, between the Times of Copernicus and Galileo: Being Notes on the Ante-Galilean Copernicans," in *Companion to the Almanac* (1855), p. 6.

[21] Burtt, *op. cit.,* p. 34. For further evidence of how widely this idea prevailed, see the "geometrical preface" of the 1578 edition of the *Sphere* of Sacrobosco, with the scholia of Vinetus, wherein are set forth "principia geometrica, ad cognitationem sphaerorum elementorum necessaria" in the first twenty odd pages. Cf. the "mathematical preface" of Clavius's *Commentary on Sacrobosco* (1607), pp. 1 ff.; John Dee's Preface to the first English translation of Euclid.

Furthermore, the mathematical tradition in which Copernicus had
worked could look to an ancient and honorable tradition in philosophy for support. In the later Middle Ages the ascendant philosophy
was that of Aristotle, recently recovered from the past and brilliantly
interpreted by Albertus Magnus and St. Thomas Aquinas. But before
the thirteenth century, of all the Greeks, Plato—or Plato as he had
come to be interpreted in the early Christian era—contributed most to
the enrichment of western thought. Nor was his influence obscured
by the rise to fame of Aristotle. It is from the place that mathematics
occupied in this tradition of Platonism that the primary philosophical
sanction for the mathematical interpretation of the universe was derived. Significantly, the one original work of Plato to have fallen into
the hands of the early medieval thinkers was the *Timaeus;* and in this
book was revealed more fully than in any other of Plato's writings, his
profound respect for mathematics and the importance of its influence
upon his system of thought.[22]

For Plato the conception of the importance of mathematics comes
ultimately from Pythagoras. Pythagoras, popularly remembered as the
champion of the doctrine of the transmigration of souls and as the
discoverer of the geometrical theorem bearing his name, is significant,
first of all, for having conceived the world as composed of "number,"
or, the doctrine that physical things "imitate" number.[23] This doctrine
apart from its association with the practice of the geometrical representation of numbers, defined above, appears nonsensical; for as Professor Taylor points out, the doctrine could have significance only as
long as "numbers" themselves were thought of as *res extensae*[24] or
if it holds that "the ultimate elements in the cosmos were limited por-
tions of space."[25]

It is this conception that comes to the fore in the *Timaeus,* and, in
fact, impregnates the whole of Plato's doctrine of ideas, which Professor Whitehead regards as the refinement or "the revised form of
the Pythagorean doctrine that number lies at the base of the real
world."[26] Through the development of the Neoplatonic tradition the

[22] Recent discussions of this subject in the light of its significance for modern
thought are to be found in the following: Whitehead, *op. cit.,* ch. ii, "Mathematics as
an Element in the History of Thought"; Burtt, *op. cit.,* pp. 40 ff.; A. E. Taylor, *op.
cit., passim.*

[23] A. E. Taylor, *op. cit.,* pp. 30, 132.

[24] *Ibid.,* p. 132. Whitehead makes the matter clear by calling attention to the "Greek
mode of representing numbers by patterns or dots" which make "the notions of number
and geometrical configuration less separated than with us."—*Op. cit.,* p. 36.

[25] Burtt, *op. cit.,* p. 30.

[26] Whitehead, *op. cit.,* p. 42.

doctrine became associated with Christian theology. Though it lost much of its mathematical significance through this association, it did succeed in establishing itself in Christian thought by suggesting that the Divine Nature is revealed to man through number and geometrical configuration. Thus, to theology and science alike was conveyed the stimulating idea that the universe is substantially a vast and wonderful harmony. For the former as well as for the latter the doctrine often became involved in mystical subtleties and assumed fantastical proportions; yet, it was preserved, and during the Renaissance it underwent a powerful revival of which Copernicus could not have been unaware when he indicated that the historical basis of his work was to be found in the doctrine of the Pythagoreans.[27]

That Copernicus's work could be regarded solely as the elaboration of a nice geometrical problem in line with the Platonic tradition for many years kept it outside the field of genuine controversy. Though historians, conceiving the new science as the force of liberalism and progress laboring to assert itself against the odds of reaction and tradition, have been accustomed, generally, to depict its rise as a period of *Sturm und Drang*, the theory of Copernicus, *as a theory*, passed through the earlier phase of its existence with little opposition. Indeed, as stated above, it was actually supported by many of the most distinguished mathematicians of Europe.[28] Only, in fact, when it was

[27] Among many thinkers associated with this movement, the names of Nicholas de Cusa and Pico della Mirandola may be singled out as representative. Platonists and Christian mystics both employed their knowledge of mathematics in interpreting the universe. De Cusa regarded God as the same as "mathematical infinity" and the world as "an infinite harmony, in which all things have their mathematical proportions." He argued against the geocentric conception of the universe on the grounds that as the universe is infinite, it has neither center nor circumference; and, therefore, the earth cannot be the center. Moreover, as motion is natural to all bodies, the earth moves. (Donne speaks of de Cusa [Cusanus] in *Pseudo-Martyr*, p. 92, and in a letter to Sir Robert Ker, Gosse, *op. cit.*, II, 245.) Pico's mathematical accomplishments, though directed toward occultism and cabalistic subtleties, enabled him to give a "thoroughgoing mathematical interpretation of the world." (Donne refers to Pico in the *Catalogus Librorum*, *Biathanatos*, *Essays in Divinity*, and in one sermon.) See Dreyer, *op. cit.*, p. 283, and Burtt, *op. cit.*, p. 42.

[28] De Morgan, *op. cit.*, pp. 7 ff. Note should be made of Tycho Brahe, whose name appears in De Morgan's list, because of my frequent reference to his work throughout the following pages of this book. Though Tycho was not a believer in the physical truth of the Copernican doctrine, he was a "mathematical Copernican," and may be regarded, as De Morgan says, as one of "the strongest of all admirers of Copernicus."—*Ibid.*, p. 12. For reasons that need not be set down here, Tycho found it necessary to design a system of his own. "This system is in reality absolutely identical with the system of Copernicus, and all computations of the places of planets are the same for the two systems." The one important difference is that "it leaves the earth at rest." It may thus be regarded "as a stepping-stone from the Ptolemaic to the Copernican system."—Dreyer, *op. cit.*, pp. 363-64.

thought that Copernicus had meant his demonstration to apply to the physical nature of things was he the subject of serious attack. In short, it was possible to be a *mathematical* Copernican without being a *physical* Copernican. Nor was this a startling fact, considering that concrete evidence to support the physical truth of the new theory was not available until a telescope capable of making an intimate survey of the heavens should be made—and no such instrument was available before 1609. Though opposition was generally leveled against the physical truth of the Copernican system, it is significant to recall that as early as 1576 Copernicus had found in England a distinguished champion in Thomas Digges, who not only accepted the new theory as a valid mathematical representation of the universe, but also affirmed that it truly represented things as they are.[29]

Apart from the fact that material evidence to support the physical truth of the new theory was wanting for so long, certain other historical reasons deterred the sixteenth-century mind from being persuaded to accept so radical a position. First of all, Copernicus's *De Revolutionibus* at the outset was deprived of much of its force by being set forth as the elaboration of a hypothesis rather than a true description of the universe. This damaging circumstance was no fault of the author, but was the direct result of liberties taken by the first editor, Osiander, the German reformer. Rheticus, the friend of Copernicus, was to have superintended the publication of the text, but when the manuscript came into his hands, he found himself unable to see it through the press. Conseqently, he turned it over to his friend, Osiander, who sensing the heresy in the doctrine expounded by Copernicus became uneasy about having a hand in such suspicious business. Thinking to safeguard his reputation, Osiander wrote an anonymous Preface to the first edition, addressed "To the reader about the hypotheses of this work." [30] "But it is not necessary," he went on to say, "that his hypotheses should be true, they need not even be probable; it is sufficient if the calculations founded on them agree with the observations" [31]—and thereby, helped to seal from any of the readers of *De Revolutionibus* any intention that its author may have had of revealing the actual construction of the heavens and the earth.

A second condition that prevented the easy acceptance of the physical

[29] See above, p. 38 n. 44.
[30] Quoted by Dreyer, *op. cit.*, p. 319. Cf. "Ad lectorem. De hypothesibvs hvivs operis," *De Revolutionibus*, sig. §4, recto and verso.
[31] *Ibid.*, p. 319. The text of "Ad lectorem" reads: "Neque enim necesse est, eas hypotheses esse veras, imo ne verisimiles quidem, sed sufficit hoc unum, si calculum observationibus congruentem exhibeant."

implications of the new system was that it contradicted the Aristotelian conception of the universe of the medieval theologians. Though we are wont to think of Copernicus as pitted against Ptolemy, in fact it is tue physical system of Aristotle into which the Ptolemaic conception had been absorbed that presented the most rigorous opposition, for it was this system that had become indissolubly associated with medieval religious thought. Implicit in the medieval conception of the universe, as we have earlier depicted it, science and theology sit easily together, each in its respective place, both interdependent parts of a great unity. The disruption of the one would naturally have meant the disruption of the other. This generalization, though it cannot be taken to include the entire realm of thought from Aquinas to the Renaissance, may be accepted, however, as the mode which generally prevailed. As evidence of the wedded ease of these two great branches of learning, the complacency with which the Ptolemaic universe was cherished for so long may be presented.

There were some minds, as Professor Dreyer points out, which in the flush of the humanistic renaissance, when the cleavage between heaven and earth had begun to be observed more acutely, would have found it possible to accept Copernicus's theory without serious qualms. To the order of theology the dues of theology could have been rendered; to the order of nature her tribute could have been paid. But by 1543, when De Revolutionibus was published, the liberality and generous spirit of the humanist had been tightened considerably by the complicating influence of the Reformation. Even Melanchthon, the great humanist of the Reformation, from whom a more liberal attitude might have been expected, frowned upon the "absurdities" of Copernicus, and later, went so far as to offer a hopelessly fatuous argument against it.[32] There was something admirable, after all, in Luther's blunt denunciation of the whole thing as the work of a fool.

Though Renaissance and Reformation may rightly be considered dual aspects of one great movement, they brought into play many forces that ran counter to one another. This fact may be observed particularly in the relations which the new science and religion were to enjoy. Catholic and Protestant alike were involved. The former, to combat the further progress of the reformed Church, reasserted its orthodox position; and as this counter reform movement was to reveal, in setting up the barrier of traditionalism against Protestant innovation, it at the same time made difficult the advancement of scientific ideas. The latter, on the other hand, caring little for the theological tradition of

[32] In ibid., p. 353.

the Church, enthroned the Holy Scriptures as the final arbiter in matters of both faith and reason; but in order to advance its cause against the learned resistance of Catholicism, it necessarily was obliged to go to school to the scholastics themselves to learn their subtle methods of controversy. Thus, as late as 1610 we find the controversialist Donne ably meeting the Jesuits on their own ground in his *Pseudo-Martyr*, and in 1608, apologizing for his extravagant show of learning in *Biathanatos*, because "scholastique and artificiall men use this way of instructing; and I made account that I was to deale with such." [33] Nor is Donne an isolated example of the way in which scholasticism participated in the non-Catholic world of thought. The strength of the influence of Aristotelianism may be measured in the work of Melanchthon and in many of the disciples of Calvin. Descartes, much later, found "Aristotle . . . as strongly entrenched in Holland as in France," and himself the object of attack by the "Calvinist scholastic Voetius," whom he was obliged to term the "world's most downright pedant." [34]

To add further complexity to the theological scene of the Reformation comes the influence of Protestant exploitation of the Scriptures upon Rome, which compelled Catholics, too, to assert the authority of the holy text in their effort to curb the growing opposition to theological dogmatism. Of this movement Sarpi gives interesting testimony in his account of Cardinal Cajetan, "a man very well read in Divinity," who went as papal legate into Germany in 1523.

[Cajetan, upon] studying exactly how those that erred might be reduced to the Church, and the Arch-heretiques convinced, found out the true remedy, which was the literall meaning of the text of the Scripture in the originall tongue in which it is written . . . [Sarpi further reports] that the good Cardinall was wont to say, that to understand the Latine text, was not to understand the infallible word of God, but the word of the translatour, subject and obnoxious unto errours. That Hierome spake well, that to prophesie and write holy books proceeded from the Holy Ghost, but to translate them into another Tongue, was a work of humane skill. And he complained and said, Would to God the Doctors of the former age had done so, and then the Lutheran heresie would never have found place. [35]

Thus, with Aristotelianism opposed to Aristotelianism, and Protestantism and Catholicism alike quoting Scripture against each other, for what would seem often to have been the devil's own purpose, the

[33] Page 23.
[34] Gibson, *op. cit.*, p. 69.
[35] Paolo Sarpi, *The Historie of the Councel of Trent . . . faithfully translated into English by Nathaniel Brent* (London, 1620), p. 155.

intelligence of the Reformation became inordinately obsessed with the futilities of controversy. Behind this screen of theological strife original thinkers like Copernicus and Vesalius or, later, like Kepler and Galileo, might work with comparative peace. But once the new doctrines of science were brought into the open, they met with resistance from both theological and narrowly conceived scriptural authority. The escape from this *impasse* would have come from disregarding the claims of the former in favor of those of the latter received in the light of a richer historical understanding—but such a point of view was slow in developing. In the meantime Luther could rail against Copernicus for upsetting the whole science of astronomy—pagan though it was in its origin—and Clavius pronounce his doctrine absurdly adverse to scriptural truth.

In such fashion might the claims of the pious canon of Frauenburg be measured against those of the pagan Ptolemy. Still and small as was the voice first raised against the deprecation of Copernicus on religious grounds, it was, nevertheless, raised—and heard. From Spain, the seat of the Inquisition, and from a Spanish monk, Didacus of Stunica, came a *Commentary on Job*, revealing how the author searched the Holy Scriptures for passages that stood in contradiction to the conventional citation of Joshua's experience in the Valley of Ajalon.[36] That was in 1584; in 1616 the *Commentary* together with the book by Copernicus which Stunica had indirectly supported, was suspended by the Sacred Congregation, "until they are corrected." [37] Other attempts to answer the traditional argument of the Scriptures are not wanting. Kepler, profoundly religious man that he was, essayed the matter in his *Introduction to Mars*, published in 1609, by arguments which speak, however, rather for Kepler's own sincere and unswerving loyalty to both the Bible and to the new astronomy, than for any ability that he may have had for effectively reconciling the two apparent contradictions.[38]

A third condition that stood in the way of the acceptance of the Copernican theory was orthodox science itself. No better than the theology was the traditional science of the day prepared to surrender itself to the claims of a world scheme put forth as a hypothesis.

[36] Cited by Dreyer, *op. cit.*, pp. 353-54. Stunica's work is included in Salusbury's *Mathematical Collections and Translations*, I, Pt. I, 468-70.

[37] *Ibid.*, p. 417.

[38] In *Joannis Kepleri astronomi opera omnia*, ed. Dr. Ch. Frisch (Frankfurt a.M., 1858-70), III, 146 ff. See especially p. 153. Inasmuch as this text is generally available, all references to Kepler are to this text, hereafter cited as *Frisch*. Kepler's *Introduction* is abstracted in Salusbury, *op. cit.*, as "Johannes Keplerus His Reconcilings of Scripture Texts," I, Pt. I, 461-67.

Though it is true that the old astronomy had not escaped modification, its fundamental conceptions remained unaltered. Furthermore, it accounted for all the celestial phenomena known at the time of the publication of De Revolutionibus. The lack of adequate instruments naturally limited the scope of the astronomers' field of investigation; and within their limited range nothing spectacular had occurred to invite suspicion of error. Predictions were as accurately made by the Ptolemaics as could have been made by the Copernicans; and the motions of the heavens could be charted with as much precision by the one system as by the other. Also, the testimony of the senses favored the old order. The empiric could not easily be led to doubt his eyes. The earth was fixed, solid, and the most secure phenomenon of the universe; while overhead, the sun wheeled its daily course, marking off the periods of light and darkness and describing through its northward and southward oscillations the procession of the seasons. The panorama of the coursing planets, of the tenuous fluid air moved by the winds and filled with the clouds, further emphasized the contrast between the stable earth and the swimming spheres.

There were many arguments of a more technical nature to strengthen the retention of the old system. For example, it was thought that if the earth moved, trees would be torn up from the roots by the violence of the centrifugal force; heavy objects dropped from a height would not fall perpendicularly to the place beneath; and if Copernicus was right, it was argued, the fixed stars ought to show an annual parallax because of the great shift in the earth's position every six months.[39] Finally, as has been pointed out, the fact that the old science had a seemingly explicit metaphysical and theological background, justified its disciples in thinking that it assured the security of man's position of dignity as well as of the primary greatness of the earth itself.

Inoffensive as the Copernican doctrine may have seemed when viewed as a geometrical problem, it, nevertheless, implied the most devastating effects upon the Aristotelian universe when regarded as a representation of the facts of the physical world. However, as earlier observed, the latter construction could carry little weight until concrete evidence was forthcoming. In the meantime, Copernicus, by his

[39] It was calculated that the earth in describing its annual orbit around the sun would be at the end of six months 186,000,000 miles from the point of reference assumed for the calculation, or that distance from the place where its motion might be assumed to have begun. As there was no clear idea of the incredible distance of the fixed stars from the earth, it was thought that a parallax should be revealed to the eye of the observer. In fact, it was not until 1836 that such a parallax was actually discovered. Without powerful instruments, it could not possibly have been discerned.

daring application of geometry to astronomy, did set at war the two great medieval traditions of science, the empirical and mathematical —the former entrenched in the metaphysical system of Aristotle, the latter fortified by an equally honorable tradition drawing its inspiration and support from Plato's *Nemo geometriae expers ingrediatur*, written, as Robert Recorde states, on "his schole house dore." [40] But even after Galileo's telescope had brought its message from the heavens, though drawing sharply the edges of controversy between the new and the old, the feeling was still so strong that Copernicus was no more than a brilliant mathematician and that his work was meant to be purely hypothetical, that as late as 1620 the Congregation of the Index mollified their proscription of *De Revolutionibus* by propounding the way "under which they could allow his book to be read as a mathematical hypothesis." [41]

The above discussion of the rise of the Copernican theory is important to this study in two ways: it exhibits the background of thought and scientific practice against which Donne, in a general way, projected the traditional matter of his inheritance and early study; again, it reveals by implication the one thing needed to give authority to the new science—the evidence of concrete fact. In following up the latter one encounters the significant development of a school of experimental scientists in the late years of the sixteenth century and the opening of the seventeenth, which was to bring to light the evidence necessary to vindicate the new philosophy; and, what is more immediately important, one encounters the fact of Donne's familiarity with the work of these men. At this point a preliminary survey of the evidence for Donne's acquaintance with this contemporary phase of the history of the new philosophy will be useful.

Donne's "hydroptique immoderate desire of humane learning" has often been invoked to account for his extensive learning, ranging as it did over as great an area of the "intellectual globe" as his own time had surveyed. However, in this appetite for knowledge he can hardly be thought unique. For us it simply means that he was in the company of the giants of those days, men like Bacon, Hooker, and Selden, for whom the province of the mind was enlarged with the expanding world of space. Pages of books like *Of the Advancement of Learning*, *Of the Laws of Ecclesiastical Polity*, and *De dis Syris*, tell the story of prodigious searching among great libraries, and their indexes disclose scores of names that awaken in us the wonder of pure discovery—of names that to us were never known. With Donne it is the same.

[40] *The Pathway to Knowledg*, sig. **2.   [41] De Morgan, *op. cit.*, p. 7.

Though we may regret the loss of those 1,400 "resultances" of learned authors which Walton says Donne left somewhere, we cannot feel that fate has cheated us entirely, for the sermon folios and the margins of *Biathanatos* and of *Pseudo-Martyr* acknowledge their indebtedness to an almost universal library—and behind a hundred poetic images lurk the ghosts of as many books and as many men.

But marvel as we may at the industry and wit enabling him with so much grace and purpose to embroider his discourse with quotation from and allusion to Fathers of the Early Church, doctors of the law, the ancient writers of the "natural story," and the poets of Greece and Rome,[42] we are excited far more to see among his pages the names of a few men whose influence has directly shaped the world in which we live. Nor is it surprising that these names are those of the men of the renaissance of science. It is they who laid the foundations of the world in which we live—a world which even now we are beginning to remodel in order to house more comfortably the infinitesimal forms of matter that swim about us and the vast nebulae of the farthest heavens. To come across the names of Copernicus, Tycho Brahe, Kepler, Gilbert, and Galileo in his books, is to note Donne's intellectual proximity to us. But Donne was not bidding for the favor of future generations when he read Galileo; nor was it by chance that for a layman he took an inordinate interest in the philosophical heresies of his day. The time in Donne's own life was right for the acceptance of the stimulus provided by his most advanced contemporaries; the time was right in the history of the new science to make the stimulus available in its most effective form.

The years preceding and following close upon the opening of the seventeenth century witnessed the rise of the experimental method in science and the publication of some of the most important books in the history of science.[43] Compared to the work done in astronomy in these later times, even Copernicus's book seems considerably like an academic exercise. In fact, it should·be remembered that Copernicus was moved as much by dissatisfaction with the old complex system of the heavens, as by the compulsion of observed facts, to set about reconstructing the world scheme. "He had, it is true, taken a small number of observations of eclipses and planets, but for the most part his results

---

[42] A recent contribution to an understanding of Donne's knowledge of some of the classical poets is that of John Sparrow, "A Book from Donne's Library," *The London Mercury*, XXV (Dec., 1931), pp. 171-80.

[43] See Charles Singer, *Religion and Science Considered in Their Historical Relations* (London, 1928), pp. 48-49.

were obtained in the study." [44] However, with the advent of Kepler, Gilbert, and Galileo there was a fuller and bolder use of the experience of the senses. Science was taken out of the study and put into the laboratory of nature.

It is this—the appeal to concrete experience—that made the new science particularly acceptable to the poetic mind. To Donne, especially, this appeal met with a sensitive response that argues how deeply the new revelations sank into the marrow of his understanding. That he grasped the all-important fact that such works as the *De Stella Nova* of Kepler and the *Sidereus Nuncius* of Galileo were the result of a direct appeal to the "stubborn facts" of the physical world cannot be denied. It was to an appeal to fact—a search for the authentic knowledge of life in real, honest experience untouched by pedantry or convention—that he had submitted himself when he got free from the trammels of formal study. It was not likely that the same appeal to factual experience addressed to the mind in consideration of matters impinging as much upon the domain of the spirit as upon the realm of physical nature could be resisted. Thus, it was inevitable that the old conception of the world, drilled into his imagination by study and tradition, should be laid siege to by the facts from which the new order was to be built, once those facts were thoroughly grasped.

That Donne laid hold upon the matter of the new philosophy his works amply testify. Not only is there the evidence of his own statement that he read some of the most important books of the new thinkers, but also there is the richer and more valuable witness of the influence of their doctrines upon his own way of thinking.

In a place where, perhaps, one would least expect it, one comes upon Donne's first direct allusion to the new science. In the "Second Part" of *Biathanatos,* in the midst of an ingenious effort to overthrow ecclesiastical prejudice against suicide, Donne attacks St. Augustine's ineffectual argument against innovation by calling to his aid the authenticated report of the new astronomers:

Had it been a good Argument in *Rome* for 500. yeeres, that Divorce was not lawfull, because (n) no example was of it? Or almost for 2000. That a woman might not sue it against her Husband, because (o) till *Herods* daughter there was no example of it? But now when the Church hath thus long persevered, in not only justifying but solemnizing many examples hereof, are not Saint *Augustines* Disciples guilty of the same pertinacy which is imputed to *Aristotles* followers, (p) who defending the Heavens to be inalter-

[44] *Ibid.,* p. 50.

able, because in so many ages nothing had been observed to have been altered, his Schollers stubbornly maintain his Proposition still, though by many experiences of new Stars, the reason which moved *Aristotle* seems now to be utterly defeated? [45]

The startling allusion to the authority of the new science is no less striking because Donne has preserved in a marginal note the specific reference to his source. In fact, because he has so carefully indicated that "*Kepplerus de Stella Serpent. cap. 23*" [46] had provided the information, he has committed himself to a kind of scholarship which frankly respects its obligations; and what is more important still, he has revealed that he is familiarizing himself with the specific details of the new philosophy by going directly to the texts in which it is expounded. Consequently, the necessity of accounting for Donne's interest in this learning, either now or later, does not lead one into the realm of critical vagueness where one attributes this and that to his subject simply because it was "in the air."

Kepler's *De Stella Nova*, a little book (*Libellus*) *Astronomicis, Physicis, Metaphysicis, Meteorologicis & Astrologicis Disputationibus*, published in Prague in 1606, contains a detailed account of the discovery on September 30, 1604, of a brilliant new star in the constellation of Serpentarius, together with a discourse on the marvelous coincidence of this star's appearance with the "great conjunction" of

---

[45] Dist. 6, sec. 8, p. 146. See marginal note 13, which reads: "S. *August.* schollers in this point of examples, as stubborne as *Aristotles*, for the heavens inalterablnes, though the reason of both be ceased."

[46] *Ibid.*, marginal reference "p." The passage in Kepler's *De Stella Nova* to which Donne alludes is the following: "Quare sic sensit Aristoteles, coelum inalterabile? Quia (inquit) a tot seculis nihil est animadversum. Ergo si quis Aristotelem doceat, succedentibus seculis compluscula nova in coelo animadversa, libentissime decedet de sententia. At hodie discipuli Aristotelis non ad rationem, sed ad nudam sententiam respicientes, ex dogmate philosophi, quod is ab experientia petebat, audent obloqui experientiae contraque eam excipere variis diverticulis quaesitis. Sed re perpensa diligentius, Aristoteles inductione usus esse videtur. De motibus stellarum constat, leges ab ultima memoria hominum mansisse easdem: et iidem hodie circumeunt planetae, qui olim fuerunt, eaedemque fixarum constellationes: nec de ipso intermedio (quod oculis non est obvium, quia pellucidum) diversum demonstrari potest. Ergo omnia in coelo sunt perpetua, ipsa etiam orbium materia. Haec inductio fallit. . . . Proponam vero aliquot hic documenta, ex quibus id quod contendo quodammodo perspici possit: ut novae fixae, quas ex materia coelesti alterabili gigno, exemplis aliis alteratae materiae coelestis confirmentur." Cap. xxiii, "Coeli materiam esse alterabilem," Frisch, II, 694. It is interesting to note that Donne, following Kepler, places the burden of error on the *discipuli* of Aristotle [Aristotle's "schollers"], not on Aristotle himself. Kepler insists on this: "Sic sententiae, dum ex ore fluunt philosophorum, facillime corrigi possunt: ubi receptae fuerint a discipulis, quovis lapide magis indurescunt, nec ullis rationibus facile revelluntur."—*Ibid.*, pp. 693-94.

Mars, Jupiter, and Saturn.[47] The treatment of its contents rightly belongs to the study of Donne's familiarity with the doctrines of the new astronomy, and will, consequently, be made when those doctrines are taken up for special consideration. That Donne as early as 1608 was alluding to a book published but two years earlier, clearly reveals how well he was keeping pace with the new learning. Furthermore, in the same book Kepler interspersed a number of leaves telling about another star, *quae usque ad annum M.DC. fuit incognita, necdum exstinguitur*. Of this part of the book, by title designated *De Stella in Cygno* Donne also shows specific knowledge.[48] The star herein described was the one which appeared first in the constellation of the Swan in 1600. In the course of his description, Kepler takes occasion to pay a tribute to his friend, Tycho Brahe, the great Danish astronomer whose death in 1601 left Kepler the legatee of the most valuable set of instruments and records of astronomical observations that had ever been made. It is from *De Stella in Cygno* that Donne quotes three years after *Biathanatos* in that rare and ingenious tract, *Ignatius his Conclave*, where he displays his knowledge of the new astronomy so completely.[49] In this work Donne also acknowledges his indebtedness to the most amazing astronomical book of his day, Galileo's *Sidereus Nuncius*.[50] Here, the first fruits of the telescope, recently invented, were brought to light. Galileo's book was published first in Venice, in 1610, and Donne's tract was written shortly afterwards, probably in the same year, though the date of publication is 1611.[51] Thus, the *Sidereus Nuncius* had hardly come from the press before

[47] The full title from which the above is taken is as follows: *De Stella Nova in pede Serpentarii, et qui sub eius exortium de novo iniit, trigono igneo. Libellus astronomicis, physicis, metaphysicis, meteorologicis et astrologicis disputationibus, παραδόξοις et παραδόξοις plenus. Accesserunt I. De Stella incognita Cygni: narratio astronomica. II. De Jesu Christi Servatoris vero anno natalitio, consideratio novissimae sententiae Laurentii Suslygae Poloni, quatuor annos in usitata epocha desiderantis.* See Frisch, II, 611. The British Museum copy bears the author's inscription in his own hand to King James I.

[48] Frisch, II, 760-72.

[49] " . . . to *Keppler*, who (as himselfe testifies of himselfe) *ever since* Tycho Braches *death hath received it into his care, that no new thing should be done in heaven without his knowledge.*" In *John Donne . . . Complete Poetry and Selected Prose*, ed. John Hayward (Bloomsbury, 1929), p. 359. In the first English edition of *Ignatius his Conclave* (1611), there is a marginal note, "De stella in Cygno," p. 3. The passage from Kepler's book is as follows: "Tychone jam mortuo equidem haec me cura incessit, ne quid fortasse novi existeret in coelo me inscio."—Frisch, II, 762. Mrs. Simpson first called attention to this quotation, *op. cit.*, p. 184.

[50] In the 1611 English edition of *Ignatius his Conclave* appears the marginal reference, "Nuncius Syderius," pp. 2, 117. The matter will be dealt with in detail later.

[51] On the date of *Ignatius his Conclave*, see Simpson, *op. cit.*, pp. 180-83.

Donne got hold of it—perhaps through his friend Sir Henry Wotton who was then in Venice [52]—and had read and digested it sufficiently to make use of practically every one of its revelations in a nimble and pointed attack upon the Jesuits.

But little less notable than Galileo's book is the great work of William Gilbert of Colchester, Donne's own countryman, De Magnete,[53] of which Donne speaks in the Essays in Divinity.[54] Gilbert's

[52] Sir Henry Wotton sent at least one copy to England, that to King James. This fact along with a valuable account of the great discoveries of Galileo are contained in a letter to the Earl of Salisbury, March 13, 1610: ". . . Now touching the occurrents of the present, I send herewith unto his Majesty the strangest piece of news (as I may justly call it) that he hath ever yet received from any part of the world; which is the annexed book [italics mine] (come abroad this very day) of the Mathematical Professor at Padua, who by the help of an optical instrument (which both enlargeth and approximateth the object) invented first in Flanders, and bettered by himself, hath discovered four new planets rolling about the sphere of Jupiter, besides many other unknown fixed stars; likewise, the true cause of the Via Lactea, so long searched; and lastly, that the moon is not spherical, but endued with many prominences, and, which is of all the strangest, illuminated with the solar light by reflection from the body of the earth, as he seemeth to say (i.e. during eclipses). So as upon the whole subject he hath first overthrown all former astronomy—for we must have a new sphere to save the appearances—and next all astrology. For the virtue of these new planets must needs vary the judicial part, and why may there not yet be more? . . . By the next ship your Lordship shall receive from me one of the above-named instruments, as it is bettered by this man."—The Life and Letters of Henry Wotton, ed. Logan Pearsall Smith (Oxford, 1907), I, 486-87.

[53] London, 1600. Quotations appearing below are taken from the Gilbert Club translation, William Gilbert of Colchester, Physician of London. On the Magnet, Magnetick Bodies also, and on the Great Magnet the Earth; a New Physiology, Demonstrated by many Arguments & Experiments (London: The Chiswick Press, 1900). Hereafter to be referred to as De Magnete.

[54] "So that this Heaven and Earth, being themselves and all between them, is this World . . . which . . . hath been the subject of Gods Labor, and providence, and delight, perchance almost six thousand yeares; whose uppermost first moving Orbe is too swift for our thoughts to overtake, if it dispatch in every hour three thousand times the compass of the Earth, and this exceeds fifteen thousand miles." Essayes in Divinity; By the late Dr Donne, Dean of S. Paul's. Being Several Disquisitions, Interwoven with Meditations and Prayers: Before he entred into Holy Orders. Now made publick by his Son, J. D. Dr of the Civil Law (London, 1651), p. 69. The passage in De Magnete on which the above is based is as follows: "Leaving out the ninth sphaere, if the convexity of the Primum Mobile be duly estimated in proportion to the rest of the sphaeres, the vault of the Primum Mobile must in one hour run through as much space as is comprised in 3000 great circles of the Earth, for in the vault of the firmament it would complete more than 1800." VI, iii, 218. Dr. Augustus Jessopp first called attention to this particular use of Gilbert by Donne in his edition of the Essays in Divinity (London, 1855), p. 86.

In the above, Donne's "fifteen thousand miles" is derived from translating into English, 1,718 German miles, the diameter of the earth given by Gilbert a few lines before the above-quoted passage from De Magnete. Actually it would be 17,990 plus, English miles; hence, the significance of Donne's statement, "exceeds fifteen thousand miles."

THE RISE OF THE NEW PHILOSOPHY

book superficially observed belongs to an entirely different class of literature from such works as *De Stella Nova* and the *Sidereus Nuncius*. It is neither astronomical, nor, save by implication, mathematical. Rather, it describes in detail with rich illustration, a great number of "laboratory" experiments with the loadstone, all beautifully organized to establish the thesis that the earth itself is a great magnet. This discovery, however, arrived at "by long experience," as Gilbert says,[55] contributed greatly to forward the new philosophy and upset the old, for to Gilbert the concrete display of magnetic energy in the earth was an inextricable part of his theory of terrestrial motion; in fact, it was the very cause of the earth's diurnal movement.[56] Gilbert's work meant definitely that by physical experiment the *Primum Mobile* could be disproved; and as Copernicus had erected a system of the planets in which this antiquated machinery had no place, Gilbert logically enough became one of the most ardent and enthusiastic supporters of a revision of the old cosmology, though, it must be remembered, he wavered in the full acceptance of the Copernican system.[57] His great Sixth Book deserves particular attention; it is more than an argument against the old order; it is a piercing shaft of wit aimed at the Peripatetics, the Aristotelians, whose arguments he regards as but "follies . . . old wives' gossip, and the rubbish of certain philosophizers, men, who when they essay to treat of the highest truths and the fabrick of the universe, and hazard anything, can scarce understand aught *ultra crepidam*. . . . Nor is it consistent with reason," he adds, "that the heavenly bodies of the Peripateticks should attend on a centre so decadent and perishable as that of the earth." [58]

Though *De Magnete* was first published in 1600, there is no evidence of Donne's direct acquaintance with the book before the com-

[55] "Preface to the Candid Reader, Studious of the Magnetick Philosophy."—*Op. cit.*, sig. * iij recto.
[56] See particularly VI, iiii, "That the Earth moves circularly," *ibid.*, pp. 220-25, and VI, vi, "On the cause of the definite time, of an entire rotation of the earth," *ibid.*, pp. 231-32.
[57] Though Gilbert refers to the doctrine of Copernicus and affirms that the earth has a diurnal motion, he does not enter upon the subject of its orbital motion in *De Magnete*. In a posthumous work, *De mundo nostro sublunari philosophia nova* (Amsterdam, 1651), according to Dreyer, "he appears to hesitate between the systems of Tycho and Copernicus."—*Op. cit.*, p. 348. De Morgan gives a more detailed account of Gilbert's conception of the earth's motion, quoting Bacon's testimony that he was definitely opposed to all but the diurnal motion, but concluding from an examination of *De mundo nostro sublunari philosophia nova*, that Gilbert "does not draw a positive conclusion," and that "he treats with contempt the notion that the earth must be at the centre."—*Op. cit.*, p. 14. Cf. *De Magnete*, p. 227.
[58] *Op. cit.*, p. 227.

position of *The first Anniversary*, probably in 1610. There, among many statements that seem to have had their inspiration in Gilbert's treatise, particularly in the Sixth Book, is the one in which Donne conceives of Elizabeth Drury's soul as endowed with "Magnetique force," able

> To draw, and fasten sundred parts in one.[59]

Gilbert's statement that "a magnetick vigour exists then in the earth just as in the terrella," [60] "without which," as he earlier remarks, "the universe would go to pieces" [61] struck Donne's imagination as the perfect analogy to the conception of the world soul that he was trying to express. Much of the imagery of the poem moves too close to the language of *De Magnete*, which suggests vividly the function Donne wished to give to Elizabeth Drury's soul, to cause one to suppose that its source was anywhere but in this book. The analogy between Gilbert's "magnetick vigour" and the cohesive force imparted to the earth by Elizabeth Drury's soul may be understood better by noting in Donne's description of the world from which this power is gone the absence of exactly that power explained fully by Gilbert under the name of "coition." Just before the line from *The first Anniversary* cited above, Donne regards the world as "all in peeces" with "all cohaerence gone," [62] and continues,

> This is the worlds condition now, and now
> She that should all parts to reunion bow,
> She that had all Magnetique force alone,
> . . .
> Shee, shee is dead.[63]

The language of the poet describing the virtue which Elizabeth Drury's death has taken from the world, is not unlike that of the scientist when considering the "grand magnetick nature of the earth" as a power "innate and diffused through all her inward parts." [64] This power, or *coition*, is

not vague or confused, not a violent inclination of body to body, no rash and mad congruency; no violence is here applied to the bodies; there are no strifes nor discords, but there is that concord (without which the universe would go to pieces), that analogy, namely, of the perfect and homogeneous parts of the spheres of the universe to the whole, and a mutual concurrency of the princi-

[59] Grierson, I, 238, l. 222.
[61] *Ibid.*, p. 67.
[63] *Ibid.*, p. 238, ll. 219-21, 237.
[60] *Op. cit.*, p. 212.
[62] Grierson, I, 237, l. 213.
[64] *De Magnete*, p. 212.

pal forces in them, tending to soundness, continuity, position, direction, and to unity.[65]

The fact that the fundamental ideas of De Magnete are structurally incorporated into The first Anniversary is certain evidence that Donne was entirely familiar with Gilbert's work considerably in advance of the time when the first specific reference to this book was made, if we are to assume that the Essays in Divinity were written just before Donne took holy orders.[66] Moreover, it should be noted, Donne would have learned of De Magnete at least as early as 1608 from Kepler; for it was in De Stella Nova that Kepler, clinging to the traditional notion that the fixed stars formed a part of a solid sphere at a limited distance from the center of the universe, criticized Gilbert (and also Giordano Bruno) for holding that the stars were at varying distances from the earth and that the idea of a sphere enclosing these bodies was a fiction.[67]

It was to the physical facts contradicting the Aristotelian world and supporting the new conception of the universe that these men of the new science directed the attention of the learned world. In no insignificant way are the books named above, particularly that of Galileo, the anchor posts of the new philosophy. That Donne was familiar with these works, evidence has been set forth; the extent of his acquaintance and its effects upon his imagination can now be analyzed with assurance.

[65] Ibid., pp. 67-68.
[66] Jessopp (op. cit., p. xliii), Gosse (op. cit., II, 63), Simpson (op. cit., p. 191), and Geoffrey Keynes (A Bibliography of Dr. John Donne, 2d ed., Cambridge, 1932, p. 76) are in agreement that the date of composition of the Essays in Divinity is 1614 or 1615. Despite the weight of their opinion, to me the matter remains pretty much of a question.
[67] "Itaque defendit illam [Copernicus] infelix ille Jordanus Brunus: nec obscure asseruit specie dubitantis et Guilielmus Gilbertus libro de Magnete, cetera praeclarissimo, religiosum tamen affectum eo demonstravit, quod existimaret, non alia re rectius intelligi infinitam Dei potentiam, quam si infinitum mole conderet mundum."—Frisch, II, 688. Cf. Gilbert's exclamation: "How immeasurable then must be the space which stretches to those remotest of fixed stars! How vast and immense the depth of that imaginary sphere! How far removed from the Earth must the most widely separated stars be and at a distance transcending all sight, all skill and thought."—Op cit., p. 215.

VI

THE MOVING OF THE CENTER

WHEN the wave of experimentation in science broke over the world at the beginning of the seventeenth century, Donne was prepared to plunge into the new study. Kepler, Galileo, and Gilbert poured their influence upon him, and it was from them, rather than from Copernicus himself, that Donne learned what he knew about the new-made universe with its moving earth. Donne did not, however, relax his interest in the old system of the world; in the work of these years Ptolemy and Copernicus jostle one another in a confusion to be explained only when the historical conditions are understood to which both Donne and the new science were being subjected.

In 1607 there was issued another of the numerous editions of the popular book on astronomy, the *De Sphaera* of Sacrobosco, with annotations and commentary by the eminent Jesuit mathematician, Christopher Clavius.[1] Although Clavius—whose revision of the calendar Donne satirizes in *Ignatius his Conclave*—was as admirably prepared in the mathematics as any living man to appreciate the grounds on which the new philosophy rested, he was still bound by his Aristotelian prejudices to attack Copernicus. By 1610 Donne had read Clavius's voluminous commentary.[2] With Kepler's *De Stella Nova*

[1] Noted above, p. 42 n. 3.
[2] The reason for holding that the above edition of Clavius's *Commentary* is the one used by Donne is based on an allusion to Clavius in *Pseudo-Martyr*, p. 16, which is accompanied by the marginal annotation, "*Comment. in Sacro. Bosc. fol. 219.*" Donne writes: "And this makes the Glosser vpon that *Canon,* where Priesthood is said to exceede the Layetie, as much as the Sunne, the Moone, so diligent to calculate those proportions, and to repent his first account as too low, and reforme it by later calculations, and after much perplexity to say, That since he cannot attaine to it, he will leaue it to the *Astronomers;* so that they must tell vs, how much the Pope exceedes a Prince: which were a fit work for their *Iesuite Clauius,* who hath expressed in one summe, how many granes of Sand would fill all the place within the concaue of the firmament, if that number will seeme to them enough for this comparison." It is into the above edition of the *Commentary* that Clavius in a "Digressio de arenae numero" (pp. 251 ff.), *first* introduces his attempt to improve upon Archimedes' efforts (in the *Arenarius*) to compute the number of grains of sand that would fill the firmament, a subject that proved fascinating to Donne from this time forward. In the Preface to the Reader of the 1607 edition of the *Commentary* Clavius states, "ut maior ex nostris Commentariis in Sphaeram perciperetur, addidimus in gratiam studiosorum, praeter Auctoris expositionem, cum multa alia, tum haec praecipue quae sequuntur." He then announces his intention of treating the four motions of the eighth sphere, the new

sufficiently digested to allow himself to declare that "the reason which moved *Aristotle* seems now to be utterly defeated," [3] he had come into possession of enough facts to make the old and the new systems stand in sharp and irreconcilable contrast. If it would seem to us that the time had arrived when he must make a definite choice of one or the other system, it did not appear so to Donne. Although the issue was drawn, the struggle into which the contending philosophies were to throw him did not come about for two or three years—not until, it may be safely assumed, Galileo contributed his devastating defeat to the old order in his *Sidereus Nuncius*, in 1610. In the meantime, Donne had engaged himself to help Thomas Morton (later Lord Bishop of Durham) wage a tractarian war against the Catholic opposition to the Oath of Allegiance. This war carried Donne into a field ever dear to him, that of legal and historical study, whereupon there seemed to be little opportunity for his interest in the new science to obtrude itself. But even here a resourceful wit led him to find in Galileo's book the means of improving the cause of the controversialist. In fact, the *Sidereus Nuncius* revealed to him a new world as apt to be exploited for the purposes of a satirical pamphlet as it was capable of involving him in the "anatomy" of his own soul.

With the fact in mind already noted, that Donne had not only turned to the study of the new science but also had refreshed his knowledge of the old through the pages of Clavius, which brought Ptolemy up to date, let us turn to an examination of just how far Donne's acquaintance with the new science was to extend during the years before he entered the priesthood. After this has been determined, we shall be prepared to consider carefully what effect it seemed to have upon his thinking and his art.

First to be considered among the images inspired by the new science which enrich Donne's prose and verse of the early seventeenth century are those drawn from the fundamental principle of the Copernican theory, the motion of the earth. Perhaps the first allusion to this principle of the new astronomy that can be dated with approxi-

---

stars (of 1572, 1600, and 1604), and the fantastic problem of the grains of sand. Donne's page reference is wrong; page 219 falls within the discussion of the new stars, a matter that was much on his mind. Though Donne does not speak of the *Commentary* before 1610, he may well have read it somewhat earlier. Certainly the fact that we can date with near exactness the time when he became acquainted with one of the most popular reviews of the old and the new philosophy makes intelligent criticism of his thought in the early years of the seventeenth century much more possible.

[3] *Biathanatos*, p. 146.

mate exactness appears in a letter to Sir Henry Goodyer,[4] with whom more intimately than with any other friend, unless it is the Countess of Bedford, Donne enjoyed talking over the nature of things and the world in general. In 1609 Donne sends his "diet" of "salads and onions of Mitcham" to Goodyer, "with as wholesome affection as your other friends send melons and quelque-choses from Court and London."[5] Addressing his friend, Donne writes,

I often compare not you and me, but the sphere in which your resolutions are and my wheel, both I hope concentric to God: for methinks the new astronomy is thus appliable well, that we which are a little earth should rather move towards God, than that He which is fulfilling, and can come no whither, should move towards us.[6]

The letter, written while Donne is thinking of the "new astronomy," is a pastiche of scientific figures, all bent toward the expression of two ideas for which the new astronomy is "thus appliable well"—first, the definition of the difference in the circumstances of the two friends, one "at Court with ambition, which would burn you, or envy, which would divest others," living "in the sun, not in the fire: and I which live in the country without stupefying . . . not in darkness, but in shadow";[7] and second, the definition of their mutual love, sustained by their concentricity to God, or their mutual aspiration toward the good life.

Here, the heliocentric universe, in which God is likened to the sun with the earth moving around it, provides the vehicle for Donne's subtle analysis of their respective fortunes. Goodyer is like the great circle through which the earth describes its annual course around the sun, whereas Donne is the "wheel" of this circle, the earth turning on its own axis on the circumference of the greater orbit; both move ever "towards" the sun, their common center.[8] In the double motion

[4] [1609], Gosse, op. cit., I, 218-20.
[5] Ibid., p. 220.
[6] Ibid., pp. 218, 219.
[7] Ibid., p. 219.
[8] Copernicus, while attributing three motions to the earth, retained some of the eccentrics and epicycles familiar to the old system. The wheel arrangement of the epicycle rolling on the circumference of the larger circle, on which Donne's figure is based, is graphically illustrated in some of the astronomy books of the day. See particularly the diagram accompanying Thomas Digges's A Perfit Description of the Coelestiall Orbes (1576), in Leonard Digges, A Prognostication Euerlastinge, etc. (London, 1576), fol. 43, sig. M 1. In Digges's diagram the "globe of mortalitye," represented as a circle about a half inch in diameter, with its conventionalized tongues of flame (representing the element of fire) pointing inward from the circumference toward a hub-like arrangement of the earth encircled by a wreath indicating the watery sphere, actually gives one the impression of a wheel. The "globe" in its plane projection appears to roll

of the earth which Donne understands, the great circle may well be conceived ever to maintain its center at the sun; it is the little circle, the path of the diurnal motion, in which he himself moves, that shifts daily from darkness into light. But at this point Donne departs from the scientific truth to compromise his vacillating moods. He accepts neither the extreme of darkness nor of light, but the mean condition of "shadow" which "is not no light, but a pallid, waterish, and diluted one" [9] as more fitting to a description of the "barbarousness and insipid dulness of the country." [10]

The second idea illustrated by the new astronomy particularly emphasizes the trend in Donne's own religious experience away from Catholicism toward Protestantism, and the evolution of the Renaissance man's idea of his own personal responsibility to God. As Donne had earlier written in *Satyre III* that one must get toward truth by the exercise of his own energies on the arduous slopes of experience, so here, he recognizes again that man is an agent in his own salvation. He does not lie composedly in the lap of heaven's influence, complacently suffering the ministrations of God and His angels, any more than does the earth rest at the center awaiting the ministrations of the sun. However, with the shift in the religious point of view and with the shift in the physical position of the earth have gone some of the old security and the sense of man's importance. The new astronomy has, in words used by Donne in a sermon at "Paul's Cross," in 1622, "reduced and brought [man] back to *God*." [11] In the "reduction" he has come to rely upon his own powers and to experience the new dignity of personal effort. "We which are a little earth" must bestir

---

upon the great circle of the orb of Venus, the planet next below the earth, which in turn surrounds the orb of Mercury, all being centered upon the Sun. This very interesting diagram, perhaps one of the most interesting to appear in an English book of the sixteenth century, fortunately has been reproduced by Johnson and Larkey, *op. cit.* See above, p. 38 n. 44.

Clavius's *Commentary* contains few illustrations; but such books as John Harris's *The Description & Uses of the Celestial and Terrestrial Globes* (5th ed.; London, 1620) (I was unable to see a first edition, though I presume it was published considerably in advance of the fifth. The *STC* does not list the work), and Thomas Blundeville's *Theoriques of the Seven Planets* (1602), both rich in geometrical illustration, must have been generally available to early seventeenth-century readers. Blundeville's book contains "a breefe Extract . . . of Maginus his Theoriques, for the better understanding of the Prutenicall Tables," the tables prepared by Erasmus Reinhold (1551) in accordance with the Copernican conception of the celestial motions.

[9] Gosse, *op. cit.,* I, 219.

[10] *Ibid.,* p. 219.

[11] *A Sermon vpon the xv. Verse of the xx. Chapter of the Booke of Ivdges . . . by* Iohn Donne, *Doctor of Divinitie and Deane of Pavls* (London, 1622), p. 44.

ourselves in order to participate in the warmth and to share in the influence of the universal light. Thus, Donne had found in cosmological fact the counterpart of the psychological experience through which he was passing in his progress to that state of independence where he could sincerely regard all religions as "virtual beams of one sun." [12]

It is not a purely voluntary motion that establishes this new relation of the earth and sun, of which in the world of religious experience the relation of man and God is the counterpart. The constraining power of the sun itself has effected the new order, for the sun is *cor mundi . . . fons lucis . . . fons caloris,* and *origo vitae motusque mundani.*[13] Nevertheless, if in the new universe the earth does not lie still but moves "towards" the sun from whence come light and life, in the new spiritual world man participates in the fulfillment of the "two-fold *Order*" of his relation with God, as he described it in the sermon referred to above. This amounts to no less than man's appreciation of the interdependence of man and God, of his awareness that not only "all creatures depend vpon *God*, as vpon their beginning, for their very *Being*"; but also, that man is "to be reduced and brought back to *God*, as to his end." [14] This is "done by meanes in this world," and the means are largely determined by man himself. Thus, does the wheel come "full center"; and though the preacher began his meditation with a line from Aquinas—*Ordo semper dicitur ratione principij,* he had anticipated much earlier the pattern that his thought should take, in terms of the "new astronomy."

It may seem to some that the explanation given of the lines in Donne's letter to his friend has been too ingenious and considerably labored. It is true that one can easily fall into the trap of making Donne appear too subtle; one is more likely, however, to fall short of the mark of Donne's meaning than to overshoot it. "Darke texts need notes," and the compression of thought so great, the manipulation of ideas drawn from his great library of learning so adroit, that until careful analysis has released the intensity the words may have no more effect upon the mind than the unexplained geometrical diagram has upon the eye.

If Donne appreciated some of the implications of the Copernican doctrine of the earth's motion, he also knew something of its history.

[12] "To Sir H. R. [Henry Goodyer]," [1609?], Gosse, *op. cit.,* I, 226.
[13] Kepler, *Dissertatio cum Nuncio Sidereo nuper ad mortales misso a Galilaeo Galilaeo* (Prague, 1610), Frisch, II, 504.
[14] *A Sermon vpon the xv. Verse of the xx. Chapter of the Booke of Ivdges,* p. 44.

By this is not meant the immediate history of Copernicus's book (though he may have had such knowledge), but the history of the idea itself. In *Ignatius his Conclave*, later to be treated in detail, Donne discloses a more objective, and at the same time more patronizing, attitude toward the new philosophy than in any other work of this early period. Though Miss Ramsay passes by the fact in the chapter of her book in which she treats the sciences,[15] it is none the less true that this masterpiece of Donne's "Lucianic art," apart from its delightfully diabolic way of showing how the Jesuits "growe harmlesse out of necessity," [16] reveals a very acute understanding of Copernicus and Galileo. It is in Donne's "best satiric vein" [17] that he takes occasion to tarnish the halo of learning which the Jesuits had proudly set upon their own heads. Of Ignatius Loyola himself Donne writes:

and though when hee died he was utterly ignorant in all great learning, and knew not so much as *Ptolomeys*, or *Copernicus* name, but might have beene perswaded, that the words *Almagest*, *Zenith*, and *Nadir*, were Saints names, and fit to bee put into the *Litanie*, and *Ora pro nobis* joyned to them; yet after hee had spent some time in hell, he had learnt somewhat of his *Jesuites*, which daily came thither.[18]

Ignatius's ignorance, however, is only less profound than that of Lucifer himself, and it is Ignatius who makes reply to Copernicus whose noble entreaty to enter hell has left Lucifer "stuck in meditation." [19] As Donne's satirical manner allows scope for the delightful play of incongruity, we are not amazed to find that the "little taste of learning" [20] with which Ignatius has "furnished" himself, amounts to about all Donne himself knew of the new astronomy, the politics of Machiavelli, and the "mineral" medicine of Paracelsus. Thus equipped, Ignatius would hope to upset the claims of Copernicus to the place of the world's greatest innovator by pointing out that "your inventions can scarce bee called yours, since long before you, *Heraclides*, *Ecphantus*, and *Aristarchus* thrust them into the world: who notwithstanding content themselves with lower roomes amongst the other Philosophers, and aspire not to this place, reserved onely for *Antichristian Heroes*." [21]

[15] *Op. cit.*, pp. 268-80. Miss Ramsay largely confines her attention to Donne and Paracelsus, pp. 272 ff.
[16] Ed. Hayward, p. 409. See above, p. 83 n. 49. All references to *Ignatius his Conclave* are to Hayward's text.
[17] Simpson, *op. cit.*, p. 187.
[18] *Ignatius his Conclave*, p. 364.
[19] *Ibid.*, p. 364.
[20] *Ibid.*, p. 364.
[21] *Ibid.*, p. 366.

Again and again, the exponents of the new theòry of the world call up these early believers in the earth's motion, ancient Pythagorean ghosts, to soften the boldness of their innovation; and with equal zeal, the reactionary Ptolemaics point with derision to these philosophers, as the advocates of a fantastic notion that time and progress have reduced to its proper place.[22] Consequently, their mention in Donne's satire throws an interesting light on his reading, and on the current tendency to reinforce the new doctrine with the support of tradition. Robert Recorde, in *The Castle of Knowledge,* enumerates the Pythagorean hierarchy of Heraclides, Ecphantus, Philolaus, Nicias (Hikitas), and Aristarchus, who thought that the earth moved;[23] but it is uncertain whether Donne ever read Recorde's astronomical discourse. In Gilbert's *De Magnete* all these names appear again,[24] and it may be assumed that Donne was reading this book at the time he wrote *Ignatius his Conclave,* for it is contemporary with *The first Anniversary,* which bears the imprint of Gilbert's influence.[25] Moreover, in no other one of the books which we are sure that he read do all the names mentioned above appear. Kepler frequently recalls the Pythagoreans in *De Stella Nova,* but singles out only Aristarchus as a forerunner of Copernicus.[26] Likewise, Clavius refers only to Aristarchus Samius who lived 400 years before Ptolemy, and whom "in recent times Nicolaus Copernicus has followed in his work on the revolutions of the heavens."[27] Copernicus himself had called attention only to Philolaus, Heraclides, Ecphantus, and Nicetas in *De Revolutionibus,*[28] but it has been discovered since that in the original manuscript of this work he did recognize his debt to Aristarchus.[29] In all probability Donne was not drawing upon any one author when he put into Ignatius's mouth the names of the old astronomers which had become familiar to him through a generous acquaintance with the books of both the old and the new philosophy.

[22] On early theories of the earth's motion, see Heath, *op. cit.,* pp. 251, 252, 254-55, 275-83, 301-3, 310.
[23] Fol. 164. Recorde regards only Philolaus and Ecphantus as Pythagoreans, "two great clerkes of Pythagoras schole."
[24] "Among the ancients Heraclides of Pontus and Ecphantus, afterwards the Pythagoreans, as Nicetas of Syracuse and Aristarchus of Samos, and some others (as it seems), used to think that the earth moves, etc." p. 214.
[25] See above, pp. 85-87.
[26] Frisch, II, 674, 686. Cf. "Praefatio," *Dioptrice seu demonstratio eorum quae visui et visibilibus propter conspicilla non ita pridem inventa accidunt* (Augsburg, 1611), *ibid.,* p. 526.
[27] *Op. cit.,* p. 80.
[28] Sig. (***) 2, verso. See above, p. 66 n.5.
[29] Dreyer, *op. cit.,* pp. 314-15. Heath prints the passage from the MS, *op. cit.,* p. 301.

That Donne was familiar also with the recent history of the new astronomy is borne out by Ignatius's further reproach to Copernicus: ". . . neither do you agree so wel amongst your selves, as that you can be said to have made a *Sect*, since, as you have perverted and changed the order and *Scheme* of others: so *Tycho Brache* hath done by yours, and others by his." [30] Though the new science was developing rapidly by the date of the composition of *Ignatius his Conclave*, it is true that nothing that properly could be called a "sect" had come into existence. But of more importance are the mention of Tycho Brahe and the allusion to the vicissitudes that had early overtaken the newly expounded doctrine of Copernicus.

Tycho Brahe, the friend of Kepler, coming shortly after Copernicus, fell just short of being one of the moderns. He was an indefatigable and accurate observer, an inventor of astronomical instruments, and a prodigious compiler of data concerning the heavens; but, in spite of these accomplishments, he was still in the shadow of tradition. The Biblical testimony against the mobility of the earth was too convincing and realistic to allow him to accept the new doctrine at its face value. Moreover, he was fettered by the popular arguments against the theory of Copernicus and was not persuaded by the evidence set forth by Copernicus himself to favor the new theory. He thought that the earth was far too clumsy and heavy to be moved, let alone to be given the threefold motion that had been ascribed to it. He still thought a body thrown perpendicularly into the air would not fall back to the ground on the spot from which it had been projected if the earth were racing beneath it. Further, he considered Copernicus's estimate of the vast distance beyond Saturn, the farthest planet, to the fixed stars, too immense to be credible; nor could he agree to Copernicus's account of the size of the stars.[31] Despite his conservatism Tycho could not forfeit the claims of his instinctively curious and scientific nature, and after careful observation of the comet of 1577 he pondered a new system which began to take form a dozen years later. But the system of Tycho, departing as it did from the Ptolemaic pattern, was far from being the radical venture of Copernicus. Briefly, he "saved the phenomena" by devising a scheme of eccentric orbits combining the revolution of the five planets around the sun and the sun around the earth. It was substantially the system suggested in antiquity by Apollonius who has been called the Tycho Brahe of the ancient Copernican system of Aristarchus.[32]

[30] *Ignatius his Conclave*, p. 366. [31] Dreyer, *op. cit.*, pp. 356, 360.
[32] Cf. above, p. 73 n. 28. Cf. Heath, *op. cit.*, p. 269.

Not only is Donne aware of the work of Tycho Brahe, but he also understands that "others" have altered his system. Where did he learn this, and who are the "others"? The answer to the first question is the same as that to the last—Kepler, beyond doubt. It was from Kepler that Donne had learned of Tycho's experiments, and of his magnificent bequest of instruments and tables to his colleague.[33] But in the *De Stella Nova* Kepler does not outline the Tychonic system; he does, however, again and again refer to Tycho, particularly, to his book, the *Progymnasmata* which gives the whole of his friend's system in detail.[34] It is not impossible that Donne's curiosity led him to investigate directly the ponderous work of this "phoenix" of astronomers, though the statement above from Ignatius is too general to permit such a specific conclusion. He would, however, have gathered enough from Kepler's book on the new star to tell him that Brahe had departed from orthodox Copernicanism.

But was it Kepler who reformed Tycho's system? As to the answer Donne is either very vague or much more particularly learned in the new astronomy than we had supposed. It would be obvious to Donne that Kepler had disavowed Tycho's system in his preference for that of Copernicus. It may be that Donne had in mind simply their disagreement or the general disagreement caused by the new philosophy, and knowing of the intimate friendship and collaboration of the two he inferred that Kepler had departed from Tycho as a student from his master's teachings. This, however, does not account for the qualification that others had "perverted and changed" Tycho's system. Truthfully speaking, no one perverted or changed Tycho's interpretation of the universe; but Kepler did make use of one of his master's suggestions—the most fertile suggestion that he offered, and the most productive of scientific progress for Kepler—namely, that the orbits of the planets may not be circular, as tradition claimed, but elliptical. It was this suggestion that Kepler took over in developing his interpretation of the planetary orbits set forth in his *De Stella Martis*, published in 1609.[35] If, then, we may assume that the transplanting of this idea from its Tychonic setting into the Copernican setting of

---

[33] *Ignatius his Conclave*, p. 359. See above, p. 83.

[34] The first edition of the *Progymnasmata*, the publication of which was supervised by Kepler himself, was brought out in 1602. In 1610 it was reissued with a somewhat altered title-page by Gottfried Tampach, the well known Frankfort bookseller who had bought up most of the 1,500 copies of the first edition. See Dreyer, *Tycho Brahe, a Picture of Scientific Life and Work in the Sixteenth Century* (Edinburgh, 1890), pp. 368-69. Kepler's references to his friend's great work are far too numerous to make citation practicable.

[35] See Dreyer, *History of the Planetary Systems*, p. 370, and *Tycho Brahe*, pp. 346-47.

Kepler amounts to perverting and changing Tycho's system, Kepler may well be said to have tampered with his friend's theory. This would mean, too, that Donne had seen Kepler's *Commentary on Mars* and had understood the historical background of Kepler's signal contribution to the theory of planetary motion. Though the evidence presented above is insufficient to warrant so startling a conclusion, it is hoped that further investigation will make possible a definitive interpretation of these interesting lines in Donne's attack upon the Jesuits.

Besides the evidence of Donne's letter to Goodyer and the references in *Ignatius his Conclave,* in many of the poems of this period there is testimony to Donne's acquaintance with the central doctrine of the Copernican astronomy.[36] In these poems Donne has become neither the advocate of the new nor the stubborn disciple of the old. [Consequently, as we view the results of his learning, caught up into the imagination and transmuted into the language of poetry, we see the imagery springing from the doctrine of the moving earth intermingled with figures of the fixed center and the spheres of Ptolemy.] Something of the state of mind into which this scientific learning has thrust Donne may be concluded; too, there may be inferred some notion of how it has become the instrument of rigorous self-analysis, or the tool of a wit within whose light lurks the shadow of a more serious spirit. With the exception of the two *Anniversaries* these poems cannot be said in any way to be directly concerned with the problems raised by the new philosophy. They disclose an appreciation of the Copernican doctrine enriched by the facile contrast it receives in the presence of allusions to the old. Both are brought into subservience to the poet's art with the same facility that Spenser and Milton exercised in their use of the classical mythology.

Thus, in *A Valediction: forbidding mourning,* after dramatically prefiguring the poet's separation from his love in terms of the separation of the soul and body of a virtuous man at death, he touches the emotional pulse of the situation by a skillful allusion to the new and the old astronomy:

---

[36] To me the following passages are worth considering, even though specific statement of the earth's motion is not made in all: *A Valediction: forbidding mourning* [1611], Grierson, I, 50, ll. 9-12, *The first Anniversary* (1610–11), *ibid.,* p. 237, ll. 207-8, p. 239, ll. 274, 281-82, *Elegie upon the untimely death of the incomparable Prince Henry* (1612), *ibid.,* p. 268, ll. 21-22, 49, *Epithalamion for the marriage of the Earl of Somerset* (1613), *ibid.,* p. 139, ll. 186-89, *To the Countesse of Salisbury* (Aug., 1614), *ibid.,* p. 224, ll. 3-4, 11-12 (?), p. 225, l. 44 (?), *To the Countesse of Bedford* [1609–1614], *ibid.,* p. 196, ll. 37-38.

Moving of th'earth brings harmes and feares,
Men reckon what it did and meant,
But trepidation of the spheares,
Though greater farre, is innocent.[37]

Of the new astronomy, the "moving of th'earth" is the most radical principle; of the old, the "trepidation of the spheares" is the motion of greatest complexity.[38] As Donne does not deny the truth of either doctrine—if he did the whole point of the argument would be wasted and futile—either might be taken to symbolize for him, in the sphere of universal things, the emotion which attends separation. As the poem is a valediction forbidding mourning, the poet must exhort his love to quietness and calm upon his departure; and for this purpose the figure based upon the latter motion (trepidation), long absorbed into the traditional astronomy, fittingly suggests the tension of the moment without arousing the "harmes and feares" implicit in the figure of the moving earth.

[37] Grierson, I, 50, ll. 9-12. The *Valediction* was probably written upon Donne's departure for France in 1611. See *ibid.,* II, 40.

[38] The history of this motion is given by Gilbert, *op. cit.,* pp. 236 ff. In Blundeville's *Exercises* (2d ed.; 1597) an explicit account of what it meant to the Elizabethans is set forth. It is the third motion of the eighth sphere, the heaven of the fixed stars. Traditionally this sphere was credited with two proper motions, one from east to west every twenty-four hours, and one from west to east with the second movable at the rate of one degree every hundred years. But, in addition, it was observed by the astronomer Thebit (tenth century) to move "sometimes towardes the south, sometimes towardes the north, by vertue of his own proper moving, called in Latine 'motus trepidationis,' that is to say, the trembling moving, whereby it is moved upon two little Circles, the poles whereof are in the beginning of that *Aries* and that *Libra* which are imagined to be in the 9th heaven, the semidiameter of which little circles is 4 degrees one minute and 8 seconds and 4 minutes and three seconds, & maketh his whole revolution in 7000 yeares." It is also called "motus accessus & recessus," that is, "the moving of approaching and returning, only proper to the eighth sphere."—p. 142. Thebit, to explain this, motion derived from some super-mover, added a ninth heaven, which as Frisch points out, Alphonsus, the Castilian astronomer (thirteenth century), retained in his tables.—*Op. cit.,* I, 195, n. 31. Once an additional heaven had been added to account for an irregularity, the process of accretion was carried to absurd lengths. Blundeville reports that "new writers say there are ten movable heavens (besides the Imperiall Heaven)," whereas the old contented themselves with but eight or nine. Moreover, "trepidation" did not pass out of existence with Copernicus. He, accepting that the starry sphere "changes somewhat," assigned "another cause for this phenomenon" deduced from the motion of the earth. See Dreyer, *History of the Planetary Systems,* p. 327, *De Magnete,* p. 237. Thus, though the "motus trepidationis" was not at once abolished by the new philosophy, the awkward and fantastic superstructure of spheres by which it had come to be explained was destroyed. As Kepler says of Copernicus, "salvat inaequalem praecessionem aequinoctiorum, et eliminat octavae fixarum sphaerae . . . motum trepidationis, illique quietem suam restituet." *Prodromus continens mysterium cosmographicum* (1596), Frisch, I, 117. Tycho Brahe spoke guardedly on the subject, but through the accuracy of his own observations revealed that the phenomenon was mainly the result of the inaccuracy of the ancients. See Dreyer, *Tycho Brahe,* p. 356.

The selection of imagery is made with discrimination and intelligence. Donne has read the reckonings of what "it did and meant" to intimate that the earth moves. He doubtless recalls Clavius's arguments against the motion of the earth: that clouds and birds would be carried in opposite directions if the earth were allowed to move on its axis from west to east and that its diurnal motion in the short twenty-four hours required to traverse so vast a distance, would violently tax the whole universal frame.[39] Furthermore, he no doubt has in mind arguments of Gilbert and Kepler, drawn from conflicting sense experience and advanced to dethrone the old order. And though the matter is presumably viewed with a fine detachment, it is not irrelevant to observe that the very intrusion upon the poem of the "harmes and feares" caused by the motion of the earth, catches an undertone of anxiety that would have been lost were the figure absent. Thus, the figure carries us behind the brave front of encouragement and the exhortation to break off mourning, to the sensitive soul of the man who has reflected upon the meaning of the separation of true lovers as well as upon the motion of the earth.

To maintain the unity of theme with which the poem begins, and to counteract the "harmes and feares" suggested by the image of the earth's motion, Donne has successfully alighted upon the very image. The "trepidation talk'd" of Milton, was the fly in the Ptolemaic ointment (*tanta esset in Ptolemaeo pernicitas*),[40] and yet, six or seven centuries had endeared it to the old system. Embalmed in tradition, it at least had become free of all disturbing connotations ("Though greater farre, is innocent"). Even those of the new school who had banished it from their thought regarded it as a thing "supported only by unrealities of arguments and by conjectures," rather than a cornerstone of the old universal structure holding up the rest of the edifice.[41]

But, for the moment Donne is outside the question of its truth or falsity. His sole concern is with the figure's aptness to convey his meaning, namely, that it should allay the "harmes and feares" threatened by his departure. "Trepidation" has the right suggestion of anxiety inherent in the situation, and common acceptance of the term has subdued its originally heretical sound. In short, along with the unsettling report that the earth moves there is provided the consolation of old familiar things. Moreover, its mitigating influence becomes effective in the same paradoxical way that recollection of last year's triumph over hardship lightens this year's trouble.

Too, it is not without significance for an understanding of Donne's

[39] Clavius, *op. cit.*, pp. 222-23.   [40] Kepler, *Prodromus*, Frisch, I, 117.
[41] Cf. *De Magnete*, p. 28.

attitude toward the new astronomy that he points his figure of the innocence of trepidation with the encouraging reminder that it is "greater
farre" in its devastating consequences than the moving of the earth.
As a matter of fact Donne is scientifically right in saying that the motion
of trepidation was "greater farre" than that assigned to the earth by the
new astronomers. Donne does not state here that that was one of the
good reasons why it was abandoned; nor does he imply that its "innocence" was compounded of picturesqueness and error. He knew, however, from Clavius that the explanation of this motion, involved in
much absurdity, entailed the erection of a ninth and even a tenth
fantastic upper story upon the already burdened universe.[42] He knew,
too, that the new theory of the world sought to eliminate the accumulation of excess baggage by introducing the simple operation of the earth's
motion. But whereas the old astronomers justified an "expanding universe" in order to preserve the structure from internal alteration, the
later thinkers, desiring to reduce the scheme to greater simplicity, threw
the whole order of the heavens into a topsy-turvy mess. The divine
juggler might add one, two, or even three more balls to his practiced
hand, because his game remained unchanged; but let him reduce their
number and change the pattern of his motions and he was apt to drop
all that remained.

Only exact knowledge of what he is doing allows Donne to make
the facile transition from the figure of the earth's motion to that of the
trepidation of the spheres. Having rapidly surrounded the facts of both
in his imagination and having in his survey taken into account the
physical breadth of both, he is able to consign to each that exact amount
of psychological truth compatible with the emotional situation dramatically prefigured in the first stanza of the poem. Nor does the rest
of the poem in any way disturb the sense, to the evolution of which
these powerful images have contributed so intimately and discriminat-
ingly. In fact the poet in the closing lines by means of the well-known
and marvelous figure of the "stiffe twin compasses," [43] while boldly
assuming that separation cleaves the lovers' souls apart, allays the
threatened anxiety by resolving their duality into the oneness of the
circle and its center, with the same absolute command of his materials
by which earlier he makes the innocence of the "trembling motion"
assert itself to absorb the disturbing influence of the figure of the moving earth.

Donne's *An Anatomie of the World* and *Of the Progresse of the
Soule* (the first and second *Anniversaries*) also provide evidence of his

[42] Clavius, *op. cit.*, p. 45.   [43] Grierson, I, 50, l. 26.

familiarity with the doctrine of the earth's motion. Here, however, the evidence is not confined to isolated images but is written into the very structure of the poems themselves. In truth, his awareness of the new astronomy with its disturbing effects upon the human imagination provides one of the principal themes on which the argument of the two poems moves: in the first, as the force which has broken up the old world scheme; in the second, as the basis on which the poet must attempt a reconciliation of the soul with the nature of things as newly described. Though we can be grateful that the occasion of Elizabeth Drury's death called forth these poems, we dare not forget Donne's debt to Galileo and Kepler, for it was they who set his wit on edge to furnish the poems with their essential cosmic significance. Because of his extravagance and presumption, glory may not be brought to Donne by his elegy as it was to Milton for writing his lament upon the death of Edward King; but it is no difficult task for the reader to forget the occasion of the *Anniversaries,* and regard them, with some reservations, for their vigorous and penetrating revelation of the poet's own soul.

Although the evidence of Donne's concern with the new philosophy is written across the entire face of the *Anniversaries,* he does delineate this concern particularly in such lines as

> The Sun is lost, and th'earth, and no mans wit
> Can well direct him where to looke for it.[44]

The word "lost" is the key to the appreciation of the physical fact to which Donne refers and also to the state of mind produced by this fact. The positions of the sun and earth were the sure and settled facts of the old astronomy. More evident to the eye of man than the places of the planets (not agreed upon entirely) were the station of the solid earth beneath his feet and the course the sun daily described above his head. The irregularities of the planetary motions might be confusing —even to the astronomer—but the certainties of the solar orbit and the stability of the terrestrial center were indisputable. But in the above lines Donne declares that these fond assurances on which the world scheme was anchored are but the tricks of a treacherous eye not to be trusted with its commonest experiences. Lost, indeed, is the sun if it does not wheel in its daily course across the heavens; and lost, too, is the earth if its stability is dissolved into illusion by a triple motion carrying it aloft among the "wanderers" of the sky. A new point of view is demanded, the adjustment of the eye to a different focus, and being without the dispassionate calm of the poet who can regard this All as

[44] *The first Anniversary, ibid.,* p. 237, ll. 207-8.

such stuff as dreams are made of, and without the heart of the discoverer which beats only with wonder at the sight of the horizon of some new world, Donne finds himself for the time being amidst the chaos of a ruined universe.

Again, as in the letter to his friend Goodyer he sees that the new astronomy has made the earth "move towards God" when he writes that "we make heaven come to us," [45] but here, it is interesting to note, the emphasis falls *unhappily* on the fact itself, as it does in a later communication to the same friend: "And I think, that as Copernicism in the mathematics hath carried earth farther up, from the stupid centre; and yet not honoured it, nor advantaged it, because for the necessity of appearances, it hath carried heaven so much higher from it; so . . ." [46] Thus, if at one time he could enlist the language of the new astronomy to symbolize man's aspirations, he can at another time call upon it to testify to his laziness and spiritual enervation. The lines.

> Loth to goe up the hill, or labour thus
> To goe to heaven, we make heaven come to us,[47]

express bitterly one of his first intimations that he appreciates the meaning of the words that Bacon declares were "aptly said by one of Plato's school *That the sense of man carrieth a resemblance with the sun, which* (as we see) *openeth and revealeth all the terrestrial globe; but then again it obscureth and concealeth the stars and celestial globe: so doth* the sense discover natural things, but it darkeneth and shutteth up divine." [48] As we may be in even better position today to inquire into the truth of these words than was Plato's disciple, or Donne, or Bacon, it is not uninteresting to record in passing the irony of Bacon's attempt to demolish the "idol" that "ignorance of second causes should make a more devout dependence upon God which is the first cause," [49] when we find an author of the twentieth century observing that the chief characteristic of the progress of modern thought has been "the shifting of creative power from God to Man." [50]

The skepticism and unrest animating the *Anatomie of the World* is not relaxed in *Of the Progresse of the Soule*. In fact, skepticism and unrest describe the condition of mind from which Donne's effort to patch

[45] *Ibid.*, p. 239, l. 282.

[46] "To my true and very good friend Sir Henry Goodere" [1615? Apr.], Gosse, *op. cit.*, II, 78.

[47] Grierson, I, 239, ll. 281-82.

[48] *Of the Advancement of Learning,* in *Works,* VI, 96.

[49] *Ibid.*, p. 96.

[50] Quoted from a review of Denis Saurat, *Blake and Modern Thought* (London, 1929), *The Times Literary Supplement,* 1929, p. 649.

up his frayed world takes its beginning. What the result was need not detain us at the present. It is sufficient to note that this skepticism springs in great part from the dissolution of the old world scheme by the Copernican innovation. That is made pretty clear to anyone who does no more than simply read the poem. But what is not obvious at first is that Donne is disturbed less by the bursting of the ancient bubble than by the fact that he ever regarded this bubble as reality. Gilbert had written in *De Magnete* that the great blunder of the old astronomy was to make the universe "attend on a centre so decadent and perishable as that of the earth." [51] Whereas Gilbert had said this to discredit the Peripatetics, not necessarily to discredit the earth, Donne evidently found in the literalness of the statement the reflex of his own mind, as is brought out in the following lines:

They who did labour Babels tower to'erect,
Might have considered, that for that effect,
All this whole solid Earth could not allow
Nor furnish forth materialls enow;
And that this Center, to raise such a place,
Was farre to little, too have beene the Base.[52]

From this double thrust—at man's idle aspirations and at the earth's fragility—Donne plunges straight forward to the conclusion:

No more affords this world, foundation
To erect true joy, were all the meanes in one.[53]

It is true that throughout the poems Donne's thought is hung on the framework of the old Ptolemaic world, but it hangs loosely, with an ill-fitting awkwardness of which he himself is too well aware. Though the physical point of reference in the poems, as far as the cosmic structure is concerned, may be taken to be the "solid Earth," the true point of reference is to be sought in the poet's mind, a mind already aware that the traditional sun and the earth are "lost" and, therefore, eager to establish another, more permanent and satisfying.

As Donne's allusions to the motion of the earth are tumbled together in the unsystematic way clearly indicated by the above illustrations, it is only through going over every inch of the language relative to this phase of the new science that one can measure the entire length to which this knowledge extended his imagination. Such a treatment, however, would be tiresome—if not for its formlessness, then because it would wind its slow length along through many pages. Nevertheless, the matter cannot well be concluded without a consideration of the

[51] Page 227.
[52] *The second Anniversary*, Grierson, I, 263, ll. 417-22.
[53] *Ibid.*, p. 263, ll. 423-24.

places wherein he lays aside the higher seriousness and spiritual earnestness to play with the idea in a way that to many is the bane of Donne's
style. While it may be put down by the Donne enthusiast for ingenious-
ness and proof of his "giant fancy," it may better be accepted candidly
as evidence of the overt torture that he could inflict upon language or
of the clever affectation to which circumstance or willfulness often
made his wit an unbecoming agent. It will appear that even in this
kind of exercise some moments could be much happier than others.

In 1612 Prince Henry, heir to the British throne, died at the "untimely" age of eighteen. At once the poets began work on the subject
of his death, and succeeded in knotting more garlands (alas, often
"with forc'd fingers rude") than, as Professor Grierson conjectures,[54]
probably ever before or since had been twined about the memory of
one man. The young Prince was the genuine hope of the Protestant
cause in Europe, and his destiny to an "unfulfilled renown," in the
light, or better, the shadow of events following upon the death of
James I, may well enough be thought to have altered the face of history.
The poets who responded to the occasion may have had an inkling of
the genuine tragedy involved in young Henry's death, but too frequently, if we are to judge from such an effusion as the *Lachrymae
Lachrymarum* in which Joshua Sylvester collected a number of the
elegies on the Prince, they capitulated to an overweening sense of their
own capacity for "distilling" tears from a rather arid wit. With an eye
that doubtless cast but a sidelong glance at the dead and a mind that
had for its purpose, according to Jonson's report of Donne's confession,
the attempt to "match Sir Ed: Herbert in obscurenesse," [55] Donne set
his pen to paper to compose his *Elegie upon the untimely death of the
incomparable Prince Henry.*[56]

To out-Herbert Herbert was an undertaking for which Donne was
eminently qualified; but the performance is less noteworthy for having
passed Herbert's obscurity than, as Professor Grierson justly claims,
for revealing how completely the poet succumbed to a "tasteless extravagance." [57] The poem starts off well with an eloquent echoing
period such as Donne could master:

> Looke to mee faith, and looke to my faith, God;
> For both my centers feele this period.[58]

[54] See *ibid.*, II, 204.
[55] *Conversations with William Drummond of Hawthornden*, in *Ben Jonson*, ed. C. H.
Herford and Percy Simpson (Oxford, 1925 ff.), I, 136.
[56] Grierson, I, 267-70.
[57] *Ibid.*, II, 205.
[58] *Ibid.*, I, 267, ll. 1-2.

But Donne early plunges into a discourse on reason and faith so inextricably involved in a tangle of images that he soon finds himself strangled by his own ingenuity. Like an exhibition swimmer more accustomed to the pool than the rough sea into which he has thrown himself, he battles his way for almost a hundred lines before becoming exhausted on the fatuous thought of

That she-Intelligence which mov'd this spheare,[59]

"Who ere thou bee" (as Donne inquires). She is, we are led to believe, the lady whom the Prince loved, here unfeelingly introduced by the poet to help him back to earth, even though it be at the expense of her subjection to the excruciating reminder that her "mutuall heaven" on earth with the Prince has been destroyed by his death.

As Professor Grierson's paraphrase of the poem makes clear,[60] Donne did have a legitimate idea to express, an idea that is certainly consistent with the temper of the poet during these troubled years prior to his reception of holy orders. Again, as in *The second Anniversary*, he shows how death has shaken his faith and unhinged his reason. The suddenness and the tragedy of Prince Henry's death, euphemistically spoken of as a "miracle," [61] is unfortunately the kind of miracle that does less to enlarge faith than to point to the impotence of man's reason and the futility of his hopes. The account given by Professor Grierson does not, however, suggest the framework of ideas on which Donne's skeptical thinking is overlaid. It is in the exploration of this inner structure of the poem that one can uncover the foundations of his disillusionment and perhaps appreciate more satisfactorily just why the poem is an imperfect realization of the synthesis of his own thought with the forced expression of grief demanded by the occasion. The parallel of the elegy to the *Anniversaries*, particularly to the second, is not extravagant; in both it is the lamentation for the dead that offends. In the former, however, the occasional element is more completely amalgamated with the personal element than in the latter; in the elegy, whether through haste, fear of seeming insincere, or, as Jonson claimed, through an effort to "match" the wit of a friend, the two are not conjoined—to the unhappy confusion of both.

It is again his preoccupation with the new astronomy and its implications of confusion that constitute the backbone of Donne's poetical thinking. And to this confusion is added Donne's own chaotic handling of the materials, amounting to a jumbling of Copernicus and Ptolemy together, with an unexpected transition from one to the other in an

[59] *Ibid.*, p. 270, l. 90.   [60] *Ibid.*, II, 205.   [61] *Ibid.*, I, 269, l. 73.

effort to maintain a single focus of ideas, namely, that of the relation of reason and faith to God. [Both reason and faith are prefigured in the geometrical relations of the sun and the earth, and the nature of both is in large measure determined by these relations. Thus, Donne begins the poem with a symbol that can be translated directly into a diagram; but a bold venture, or perhaps a blunder, turns the pattern into something as freakish as a cubistic drawing. Let us examine the imposition of a conception of relativity upon a Euclidian diagram.]

> Looke to mee faith, and looke to my faith, God;
> For both my centers feele this period.
> Of waight one center, one of greatnesse is;
> And Reason is that center, Faith is this;
> For into'our reason flow, and there do end
> All, that this naturall world doth comprehend:
> Quotidian things, and equidistant hence,
> Shut in, for man, in one circumference.
> But for th'enormous greatnesses, which are
> So disproportion'd, and so angulare,
> As is Gods essence, place and providence,
> Where, how, when, what soules do, departed hence,
> These things (eccentrique else) on faith do strike;
> Yet neither all, nor upon all, alike.
> For reason, put to'her best extension,
> Almost meetes faith, and makes both centers one.[62]

It is evident that Donne had in mind some pattern of the relations of the circles used by the astronomers and mathematicians to represent the relative positions of the planets, when he wrote these lines. Let us begin at home, with man. Man is given two centers, one of "waight," and one of "greatnesse," corresponding respectively to his two faculties of reason and faith. It is round these centers that man's natural life and spiritual life revolve, and, thus, both centers are somehow comprehended in the orbit of his life. What kind of diagram will represent this condition? In the Ptolemaic astronomy, man himself is the center of the universe, and all the rest of the world is referred to this center. Even God may be thought of as some all-seeing eye directing its glance particularly upon this planet. In Donne's poem, however, is the expression of a different point of view, one directed away from homocentricity. Though both of man's centers are psychologically within himself, they are objectified as the centers of circles without himself, communicating radially with the circumference of human experience.

[62] *Ibid.*, p. 267, ll. 1-16.

It is the Copernican scheme that provides the right figurative illustra-tion of this relationship. As in the letter to Sir Henry Goodyer Donne made the new astronomy "appliable well" to the description of a friendship of two men thriving under different worldly conditions, so again, he finds its application appropriate—this time to the representa-tion of the effective relations of reason and faith to God.

Donne has nothing to do with the third motion of the earth, de-veloped by Copernicus to explain the precession of the equinoxes. It is hardly to be doubted, however, that he could have found in this complexity an "appliability" to some subtle relationship had he so desired; but now, as before, he is content to use the circular course of the daily rotation and of the annual orbit, by which the paths of the first and second motions of the earth were described.

In his letter to Goodyer the center of the smaller circle, the "wheel," is reason, the faculty that exercises itself upon all that "this naturall world doth comprehend." It is the immediate center of the earth's activities and measures "quotidian things" and things "equidistant hence," a figure chosen to suggest the physical reality of space and at the same time to show how reason, symbolized as the center of the circle on which the earth describes its daily course, is confined to the objects of the natural world. It is the faculty by which we are made aware of the "rags of time"—in short, it is the means by which we know time and space.

Of the "enormous greatnesses" of the orbit of which faith is the center, the deferent, or circumference of the circle on which the diurnal motion is described, is the counterpart in the geometrical diagram. Its startling novelty and bewildering enormity strike Donne's imagination as apt to connote the equally elusive and ineffable realities as "Gods essence, place, and providence." Why, we may ask, are these "enormous greatnesses" regarded as "so disproportion'd, and so angulare"? First, these particular words indicate the feebleness of reason to get hold of the incomprehensible and inexpressible objects of faith which stretch out toward God and infinity, for reason knows only "quotidian things, and equidistant hence," and therefore can appreciate only quantitative knowledge of phenomena extended in time and space. A similar image in *The second Anniversary*, a poem carrying many images that are echoed in the elegy,[63] reveals Donne's same predilection for the use of mathematical abstractions to convey the vaster abstractions of Divinity:

[63] Cf. particularly, the *Elegie*, ll. 71-74 (*ibid.*, I, 269) with the *Anniversary*, ll. 143-46 (*ibid.*, p. 255).

> To whose proportions [of Elizabeth Drury's soul
> conceived as the world soul] if we would compare
> Cubes, th'are unstable; Circles, Angular.[64]

Is there any basis in astronomical fact for Donne's choice of the particular phrase, "so disproportion'd and so angulare"? It is not too daring to intimate that Donne, in contemplating the greatness of the period of faith, recalled the vast circle of the annual orbit of the earth, some 95,000,000 miles according to computation, a distance in bewildering "disproportion" to the simpler reckoning of the old astronomers. Both in Kepler and in Gilbert he became acquainted with the measurements recently made of the terrestrial orbit, and it is not unlikely that the recollection of these astonishing numbers together with Clavius's fantastic computation of the size of the concave of the firmament and Galileo's proof of the great extension of the heavens was in his mind when he coined the figure.

One gathers from Donne that it is only in a relative sense that reason and faith, like the two circles by which they are represented, are not concentric. Put to its "best extension," reason, in the full journey that it runs, like the circle of the earth's diurnal motion whose immediate center is on the circumference of the greater circle, describes its course round the God-centered universe. Thus, Donne achieves a literal translation of abstract idea into language which deprives the idea of none of its intellectual glitter and at the same time endows it with a graphic vividness that carries it into the reader's imagination.

The figure of reason and faith, derived from Donne's astronomical lore, is, however, extended still further. "These things," he writes, namely, "Gods essence, place, and providence," and other mysteries enumerated, "eccentrique else," "on faith do strike." That is to say, if these mysteries are not to be comprehended by faith, faith is not the true center of the scope of man's spiritual experience. The phrase, "eccentrique else," it will be remembered, is enclosed in parentheses; and it is this simple parenthetical expression that calls attention to Donne's understanding of one of the details in Copernicus's modification of the world scheme. Eccentrics, epicycles, deferents, and equants had burdened the old Ptolemaic system, but in reducing the world picture to greater simplicity Copernicus had not been able to do away entirely with some of these devices. Because he still held to the antique postulate of uniform circular motion of the planets and as the heliocentric system was "not sufficient to explain the varying velocities of the planets in their orbits"—the so-called "first inequalities"—he re-

[64] *Ibid.,* I, 255, ll. 141-42.

sorted to the use of the old machinery. Consequently, "as regards the motion of the earth round the sun Copernicus had of course nothing essential to add to the excentric circle (or concentric circle with an epicycle) which Ptolemy had used for the motion of the sun." [65] In this way a little epicycle placed on the circumference of the circle used to describe the annual orbit of the earth (a circle with its true center at the sun) allowed for the eccentricity in the relation of the motions of these planets that Copernicus accepted from earlier observations.[66] Thus, Donne's conception of the relation of man to faith and God is satisfied. The true center of the spiritual life—a center coincident with God himself—is faith; and it is the Copernican analogy that provides both for the figurative representation of this and for the deviation (the eccentricity) from the perfect course which man in the circle of his "natural" experiences (as a rational creature) follows.

It should be noted that by making the "enormous greatnesses" of "Gods essence . . ." strike upon faith, the center of the great orbit of man's experience, the place in the physical world occupied by the sun, he seems, as stated above, to make God the analogue of the sun, if the full weight of the figurative representation be allowed. That such an idea should have entered Donne's mind is neither shocking nor strange. The identification of the sun with God is one of the concomitants of the Neoplatonic metaphysics, adduced to justify the new astronomy, appealing rather to the esthetic than to the mathematical demand made upon the new system. The place of the sun in the universal construction of the Christian Neoplatonic St. Augustine at once comes to mind. Though Donne was familiar enough with Augustine, much nearer home, in Kepler himself, there is evidence of the divine regard of the new philosophers for the solar planet. One of the elements in the Copernican scheme which evoked Kepler's enthusiastic support as completely as any other, was the place of dignity and exaltation given to the sun. In a youthful eulogy of the new system he glows with extravagance over the sun as the most excellent "of all the bodies of the universe," that body "which alone we should judge worthy of the Most High God, should He be pleased with a material domicile and choose a place to dwell with the most blessed angels." [67]

That Donne ever saw the particular words quoted above cannot be ascertained, but that he was familiar with the idea, often repeated by

[65] Dreyer, *History of the Planetary Systems*, p. 331.
[66] Cf. "Ptolemaeus Solem collocat in eccentrico, eccentricum includit duobus deferentibus; Copernicus epicyclo affigit planetam, epicyclum concentrico."—Kepler, *Prodromus*, Frisch, I, 120.
[67] *Fragmentum orationis de motu terrae*, Frisch, VIII, 267.

Kepler, is hardly to be questioned. In the *Commentary on Mars* Kepler attributes to the sun the impelling power of all the planets; and in the *Mysterium Cosmographicum*,[68] a book which Donne may very well have seen, he identifies the sun with God the Father, the fixed stars with God the Son, and the intervening ethereal medium through which the power of the sun is communicated to move the planets in their orbits, with the Holy Ghost. Donne in no way shares Kepler's mystical allegorizing imagination which allows him to pursue trinities—or, as with Sir Thomas Browne, quincuncial arrangements—throughout the phenomena of all the natural world; but, always, as in the poem under consideration, he reveals himself sensitive to any phase of learning that may be "appliable" to his purpose. Neither to Donne nor to Kepler can be imputed the idolatry of sun worship. The latter found in the new astronomy a sun that by virtue of its central position could be made the focus of his thoroughly mystical interpretation of the universal harmony. For Donne the conception does not become a part of some great allegorical fabric woven by his imagination; it serves only as a means of translating an abstraction into concreteness, as a way of giving to a set of relations the same graphic quality that the geometer gives to a theorem when he describes it by a figure composed of lines and points.

After the above quotation from the *Elegy on Prince Henry,* Donne digresses from the pattern on which thus far the poem has been constructed to introduce an idea deemed necessary to the theme, namely, that of universal confusion as a result of the Prince's death. By making this shift he incidentally introduces confusion into his poem. After line fifteen, bringing to a close the ingenious demonstration of the ultimate concentricity of faith and reason, Donne states that what he has been saying is applicable to the Prince:

> And nothing ever came so neare to this,
> As contemplation of that Prince, wee misse.
> For all that faith might credit mankinde could,
> Reason still seconded, that this prince would.[69]

From this he proceeds as follows:

> If then least moving of the center, make
> More, then if whole hell belch'd, the world to shake,
> What must this do, centers distracted so,
> That wee see not what to beleeve or know?[70]

With Henry's death the centers of mankind's experience have been "distracted so" that faith has become "heresie" and reason a chain of

[68] Frisch, I, 11.   [69] Grierson, I, 267, ll. 17-20.   [70] *Ibid.,* p. 268, ll. 21-24.

cause and effect made ineffectual by the intrusion of the accidents of Fate, or as Donne speaks of it, of "miracle" which thrusts the mind into the darkest kind of skepticism. It is the lines,

> If then least moving of the center, make
> More, then if whole hell belch'd, the world to shake,

so obviously reminiscent of the effects of the new astronomy upon the mind nurtured by tradition, that seem to upset the progress of the poem. The words have the structural function of a transitional element, but as a transitional element they bear no causal relation to the preceding lines. Donne has laid out an ingenious conception of the relations between reason and faith and God and has found the geometry of the new astronomy appropriate to represent this pattern of relations; but the Prince's death has disturbed the pattern, and now the poet is obliged to explain just how this has been done. In other words, he must show how the world of concrete and tragic human experience cuts across the grain of our symmetrical and harmonious metaphysical conceptions. Thus, to sound the contradiction that he discovers to exist between the theory and the facts, so to speak—a contradiction that would not be had the Prince lived—and to set the emotional and intellectual tone of the situation caused by the disturbing effects of reality upon our idealizations, he introduces the pertinent allusion to the most disturbing contemporary cosmic fact—the moving of the earth. Because the figure used to effect this end is materially related to what has gone before, we instinctively expect it also to be related logically. In fact, it is not, for it is with a psychological situation that Donne is concerned, not with a scientific one. Thus, there is no particular incongruity involved here if we are able to dissociate the levels of psychological and physical connotation evoked by the imagery.

Consequently, it is as an effective bit of dramatic symbolism that Donne intends the figure. Like a screen dropped in the path of a bright light to absorb and dissipate its brilliance, the idea is meant to project the rest of the poem into an atmosphere of shadow and half-light. There is no deliberate attempt to exploit the idea implied by the allusion to the misplaced earth for other purposes than this. When it is introduced some twenty lines farther on,

> As, for the earth throwne lowest downe of all,
> T'were an ambition to desire to fall,[71]

it would seem that art demands only that Donne reaccent the motive of gloom and skepticism established by the "transitional" lines above.

[71] *Ibid.*, p. 268, ll. 49-50.

One begins to recognize that what should have been entirely subordinate to the theme of Prince Henry's death actually comes to the front as the most significant element in the poem. As Elizabeth Drury's ghost retires before Donne's rigorous analysis of himself, here, too, the elegiac theme is dissolved in the perplexity and doubt urged upon Donne by his own thinking. It is very much as if the "Angell" which Donne accepts himself to be in the final line of the poem were singing words presumably meant for the Prince, but set to a gloomy tune by the poet's own reflections.[72] Mention of the "moving of the center," and reflection upon such disillusioning and uncomfortable thoughts as "the earth throwne lowest downe of all," provoke the "harmes and feares" spoken of by Donne in *A Valediction: forbidding mourning.* It is true that the departed soul of Prince Henry intrudes itself to account for the corruption into which the world has fallen, the shattering of faith, and its inevitable consequence, the destruction of reason; but animating this progress of the imagination is the motive to which attention has been called. The result could hardly be anything but confusion and disappointment. By a close analysis we can deduce an over-subtle and tortured treatment of the vicissitudes encountered by our idealized conceptions of the perfect relations of faith and reason in a world of genuine experience; we cannot deduce an elevated and unified memorial to the death of a prince. Perhaps the elegy would have been better had Copernicus and the moving earth not appropriated the foreground of Donne's imagination when his mind was turned to the knotty problems of life and death; certainly it would have been simpler. But then, the poem might still be preferred with all its entanglements of thought to some of the innocuous and vapid utterances which keep it company in old Sylvester's distillation of tears for the untimely death of England's Prince.

The last illustration of the use Donne makes of the figure of the moving earth will be drawn from a poem of the year 1613. By that year Donne could look upon the new philosophy with temporary levity at least. The year preceding had been marked by his efforts to escape or to solve its troublesome implications—in fact, to solve the entire problem of doubt and uncertainty imposed upon the mind by our feeble attempts at knowledge. He had bent his contemplative energies —never too strong in Donne—upon the "essentiall joyes" of heaven to which Elizabeth Drury's soul had but recently attained. But now, with the unfortunate occasion for advancing his secular ambitions once

[72] *Ibid.,* p. 270, 1. 98.

more before him, he was able to wave aside, indifferently, the claims made by speculation upon the serious themes of the *Anniversaries* and write the *Epithalamion* in honor of the anticipated marriage of the Earl of Somerset to Lady Howard.[73]

Nor is this poem without its virtue. There is fluency, more dignity than the subject deserved, and an echoing tenderness provoked by the refrain, ". . . of thy inflaming eyes, and of thy loving heart," that reveal the certain stamp of the poet's experience and maturity in handling an unwelcome subject in a manner that convention decreed. Indeed, the *Epithalamion* was a more "perfect sacrifice" than Donne's muse should have felt obliged to make; but then, a numerous family and a bleak prospect may justly make unseemly demands. In addition to the grace and unexpected restraint and tenderness of the piece there is a fourth element which should not be wanting in a poem designed to arouse good feeling and evoke response, and this is gaiety.

For Donne the gaiety results from the exercise of an ingenious mind and subtle wit in novel ways. Thus, the old wit which nibbed his pen in the sonnet days moves again upon his language to bring forth such figures as "their easy liquid jawe," [74] the "gellie" of a fallen star,[75] and allusions to the lamp that "burnt cleare" "in Tullias tombe," [76] and to his own "undiscerning Muse." [77] But nowhere is the mark set stronger than upon the lines gently mocking his own seriousness over the doctrine of the moving earth. In the stanza on "Feasts and Revells" (VIII), he writes:

> And were the doctrine new
> That the earth mov'd, this day would make it true;
> For every part to dance and revell goes.
> They tread the ayre, and fal not where they rose.
> Though six houres since, the Sunne to bed did part,
> The masks and banquets will not yet impart
> A sunset to these weary eyes, A Center to this heart.[78]

At once one marks the levity of the poet playing with one of the common arguments against the motion of the earth and the familiarity with the matter which makes this levity possible. His mind, but lately too much upon the "world emploi'd," has with spontaneous indifference, submitted the traditional reason why the earth does not move as an explanation of its motion.

[73] *Ibid.*, pp. 131-41, including the *Ecclogue*, pp. 131-35. See also, *ibid.*, II, 94.
[74] *Ibid.*, I, 135, l. 112. [75] *Ibid.*, p. 139, ll. 204, 205.
[76] *Ibid.*, p. 140, l. 215. [77] *Ibid.*, p. 135, l. 116.
[78] *Ibid.*, p. 139, ll. 186-92.

For every part to dance and revell goes.
They tread the ayre, and fal not where they rose.

Here, astronomical theory, right or wrong, is beneath his concern. He is neither approached by doubt nor by the demands laid upon him by his impoverished condition. Once more he is the poet practicing the art of removing himself from the materials with which he is working, as in many of his early love poems, where he could be the spectator of his own amours and listen to the drama of his soul. It is this ability to be objective that allows him to mingle freely the apparent incongruities of misplaced cause and effect and provides him with the license to appropriate the seemingly uncongenial arguments of science to adorn a marriage feast. Note the success. The contradiction of new and old astronomy, fitting ill with one another and confused in the popular mind, suggests, when treated lightly, exactly the careless, incoherent revelry of the marriage—and perhaps even imparts a note of irony to the occasion.

Over and over again in his mind Donne has turned the arguments for and against the doctrine of Copernicus. From Kepler, Galileo, Clavius, and Gilbert he has learned them all. That trees would be uprooted, birds frustrated in their flight, and animals precipitated into the air if the earth actually whirled about as the new philosophers teach have become a part of the "welter of experience" flooding his mind. From these arguments and many more he selects one to decorate the epithalamion for his prospective patron. Bodies thrown vertically into the air will not return to the spot from which they were thrown, if the earth moves. Copernicus had undertaken a reasonable refutation of this argument. But why, Donne must have thought—why be bothered for the moment with the subject of argument, for he grants to both parties of the debate their cherished premises. The result is what we have quoted above—a pretty piece of witty playfulness.

All the evidence presented in this chapter to account for Donne's familiarity with the principal doctrine of the new philosophy, the motion of the earth, reveals that his acquaintance extended beyond the simple generalization that such a theory existed. His study of the doctrine had taught him something of its history; he knew that it had suffered rebuff and revision as well as enjoyed acceptance by some during the years that followed its promulgation. The arguments pro and con, more exact than those bandied about in the popular imagination, were a part of his knowledge. And, what is truly important, he understood the alteration of the old system that the geometer effected in his diagrams made to represent the new order of the universe.

In anticipation of the question that may be raised as to whether or no Donne accepted the doctrine of the earth's motion, it is well to state that a categorical affirmative or negative cannot be recorded. The evidence given above illustrates Donne's ability to absorb with varying degrees of success the scientific matter into his expression. As it is the poet's imagination that attempts to command the material for some particular purpose, a study of his response to the new science should be directed upon the analysis of this imagination—not upon the subject of his acceptance or denial of a doctrine based upon the material. At present no generalization concerning the nature of the response dare be undertaken. [The motion of the earth is not the full story of the new astronomy.] A great many attendant ideas were not only in the air but also in the books Donne was reading; and for this reason an account of the ultimate contribution of the new philosophy to his imagination cannot be given before we consider the extent to which he participated in the knowledge of these ideas.

VII

THE NEW HEAVENS

THE year 1609 is one of the great years in the history of science, and, therefore, great in the history of human thought. In that year the genius of Kepler brought to completion his greatest work, *De Motibus Stellae Martis,* in which the scientist as mathematician experienced his greatest triumph. Kepler in his book on the motions of the planèt Mars proposed not merely a new hypothesis able to enjoy the reputation of being mathematically true regardless of whether or no it represented the physical facts but propounded a theory which satisfied the observations and proved that no other hypothesis could be made to agree with the observations.[1] He demonstrated the fact that the planets move round the sun, not in circles, but in ellipses; furthermore, he formulated the law governing this elliptical motion.[2] Thus, Kepler corrected Copernicus and forever laid the ghost of circular motion that from antiquity had been accepted as axiomatic.

A work that, because of its very nature, inevitably was to have a greater and more striking *immediate* influence than Kepler's book was begun by Galileo in the same year, namely, his experiments with the telescope.[3] The import of Kepler's voluminous treatise in no sense save in that of its most general implications can ever be communicated to anyone but the skilled mathematician. This fact, though not depriving it of a place alongside *De Revolutionibus* and the *Principia Mathematica,* does, nevertheless, withhold it from the reader without this skill, and consequently greatly lessens its popular appeal. Quite different, however, was the character of Galileo's work, as we learn about it from the slender volume of the *Sidereus Nuncius* which was issued from the Venetian press in mid-March of 1610. The title itself, free from any technical connotation, stirred the imagination; and the subtitle, describing the contents of the book, fulfilled the anticipations of the reader by inviting him to share in an adventure not only rivaling but surpass-

[1] Dreyer, *History of the Planetary Systems,* p. 392.
[2] Known as Kepler's first two laws of planetary motion. For specific statement of, see Singer, *Religion and Science Considered in Their Historial Relations,* p. 67. Kepler's third law was announced in 1618.
[3] For the history of the telescope, see Charles Singer's essay in *Studies in the History and Method of Science,* ed. Charles Singer (Oxford, 1917, 1921), II (1921), 385 ff., and J. J. Fahie, *Galileo: His Life and Work* (1903), pp. 74 ff.

ing the most fantastic accounts of a Guiana, of the search for the Northwest Passage, or of the discovery of new worlds beyond the sea. In full the title in translation reads: *The Astronomical Messenger: Containing and setting forth Observations lately made with the aid of a newly invented Telescope respecting the Moon's Surface, the Milky Way, Nebulous Stars, an innumerable multitude of Fixed Stars, and also respecting Four Planets never before seen, which have been named the Cosmian Stars.*[4]

In this book there was the promise of the truth that was stranger than romance. Beside it the tales of search for the treasure of the Indies and the fable of the lost Atlantis must have paled, for here was adventure in worlds to which ships had never sailed. It was as if the metaphysical world had been invested miraculously with qualities comprehensible by sense, as if the diagrams and abstractions of the geometers suddenly had been endowed with life. It is reported that in Florence a public fête was made in honor of the great discoveries, to which poets lent their grace and art to glorify a fellow citizen. Venice was in a frenzy. And when the report of the discoveries together with a telescope was carried to France, Queen Marie de' Medici fell to her knees in a fit of excitement while waiting on her servants to fix the instrument to a window so that she might view the new heavens. But shortly after this event a message went out from the French Court to Galileo requesting him to call "any other fine star" that he might discover "by the name of the Great Star of France, as well as the most brilliant of all the earth." [5]

The great enthusiasm that greeted Galileo's discoveries should not be taken to indicate universal acceptance and approval—not even by those who presumably were competent to judge of such matters. In August of 1610 Galileo wrote to Kepler that "you are the first and almost the only person, who, after a cursory investigation, has given entire credit to my statement." He then alludes to popular abuse which he can, nevertheless, dismiss, and even laugh at, "for against Jupiter even giants, to say nothing of pygmies, fight in vain." But if he and Kepler could laugh at the "extraordinary stupidity of the multitude," we can hardly look with less than contempt upon the professors who would not even look through the telescope out of a "lazy obstinacy"

---

[4] A translation of *Sidereus Nuncius* under the above title by Stafford Carlos was published in 1880 (London, Oxford, Cambridge: Rivington's). The book also contains an introduction, notes, and in translation, "A Part of the Preface to Kepler's Dioptrics." All references to *Sidereus Nuncius* will be to the Carlos translation, cited as *Sidereus Nuncius*.

[5] Fahie, *op. cit.*, pp. 99-100.

like that "of a serpent who has eaten his fill." Galileo concludes the letter with an example of this obstinacy set by the leading philosopher of the faculty of Pisa who attempted to turn the Grand Duke from him by discrediting the new discoveries with "logical arguments, as if with magical incantations to tear down and argue the new planets out of heaven." [6]

In the *Sidereus Nuncius* Galileo makes no effort to indicate the connection between his discoveries and the doctrine of Copernicus. In fact he mentions the name of Copernicus but once in the book.[7] In his conversations and lectures, however, he did not hesitate to point out the bearing of his work upon the establishment of the new theory; [8] nor did the orthodox-minded miss its implications. Thus, at last, sixty-seven years after the publication of *De Revolutionibus*, evidence supporting the physical truth of the Copernican theory was provided; no longer were the champions of the old and the new systems of the world without a realistic basis for their disagreement.[9] The comforting and rationalistic dichotomy of truth, effected by a tradition that permitted the dissociation of the mathematical and physical truth of Copernicus, Galileo rendered both disturbing and unintelligent. No longer were the problems of astronomy a matter to be settled solely by the geometer's pencil and compasses. His figures and diagrams were strangely metamorphosed into a skeleton of physical fact and threatened to assume even more lifelike aspects. Moreover, the telescope made what had been largely the property of the scientist the property of the public. In fact, as Professor De Morgan writes, "the exhibition of Jupiter and his satellites was an argument which was not only worth much, but was soon to go for more than it was worth with the whole of the educated community." He refers also in this statement to the more active and pertinent interest that the theologians were to take in the matter of the new science. As long as Copernicus's doctrine was set forth as a "hypothetical," or a problematical view of the universe, the book in which it was expounded was allowed to go unmolested; but

[6] *Ibid.*, p. 102.
[7] Page 69.
[8] Fahie, *op. cit.*, p. 100.
[9] De Morgan, in reviewing the history of the theory of Copernicus up to Galileo, says that before the discoveries of Galileo there was no "genuine controversy" on the subject. "The question was not, properly speaking, discussed. Various writers gave opinions [Kepler always uses the word *sententia* when speaking of any doctrine concerning the universe expounded by another philosopher], but no book was written against another book." Recall in this connection, as De Morgan points out, that Clavius as early as 1570 regarded Copernicus as "the excellent restorer of astronomy," and admired him as a second Ptolemy; at the same time he thought the theory of the motion of the earth rash, absurd, and contrary to the senses. See *op. cit.*, pp. 5, 15

once men began reading it "through Galileo's glass," it aroused so much excitement that the cardinals of the Index thought it necessary to proscribe it.[10]

Evidence of the alarm that spread through the ranks of the mathematicians may be gathered from the remarks of Clavius who laughingly declared that Galileo had put something into the telescope before he turned it toward the heavens [11] and from the fact that the young German mathematician, Martin Horky, within but a few months after the publication of Galileo's book was moved to write his presumptuous *Brevissima peregrinatio contra nuncium sidereum*.[12] One more example of the kind of reception given Galileo by his learned colleagues will suffice to test the soundness of De Morgan's contention that the whole question of the two systems of the world was now open to the warmest controversy. One of the gentlemen who doubtless argued against Galileo before the Grand Duke with "logical arguments" and "magical incantations" was Francesco Sizzi, from whose *Dianoia Astronomica,* published in Venice, 1611, one can obtain a sample of the depth of his logic and the efficacy of his magic.

There are seven windows given to animals in the domicile of the head [declared Sizzi] . . . two nostrils, two eyes, two ears, and a mouth. So in the heavens . . . there are two favourable stars, two unpropitious, two luminaries, and Mercury undecided and indifferent. From this and many other similarities in nature . . . we gather that the number of planets is necessarily seven. Moreover, these satellites of Jupiter are invisible to the naked eye, and therefore can exercise no influence on the earth, and therefore would be useless, and therefore do not exist.

In further support of his opinion he "argues" that as we have seven days in the week, and so on, it follows that the admission of any more planets would cause "this whole and beautiful system to fall to the ground." [13] One might add that it likewise follows that Sizzi had not looked through the telescope; and it is hard to find on the grounds of such "logic" as he practiced any great inconsistency in the fact that he was executed a few years later in Paris for political crimes which, obviously, he could not deny as easily as he could throw out the new planets from the heavens.

It is not the purpose of this work to write the history of Galileo's

[10] *Ibid.,* p. 23.

[11] See Fahie, *op. cit.,* p. 101.

[12] In *Le opere di Galileo Galilei, Edizione Nazionale,* ed. Antonio Favaro (Florence, 1890 ff.), III (1892), Pt. I, 129-45. Horky's *Peregrinatio* bears the "imprimatur" of "Die 18. Iunii, 1610." Upon the advice of his friends, Galileo did not undertake a reply. Favaro's edition of Galileo will later be referred to as *Edizione Nazionale.*

[13] Fahie, *op. cit.,* p. 103.

great contribution to modern science—a work that has been done so admirably by the editor of the *Sidereus Nuncius* in the fine *Edizione Nazionale* of his writings [14]—but it is necessary to review, as we have done, the response that the book met in order to place it significantly among the body of influences which helped to enrich Donne's thought. In fulfilling this introductory obligation we should also call attention to the reception that was given to the *Sidereus Nuncius,* not only by Donne, but by some of his countrymen.

England, it is pleasant to recall, was more hospitable to the new science than any other country,[15] and for this reason it is not surprising to find some of the countrymen of Recorde, Dee, and Thomas Digges, commenting upon the discoveries of Galileo with an enthusiasm that at once speaks for a great sympathy with the new learning and an intelligence not heavily burdened by the trammels of authority. Above we have noted the letter of Sir Henry Wotton, ambassador at the Venetian Court, to the Earl of Salisbury, accompanying the copy of the *Sidereus Nuncius,* "come abroad this very day," which he had obtained for James I.[16] That Wotton did not grasp the full import of the work of Galileo may be argued; but that he was ready to wonder at it as "the strangest piece of news . . . that he [the King] hath ever yet received from any part of the world," without deriding it as the absurdity of the age is, indeed, significant of an open and eagerly inquiring mind. Furthermore, after bravely affirming that "upon the whole subject he hath first overthrown all former astronomy . . . and next all astrology," he ventures to ask, "why may there not yet be more" new planets than Galileo has already discovered? At least, he acts on the assumption that it would do no harm to investigate the matter, for the letter ends with a note to the effect that "by the next ship your Lordship shall receive from me one of the above-named instruments, as it is bettered by this man."

During the Renaissance many English and Scottish students attended the University of Padua, where between 1592 and 1610 Galileo held a professorship.[17] Among these men who journeyed to the famous

[14] See above, p. 119 n. 12.

[15] See De Morgan, *op. cit.,* and "Notices of English Mathematical and Astronomical Writers between the Norman Conquest and the Year 1600," *Companion to the Almanac* (1837), pp. 23-44. The number of Englishmen who may be regarded as in some way sympathetic with the Copernican doctrine is proportionally greater by far than that of Continental scientists reported.

[16] See above, p. 84 n. 52. Wotton's date, March 13, 1610, is correct. Galileo writes on the same day that he is sending "a Belisario Vinta la prima copia del *Siderius Nuncius.*" *Edizione Nazionale,* III, Pt. II, 404.

[17] See Io. Aloys Andrich, *De natione Anglica et Scota iuristarum universitatis Patavinae, ab a. MCXXII P.Ch.N.usque ad a. MDCCXXXVIII* (Padua, 1892).

Italian university were at least two who achieved a degree of fame incident to the publication of *Sidereus Nuncius,* John Wedderborn and Thomas Seggett [Seget]. Shortly after Martin Horky published his *Brevissima peregrinatio contra nuncium sidereum* in June, 1610, an answer was forthcoming by a young Scotch friend and pupil of Galileo, one John Wedderborn, then in Italy. Wedderborn's book, a *Confutatio* of Horky's four problems posed against the Galilean discoveries, borrowed generously from Kepler, but in this very process of going directly to the greatest Copernican authority in Europe, the author showed a discretion far in excess of his opponent's.[18] From one source we learn of Thomas Seggett, the other student, only that he "was in prison on the charge of libeling a Venetian noble"; and finally acquitted, "after the great persistence" of the English Ambassador.[19] Of more substantial note is his title to the authorship of a group of laudatory epigrams to Kepler's *Narratio de Jovis Stellatibus,* issued in 1611 as a defense of Galileo's discoveries.[20] In these epigrams Seggett praises not only the genius of Kepler and Galileo but also the magnificence of Cosmo the Second, Galileo's patron, in whose honor the Jovian satellites were named the Medicean Stars. Of particular note is the sixth epigram, beginning, *Keplerus, Galilae, tuus tua sidera vidit,* because it contains the famous exclamation *Vicisti Galilaee,* which so frequently has been attributed to Kepler himself.

That the fame of *Sidereus Nuncius* was spread abroad in England, perhaps through Wotton's prompt enthusiasm, is further evidenced by the interesting letter of Sir William Lower to the mathematician, Thomas Hariot, in June, "the longest day of 1610." Hariot had evidently become familiar with the book some time before, for Lower wrote:

I gave your letter a double welcome, both because it came from you and contained newes of that strange nature . . . Methinks my diligent Galileus hath done more in his three fold discoverie than Magellene in opening up the streightes to the South sea or the dutch men that weare eaten by beares in Nova Zembla.[21]

[18] Wotton's biographer, Logan Pearsall Smith, fails to note that Sir Henry was honored by the dedication of this early tribute to Galileo, "Illustrissimo domino D. Henrico Woton potentissimi Magnae Britanniae regis apud senatum Venetum oratori, domino meo colendissimo," *Edizione Nazionale,* III, Pt. II, 151. The *Confutatio* was published in Padua, Nov. 17, 1610.

[19] Smith, *op. cit.,* I, 68.

[20] There are nine epigrams in all, entitled *Thomas Segethi Britanni in illustrissimi viri Galilaei Galilaei, patricisi et Florentini et sereniss. magni Hetruriae ducis Cosmi II philosophi et mathematici, observationes coelestes epigrammata,* in *Edizione Nazionale,* III, Pt. I, 188-89.

[21] In Henry Stevens, *Thomas Hariot* (London, 1900), pp. 116-18.

To this may be added the letter of John Wells to Galileo in October of 1613. Though a delay of three years from the date of publication of *Sidereus Nuncius* occurred before Wells received the book, his enthusiasm and gratitude were not diminished: *Tuus ad meas devenit manus, ab hinc triennium fere, Sidereus Nuncius quem quidem gratissimum accepi, non tam mellifluo captus (quo polles) styllo, quam quod avidus eram abstrusissima illa naturae (de quibus loqueris) invisendi.*[22]

Thus, with England providing a congenial climate for the ideas of the new astronomy it is not very strange that Donne should have read Galileo's book shortly after its publication. As pointed out above,[23] the first reference made by Donne to this book that can be dated specifically occurs in the Latin edition of *Ignatius his Conclave*, which was entered in the Stationers' Register on the 24th of January, 1611.[24] This work, however, is not the only book on which Galileo's influence left its impress. Both of the *Anniversaries*, likewise, record the knowledge that Donne gleaned from his reading about the discoveries of the telescope. Though these pieces afford the principal sources for the study of Donne's familiarity with *Sidereus Nuncius*, it would be a mistake to think that its influence went no further. As the subtitle of *Sidereus Nuncius* indicates, the book brought before the eyes of the world four new facts, amounting to as many singular experiences for Donne: that the moon's surface is irregular, with mountains and valleys like those of the earth; that the fixed stars are countless; that the Milky Way may be resolved into a "congeries" of innumerable fixed stars; and that there exist four new planets, the satellites of Jupiter. Of each of these discoveries, either directly or indirectly, Donne takes cognizance. Furthermore, though the *Sidereus Nuncius* makes no mention of the Copernican system, all of the discoveries therein described are in tacit agreement with the new conception, a correlation which Kepler's short *Dissertatio cum Nuncio Sidereo*, published but shortly after Galileo's book in the same year, sought to establish.[25]

Donne did not have to go to Galileo for information on the doctrine of the moving earth, but that Galileo's book carried the new doctrine deeper into his imagination is made certain by the fact that it is after 1610 that most of the allusions to the earth's motion appear, and then in surroundings richly indebted to the author of *Sidereus Nuncius*. In like manner, the *Sidereus Nuncius* gave a new and realistic meaning

[22] In *Edizione Nazionale*, XI, 585.
[23] See above, p. 83.
[24] See Simpson, *op. cit.*, p. 181.
[25] Frisch, II, 485-506. The *Dissertatio*, published in Prague, is dated by Kepler in the dedication, "Non. Majas. anno Christi Domini MDCX."

to other phases of the new astronomy already familiar to Donne, such as the new stars of Tycho Brahe and Kepler, the argument raised by the new science against the old disposition of the four elements, and the speculation on the habitability of other planets. The book, in short, did for Donne what it must have done for many—it projected against a world of factual experience his store of cosmological and astronomical learning pertaining to the new and the old orders alike, it gave to the new order a concreteness and reality that removed it from the category of problematical and theoretical things, and it set up a body of facts that would forever disturb the mind accustomed to the security of the old world scheme. Galileo's account of his discoveries reads like a clean vindication of Kepler's bold announcement in *De Stella Nova* that the *alteratae materiae coelestis confirmentur,* and strengthened Donne's regard for these words as proof that "the reason which moved Aristotle seems now to be utterly defeated." [26] Though the material set forth by Galileo was divided into four parts, it definitely contributed to the establishment of but one idea and its corollary—that there is a new heaven, and a new earth. The principle of the old philosophy affirming the heavens to be subject neither to "corruption" nor "generation," because *a tot seculis nihil est animadversum,* was rendered invalid; and as if creation had begun its work again a new heaven and a new earth were called into existence. With this as a unifying thought, let us consider how fully Donne appreciated the words of Galileo's "sidereal messenger."

First the new stars. In an early poem Donne had declared his mistress's beauty to be like the "unchangeable firmament," [27] thus revealing his familiarity with the old philosophers who held that the eighth heaven, or the firmament of the fixed stars, was immutable.[28] In fact, the stars had been counted, and their number definitely fixed at 1,022. In 1572, however, Tycho Brahe had observed, what he was at first inclined to doubt, or if true to regard as among the greatest miracles that "have occurred in the whole range of nature since the

---

[26] See above, pp. 81-82.

[27] *A Feaver,* Grierson, I, 21, l. 24.

[28] Tycho Brahe summarizes the matter very well in the following words: "For all philosophers agree, and facts clearly prove it to be the case, that in the ethereal region of the celestial world no change in the way either of generation or corruption, takes place; but that the heavens and the celestial bodies in the heavens are without increase or diminution, and that they undergo no alteration, either in size or in light or in any other respect, etc." From Tycho Brahe's *De Stella Nova,* translated in Harlow Shapley and Helen E. Howarth, *A Source Book in Astronomy* (New York, 1929), p. 13. Tycho's treatise on the new star was first printed in 1573 in Copenhagen and later incorporated in part in his *Progymnasmata.* See Dreyer, *Tycho Brahe,* pp. 44, 368-69.

beginning of the world, or one certainly that is to be classed with those attested by the Holy Oracles"—a new star in the constellation of Cassiopeia.[29] Not since the time of Hipparchus, as reported by Pliny,[30] had a new star appeared in the heavens, and this was far too long ago to˙give serious cause for anxiety to the sixteenth-century observer. The star that had guided the Magi had been interpreted as a miraculous light, and thus it could hardly be the subject of comparison with Tycho's new discovery. The star in Cassiopeia, though at first of amazing brightness, surpassing Venus, gradually lost its intensity, changed its color, and by the end of March, 1574, became invisible. Again, as pointed out above, another new star, observed first in 1604 in Serpentarius, had become the subject of Kepler's treatise, De Stella Nova,[31] to which he added his description of the new star seen four years earlier in the constellation of the Swan. The former of the two, like Tycho's star, had shone brightly for a while and then had faded out completely.[32] These sporadic occurrences and temporary phenomena were made to seem like matters of little consequence, however, until at last, Galileo, turning his telescope to the heavens, saw revealed for the first time the numberless multitudes of stars of which man never before had even dreamed.[33]

Though Donne frequently alludes to "new stars," it is quite impossible to regard these allusions as applying particularly to the stars of Tycho Brahe or Kepler or Galileo. This in itself is not strange, as Donne at no time was compiling a star catalogue or composing astronomical poems like those of Palenginus and Manilius. His first purpose was the expression of his own thoughts and feelings as they were

[29] Ibid., p. 13. So popular and widespread was the fame of Tycho Brahe that Donne would have known of his new star even had he not read so much about it in Kepler's De Stella Nova. It was Kepler's book, however, that contributed so greatly to his knowledge of the subject. See particularly De Stella Nova, Frisch II, pp. 620, 686, 692, 702, 703, 726, 747, 765, where Kepler discusses the star of 1572. Tycho himself predicted the disappearance of his star: "It does not seem likely that it will last beyond September, or at most, October, 1573, and it would be far more marvellous if it remained, for things which appear in the world after the creation of the universe ought certainly to cease again before the end of the world."—Dreyer, Tycho Brahe, p. 45.

[30] Natural History, Bk. II. Hipparchus flourished 160-125 B.C.

[31] In comparing the relative duration of the stars of 1572 and 1604, Kepler writes: "Nec ulla diversitas in duratione, qua de quis testari posset. Incensa erat illa mense Octobri vel Novembri anni 1572: incensa haec Octobri anni 1604. Illa exstincta post 16 menses, Martio scilicet anni 1574; nostra cum Octobri anni 1605. adhuc videretur, postquam 12 menses jam durasset, sequentibus quatuor mensibus ob Solis praesentiam videri non potuit; Februario et Martio anni 1606. disparuerat."—Frisch, II, 702.

[32] The star in the Swan had not disappeared when Kepler published his account, as the title states: De stella . . . in Cygno, quae usque ad annum MDC. fuit incognita, necdum exstinguitur, Frisch, II, 759. See also p. 761.

[33] Sidereus Nuncius, pp. 40-43.

affected both by the philosophical outlook as altered by the new stars and by circumstances which the imagery drawn from the stars could clearly illustrate. For instance, in *A Funerall Elegie*, without doubt composed in 1610 shortly after he had read Galileo's book, he makes use of a figure drawn from the controversies raised over the new stars to suggest the inexplicable mystery of Elizabeth Drury's short but perfect life:

> But, as when heaven lookes on us with new eyes,
> Those new starres every Artist exercise,
> What place they should assigne to them they doubt,
> Argue, and agree not, till those starres goe out:
> So the world studied whose this peece should be,
> Till shee can be no bodies else, nor shee:
> But like a Lampe of Balsamum desir'd
> Rather t'adorne, then last, she soone expir'd.[34]

Here, the general reference to "new starres" as aptly applies to the transient luminary which appeared in Cassiopeia, as to that observed by Kepler in Serpentarius; nor could his imagination have failed to be stimulated by his recent acquaintance with the *Sidereus Nuncius*. Such arguments as Donne alludes to could have been found in both Tycho Brahe and Kepler. The former's projected *Astronomiae Instauratae* was almost completely postponed by his ever-growing and voluminous introductory discourse on the Cassiopeian star which lasted less than two years. The latter's book of the new star, while arguing for its authenticity, treats fully the contentions raging among the astronomers over the new phenomenon. In the *De Stella Nova* to the confusion of opinion over whether the new star is in the elementary sphere below the moon or in the remote region of the ether is added the question of its astrological import, and it is to Donne's credit that he shows no signs of having become excited with Kepler over the apparently amazing fact that the new star in Serpentarius appeared at the time of the conjunction of Saturn and Jupiter *in principio Sagittarii*.[35] But a more convenient account of the arguments raised by the discovery of the new stars, such as Donne speaks of above, particularly the issues raised by Tycho's star of 1572–74, was that given by Clavius in his commentary on Sacrobosco of 1607. According to Clavius some thought that the new star was not a new star at all but one of the thirteen stars of the constellation of Cassiopeia enlarged beyond famil- iarity; some thought it to be a little star of the firmament, temporarily

---

[34] Grierson, I, 247, ll. 67-74.

[35] See cap. xxvi, "An fortuito concurrerit sidus hoc cum tempore et loco conjunc- tionis magnae," Frisch, II, 705 ff.

magnified; and others regarded it as a comet flashing in the upper regions of the air. Following the presentation of these opinions is Clavius's own conclusion that the new star existed in the eighth heaven, possibly a new creation of Almighty God.[36]

For us the interesting thing is that Donne could make poetry out of the arguments of the philosophers. In the passage from *A Funerall Elegie,* cited above, coming near the close of a strophe in which Donne has implied a striking parallel between Elizabeth Drury and Jesus Christ, the poet finds the new stars and the arguments they provoked apposite symbols of the brief life of perfect goodness and beauty with which Elizabeth Drury, like Christ, her prototype, adorned the earth and the fatal error of mankind in responding to this ideal, this "new eye" of heaven, with contention and disputation rather than with the simple devotion it deserved.[37] While paying tribute to the Renaissance conception of the "immortality" conferred by art on nature, Donne does not go the whole way of Shakespeare in affirming that verse will outlast enduring brass and stone. For Donne the world of sense must be sustained by an animating soul of goodness and beauty, and with Elizabeth Drury's death this soul has gone from the earth and her body "turned to dust":

> Yet she's demolish'd: can wee keepe her then
> In works of hands, or of the wits of men?
> Can these memorials, ragges of paper, give
> Life to that name, by which name they must live?
> Sickly, alas, short-liv'd, aborted bee
> Those carcasse verses, whose soule is not shee.
> And can shee, who no longer would be shee,
> Being such a Tabernacle, stoop to be
> In paper wrapt; or, when she would not lie
> In such a house, dwell in an Elegie?
> But 'tis no matter; wee may well allow
> Verse to live so long as the world will now,
> For her death wounded it.[38]

Like Christ, Elizabeth Drury was heaven looking upon us with "new eyes"; earlier in the poem Donne had described the attitude that should arise in the beholder of such a wonder:

> But those fine spirits which do tune, and set
> This Organ, are those peeces which beget
> Wonder and love.[39]

[36] *Op. cit.,* pp. 217-20. On p. 221 the new stars of 1600 and 1604 are mentioned; Clavius says that what has been said about the earlier new stars holds also for these.
[37] For a further treatment of Elizabeth as a symbol of Christ, see below, ch. xiv.
[38] Grierson, I, 246, ll. 9-21.
[39] *Ibid.,* ll. 27-29.

But, instead of "wonder and love" in which for Donne "all divinity" is comprised—embracing the ideals, both of devotion and of noble living, Elizabeth Drury received as did Christ the tribute of warped and misleading interpretation and pitiable neglect. As Christ's teachings became obscured by doctrinal superfluities, so beauty is forsaken for irrelevant argument. In the poem the arguments waged for and against the new stars in the lengthy discourses of Tycho and his opponents and in the treatises of Kepler and Clavius are like the wranglings of the schools, the gloss and supergloss of pedantic divines, and the digressions of frail humanity from the force of the plain text of experience into fatuous sophistications. Nowhere has Donne more insistently and more courageously set forth the claims of a spiritual ideal, unspoiled by the rubbish of irrelevancy, upon the human mind. The use of language drawn from so precarious and uncertain a realm of experience as that of scientific controversy testifies not only to his boldness but also to his thorough command of his materials. No more apt figure could have been chosen to suggest the fragility of beauty and goodness in a world of mutability; and nothing less than an allusion to the dissension over the heavens, a subject next to divinity to be held in the greatest awe and respect, could have been called into use to disclose the folly of perverted enthusiasm.

Nor do the above lines about the new stars fall unexpectedly into the text. Donne has led up to the ironical climax of one phase of the exposition of the poem,

. . . they doubt
Argue, and agree not, till those starres goe out,

through the use of a figure which anticipates clearly the passage referring specifically to the "Artist" and the "new starres." In attempting to indicate the mysterious relationship enjoyed by Elizabeth Drury's body and soul, Donne writes that she was

One, whose cleare body was so pure and thinne,
Because it need disguise no thought within.
'Twas but a through-light scarfe, her mind t'inroule;
Or exhalation breath'd out from her Soule.
One, whom all men who durst no more, admir'd:
And whom, who ere had worth enough, desir'd;
As when a Temple's built, Saints emulate
To which of them it shall be consecrate.[40]

In the above lines there are three images which seem to have come out of the books Donne had been reading about the new stars: "whose cleare body was so pure and thinne," " 'twas but a through-light scarfe,

[40] *Ibid.*, p. 247, ll. 59-66.

her mind t'inroule," and "exhalation breath'd out from her Soule."
Next in importance to the question of their place in the heavens, and
closely dependent upon it, is that of the material of the new stars.[41]
Thus, in casting about in his memory for language that would best
describe the mysteriously beautiful and fragile nature of Elizabeth
Drury's body, Donne recalls the astronomers' opinions of the matter
of the stars. The poet makes no attempt to be technically exact or
to follow consistently the interpretation of any one author, but he
allows the suggestion given by particular words and theories to be translated into the imagery of poetry. "Whose cleare body was so pure
and thinne," so definitely allusive to some kind of celestial phenomenon, recalls that Tycho had affirmed the stars to be celestial matter
and the new one of 1572 only less pure than the others because it vanished shortly from the sky.[42] That Tycho thought it less pure, however,
in no way nullifies the power of his description to fix itself upon the
poet's imagination. Again, Kepler thought his star of 1604 had been
generated in the highest ether; being of matter run together from the
starry sphere,[43] it was more dense than the surrounding ethereal medium. It is in this fact itself that one discovers the thing that suggested
Donne's idea of bodily substance as something tangible and real
enough to be perceived, yet akin to the invisible and the transparent
—"cleare . . . pure and thinne."

The figure immediately following, "A through-light scarfe, her mind
t'inroule" confirms the poet's conception of bodily substance as something verging narrowly upon incorporeality and adds the further idea
of the relation enjoyed by body and mind. They are interfused, participating in one another, sharing alike their respective substantiality
and immateriality, and at the same time retaining their own peculiar
attributes. But the "through-light scarfe" cannot be explained so readily. The phrase seems to have a more specific origin than the general

[41] In treating the subject of the matter of the new star, Kepler says, "omnis de
materia stellae disputatio ab iis dependet, quae hactenus diximus."—*De Stella Nova*,
cap. xix, "De materia novi sideris," Frisch, II, 682. In the three chapters immediately
preceding he has proved from the agreement of its motion with the fixed stars, from
the quality of its light, and from its "scintillation," that its place is in the highest
heavens among the fixed stars. If that is its place, and he understands the stars to be
vastly removed from the earth (see cap. xvi, "De immensitate sphaerae fixarum in
hypothesibus," *ibid.*, pp. 672 ff.), the matter of the new star must be ethereal. "What
is to prevent me," he asks, "from affirming these [the new stars] to be composed of
the ethereal essence?"—*Ibid.*, p. 692.
[42] See Dreyer, *Tycho Brahe*, p. 193.
[43] *De Stella Nova*, cap. xxii, "Materiam novi sideris fuisse coelestem, et de ortu
ejus," Frisch, II, 692. Kepler cites the opinion of Tycho that the star of 1572 was
condensed from the Milky Way, and flowed back into it when it disappeared. See also,
ibid., pp. 693, 687.

observation that Kepler considered his new star composed of ethereal substance, and that Tycho found his to be composed, as he put it, of celestial matter.[44] One is inclined to find in the figure, particularly in the word "scarfe," a reminiscence of some of the notes made upon the nature of the Milky Way.[45] In the minds of the astronomers the Milky Way was closely related to the new stars. Tycho, observing the new star in Cassiopeia to be situated near the Milky Way, supposed that the matter of which the star was composed had been drawn from that source and that it was to the Milky Way that it returned when it became invisible. The belt of nebulous stars, compared by Donne himself to a "girdle"[46] veiling but not obscuring some of the stars of the many constellations through which it passed, temptingly suggests that the poet derived his image from these reflections.[47] Though the Milky Way suggests the quality of luminous transparency associated with Elizabeth Drury's body, it is probable that Donne was also thinking of the stars themselves when he conceived the image likening it to a "through-light scarfe." At least, Kepler's interpretation of the light of the stars may be adduced to enrich our explanation of the figure. Until Galileo's discoveries acquainted him with his error, Kepler held that both the planets and the stars were self-luminous. Consequently, when the new star appeared he declared that it was an ethereal body scintillating with its own light.[48] His word, *pellucida*, used so frequently to describe the new luminary, is suggestive of Donne's "through-light," though, of course, not an exact equivalent. Nevertheless, the description of the paradoxical state that Donne has in mind, that of substance made almost invisible and transparent by the influence of its inherent luminosity, might well have followed from Kepler's account of the star as an ethereal body, pellucid and interfused with light.[49]

The third figure cited above is less difficult to account for, as it

[44] Dreyer, *op. cit.*, p. 193.

[45] See below, pp. 148, 149 nn. 98-99.

[46] "Off with that girdle, like heavens Zone glittering," *Elegie XIX. Going to Bed*, Grierson, I, 120, l. 5.

[47] Cf. *Sidereus Nuncius*, pp. 42-43 with Clavius: "Cum enim ubique terrarum per eadem sidera Firmamenti, Cassiopeiam, Cygnum, Aquilam, Sagittarium, Geminos, & alia, lactea via ducta videatur, etc."—*op. cit.*, p. 219.

[48] See *De Stella Nova*, Frisch, II, pp. 619-20. In cap. xviii, where Kepler discourses on the purity of the light, the color and the scintillation of the new stars, he states that he does not know the cause of the sparkling of the fixed stars.—*Ibid.*, p. 679. In his *Astronomiae pars optica* (the *Optics*), to which Kepler refers the reader on the light of the stars, he concludes that all of the stars, and the planets (except the moon) are self-luminous. He agrees, however, with Albategnius and Vitellio that "stellis omnibus a Sole suum esse lucis modulum."—*Ibid.*, p. 293.

[49] *Ibid.*, pp. 619-20, 682, 684.

130 THE NEW HEAVENS

appears to be a direct adaptation of Clavius's report of Aristotle's explanation of the Milky Way. In his *Commentary* on Sacrobosco, Clavius says that those philosophers and astronomers who think the new star to be a comet in the highest region of the air, by their argument contradict Aristotle's opinion that the Milky Way is generated in the upper air from vapors and exhalations continually attracted to that region by the energy of the stars which are visible in the *circulo Lacteo*.[50] Donne's idea of the body as "an exhalation breath'd out from her Soule," analogous to the "congregated vapours" and celestial exhalations "kindled" *ex vaporibus, & exhalationibus . . . excitatis* by the energy of stars, is a perfect example of the subtle transformation worked upon the "scientific fact" by the poetic imagination. Furthermore, though this figure is not anticipated by the preceding image of the scarf, the two are clearly related by association. The "scarfe," so definitely reminiscent of the Milky Way, doubtless served to conjure up in the mind the "exhalation breath'd out from her Soule," springing, as it does, from the philosopher's account of the nature of the phenomenon already in his mind. That such was the way in which the sequence of images was generated is reinforced by the fact that the matter from which they are derived is set forth in one and the same section of Clavius's *Commentary*, that is, the part dealing with the new stars,[51] the subject from which the first of the three images is definitely drawn and to which all lead in the climactic strophe treating the arguments that ensued upon the discovery of these stars.

Though the "new stars" come again and again into the poems after 1610, there is no consistent use made of the star imagery; and for this reason it would be as foolish as useless to attempt to make a classification of this imagery in an arbitrary way. Only by study of the particular passages in which it appears, as in the treatment of Donne's references to the motion of the earth, can one learn how completely he had absorbed the accounts of the new discoveries. Following *A Funerall Elegie* are the *Anniversaries*, wherein Donne's crumbling world is analyzed—often with the help of his knowledge of the stars. For instance, in contrast to the effect of mutability and transiency in the upper heavens which Donne associates with the temporary life of the new stars, in the passage cited above from *A Funerall Elegie*, is that of the relative shortness of human life in the following lines, gained by an allusion to some "slow pac'd starre." The allusion falls within a passage marking the ironical decline of the present times from the glories of the Golden Age:

[50] Page 219.   [51] Pages 217 ff.

There is not now that mankinde, which was then,
When as, the Sunne and man did seeme to strive,
(Joynt tenants of the world) who should survive;
When, Stagge, and Raven, and the long-liv'd tree,
Compar'd with man, dy'd in minoritie;
When, if a slow pac'd starre had stolne away
From the observers marking, he might stay
Two or three hundred yeares to see't againe,
And then make up his observation plaine;
When, as the age was long, the sise was great;
Mans growth confess'd, and recompenc'd the meat;
So spacious and large, that every Soule
Did a faire Kingdome, and large Realme controule:
And when the very stature, thus erect,
Did that soule a good way towards heaven direct.
Where is this mankinde now? [52]

Obviously the "slow pac'd starre" is not one of the recently discovered new stars, but it is just as obvious that the recent discoveries
were in Donne's mind when he associated the well-worn notion of
the world's decay with such scientific matters as "slow pac'd" stars,
the "observer," and his "observation plaine," the table or chart on
which the observer projects the positions and movements of the stars.[53]
That this particular association of ideas and facts should have been
made is the result of two apparent causes—and, doubtless, many not
apparent. First, Donne was absorbed in the new astronomy when he
wrote the Anniversaries, and it is natural enough to find the arguments, facts, and images of the new science coming to his assistance
at every turn of thought; second, the vehicle here used by Donne to
express the idea of human frailty and decay had been for centuries
closely linked with the implications of astronomical study.
    The thought of man's mortality—an eternal theme of poetry—com-
monly haunted the imaginations of the late Elizabethans and the writers
of the Jacobean age; and for Donne it became increasingly stimulating
to the sensitivity of his maturing mind. In the above lines from The
first Anniversary Donne sets forth the thought of the temporary and
ephemeral condition of human life in terms of a traditional contrast

[52] The first Anniversary, Grierson, I, 234-35, ll. 112-27.
[53] See, for example, Kepler's "Catalogus quarundam stellarum in constellationibus
Serpentarii, Serpentis et Scorpionis, quae a Tychone vel etiam a Ptolemaeo omissae
sunt, ad annum 1604, accommodatus, etc."—De Stella Nova, Frisch, II, 667-68; and his
catalogue of the stars in the Swan, ibid., pp. 766-67. Cf. Tycho's table of the stars in
Progymnasmata frequently referred to by Kepler, and Galileo's record of his observations of the satellites of Jupiter.—Sidereus Nuncius, pp. 44 ff.

made between the primitive sturdiness and longevity of man and his
present feebleness. One of the sources of his tradition is Josephus,
with whom Donne was well acquainted long before *The first Anniversary* was written.[54] In the meantime, however, Donne has renewed
his acquaintance with this tradition elaborated amidst surroundings
that emphasize its relation to the history of astronomy—in Clavius's
Commentary on Sacrobosco. In Clavius's summary of the history of
astronomy from its beginnings down to 1606 he draws heavily upon
Josephus's story of the origins and rise of the science, wherein occurs
the account of the long lives of the patriarchs.[55] According to the
legend their lives were prolonged not by reason of their native sturdiness but out of necessity to give them time to gain a competence in
the understanding of the mysteries of the heavens. As the "art" was
young much time was required to bring it to a state of perfection.
It is this legend of long life and hardihood that is projected by the
poet against a background of experience colored by the discoveries of
the new observers, implying that the heavens are alterable and the
span of man's life as narrow as that of the new stars. Thus, by bal-
ancing a reference to a "slow pac'd starre" of an age in the mythical
history of astronomy against the suggestion of the uncertain destiny of
man in a world of new thought Donne imparts to his lines a vitality
that relieves him of the charge of being thought another borrower of
an idle chapter in the story of mankind's mortal progress.

In that portion of *The first Anniversary* devoted to an account of
the disproportion and decay [56] of all nature Donne continues to bend
to his purpose his knowledge of the recent observations of new
heavenly bodies. Among the noteworthy places in which this may be
studied is that passage, so frequently cited, but so seldom "anatomized,"
beginning, "And new Philosophy calls all in doubt." Above, we
have drawn upon these lines to illustrate Donne's acquaintance with
Copernicus's disposition of the sun in the new universe; now, though
we shall return to the lines again, we find them interesting for their
reference to the new stars as a contributing cause of the "doubt" into
which the new philosophy has plunged the world:

>   And new Philosophy calls all in doubt,
>   • • •
>   And freely men confesse that this world's spent,
>   When in the Planets, and the Firmament

[54] See n. on l. 9 of *The Progresse of the Soule,* Grierson, II, 219.
[55] Pages 3-4.
[56] Grierson, I, 237, ll. 191 ff. For a discussion of the idea of the world's decay, see
below, ch. xiv.

They seeke so many new; they see that this
Is crumbled out againe to his Atomies.
'Tis all in peeces, all cohaerence gone;
All just supply, and all Relation.[57]

This passage, though generally applicable to the discoveries of Tycho
and Kepler, more particularly takes into account the work of the
telescope as reported in *Sidereus Nuncius*. It is Galileo to whom Donne
can attribute "so many" new stars, and it is only to him that he can
ascribe the discovery of new planets. But with the recognition of these
discoveries Donne's indebtedness stops and something like perversion
appears to begin, if one is to consider solely Donne's interpretation of
the historical facts. To these observers he attributes the same despair
over the explosion of the Aristotelian doctrine of the inalterability of
the heavens that affected the popular mind. Men did "freely confesse
that this world's spent," but they were not the same men, as Donne
implies, who "seeke so many new" bodies in the heavens. It was not
they who searched for confirmation of any fears they may have had
over the breakdown of the old order. Tycho had discovered the new
star in Cassiopeia in 1572 by the happy chance favoring men who are
always looking for something new and who are not blind to it when
it appears. To him the star was the greatest miracle since creation.
With enthusiasm and like reverence Kepler regarded the stars in the
Swan and in Serpentarius. Galileo at no time seems to have been
troubled by thoughts of the world's decay; instead, he wrote that
his discoveries excited him with "astonishment" and gave him "incredible delight." [58] Furthermore, Galileo considered the discovery of the
planets of Jupiter, born in the new space of the new cosmos, along
with the stars in and beyond the Milky Way the most important contributions of his telescope.[59] The record of his observation of the new
planets in its concreteness, in the sense of unexpectedness that it con-
veys, is touched with the feeling of pure wonder that accompanies the
experience of discovery and revelation. That new stars should have
been revealed was not unanticipated; and that spots on the moon
could be resolved into the concrete shapes of mountain and valley was
the confirmation of ancient fantasy. Too, the Galaxy had been thought
to be composed of a multitude of small stars. But that "alterability"
of the heavens should invade the sacred precincts of the planetary
spheres was absolutely new. Even Galileo was somewhat in doubt,
"afraid lest the planet [Jupiter] might have moved differently from

[57] *Ibid.*, p. 237, ll. 205, 209-14.
[58] *Sidereus nuncius*, pp. 9, 11.
[59] *Ibid.*, p. 44.

the calculation of astronomers," before he finally determined through patient watching that here was something never seen before, "from the very beginning of the world up to our own times." [60] Kepler, whose entire conception of the world, based on the relation of the planets to the five regular solids, was upset by the discovery of the four satellites of Jupiter, after reviewing the matter cautiously concluded that a new set of relations was necessary and possible, and he even went so far as to prophesy that the new arrangement would be completed by the discovery of still more planets.[61]

Again, when Donne says,

> . . . they see that this
> Is crumbled out againe to his Atomies,

he is not only questioning the ultimate fate of the world by fire but also is continuing his practice of making the new astronomers share the burden of his own skepticism. In reckoning the astrological import of the occurrence of the new star in 1604 at the time of the "great conjunction" Kepler did refer to the Epicurean theory that stars are formed by a flowing together of the atoms.[62] But this is no good reason for Donne's use of a witty inversion of theory to make it appear that the countless stars observed by Galileo betoken a disintegration of the universe. That these lines should be read as the reflection of Donne's gloomy mind, not simply as a report of scientific discovery, is made quite clear further on in the poem where he treats matters familiar to the old astronomy as if they were the most daring innovations of the day. In carrying forward the idea of the broken harmony of the universe Donne calls attention to the confusion brought about by "tearing" the firmament into constellations. In addition to the multiplication of "so many Eccentrique parts," and the discovery of "such divers downe-right lines, such overthwarts," astronomy seeks further ways to "disproportion that pure forme":

> . . . It teares
> The Firmament in eight and forty sheires,
> And in these Constellations then arise
> New starres, and old doe vanish from our eyes:
> As though heav'n suffered earthquakes, peace or war,
> When new Towers rise, and old demolish't are.[63]

[60] *Ibid.*, pp. 46, 44.
[61] *Dissertatio cum Nuncio Sidereo,* Frisch, II, 505-6. Cf. Delambre, *Histoire de l'astronomie moderne,* I (Paris, 1821), 469-70.
[62] ". . . ipsa etiam stella ex atomis confluxit,"—*De Stella Nova,* Frisch, II, 706.
[63] Grierson, I, 239, ll. 255, 256, 257-62.

Donne knew that the "eight and forty sheires" were as old as Hipparchus, and that from his time the number of the fixed stars had been put at 1,022.[64] Though he is perverse in dealing with the number of constellations, he is once more the sensitive observer of contemporary scientific discovery in speaking of the appearance of new stars in the constellations and the disappearance of some of the old. Donne's statement signifies something more than the fact that he noted the new stars in Cassiopeia, Serpentarius, and the Swan. Tycho actually had reduced the number of constellations, and in his famous star catalogue, which Kepler called to Donne's attention, he had listed but 777 stars. Though stars were thus lost that had been honored from antiquity, new ones were added. Kepler says that Tycho collected stars from everywhere (*undique*) to bring his number up to 1,000 (the number appearing in the unpublished manuscript catalogue in Kepler's possession); [65] and in 1603, John Bayer issued his famous *Uranometria*, frequently mentioned by Kepler, containing more than 1,700 stars and twelve new constellations.[66] However, when we read further on in Donne, that

> They have impal'd within a Zodiake
> The free-borne Sun, and keepe twelve Signes awake
> To watch his steps,[67]

we realize that the traditions of science by no means escaped the sting of his skepticism, a fact that has generally been overlooked by his critics. Thus, in lumping together the old and the new philosophies as a cause for his uncertainty about the world, he underscores the embracing literalness of his well-known affirmation that "new Philosophy calls *all* [italics mine] in doubt."

To the idea of the alterability of the heavens inferred from the "generation" of the new bodies of stars and planets, it should be noted that a few lines further on Donne alludes to a popular notion of the decay of the universe based on a discrepancy among ancient and modern astronomers in their observations of the declination of the sun:

[64] See Clavius, *op. cit.*, pp. 174-75.
[65] "Et tamen haec nostra neque in libro Progymnasmatum inter 800 neque in catalogo 1000 fixarum manuscripto reperitur."—*De Stella in Cygno*, Frisch, II, 765. Immediately above Kepler calls attention to the fact that though Tycho could not see all of the stars recorded by the ancients, he described many that they had never observed. Kepler is in error in giving Tycho's number as 800. See Dreyer, *Tycho Brahe*, p. 227.
[66] Though Kepler refers to Bayer in both *De Stella in Cygno* and *De Stella Nova*, he does not mention the total number of stars recorded in *Uranometria*. See Frisch, II, 662, 762, 770, 776, 824.
[67] Grierson, I, 239, ll. 263-65.

. . . nor can the Sunne
Perfit a Circle, or maintaine his way
One inch direct; but where he rose to-day
He comes no more, but with a couzening line,
Steales by that point, and so is Serpentine:
And seeming weary with his reeling thus,
He meanes to sleepe, being now falne nearer us.[68]

It is no novelty of the new science that the sun cannot "perfit a Circle, or maintaine his way one inch direct." From antiquity the inequalities in the [apparent] annual motion of the sun, which Donne has in mind, had been noted. Hipparchus discovered "from a comparison of his own observations with the more ancient ones of Timochares, that the intersections of the ecliptic with the equator were not fixed, but variable points." [69] These inequalities, translated into terms of the obliquity of the ecliptic, or the precession of the equinoxes (as they were observed in the positions of the stars through which the sun described its annual course) were diversely explained and calculated throughout the ages. Copernicus, considering the matter fully in the third book of De Revolutionibus, with too great confidence in the old observations, reckoned a variation in the obliquity between 23° 52' to 23° 28' (the maximum declination in his own time) to have occurred periodically in 3,434 years. Tycho saw no need to assume the irregularity in the precession of the equinoxes, and taking into account a constant of variation and the influence of refraction, produced still other and more accurate results. In fact, as early as 1538 Fracastoro had asserted that from the beginning of time the obliquity of the ecliptic had diminished at a regular rate.[70] This observation provided the basis for computing the ultimate date when the plane of the ecliptic would be drawn into coincidence with that of the equator. Popularly, the diminishing declination of the sun meant that "the Sun in our time goeth not so far Southernly from vs in Winter, as it did in the time of Ptolomy and Hipparchus, neither in Summer cometh so much Northernly towards vs, as then." [71]

Closely associated with this idea is the notion, apparently transmitted widely by Bodin and Melanchthon, that the sun actually is nearer the earth than in the past.[72] How baseless the notion was may be de-

[68] Ibid., p. 239, ll. 268-74.
[69] Robert Small, An Account of the Astronomical Discoveries of Kepler (London, 1804), p. 7. See also Dreyer, Tycho Brahe, pp. 354-55.
[70] See Dreyer, op. cit., pp. 354-55, and History of the Planetary Systems, p. 300.
[71] G[eorge] H[akewell], An Apologie of the Power and Providence of God in the Government of the World (Oxford, 1627), pp. 94-95.
[72] Ibid., pp. 93, 94.

THE NEW HEAVENS 137

duced from the general disagreement among the observers of the past
and from Kepler's calculation of the vastly remote distance of the sun
from the earth.[73]

Donne appears to accept both the inequality of the sun's motion
and its reputed approach to the earth in the way these opinions were
currently interpreted to argue for the general decay of the earth. Particular significance is given to his utterance by the fact that these conventional opinions are boldly merged with the discovery of new stars
and planets and the displacement of the sun and earth in the Copernican
reconstruction, to which he earlier alludes,

> The Sun is lost, and th'earth, and no mans wit
> Can well direct him where to looke for it.[74]

In writing thus Donne is not simply versifying a popular pessimistic doctrine, but rather exploiting that doctrine in his original way
to make clear the fit of disillusionment which has seized him. Nor is
this to deny that his gloom was deepened by the influence of the scientific discoveries alluded to. Always there is a reciprocal action to be
taken into account: though the materials from which the imagery is
drawn are properly subordinated to the major purpose of analyzing
a condition of mind, they nevertheless are made to share the responsibility for the existence of that condition.

In *The second Anniversary* there is, superficially, little that bears
the impress of Donne's study of the new astronomy; the imagery
present that is derived from scientific learning harks back to the old
order.[75] The new stars, the Galaxy, the planets of Jupiter, the aspect
of the moon, the conception of new worlds, are absent; but this
absence of imagery based on the recent discoveries should not be taken
to mean that Donne has abandoned his interest in the new science. Its
significance lies, as we shall see, in the fact that the purpose of the
poem demanded the exclusion of this material. The end Donne sought
to effect is anticipated in the opening lines:

> Nothing could make me sooner to confesse
> That this world had an everlastingnesse,
> Then to consider, that a yeare is runne,

[73] *De Stella Nova*, Frisch, II, 671-72.   [74] Grierson, I, 237, ll. 207-8.
[75] Cf. the following lines (written in 1612 while Donne was meditating *The second
Anniversary*) from *A Letter to the Lady Carey and Mrs Essex Riche, From Amyens*,
wherein he reverts to a figure based on the doctrine of the inalterability of the heavens
to compliment the two ladies. They are addressed as,

> . . . a firmament
> Of virtues, where no one is growne, or spent.
> *Ibid.*, p. 222, ll. 13-14.

> Since both this lower world's, and the Sunnes Sunne,
> The Lustre, and the vigor of this All,
> Did set; 'twere blasphemie to say, did fall.[76]

This is the note of hope, at least, the note of courageous striving for the assurance and faith-inspired vision which had been eclipsed by doubt in *The first Anniversary*. For the successful development of this theme the matter of the new philosophy, with its disconcerting connotation, can make no contribution. It is true that there is a repercussion of the doubt and uneasiness pervading *The first Anniversary*, but over the conditions inducing the former skepticism there triumphs an expression of positive and constructive faith. Consequently, into this atmosphere there is no place for the introduction of the "blazing stars," the temporary luminaries which flitted across the heavens with their popularly conceived portent of disaster, or, at best, of uncertain event. In short, the stars of *A Funerall Elegie* and *The first Anniversary*, proper symbols of transiency and uncertain reality are here effectively excluded to the advantage of imagery on which the structure of ideas representing the permanent and enduring qualities of a genuine faith may be raised.

Though the new stars do not appear in *The second Anniversary*, Donne does not hesitate to call them into use in other poems of the same period when the proper occasion arises. In *An Epithalamion, Or marriage Song on the Lady Elizabeth, and Count Palatine*, he invites the Lady Elizabeth, the daughter of King James, to be

> . . . a new starre, that to us portends
> Ends of much wonder; And be Thou those ends.[77]

The lines occur as the climax of a beautifully constructed stanza, remarkable for the effective arrangement of its matter:

> Up then faire Phoenix Bride, frustrate the Sunne,
>   Thy selfe from thine affection
>   Takest warmth enough, and from thine eye
> All lesser birds will take their Jollitie.
>   Up, up, faire Bride, and call,
> Thy starres, from out their severall boxes, take
> Thy Rubies, Pearles, and Diamonds forth, and make
> Thy selfe a constellation, of them All,
>   And by their blazing, signifie,
> That a Great Princess falls, but doth not die;
> Bee thou a new starre, that to us portends
> Ends of much wonder; And be Thou those ends.

[76] *Ibid.*, p. 251, ll. 1-6.
[77] *Ibid.*, p. 128, ll. 39-40. Feb. 14, 1613.

Since thou dost this day in new glory shine,
May all men date Records, from this thy Valentine.[78]

Even the trite and familiar comparison of jewels to stars takes on freshness from its power to call up in the poet's mind the livelier allusions to "blazing" stars and new luminaries of recent fame. In the expansion of the star figure the imagination moves forward with increasing originality. The meaning comprehended by the figure, likewise, is of increasing penetration and beauty. The mind passes from a conception of womanhood, radiant with external beauty, to a vision of pure wonder. The images are stripped of all unhappy connotation. All suggestion of the evil portended by the temporary duration of comets and new stars is suppressed; and in the face of popular fear and superstition the new stars with their glittering brilliance become symbols of beauty worthy of a princess and a presage, as the climax of the poet's compliment reports, of "ends of much wonder."

Again, in a verse letter to the Countess of Bedford, of doubtful date,[79] occurs a reference to "new starres," recalling an ancient pagan belief that the souls of illustrious persons after death appear as new stars in the heavens:

We'have added to the world Virginia, 'and sent
Two new starres lately to the firmament;
Why grudge wee us (not heaven) the dignity
T'increase with ours, those faire soules company.[80]

At least, this is the construction that Professor Grierson, following Norton and Chambers, places upon the lines when he states that "the poem probably belongs to 1614," tentatively agreeing with Norton that the two stars are "Prince Henry (died November 6, 1612) and the Countess's brother, Lord Harrington who died early in 1614," because "public characters like these are more fittingly described as stars" than Lady Markham (died May 4, 1609) and Mrs. Boulstred (died August 4, 1609) whom Chambers conjectures to be the two stars "sent . . . lately to the firmament." To corroborate the latter date, however, is the allusion to Virginia "in which there was a quickening of interest in 1609." [81] Thus, as all these authorities base their opinion for the date of the poem on the above lines, careful inquiry into their meaning becomes doubly important.

If the above explanation is the only one that may be applied to

[78] *Ibid.*, ll. 29-42.
[79] *Ibid.*, pp. 195-98. [1609–14.] Grierson inclines toward the latter date.—*Ibid.*, II, 160.
[80] *Ibid.*, I, 197-98, ll. 67-70.
[81] *Ibid.*, II, 132. Cf. Chambers, *The Poems of John Donne*, II, 219.

the lines, the figure of the new stars is a unique instance of Donne's reference to new stars unassociated with the recent discoveries. But can we be certain, even if it is assumed that the two "new starres" refer to souls of the departed changed into stars, that in Donne's mind the figure does not spring from a recollection of the new stars of the astronomers—that, in fact, it was not Kepler's stars that he was thinking about when he wrote the lines? Certainly the new philosophy was stirring Donne's imagination when he wrote to the Countess, for earlier he has called into use the motion of the earth to symbolize the wanton conduct of the body:

> Oh! to confesse wee know not what we should,
>   Is halfe excuse; wee know not what we would:
> Lightnesse depresseth us, emptinesse fills,
>   We sweat and faint, yet still goe downe the hills.
> As new Philosophy arrests the Sunne,
>   And bids the passive earth about it runne,
> So wee have dull'd our minde, it hath no ends;
>   Onely the bodie's busie, and pretends;
> As dead low earth ecclipses and controules
>   The quick high Moone: so doth the body, Soules.[82]

Though a definite answer to the above question is perhaps impossible, an approach to a more convincing explanation of the lines may be made by considering them in their setting and in their relation to the theme of the letter. According to Professor Grierson the theme of this letter—"one of the most difficult of Donne's poems," from which emerges "the deepest thought of Donne's poetry, his love poetry, and his religious poetry"—is "the degradation of the soul by our exclusive regard for the body." Donne, however, "will not accept the antithesis between soul and body," Professor Grierson continues. "The dignity of the body is hardly less than that of the soul. But we cannot exalt the body at the expense of the soul. If we immerse the soul in the body it is not the soul alone which suffers but the body also. In the highest spiritual life, as in the fullest and most perfect love, body and soul are complementary, are merged in each other; and after death the life of the soul is in some measure incomplete, the end for which it was created is not obtained until it is reunited to the body. . . . The body is not essentially evil. It is not the body as such that weighs down the soul (*aggravat animam*) [St. Augustine], but the body corrupted by sin." [83]

How, it may be asked, does the idea of the souls of Prince Henry,

[82] *Ibid.*, I, 196-97, ll. 33-42.   [83] *Ibid.*, II, 160, 161, 162.

Lady Markham, or of whoever they may be, reappearing in the heavens as siars fit into this development of the theme? We dare not presume upon Donne's devotion to the Countess to suppose that he is implying that the two should die and thus remove the "grudge" and leave their souls free to join the stellified company above. Yet, if the interpretation given above is accepted, how else can the company of those "faire soules" be increased by "ours"? In fact, Donne mentions death but once, and then in a way that concurs with Professor Grierson's understanding of the poem as the means by which the corruptible body is put off, by which bodies are restored to their "proper dignity" as the "Caskets," "Temples, and Palaces" of souls:

> Wee (but no forraine tyrants could) remove
> These not ingrav'd, but inborne dignities,
> Caskets of soules; Temples, and Palaces:
> For, bodies shall from death redeemed bee,
> Soules but preserv'd, not naturally free.[84]

Following immediately upon the above lines Donne names some of the strange symptoms of man's viciousness and suggests that there are, however, miracles of goodness that "nature can worke soe." Among these are the riches of which Virginia and the two new stars "sent . . . lately to the firmament" are symbolic: the former, of material good that may accrue to man; the latter, of a heavenly source of spiritual inspiration. If this is the meaning of the passage in question, that is, to regard the two new stars as the gleaming souls of certain dead persons, this is to allow the conventional meaning of the figure to strip from Donne the originality that finds in the triumphs of Renaissance exploration and discovery tokens of a promise of good to both the body and the soul. The new stars, associated in the poet's imagination with lands in the new world to which the year 1609 sent a wave of hopeful colonists, would seem beyond doubt to be the new discoveries made in the heavens, suggesting the miraculous extension of man's spiritual destiny and portending "ends of much wonder."

But what are the "two" stars? Evidently Donne means to be specific. If we are to assume that the stars are the metamorphosed souls of some particular persons, there is really little choice between the two pairs offered for identification by Norton and Chambers, respectively. Though Lady Markham and Mrs. Boulstred are not so illustrious as the Prince and Lord Harrington, they might be preferred, because both were the first cousins of Lady Bedford to whom the letter is addressed, and both died at Twickenham Park, where the Countess took up

---

[84] *Ibid.*, I, 197, ll. 54-58.

residence in 1608. Again, the allusion to Virginia would seem to point to the year in which these ladies died as the date of the composition of the letter, for it was early in that year that Donne sought to be "Secretary at Virginia." [85]

However, there are two specific stars of another kind with which Donne but a year before (1608) had confessed his acquaintance: the stars in the Swan and in Serpentarius, described by Kepler in *De Stella Nova*. Thus, 1609 would not antiquate the reference to "two new starres lately [sent] to the firmament," nor would their association with the allusion to Virginia—a subject fresh in Donne's mind at the time—be unlikely. Moreover, Kepler's stars are two specific stars seen in the "firmament" of the fixed stars, not any two of a number of persons known to Donne and Lady Bedford who died between 1609 and 1614. In the light of this argument, the two stars, understood as the souls of Prince Henry, Lord Harrington, or of any others, seem a trifle nonsensical, the victims of a certain kind of literalness not characteristic of Donne's poetic method. It should be remembered that Donne has made no suggestion that the Countess and he join the eager colonists to Virginia. But Donne does identify the "two new starres" with "soules." As "soules," though they may be the luminous representatives of any good persons, they are objects of wonder, and the promise of heaven's goodness to mankind to which the poet invites his friend to direct her aspirations.

As Donne is fond of the stellar imagery in his letters to women, we may cite another verse letter, one to the Countess of Huntingdon,[86] in which he painstakingly elaborates a figure based on his knowledge of the new stars, to celebrate the essential quality of womanly virtue. The piece, as a whole, is dull and forced, with a too-thorough observance of the spirit of the closing lines:

> I was your Prophet in your yonger dayes,
> And now your Chaplaine, God in you to praise.[87]

It is saved, however, from falling completely into the shadow by occasional flashes of brilliance, of which his treatment of the Countess's innocence is an example. To Donne, who has not entered her ladyship's chaplaincy without experiencing first a rather worldly apprenticeship, her innocence is a thing both rare and marvelous, only to be excelled by her "active good." Where, then, is language to be

---

[85] "News is here none at all, but that John Donne seeks to be Secretary at Virginia." From "a letter, dated February 14, 1609."—Gosse, *op. cit.*, I, 209.

[86] Grierson, I, 201-3. [1614–15.]

[87] *Ibid.*, p. 203, ll. 69-70.

found to smooth the rough prosaic edges from his thought and to draw with delicacy not only the wanted contrast between womanly purity and the grossness of the world, but also the far more subtle difference separating the idea of purity from positive goodness? It is again to his scientific books that he turns:

MADAME,
Man to Gods image; *Eve*, to mans was made,
    Nor finde wee that God breath'd a soule in her,
Canons will not Church functions you invade,
    Nor lawes to civill office you preferre.

Who vagrant transitory Comets sees,
    Wonders, because they'are rare; But a new starre
Whose motion with the firmament agrees,
    Is miracle; for, there no new things are;

In woman so perchance milde innocence
    A seldome comet is, but active good
A miracle, which reason scapes, and sense;
    For, Art and Nature this in them withstood.[88]

As is Donne's frequent manner, he mingles in a curiously original fashion facts and fancies gleaned from his astronomical learning. Here, for instance, is a recollection of the comets of Tycho Brahe,[89] the

[88] *Ibid.*, p. 201, ll. 1-12.

[89] Tycho Brahe is responsible for the great interest in comets in the late sixteenth century, and to him, perhaps more than to any other person, this period is greatly obliged for any intelligent understanding that it may have had of these phenomena. In 1577 Tycho observed the "great comet," which, according to Dreyer, "gave rise to a perfect deluge of pamphlets, in which the supposed significance of the terrible hairy star was set forth, and," he continues, "for more than a century afterwards every comet was followed by a flood of effusions from numberless scriblers." Between 1580 and 1596, Tycho saw five other comets, and a sixth, observed only by a former pupil, Christen Hansen, in 1593 at Hveen, is usually counted among those of Tycho himself. In contradiction to the prevailing Aristotelian notion that comets, like meteors, were of atmospheric origin, Tycho proved conclusively that the very small parallax exhibited by comets argued for their very great distance from the earth, beyond the moon, whose orbit "was still considered the limit of the elementary world." Further, Tycho disturbed the complacency of those who thought that all motion in the heavens was circular, by suggesting, after attempting to calculate the orbit of the great comet, that the course it described "may not have been 'exactly circular but somewhat oblong, like the figure commonly called oval.'" How important this conclusion was may be gathered from the fact that it was "the discussion of the motion of the comet of 1577 [that] gave Tycho the opportunity of promulgating his system [of the universe]." The results of Tycho's investigations of the great comet did not appear until 1588, when at his own press he published his *De mundi aetheri recentioribus phaenomenis liber secundus, qui est de illustri stella caudata ab elapso fere triente Nouembris anno MDLXXVII usque in finem Januarii sequentis conspecta*, a work not widely circulated until after its regular publication as the second volume of the *Progymnasmata* (1602). See Dreyer, *Tycho Brahe*, p. 171, and *History of the Planetary Systems*, pp. 365-66. As Kepler had re-

opinion of the astronomers on the motion of the new stars,[90] and the
verdict of the Aristotelian theologians upholding the continuation of

---

ceived the manuscripts of Tycho upon the latter's death and had himself supervised the
publication of the *Progymnasmata*, he was thoroughly familiar with Tycho's work on
the comets, and of this familiarity his works bear repeated evidence. See "cometa" in
Index, Frisch, Vol. VIII. In *De Stella Nova*, with which Donne was particularly familiar, four of the comets mentioned above as observed by Tycho Brahe are considered
by Kepler: (1) the "great comet" of 1577, Frisch, II, 686; (2) the comets of 1580
and 1585, *ibid.*, p. 704; (3) the comet of 1596, *ibid.*, p. 693. In *De Stella Nova* Kepler frequently refers to his work on the optics, *Astronomiae pars optica* where the
nature of comets is treated at length. See especially, cap. vi, "De cometarum lumine,"
ibid., pp. 295 ff.

[90] On the basis of the difference in their movements Donne significantly draws a
distinction between the "vagrant" and "transitory" comets and the stars "whose motion with the firmament agrees," a distinction thoroughly technical and all the more
remarkable when one recalls that many regarded the new stars and comets as one and
the same: "Sunt enim qui cometam appellent, Guntherus, Mollerus, Bütnerus et alii."—
De Stella Nova, Frisch, II, 703. See also Clavius, *op. cit.*, pp. 219, 220. It is true, the
new stars as well as the comets had been "transitory"; but, whereas stars were generally
permanent, the comets were always temporary. Furthermore, the authenticity of the
new stars depended on causes other than their duration. The transitory nature of
comets had been noted by Aristotle and by Seneca (who, however, thought that they
would return again), as well as by Tycho and Kepler. Johan Alsted, in his *Encyclopaedia* (Herborn, 1630), remarks that the comets, ". . . incerto: vagabundo motu
volvuntur, sulphureo halitu constant & combustible, & non ita diu durant, sed absunta
materia evanescunt."—p. 982. Because the new stars and the comets were so frequently
confused, Tycho and Kepler took great care to point out their differences. Thus, in the
first chapter of *De Stella Nova*, he proceeds to disillusion those who regarded the star
of 1604 as a comet. The new star, he writes, ". . . fuisse exacte rotundam, nullo crine,
nulla barba vel syrmate in ullam partem projecto, quare nulli crinitarum speciei, neque
pogoniae neque cometis accensendam, sed stellis fixis simillimam, radiis undiquaque ut
fixarum emicantibus, etc."—Frisch, II, 619-20. In short, the new star exhibited none
of the characteristics of a comet: it was not "hairy," had no "beard," and was without
a "tail"; and it definitely bore all the appearances of a true star.

But apart from appearances, the new stars differed from comets in being without
motion, and in this resembled all other fixed stars. When Donne writes, "whose motion
with the firmament agrees," he can only mean that the new star retained its place in
the heavens relative to the other stars throughout its duration, and did not, like the
comets, appear like a vagrant of the sky, marking out an irregular (not circular)
course. "Toto tempore durationis stetit eodem loco sub fixis; schematismos cum stellis
pedis, tibiae, genuque dextro Serpentarii, cumque triangulo in spira Serpentis ne
minimum quidem quod in sensus incurrat mutavit. Non ea cometarum natura, qui per
mobilium regionem inveniuntur."—*Ibid.*, Frisch, II, 677. Tycho's new star in Cassiopeia, according to Clavius, likewise, was one "whose motion with the firmament
agrees," "Quodsi in orbe alicuius planetae fuisset, cum orbis ille sane alienum a stellis
fixis motum habeat, proculdubio, & stella ipsa eundem motum, cursumq[ue] habuisset;
secus autem evidenter concludit, multo minus stellam illam in elementari regione ex-
stitisse: quod ibi nulla ratione eandem semper situm, *ac distantiam cum stellis fixis
potuisset retinere* [italics mine]."—*Op. cit.*, p. 220.

On the other hand, the independent motion of the comets was obvious. Tycho, placing the comets in the planetary sphere, calculated the path of their motion to be that
of an ellipse; and Kepler, agreeing with his friend on the remoteness of the comets
from the earth, thought, however, that they moved in a straight line which the motion

God's miracles to account for the apparent mutability of the heavens.[91] Out of this seeming welter of ideas Donne compels his meaning to emerge, clear, yet paradoxical. He indicates what "milde innocence" and "active good," the "seldome comet" and the miraculous new star, are like when found in woman; and in doing this, he bends the "stubborne language" to mark the shadow-line distinction that divides the two. In coming to this end a reversion of the expected use of the imagery has been made. Of the transitory nature of the new stars Donne is silent; now, it is the comets that are described as "vagrant," "transitory," and "seldome." The terms are not used to provoke the sense of fear, but to suggest the wonder and admiration which rarity commands, for here Donne is writing in the spirit of the ninth elegy:

If we love things long sought . . .

· · ·

If transitory things, which soone decay,

Age must be lovelyest at the latest day.[92]

Having trespassed so far upon the realm of marvels to suggest the sense of womanly innocence, he can find no epithet adequate for goodness, but "miracle" itself, "which reason scapes, and sense." To enrich

---

of the earth made to appear curvilinear. See Dreyer, *History of the Planetary Systems,* pp. 411, 412, and *De Stella Nova,* Frisch, II, 686. Kepler's question, "Nam quid motui cometarum cum immobilitate hujus Novae fixae?" directed against the argument of his reactionary friend David Fabricius, that the new stars were like the comets whose temporary appearance was but the periodical reappearance of bodies that always existed in the heavens, indicates clearly the importance of the distinctly different movements of these bodies, which Donne so carefully observes. Kepler gives a complete refutation of that "alterum argumentum ducit [Fabricius] a motu cometarum," *ibid.,* p. 686.

[91] In declaring that "there [in the heavens] no new things are," Donne is repeating the traditional doctrine of the inalterability of the celestial world. However, as he accepts the reality of the new stars, he falls into an apparent contradiction from which there is but one route of escape—by way of miracle. By the time of the composition of this poem, it is difficult to believe that Donne any longer regarded the Aristotelian doctrine with seriousness, and it is likewise difficult to believe that he did not think that the day of miracles had ceased. Nevertheless, he doubtless recalled Clavius's conjecture that the new star in Cassiopeia may have been a miracle of Almighty God: ". . . ita mihi persuadeo, stellam illam vel tunc a Deo. Opt. Max. procreatam esse in cælo octavo, ut magnum aliquid portenderet . . ." (*Op. cit.,* p. 220), and Kepler's rebuke of his friend Fabricius for arguing like an imbecile in agreeing with the theologians that God's creative powers were put to rest after the week of creation: "Primum exorsus ille a theologis, rationem eorum de requiete Dei post diem septimum ipse quoque imbecillem arguit."—*De Stella Nova,* Frisch, II, 685.[The thing of importance to note, however, in Donne's paradoxical use of the controversy of the philosophers, is not that he agreed or disagreed with this or that opinion, but that he found in the suggestion of miraculous change in an unchangeable world the right device for emphasizing the marvel and wonder of woman's "active good."]

[92] *Elegie IX. The Autumnall,* Grierson, I, 93-94, ll. 33, 35-36.

146 THE NEW HEAVENS

the figure he naturally turns to the comparison of *this* star ("active good") in woman to that great miracle of stars, the one that

> . . . the *Magi* led to view
> The manger-cradled infant, God below: [93]

hoping that

> By vertues beames by fame deriv'd from you,
> May apt soules, and the worst may, vertue know.[94]

But, as suggested above there is something paradoxical in praise so glorious as this. It is the paradox of insidious satire lurking behind the glittering external imagery wherein innocence and virtue hold poetic commerce with comets and stars. Donne does not indulge in the vice of damning by faint praise; his method is the very converse: the glowing adulation heaped upon the Countess of Huntingdon has become a foil to set off the essential weakness of her sex. A score of years before this letter was composed one· would have found a more forthright declaration of the poet's perverse attitude toward woman-kind; quotation is unnecessary to call to mind the savagery with which he attacked these "principals" to man's undoing. Here, it may be a bit disturbing to those who think that Donne had undergone, or was undergoing, a translation into something, if not "rich and strange," then something pious and ministerial, to find him still troubled by the "seldome comets" of innocence in woman. As a matter of fact, a deepening interest in the Scriptures, which certainly Donne was cultivating in these years, might easily have strengthened, though for reasons at variance with his early motives of bitterness and cruel delight, his appreciation of the doctrine that

> . . . The mother poison'd the well-head,
> The daughters here corrupt us, Rivolets.[95]

[93] *To the Countesse of Huntingdon, ibid.,* p. 201, ll. 13-14. Reference to the star of the Magi comes with a certain inevitability after Donne has indicated the miraculous nature of new stars in the second stanza of the above poem. In this respect the allusion becomes an interesting example of the way in which a poetic theme grows through an accumulation of ideas associated imaginatively. Though the new stars were popularly likened to the miraculous star of Bethlehem, Donne would not have found in the authorities with which he was familiar reason for believing that they were similar. Tycho thought it necessary to specify in what ways his star of 1572 was different. See *Progymnasmata* (1610), section "De Stella Nova," p. 324. Beza believed that the new star of 1572 was the reappearance of the star of the Magi, but this view received no support among the astronomers, who generally held that it was something in the elementary sphere. However, with the appearance of the new stars, naturally enough the mind turned to the unconventional stars of antiquity. Kepler recalls Pliny's report of a new star seen by Hipparchus and also those rumored to have been visible in the time of the Emperor Adrian [Hadrian], of the Emperor Otto, and in the year 1264. See *Prodromus . . . mysterium cosmographicum,* Frisch, I, 319, 331.

[94] *Ibid.,* p. 201, ll. 15-16.

[95] *The Progresse of the Soule, ibid.,* p. 298, ll. 93-94.

In the letter to the Countess of Huntingdon there is no implication of hypocrisy; and it is beside the point to think that Donne was insincere. In fact, making allowances for the overstatement burdening most complimentary verse Donne seems to be particularly sincere because he has been honest; he has not allowed an illusion (if it is illusion, it is one Donne shared with many of his fellow poets) of the frailty of womankind to darken the character of one virtuous woman. The Countess—or it could have been Lady Magdalen Herbert or Lucy, Countess of Bedford—is not maligned. The Ophelias and Violas of the age are no less miracles of goodness because their virtue is paid for largely at the expense of those mothers of Hamlet and Lady Macbeths—"daughters here [who] corrupt us." Such is humanity at any time.

To the transient stars of Tycho Brahe and Kepler and to the innumerable new fixed stars brought into the range of human vision by Galileo's telescope must be added the "numberless infinities" of the Milky Way as a source of stimulation to Donne's imagination. Again, it was the telescope that brought about the revision of the poet's conception of the nature of this traditionally disputed phenomenon. In the *Sidereus Nuncius* Galileo declares that

by the aid of a telescope anyone may behold this [the Milky Way] in a manner which so distinctly appeals to the senses that all the disputes which have tormented philosophers through so many ages are exploded at once by the irrefragable evidence of our eyes, and we are freed from wordy disputes upon this subject, for the Galaxy is nothing else but a mass of innumerable stars planted together in clusters (*est enim GALAXIA nihil aliud quam innumerarum Stellarum coacervatim congeries*). Upon what ever part of it you direct the telescope, straightway a vast crowd of stars (Stellarum ingens frequentia) presents itself to view; many of them are tolerably large and extremely bright, but the number of small ones is quite beyond determination (*sed exiguarum multitudo prorsus inexplorabilis est*).[96]

To have resolved the "Galaxy," the name Galileo is accustomed to use, into a "congeries" of little stars, and to have discovered the consistency of the nebulous stars was not, however, to alter the heavens in the same way that the discovery of absolutely new and unknown stars changed the celestial regions. The Galaxy and the nebulous stars had long been known, if not understood. Consequently, if this phase of Galileo's work does not by itself substantially refute the Peripatetic doctrine of inalterability, it does, at least, as Galileo affirms, "explode" "all the disputes which have tormented the philosophers through so many ages."

[96] Pages 42-43. Latin text in Petri Gassendi, *Institutio Astronomica* (London, 1683), p. 32.

A notion of how thoroughly the philosophers were tormented by this subject may be gained from the account of the Galaxy in Alsted's ponderous *Encyclopaedia,* which begins with the question, *De Galaxia, seu viâ lacteâ quanta est opinionum varietas?* [97] Inevitably, in a universe conceived as a series of closed compartments housing the various elementary and celestial phenomena the place and matter of the Galaxy would be as uncertain as the place and matter of the new stars. But without availing ourselves of Alsted's help to recount the opinions of Anaxagoras, Possidonius, or Diodorus, we may profitably take note of those of the writers under whose direct influence Donne fell. Both Tycho and Kepler thought that the Milky Way was a path of nebulous substance in the highest ether.[98] In disagreement with Aristotle, Clavius, too, regarded the Milky Way as removed from the elementary sphere where his master had consigned it along with the meteors and comets. Unlike the stars, which are of much greater density and scattered throughout the heavens, it is a continuous part of the firmament, denser than the surrounding medium, made visible by its capacity to receive illumination from the sun, and like a path of filmy whiteness it passes across the heavens through the constellations.[99] Clavius then invokes the art of Manilius and Ovid to enrich his description.

[97] Page 2016.

[98] Kepler, recalling Tycho's opinion that the new star of 1572 was formed by the condensation of matter from the Milky Way, concludes that the new star in Serpentarius likewise had its origin in the region of the Milky Way: "Hic jam supra mentio facta est pulcherrimae sententiae, quam Braheus dixit: stellas hujusmodi procreari ex via lactea. Et visus est confirmare rem sensu oculorum, ostensa lacuna eo loco, quo sidus anni 1572. effulsit; quasi portio illa materiae in corpus sideris coacta fuerit, quae postmodum fortasse conflagraverit aut dissipata fuerit. Cui experimento accedit et nostra haec nova stella, cujus exortus rursum in confinium viae lacteae cecidit. Quae vero anno 1600. in Cygno effulsit (. . .) plane in ipso pleno lacte fulget etiamnum. Et possis huc trahere traditionem Aristotelis et Plinii, qui cometas ut plurimum ajunt sub lactea existere; si certum esset, loqui illos etiam de fixis novis. Ut vero fidem faciam nostrae Novae de vicinia viae lacteae, . . . Aut igitur in ipsam lacteae latitudinem incidit locus novi sideris, aut marginem ejus sinistrum et orientalem proxime attingit, vergens versus alteram lactis portionem; sic ut in illo angusto limite sit comprehensus, qui inter utrumque arcum limitis lactei eo loco distinguit ceu insula inter duos fluvii alveos. Itaque consentaneum, materiam novae esse ex via lactea. Idque etiam naturalis contemplatio confirmat. Nam si essentia viae lacteae pars est densior aetheris (materiam enim aliquam tantis coruscationibus subesse necesse est) nemini non verisimile erit, aptissimam esse illam materiam novis phaenominis."—*De Stella Nova,* Frisch, II, 692-93. See also Preface to the *Dioptrics, ibid.,* II, 524, and Dreyer, *History of the Planetary Systems,* p. 365.

[99] "Ego tamen cum aliis probabilius existimo, Lacteum circulum esse partem Firmamenti continuam, & densiorem aliis partibus caeli, ita ut lumen Solis recipere possit, non tamen sicut aliae stellae, quae sunt partes Firmamenti multo densiores & inter se distantes; . . . Itaque lacteus circulus vere existit in Firmamento, non autem in regione aeris, ut Aristoteles volebat. . . . Incedit enim lacteus circulus perpetuo, ut videre est apud Ptolemaeum loco citato, & experientia docet, per Cassiopeiam, Cygnum, Aquilam

There is one opinion among these early writers on the Milky Way that should not be overlooked, not because it was based on surer evidence than many other notions. commonly held, for it was not, but because it anticipated the facts which Galileo's telescope revealed. It is the opinion that the Galaxy was made up of many small stars. Clavius calls attention to it in the following words: *Candor vero eius, à quo lactei nomen habet, provenit, ut nonnullis placet, ex multitudine nimia stellarum exiguarum, quae in ipso continentur, & ad nostrum visum distinctae non perveniunt, sicut caeterae stellae.*[100] Of the philosophers who held this opinion, Alsted is more specific, assigning it particularly to Democritus and Scaliger; "in more recent times," he adds, "a great many others" have held that the Galaxy is *congerie[s] stellarum minutissimarum.*[101] As Alsted was writing in 1630, the "great many others" are, beyond doubt, the followers of Galileo, who had learned the truth from *Sidereus Nuncius.* In view of the fact that in the past the Milky Way had been considered an assemblage of small stars, it is not surprising that some of Galileo's detractors brought out the old doctrine to discredit the value of the new discovery.[102] On the other hand, Kepler's enthusiastic greeting of the solution of the traditional problem of the nature of the Milky Way makes it eminently clear that the old belief, apparently originating with Democritus, either was not widely held or was generally submerged in the chaos of contradictory opinion.[103]

---

volantem, Sagittam Sagittarij, & caudam Scorpij, Centaurum, Argonavem, pedes Geminorum, Heniochum sive Aurigam, & Perseum, ut clarissime constat in globo aliquo Astronomico."—*In sphaeram Ioannis De Sacrobosco commentarius,* pp. 369-70.

Clavius's description, on the whole, accords favorably with that given in English in Blundeville's popular *Exercises.* Blundeville says that the Milky Way is a "Milk-white impression," "in heaven," resulting from the condensation of the celestial matter itself. The celestial matter, being "most pure, thinne, transparent and without colour," is naturally invisible; whereas the substance of the Milky Way, "thicker than anie other part of heaven," except the stars themselves, is "apt to receive and return the light of the Sunne" (p. 158), and, therefore, is rendered visible as a nebulous veil-like form passing across the heavens.

[100] *Op. cit.,* p. 369.

[101] *Op. cit.,* p. 2016. Alsted speaks of the *Sidereus Nuncius* on the same page.

[102] Martin Horky, for instance, in his *Peregrinatio,* writes: ". . . in via lactea, Nuncium nil novi attulisse, sed esse haec velutissimum cantilenam et consensum omnium Philosophorum et Mathematicorum, quod sit congeries infinitatem stellularum, omnes scimus."—*Edizione Nazionale,* III, Pt. I, 135.

[103] "Pena has noticed how astronomers, using the principles of optics, have by most laborious reasoning removed the Milky Way from the elementary universe, where Aristotle had placed it, into the highest region of the ether; but now, by the aid of the telescope . . . the very eyes of astronomers are conducted straight to a thorough survey of the substance of the Milky Way; and whoever enjoys this sight is compelled to confess that the Milky Way is nothing else but a mass of extremely small stars."—

Of all the features of the celestial world, the great "net" of meridians and parallels "weav'd out" by the astronomers, the planets and the constellations, the Milky Way added least to Donne's store of imagery. It proved less frequently than other aspects of the heavens to be a ready tool for the shaping of his thought. The reason is not hard to discover; it was really a less significant part of the heavens to the astronomers than were the stars, the planetary orbs, and the great circles on which were charted the courses of the heavenly bodies and were indicated the positions of the constellations. The Milky Way cast no influence upon the lives of men. It was a decorative phenomenon entirely, a path of whiteness thrown across the skies enhancing the beauty of a beautiful universe. Consequently, it is the decorative quality of the Milky Way that strikes Donne's imagination when he first calls upon its use:

> Off with that girdle, like Heavens Zone glittering,
> But a far fairer world incompassing.[104]

The couplet occurs in a poem of early date, *Elegie XIX*, one poem, at least, in the English tongue which needs no apology for treating love, unattenuated and unrefined by spiritual encumbrances, in a robust and downright manner. The refreshing realism is saved from being objectionable—though perhaps not sufficiently for those who always regard Donne in ecclesiastical perspective—by the native vigor of the poet. Further, the emotion imparted is kept free from grossness by the witty and learned imagery through which it is communicated. Compared with a similar, yet vastly different poem, Carew's *A Rapture*, Donne's elegy is a revelation of the worlds separating passion from lust, separating the pure joy of the physical from sensualism abandoning itself to the language of luscious suggestion. To Donne the body is something beautiful and strange, to be explored and to be possessed; and it is with the eagerness of the voyager who sights new continents beyond the seas,

> O my America! my new-found-land,

Indies, and mines of "precious stones," and "Emperie," that each line, tearing away some concealing veil, brings us nearer to the pure beauty of "full nakedness," to which "all joyes are due." [105]

Preface to the *Dioptrics* in Carlos's translation of the *Sidereus Nuncius*, p. 83. I have not observed that Kepler ever calls attention to an earlier belief that the Milky Way was composed of a mass of small stars.

[104] *Elegie XIX. Going to Bed*, Grierson, I, 120, ll. 5-6.
[105] *Ibid.*, ll. 27, 33.

The theme of the elegy is implicit in the lines first quoted. "Heavens Zone glittering" is doubtless the Milky Way, and as such it is understood by Donne to veil the more glorious beauty of the heavens as the girdle of his mistress conceals her own naked beauty. Beautiful as the Milky Way may appear to the eye, it covers greater beauty beyond or within, and it is to the greater beauty that Donne would penetrate. Though the source of the image cannot be determined, and though the poem was doubtless written early in Donne's life, it would seem that he had in mind some such visualization of the heavens as Clavius gives in his description of the Milky Way as a continuous white path advancing across the sky through the constellations.

Of probably later date is another allusion to the Milky Way, again chosen for the sense of concrete beauty that the image arouses rather than for its contribution to the thought of the poem. Sapho addresses Philaenis:

> So may thy cheekes red outweare scarlet dye,
> And their white, whitenesse of the Galaxy,
> So may thy mighty, amazing beauty move
> Envy'in all *women*, and in all *men*, love,
> And so be *change*, and *sicknesse*, farre from thee,
> As thou by comming neere, keep'st them from me.[106]

Though the image might well have come from experience, the fact that Donne's language so seldom suggests the apprehension of nature through the eye or ear makes it all the more likely that it rests on the descriptions of the Milky Way to be found in the books that he had been reading. The "whitenesse" of the Milky Way is generally noted; but among the authors whom we are certain Donne studied only Clavius seeks out the aid of the poet to accent this particular quality of beauty which Donne finds worthy of his "Philaenis." [107]

That Donne knew Galileo's resolution of the problem of the Milky Way as described in *Sidereus Nuncius* is certain; how thoroughly the discovery of the multitude of little stars in the Galaxy took hold of his mind is established by the fact that twenty years after he had read

[106] *Heroicall Epistle, ibid.*, p. 126, ll. 59-64. Grierson thinks this poem was probably written about 1597 or 1598, possibly inspired by Drayton's Ovidian epistles.—*Ibid.*, II, 91.

[107] Cf. Clavius, *op. cit.*, p. 370, where he cites Ovid's figure describing the Milky Way, "candore notabilis ipso" (*Metamorphoses*, I, vi). I realize that the suggestion that Donne drew the image from Clavius is dangerous. Donne undoubtedly knew Ovid before he read Clavius, if we assume that it was the 1607 edition of the *Commentary* that Donne made use of. 1607, or any date thereafter, is probably too late for the poem. Nevertheless, it is interesting to note that the image appears in Clavius's description of the Milky Way, and that the *Epistle* appears in the editions of 1635-69 of Donne's poems, "among the sober *Letters To Severall Personages.*"—Grierson, II, 90.

Galileo's book he recalls, as if he had but refreshed his mind on the subject, the concrete details of this phase of the new heavens:

In that glistring circle in the firmament, which we call the Galaxy, the milky way, there is not one Star of any of the six great magnitudes, which Astronomers proceed upon, belonging to that circle. It is a glorious circle, and possesses a great part of heaven: and yet is all of so little stars, as have no name, no knowledge taken of them.[108]

Though Galileo's discovery may be invoked to ennoble the efforts and aspirations of those "good and blessed souls, that have religiously performed the duties of inferior callings, and no more," of whom Donne is preaching, it is interesting to observe that nowhere in Donne's poems does an allusion to the Galaxy itself, as described by Galileo, appear to deepen the thought and complicate the theme. The one certain allusion to this part of Galileo's work that does appear in the poems is, however, of considerable importance. Because it helps to fix the date of the poem, it becomes a key to the appreciation, if not the understanding, of the baffling variety of his interests and tastes and of the venturesomeness of his imagination, even as late as 1610. In one of the "examples of his subtler moods," [109] *The Primrose*, thought by many to have been addressed to Lady Herbert, because of the late addition to the title of " . . . *being at Montgomery Castle, upon the hill, on which it is situate*," [110] appear the following opening lines:

Vpon this Primrose hill,
Where, if Heav'n would distill
A shoure of raine, each severall drop might goe

[108] *Fifty Sermons* (1649), 29, fol. 252. Cf. "many of them are tolerably large and extremely bright."—*Sidereus Nuncius*, p. 43.

[109] Grierson, II, 10.

[110] *Ibid.*, I, 61-62. In one place Grierson remarks that, "it is noteworthy that the addition 'being at Montgomery Castle' &c. was made in *1635*. It is unknown to *1633* and the MSS. It may be unwarranted. If it be accurate, then the poem is probably addressed to Mrs. Herbert and is a half mystical, half cynical description of Platonic passion."—*Ibid.*, II, 48. In another place Grierson speaks less cautiously: "And to her [Lady Herbert] also it would seem that at some period in the history of their friendship, the beginning of which is very difficult to date, he wrote songs in the tone of hopeless, impatient passion, of Petrarch writing to Laura, and others which celebrate their mutual affection as a love that rose superior to earthly and physical passion. The clue here is the title prefixed to that strange poem *The Primrose, being at Montgomery Castle, upon the hill, on which it is situate*. It is true that the title is found for the first time in the edition of *1635* and is in none of the manuscripts. But it is easier to explain the occasional suppression of a revealing title than to conceive a motive for inventing such a gloss. The poem is doubtless, as Mr. Gosse says, 'a mystical celebration of the beauty, dignity and intelligence of Magdalen Herbert'—a celebration, however, which takes the form (as it might with Petrarch) of a reproach, a reproach which Donne's passionate temper and caustic wit seem even to touch with scorn."—

To his owne primrose, and grow Manna so;
And where their forme, and their infinitie
Make a terrestriall Galaxie,
As the small starres doe in the skie:
I walke to finde a true Love; and I see
That'tis not a mere woman, that is shee,
But must, or more, or lesse then woman bee.[111]

In the minds of some there may be a doubt as to whether the figure of the "terrestriall Galaxie" actually is derived from Galileo; but a recollection of the historical facts will certainly serve to dispel this uncertainty. Above, we have noted that Donne was familiar before 1610 with the opinion held by some of the ancients that the Milky Way was made up of small stars. However, it was only as an opinion that Clavius recalled Democritus's explanation of the Galaxy; it was regarded favorably only by some (*nonnullis*), and Clavius himself took no stock in it, preferring rather to think that *Lacteum circulum esse partem Firmamenti continuam*. Moreover, Kepler, to whom Donne is always greatly indebted, never speaks of this old doctrine; and Blundeville's *Exercises,* a book which may be assumed to present the popular stock of astronomical lore circulating in England in Donne's time, knows nothing of it. Donne's reference is specific, without a suggestion of doubt,

> . . . and their infinitie
> Make a terrestriall Galaxie,
> As the small starres doe in the skie.

Ibid., II, xxiv. With his usual credulity, Gosse assumes without question, that the poem was addressed to Lady Herbert. "It was at Montgomery Castle, and (I do not question) at this very time [sometime when Donne visited the castle], that Donne wrote the singularly beautiful poem of 'The Primrose.' . . . The whole is a mystical celebration of the beauty . . ."—*Op. cit.,* II, 26. Pierre Legouis attempts a refutation of Grierson's conjecture that this poem as well as the four others with which it is associated (*The Funerall, The Dampe, The Relique,* and *The Blossome*), because "all these poems recur so repeatedly together in the manuscripts as to suggest that they have a common origin (Grierson, II, xxiv), is to be identified with the name of Lady Herbert. His argument is based on his interpretation of the poem as being "simpler and coarser" than Grierson makes it out, and on the assumption that a "revealing title" carries little or no weight because Grierson himself does not apply consistently his principle that "it is easier to explain the occasional suppression of a revealing title than to conceive a motive for inventing such a gloss." "This remark carries some weight," Legouis admits, "but is answered elsewhere by the same editor (II, cxxxix): 'I do not attach much importance to this title [Sir Walter Aston to the Countesse of Huntingtone]. Imaginary headings were quite common in the case of poems circulating in manuscript.' May it not be that the 1635 editor, aware of Donne's friendship with Mrs. Herbert, made a guess at random? If so, the later editors merely followed him, as they usually do."—*Op. cit.,* Appendix B, pp. 94 ff.
[111] Grierson, I, 61, ll. 1-10.

Furthermore, the word "infinitie," describing the number of the small stars, comes much nearer Galileo's "innumerable" (*innumerarum Stellarum . . . congeries*) than to Clavius's word, "multitude" (*Ex multitudine nimia stellarum exiguarum*). Such definiteness and concreteness as Donne's statement exhibits can hardly be said to rest on an author's incidental citation of an opinion that remained highly suspect until after Galileo's discovery.

As *The Primrose* is one of a "group" of poems subject to widely varying interpretation,[112] it will be profitable to give it particular consideration in the light of its late composition—and there is no substantial evidence to refute the date argued by the allusion to the Galaxy. The subject matter of the poem is itself a debated and debatable thing, greatly confused by the autobiographical complication noted above, as well as by the tendency of Donne's critics to see in the poem his peculiar conversion of the Platonic and Petrarchian conventions. Obviously, if the identification of the "true love" for whom the poet is looking while gathering flowers upon the "primrose hill" of Montgomery Castle with Lady Herbert is allowed, the poem must be an expression of refinement and compliment. If the poem is not addressed to Lady Herbert, it becomes exposed, at least, to such a disillusioning treatment as M. Legouis's propensity to discover coarseness in Donne, encourages.[113] However, at the outset it does seem desirable to accept M. Legouis's approach to the study of the poem, when he says that it (and the others with which it has been associated) "should be studied as artistic handlings of lyrical themes, not as biographical documents in the narrower sense of these words," [114] and temporarily, to omit Lady Herbert's name from the discussion. If an interpretation is undertaken from this point of view, though it is impossible to reach M. Legouis's conclusions, it will be seen that neither is there anything in it that would not comport with the late date of its composition nor that would definitely rule out the assignment of the poem to Lady Herbert.

The theme of the poem is "true love," and the particular attitude of the poet is suggested in the line,

I walke to finde a true Love . . .

[112] In Grierson's classification of Donne's poems into three groups, in which he admits "there is much overlapping," he places "in the third and smallest group," "such fine examples of his subtler moods as *The Funerall, The Blossome, The Primrose*," to which must be added, *Twicknam Garden* and *A nocturnall upon S. Lucies day*, "the two most enigmatical poems in the *Songs and Sonets*." The first three, together with *The Relique* and *The Dampe*, Grierson associates with the name of Lady Herbert, as pointed out above. He states that "some of these must, I think, have been written after Donne's marriage."—*Ibid.*, II, 9, 10.

[113] Legouis, *op. cit.*, p. 97.

[114] *Ibid.*, p. 98.

As one of Donne's "subtler moods," as the development proves, it is a mood wherein subtlety is enlivened by grace and playfulness that might intimate a moment of genuine delight were it not "star-crossed" by his abiding satire. Though the particular course followed, leading to the cynical snag at the end, does not necessarily suggest that Lady Herbert, Lady Bedford, or any other particular lady of quality set him on his way, it does afford an opportunity, nevertheless, for Donne to regard a very human matter in a way destined to be concluded almost as satisfactorily as *The Extasie*. But the intrusion of exactly the same kind of skepticism toward virtue in woman as that which shadows his tribute to the Countess of Huntingdon, noted above, cannot be overlooked.[115] Considered as a work of the imagination alone, not directed to or against any real person, the poem strives to discover the grounds of harmonious adjustment between woman and man and to express at the same time Donne's gloomy attitude toward the vain and mawkish generalities, removed from experience, which the conventions of love are prone to encourage. In these respects, *The Primrose* is hardly to be described as a poem in which Donne "adopts the tone (as sincerely as was generally the case) of the Petrarchian lover whose mistress's coldness has slain him or provokes his passionate protestations." [116]

As Donne proceeds he makes a plea to lovers for a genuine devotion in which the body with the mind shall share equally the happiness of the experience of their union. The flower setting may offer a partial explanation of the situation, for whether it is at Montgomery Castle or in the garden of the mind the figures are weighted with significance. The primrose growing out of the earth of the hillside does not flourish without heaven's rain. Because of the refreshing showers the primroses "grow Manna so." Thus is prefigured in language of delicate pastoral beauty the metaphysical conception of the necessary conjunction of heaven and earth, soul and body, if the "manna," true love, is to be created. Love has its roots in the soil, but it is transformed into "manna" by the action of the spirit. It would be more exact, perhaps, to speak

[115] See above, pp. 142 ff. Compare the following lines in the verse letter with those subjoined from *The Primrose:*

"In woman so perchance milde innocence
   A seldome comet is, but active good
A miracle, which reason scapes, and sense;
   For, Art and Nature this in them withstood."

Grierson, I, 201, ll. 9-12.

"... Since there must reside
Falshood in woman, I could more abide,
She were by art, then Nature falsify'd."

Ibid., p. 61, ll. 18-20.

[116] Grierson, II, 10.

of woman than of love, but "true love" here, is the model woman. She has her roots of beauty in the earth, but to crown her perfection, the influence of heaven must be conjoined. The primrose with five petals signifies the true and perfect woman, the natural woman, neither undeveloped by lack of spiritual nourishment nor grown lush from having partaken in excess of the food either of the spirit or of the flesh —"both these were monsters." [117] It is in the union of the normal woman, in whom body and soul are harmoniously mingled, with the normal man, that the ideal relationship of the two sexes is to be found.

Nowhere, however, is he likely to find the perfect woman: she is apt to be either less than woman, a primrose with four petals; or more than woman, a flower with six. If the former, "she were scarce any thing," [118] immature, undeveloped, still "suck'd on countrey pleasures," wanting the richness of the spirit needed to endear her to the heart of man. If the latter, she is the unreality beyond sex, in whom the vital fiber of life has grown lax and wan, and thus, fit object only of "Platonic affection and Petrarchian adoration." [119] In conclusion, and it is the conclusion that perplexes the reader, Donne exhorts the primrose, "women, whom this flower doth represent," to live with its "true number five," and be content, "five," the number of petals of the normal primrose, being a symbol of natural perfection in woman, as suggested above. Thus far the meaning is obvious enough; but from this point on it becomes complicated by Donne's indulgence in the "mystical" meaning of numbers:

> Live Primrose then, and thrive
> With thy true number five;
> And women, whom this flower doth represent,
> With this mysterious number be content;
> Ten is the farthest number; if halfe ten
> Belonge unto each woman, then
> Each woman may take halfe us men;
> Or if this will not serve their turne, Since all
> Numbers are odde, or even, and they fall
> First into this, five, women may take us all.[120]

This is not pure caprice. As throughout the poem, whatever is the source of its imagery—science, theological doctrine, or fantastic learning—the use to which it is put is not devoid of significance. While both appreciate the sting of aspersion in these lines, Professor Grierson and M. Legouis are otherwise worlds apart in their respective

---

[117] *Ibid.*, I, 61, l. 18.   [118] *Ibid.*, ll. 1-14.   [119] See *ibid.*, ll. 14-17.
[120] *Ibid.*, pp. 61-62, ll. 21-30.

interpretations.[121] The gross literalness of Legouis, with no accounting for the poet's imaginative use of the learning on which the thought depends, may be dismissed as ridiculous. Professor Grierson's interpretation, though sound, needs some expansion to make it entirely clear. As ten is the "farthest number," the sum of human perfection as represented by the combination of perfect woman and man, woman may reach her full glory in union with man by adding to her own five another five which is man's number. In "each woman may take halfe us men," then, Donne does not mean "half the males of her species," as Legouis ventures (if so, why should her exploits be confined to this particular fraction? Why not two-thirds, or three-fourths?), but rather means that she may take "from" us men, half of her complete perfection which is reached only in union with man. But, respecting the fact that woman is as often by *art* as by *nature* "falsify'd," Donne admits that she may argue subtly that as five contains all that perfection demands (both the first even and the first odd number), she may "take us all." Professor Grierson says that "take us all" means

[121] "The perfect primrose has apparently five petals, but more or less may be found. Seeking for one to symbolize his love, he fears to find either more or less. What can be less than woman? But if more than woman she becomes that unreal thing, the object of Platonic affection and Petrarchian adoration: but, as he says elsewhere,

> 'Love's not so pure and abstract as they use
> To say, which have no Mistresse but their Muse.
> [*Loves growth*, I, 33, ll. 11-12.]

Let woman be content to be herself. Since five is half ten, united with man she will be half of a perfect life; or (and the cynical humour breaks out again) if she is not content with that, since five is the first number which includes an even number (2) and an odd (3), it may claim to be the perfect number, and she to be the whole in which we men are included and absorbed. We have no will of our own."—*Ibid.*, II, 48-49. Legouis's answer to Grierson's interpretation runs as follows: "The conclusion, wrapped up in a mystical theory of numbers, advances two propositions, the second of which improves upon the first:

> 'Each woman may take halfe us men;
>   . . .
>   . . . women may take us all.'

. . . I do not deny that the lines may be so construed [that is, as Grierson construes them], but think their meaning is both simpler and coarser: (1) each woman has a right to half the males of her species; (2) 'Or, if this will not serve her turne,' each woman may take to herself as mates all men. This explanation is supported by the maxim in *Communitie*, 'All, all may use.' . . . And as regards his [Grierson's] general explanation of the cynical element (which he minimizes but does not wholly exorcize) in *The Primrose* and its companion pieces, to wit that Donne has difficulty 'in adjusting himself to the Petrarchian convention' and that 'his passionate heart and satiric wit' tend 'to break through the prescribed tone of worship,' it is no doubt true, so far as it goes; but while it accounts for the internal contradictions of these poems, can it reconcile the indecencies in them with the reputation of the lady [Lady Herbert] for whom they are supposed to have been written?"—*Op cit.*, pp. 96-97.

"our will counts for nothing." Above, the "halfe" in "halfe us men"
refers to the contribution man makes to the full perfection of woman
in union with him; the "all" in "women may take us all," refers to the
complete personality of man. "Our will counts for nothing"; woman
may take all from us, in the sense of deprive us of all, make us completely subject to her will. Thus, in the guise of witty gymnastics and
in imagery appropriate to convey the cynical glance which his eye
casts upon feminine nature Donne conceals from ready observation
what to him is a fundamental human truth. Accept it or not, it must
be admitted that he has tried to penetrate to the psychological truth
involved in every human situation in which the clean singleness and
independence of either the man or the woman is violated in their
assumed relations.

Though the question as to whether *The Primrose* should be identified with Lady Herbert cannot be answered with certainty, the basis
for any conjecture on that matter has been set forth. If we accept the
addition to the title as accurate, though the addition states no more
than that the poem was written at Montgomery Castle, we should
naturally assume that in some way Lady Herbert was in Donne's mind
when he wrote the piece. As the emphasis falls on the defects of
womankind rather than on the virtues, it is difficult to accept in full
the strained interpretation that Gosse gives: "The whole is a mystical
celebration of the beauty, dignity, and intelligence of Magdalen Herbert." But it cannot be doubted that a visit to this admirable friend
may have forced upon him again that cynical mood in which the
excellence of one but serves to remind him of the weakness of the
many, as did his reflections upon the "active good" of the Countess
of Huntingdon. Moreover, he has laid down in the poem the grounds
on which such true excellence as was Lady Herbert's rests. It is pretty
certain that Donne journeyed to Montgomery Castle in 1613 to visit
his friend,[122] then Lady Danvers, and, as *The Primrose* was written after
1610, it may be this very visit that inspired its composition.

We have been brought far afield from the "new starres" and the
Milky Way, seemingly carried along on a voyage among the nebulae of
poetic invention. But no apology need be given. Poems do not begin

[122] "On Good Friday, 1613, Donne wrote his poem 'Riding Westward' as he was
journeying from Polesworth, where he had visited Sir Henry Goodyer, on his road to
Montgomery Castle and its delightful inmates, Magdalen Herbert and her son Sir
Edward."—Gosse, *op. cit.*, II, 25-26. Montgomery Castle, according to Gosse, had
been transferred under James I to another branch of the family, "that of Philip Herbert," but was sold back to Sir Edward in July, 1613, several months after Donne's
reported visit. Gosse thinks, however, that Lady Herbert may have taken up residence
in the castle sometime "before she was actually the owner."

and end with telescopes and astronomical treatises; and it is in just such "wild pursuits" of words and images suggested by these means that we arrive at the "heavens" of the poetic mind. Though Donne's studies of the discoveries made by Galileo's glass did not stir his imagination to the composition of a work of cosmic greatness, they did provide an effective means for the adornment of compliment and tribute, and, what is more important, they brought to a nature already complex the cause for further complication, the analysis and expression of which, in turn, they help to realize. Thus, experiences of the poet, associated with learning that is always encroaching upon the realms of philosophy and religion, are thrown into a deeper perspective wherever the figures of heaven and earth merge to elicit their true poetic value.

VIII

THE FIRST ELEMENTS

IN A day that has seen so much water pass under the bridge of scientific discovery, the old is apt to be scorned out of existence, if not actually forgotten. The search for the ultimate components of matter has gone so far that atoms have had to give way to electrons and even they, to such fanciful realities as ions, neutrons, and protons. So completely has the work of the scientific analysts got hold of the imagination that the average intelligent person is much more inclined to regard his universe as disposed into atoms and molecules—even the lesser entities named above—than into the more tangible substances of mineral and gaseous composition. If he happens to be of a venturesome disposition, and if he has been listening to some of the high priests of modern scientific research, he may question his senses to the last and talk about radioactivity or energy, or think in his uninitiated way of the utter nothingness of things which only the imagery of mathematics can describe. The day of "I refute it thus" by thumping a stone with one's great toe is past; and the mystical conception of the "world in a grain of sand" has the tang of ancient literalness beside some theories of the present time.

Thus, though the figure of "the four elements," drawn from old science, may remain with us, it is in the realm of poetic fiction that we keep it, unmindful of the fact that therein is expressed a "truth" to the "pre-scientific" thinkers as genuine and concrete as that described for us by the table of atomic weights hanging in every college lecture hall where chemistry is taught. The solemn statement of Robert Recorde's schoolmaster in *The Castle of Knowledge,* in 1556, is not to be regarded lightly: " . . . these foure, that is, earth, water, ayre and fyer, are named the foure elements . . . the fyrste, symple and original matters, whereof all myxt and compounde bodies be made, and into whiche all shall retourne againe." [1] Recorde was an intelligent man whose thinking was advanced far enough to allow him to see the advantages of the Copernican system less than a quarter of a century after the publication of *De Revolutionibus.* Nor should the sincerity of Milton's thought, expressed more than a hundred years later, be

[1] Fol. 6.

obscured by the brilliance of his dramatic account of the endless warfare of the elements,

> . . . where eldest Night
> And *Chaos,* Ancestors of Nature, hold
> Eternal *Anarchie* . . .
>
>   . . .
>
>   this wilde Abyss,
> The Womb of nature and perhaps her Grave.[2]

The doctrine of the four elements, derived mainly from Aristotle,
was challenged in the years of the scientific renaissance, not only by
the chemists who were busy with their minerals and the problem of
transmuting metals, but also by the astronomers and mathematicians.
It will be recalled that, according to the traditional world scheme the
universe was cleft in twain into the celestial and elementary worlds;
in the former, the planets and the stars had their places; in the latter
were disposed the elements according to their peculiar natures. The
earth, being the heaviest of the elements, occupied the center, and surrounding it were the water, air, and fire, in the order named, respective
of their diminishing weight and increasing lightness. Thus, as the elements of air and fire presumably filled all the sublunary space, they
inevitably came under the astronomer's consideration as his attention
was drawn to the phenomena of the superterrestrial regions. The challenge given to the old system by the discovery of new celestial phenomena and by the improvement of the science of optics, shook the
old doctrine of the inalterability of the heavens. The existence of the
traditional solid orbs and of the element of fire was denied. Furthermore, when comets and meteors, along with new stars, were removed
to the pure and indestructible heavenly sphere, the elementary regions
—long accepted as the sphere of change, of growth, and of decay—
lost the distinction of being the breeding place of these transient
phenomena.

The doctrine of the elements plays an intimate and important rôle
in the unfolding of Donne's thought. At times he literally translates
the idea into poetry. Again, as the symbol of the ultimate to which
matter or experience may be reduced, it serves as the vehicle whereby
the poetical analysis is accomplished, and also stands as the figurative
representation of that analysis. In an early poem, *The Dissolution,*[3]
these uses of the elements are well set forth. *The Dissolution* is concerned with one of Donne's favorite themes—the separation of lovers.

[2] *Paradise Lost,* II, ll. 894-96, 910-11.   [3] Grierson, I, 64-65.

Here it is death that has worked the separation; and it is with the analysis of the mind of the man who has thus suffered irreparable loss that the poem proceeds after the opening dramatic words abruptly and poignantly announce the fact that

> Shee'is dead; And all which die
> To their first Elements resolve.[4]

One need not recall the compelling force of Milton's

> For *Lycidas* is dead, dead ere his prime,

and Wordsworth's announcement of the death of Lucy, to appreciate that Donne is with the first poets in his ability to make simple, direct language carry the burden of great human emotion and poetic truth. But, whereas Milton makes the death of Edward King the occasion for treating one of the signal problems of all time and Wordsworth leaves the bare facts of Lucy's death and her translation into the "first Elements,"

> Rolled round in earth's diurnal course,
> With rocks, and stones, and trees,

to impart the effect of tragedy to the imagination, Donne sets out to inquire into the psychology of the matter and to find out just what happens to a man when his beloved dies. And it is this first observation, the fact that the body in death is resolved into the elements themselves, that furnishes the clue to the analysis that follows.

The conclusion reached is that to be expected from Donne, for he comes to it again and again in his treatment of a similar situation —the lover himself is also brought to death, and there follows the dissolution of soul and body:

> And so my soule more earnestly releas'd,
> Will outstrip hers; As bullets flowen before
> A latter bullet may o'rtake, the pouder being more.[5]

This conclusion is reached in a most unusual way. The conventional treatment would have it that the lover dies because of his loss—killed by the tragic blow; but this is not Donne's paradoxical way. It is not the loss that kills, but the gain—but the gain of what? In life, Donne says, their love was so complete and harmonious that

> . . . wee were mutuall Elements to us [ourselves],
> And made of one another.[6]

Consequently, though she is dead the mystical union is continued;

[4] *Ibid.*, p. 64, ll. 1-2.   [5] *Ibid.*, p. 65, ll. 22-24.   [6] *Ibid.*, p. 64, ll. 3-4.

THE FIRST ELEMENTS   163

and whereas in life they shared one another mutually, he finds himself
now in possession of *all* that she was:

> My body then doth hers involve,
> And those things whereof I consist, hereby
> In me abundant grow, and burdenous,
> And nourish not, but smother.[7]

As the lover looks into his heart to discover the elements that compose his earthly life, he finds, not the four elements of the physical
body, but the materials of their former love, that is, passions, sighs,
tears, and despair, now made "burdenous" and "smothering" by the
transforming influence of death. The analogy to the four elements is
skillfully worked out:

> My fire of Passion, sighes of ayre,
> Water of teares, and earthly sad despaire,
> Which my materialls bee.[8]

Thus, "elemented" of impassioned grief he passes his bodily life.
While she lived, the secure love they enjoyed "wore out" these materials;
but now that she is dead they are no longer worn out—the loss ironically is repaired. A burden formerly shared by both must now be
borne by him alone. Thus, his passions diverted from their natural
channels of expression (that is, the reciprocal interchange of emotion
which preserved the balance and proportion of a happy life) find no
outlet and consequently wear out the body:

> Shee, to my losse, doth by her death repaire,
> And I might live long wretched so
> But that my fire doth with my fuell grow.
> Now as those Active Kings
> Whose foraine conquest treasure brings,
> Receive more, and spend more, and soonest breake:
> This (which I am amaz'd that I can speake)
> This death, hath with my store
> My use encreas'd.[9]

All this is pure circumlocution and ingenuity if we assume that a
poem on death should tread the beaten way of grief and sorrow.
However, Donne has chosen to penetrate the region of consciousness
where effects of experience are poignantly recorded but vaguely comprehended. The analysis is difficult but not obscure. A few controlling
facts such as we have suggested make the meaning clear and keep the
progress of the thought on solid ground where its development can be

[7] *Ibid.*, ll. 5-8.   [8] *Ibid.*, p. 65, ll. 9-11.   [9] *Ibid.*, ll. 13-21.

observed. "What is not mix'd equally, dies"; and as in life the elements of true love are harmoniously commingled to the preservation of both lovers alike, so in death the subtle balance is broken and the flesh, consumed by its grief, sets free the soul. So thorough has been Donne's adherence to the doctrine of the elements that he has even preserved the relation that the elements themselves bear to the incorruptible ethereal world. The bodily constituents are consistently analogous to the mutable materials of the elementary sphere. They cannot escape the corruption to which nature is heir; but the soul, identified with the celestial sphere, is not only the symbol of immutability, but also the very part of the world's form in which permanence and security abide.

The Dissolution, because its entire structure depends upon an understanding of the doctrine of the elements, represents more fully than any other of Donne's early poems the kind of use which he made of this doctrine. As observed above, the elements come into the poem primarily as a means of analysis, as a scheme whereby things may be reduced symbolically to their ultimates and by which a figurative representation of this analysis may be effected. Other examples, however, are not wanting, but they tend only to confirm with varying degrees of emphasis the statement that has been made.[10]

Now and then it is some special phase of the doctrine that captures Donne's imagination, as in a verse letter to his friend Sir Henry Wotton that can be assigned approximately to the year 1598.[11] In this letter Donne shows no concern for the doctrine as a matter of philosophical importance; it becomes only a means for the more specific definition of his satirical thought. The letter deals with a conventional enough theme, the relative merits of life in the country and life in the city and the court. Nevertheless, it gives Donne scope for the expression of two things: the disillusionment that was spreading its pall over the later Elizabethan days of

> Utopian youth, growne old Italian; [12]

and a note consistent in Donne, akin to the *nosce teipsum* theme, that in the discovery of self-knowledge and in the realization of a soul independent of cramping and outworn conventions exists man's happiness:

> Be thou thine owne home, and in thy selfe dwell.[13]

---

[10] See *Elegie II. The Anagram, ibid.,* p. 80, l. 10; *A Valediction: of the booke, ibid.,* p. 30, ll. 19-22.
[11] *Ibid.,* pp. 180-82. [12] *Ibid.,* I, 182, l. 46.
[13] *Ibid.,* l. 47.

It is in the course of the development of this theme that the poet finds in the doctrine of the elements the reflection of his own conception of the troubled and orderless life of the world:

> . . . of all three [country, city, court]
> (O knottie riddle) each is worst equally.
> Cities are Sepulchers; they who dwell there
> Are carcases, as if no such there were.
> And Courts are Theaters, where some men play
> Princes, some slaves, all to one end, and of one clay.
> The Country is a desert, where no good,
> Gain'd (as habits, not borne) is understood.
> There men become beasts, and prone to more evils;
> In cities blockes, and in a lewd court, devills.
> As in the first Chaos confusedly
> Each elements qualities were in the'other three;
> So pride, lust, covetize, being severall
> To these three places, yet all are in all,
> And mingled thus, their issue incestuous.[14]

In this letter the chaos of the warring elements is a figure of man's unwitting efforts to undo the work of creation. In another poem of the same period, *The Progresse of the Soule*,[15] the growth of the plant, "thus abled" by the infusion of the erratic and vagarious soul, is described in terms of the habits of air and water which seek their proper places, according to their respective qualities:

> The plant thus abled, to it selfe did force
> A place, where no place was; by natures course
> As aire from water, water fleets away
> From thicker bodies, by this root thronged so
> His spungie confines gave him place to grow.[16]

Further on, in the same poem, the whale, in whose body the soul has taken temporary residence,

> . . . ever as hee went
> . . . spouted rivers up, as if he ment
> To joyne our seas, with seas above the firmament.[17]

The technical aspects of the doctrine continue to appeal to Donne for the rest of his life; again and again he finds it useful as a means of representing his resolution of thought and emotion into their first principles. The frequent use of a doctrine so widely known and so

[14] *Ibid.*, p. 181, ll. 19-33.   [15] *Ibid.*, pp. 293-316.
[16] *Ibid.*, p. 300, ll. 131-35.   [17] *Ibid.*, p. 308, ll. 318-20.

commonly employed in poetic imagery may at times suggest the over-working of a threadbare convention; but usually his paradoxical wit and fertile invention endow the allusions to the elements with a freshness that is stimulating and effective, as in the *Elegie on the Lady Marckham,* where he writes,

> Man is the World, and death th'Ocean,
>   To which God gives the lower parts of man.
> This Sea invirons all, and though as yet
>   God hath set markes, and bounds, twixt us and it,
> Yet doth it rore, and gnaw, and still pretend,
>   And breaks our bankes, when ere it takes a friend.
> Then our land waters (teares of passion) vent;
>   Our waters, then, above our firmament,
> (Teares which our Soule doth for her sins let fall)
>   Take all a brackish tast, and Funerall,
> And even these teares, which should wash sin, are sin.
> We, after Gods *Noe,* drowne our world againe.[18]

The most familiar passage in Donne witnessing his interest in the new science, so often cited that now it has the taint of staleness for the critic, is that to which we too already have referred, in *The first Anniversary,* beginning,

> And new Philosophy calls all in doubt,
> The Element of fire is quite put out . . .

The attention of the critics usually has not paused here long but moved on to the ensuing lines to take note of Donne's report of the revolution accomplished in astronomy. The lines, however, are impor-tant in themselves, because the fact that Donne places first in his cata-logue of "doubts" the explosion of the belief in the existence of the element of fire argues for the significance he attached to the place of the doctrine of the elements in the old philosophy. In this passage he acknowledges that judgment has been passed upon the old world scheme in ways other than that sounded by the discovery of new stars or by the promulgation of the doctrine of the moving earth. The elementary world, already thought corruptible, has been made to reveal to the very eyes of men its corruptibility, and as vividly has the "in-alterable" celestial sphere been forced to expose its symptoms of decay and change. The element of fire has been put out, and the solid orbs have vanished. It is not without a close and exact knowledge of the work of the scientists that Donne could have reached the conclusion expressed in his fit of disillusionment.

[18] *Ibid.,* pp. 279-80, ll. 1-12. May 4, 1609.

It was not the telescope that conveyed to man that there was no such thing as a fiery region beneath the moon nor confining crystalline spheres—though doubtless Galileo's discoveries stamped the fact on Donne's mind—but the more purely mathematical science of the optics.

As evidence for the dismissal from its universal rôle of the element of fire was certainly not generally known nor the knowledge that it had been dismissed commonly recognized by 1611, it becomes extremely interesting to inquire into the source of Donne's information and into the particular form in which it was conveyed to him. Robert Burton writes in *The Anatomy of Melancholy* that "Cardan, Tycho, and John Pena, manifestly confute by refractions, and many other arguments, there is no such element of fire at all." [19] When Donne wrote the *Catalogus Librorum,* he was already familiar with Cardan's popular omnibus of physical learning, *De Subtilitate,* in which the denial of the existence of the element of fire appeared.[20] Again in 1608, in *Biathanatos,* he took note of Cardan's book, but then only to support his contention that self-homicide is not against the law of nature.[21] From Clavius also he learned of Cardan's attitude toward the element of fire.[22] However, it is doubtless from Kepler, who taught Donne so much about the new philosophy, that he derived the full import of Tycho's and Pena's "confutation" of the element of fire, as well as of Kepler's own detailed and critical examination of the problem. At least, it is not until after Donne had come to know Kepler that he saw fit to make his own declarative statement that "the Element of fire is quite put out." [23] If we assume, then, that it was Kepler who persuaded

[19] Part II, sec. ii, mem. iii, "Digression of Air."

[20] Donne casts a sidelong witty glance at Cardan's pseudo-medical learning by recommending that all politely learned gentlemen should read "Cardan, *On the nullibiety of breaking wind.*" Item no. 23, p. 50. *De Subtilitate,* first published in 1550, was one of the most popular sixteenth-century books on physical learning. I have noted offhand ten different editions in the British Museum *Catalogue* dated between 1550 and 1611. Cardan's *De Varietate Rerum,* first published in 1557, supplements the earlier work and extends his conquest of the natural world. It is in the second book of *De Subtilitate* that Cardan denies the existence of the element of fire.

[21] "And as (a) *Cardan* sayes it, [*Mettall is planta sepulta, and that a Mole is Animal sepultum.*] So man, as though he were *Angelus sepultus,* labours to be discharged of his earthly Sepulchre, his body." Part I, dist. 2, sec. 3, p. 50. The reference in the margin is to Cardan's *"De Subtil. lib. 5."*

[22] "However, there are some," Clavius writes, "who deny that the region of fire exists above the air, because it is not perceptible by our senses. They say, if it exists, it would consume all things below it. Thus, they do not allow any elementary fire other than that which we enjoy on earth. . . . It is sufficient to know the more probable and more common opinion of those, who with Aristotle hold that the element of fire exists in its natural place under the concave of the moon."—*Op. cit.,* pp. 37-38.

[23] The influence of Gilbert's enthusiastic attack upon the heavens of the old philosophy should not be disregarded. See particularly *De Magnete,* pp. 214-20.

Donne to deny the existence of the fourth element, it is necessary to have some understanding of the nature of the arguments used to establish this heretical doctrine.

Donne's repeated mention of the "optics," as well as his frequent use of imagery and illustration based on the conclusions reached by this science—particularly in the *Sermons*—demonstrates a familiarity with the optical science that in itself could be made the subject of extended study.[24] Though at no time does he refer to specific books or authors, contenting himself rather with general allusions to the "old Writers in the Optiques," or to the "later men," [25] it is not difficult to establish his most fertile source of information. In his *De Stella Nova* Kepler again and again calls upon his own work on the optics in expressions such as *quod in Opticis putavi, ut in Opticis explicatur,* and *ut in Opticis docetur* to explain the distance of the new star, the nature of its light, the density of the ether, and kindred matters. Likewise, the achievements of his master, Tycho Brahe, who was the first to measure with any degree of accuracy the amount of refraction observed in the sun at different altitudes, are referred to. The book to which Kepler alludes and whose use he invokes, is his *Ad Vitellionem Paralipomena,* a voluminous discourse on the optics published in Frankfort in 1604.[26] As the title indicates, Kepler's book purported to be a supplement to the work of Vitellio [Vitello], a thirteenth-century writer on the optics. Vitellio's treatise *praecipuum fuerit fundamentum opticorum* (in the main a digest and simplification of a treatise of the eleventh-century Arabian, Alhazen, the most noteworthy medieval writer on the optics), had not been printed before 1572, the year of Tycho's new star.[27] In 1611 appeared Kepler's second significant work on optics, the *Dioptrice,* a continuation of his own *Dissertatio cum Nuncio Sidereo* (1610), repeating much that had formerly been expressed in *Ad Vitellionem,* in which he hoped to demonstrate the theory of Galileo's new telescope.[28] It is in the Preface to the *Dioptrice* that Kepler conveniently summarizes the arguments of Vitellio and Pena against the existence of a fiery sphere above the earth and explains by the

[24] See, for example, the following: *The Progresse of the Soule,* Grierson, I, 306, ll. 271-73; *To Mr Rowland Woodward, ibid.,* p. 186, ll. 19-21; *To the Countesse of Bedford, ibid.,* p. 219, ll. 28-30; *The first Anniversary, ibid.,* p. 242, ll. 353-55; *The second Anniversary, ibid.,* p. 259, ll. 291-94; *Biathanatos,* pp. 154, 214; *Devotions vpon Emergent Occasions* (London, 1624), p. 47; *LXXX Sermons,* 16, fol. 162; *ibid.,* 23, fols. 224, 225, 226, 227; *ibid.,* 75, fols. 760, 761; *ibid.,* 29, fol. 289; *ibid.,* 12, fol. 121; *ibid.,* 30, fol. 302.

[25] *LXXX Sermons,* 23, fol. 226.

[26] Cited above as *Astronomiae pars optica,* pp. 129, 144 nn. 48, 89.

[27] "In opticam notae editoris, 1," Frisch, II, 399.

[28] See above, p. 94 n. 26.

use of a remarkably simple experiment the nature of the process of observation which established the earlier conclusion. Kepler's argument runs thus: rays of light are bent out of their straight course when passing through different media from the object from which they are emitted, such as a star, to the eye of the observer. As this is true, if there were a sphere of fire under the moon, considerable refraction of the rays emitted from the stars should be evident. This may be demonstrated by a single experiment: if a vessel containing live coals is placed between the eye and a wall against which the sun is shining, the stream of heat issuing upward from the vessel, though invisible, when agitated by a little wind, can be observed in shadow on the bright wall. This trembling shadow is really a reflection of the rays of light which are broken or bent upon passing through the stream of heat rising from the coals. As the best observations do not reveal any considerable refraction of the light of the stars, it is proved that no fiery sphere exists in the sublunary heavens.[29]

[29] For those who care to follow the argument in detail I have made the following translation:

"But I shall turn to a number of doctrines that Pena established most truly from the optics, of which the fourth is that it has been argued most correctly from optical phenomena that there is no fiery sphere above us. With this fundamental undermined, how great is the ruin of the Aristotelian Meteorology cannot be unknown to any philosopher of this age. If, indeed, under heaven there is fire, either visible or invisible, there would be a very great refraction of the rays of light from the heavenly bodies. For the fire seeks to go upwards because it is a more tenuous substance than the air, just as an inflated bladder bobs up from the depth of water into which it has been submerged, being forced from below by the weight of the water. Likewise, the fiery substance, having the cause of its upward moving tendency in its lightness, is driven from the heavier body of the surrounding air.

"If the physicists affirm that there is round and about above our heads a transparent substance lighter than the air, they cannot deny that rays of light would be broken in crossing from the confines of the heavier air to the surface of the lighter fire. Moreover, all cross obliquely to the place of the observer, whence results the great refraction of the rays.

"The force of the argument can be made clear to the eye by an experiment. Suppose the sun to be shining against a wall. Place a thurible filled with living coals between the eye and the wall. If the air is still, a stream of fiery substance ascends straight up from the thurible, with no fumes intermixed. If a little wind comes up, the stream is deflected somewhat to one side, flowing upwards with an undulation. Though you do not follow this stream with the eyes, as it is certainly transparent and without color, if you glance at the wall opposite, you will see in the sun the shadows of these things thrown against the wall by the flowing of the fire. This undulation is truly a species of motion. And thus the rays of the sun circumscribing the shadow, tremble, because they are broken while crossing the fiery ebullition, and this is always changing in accordance with the varying transformation of the surfaces of the fiery stream. From this uneven inflection of the rays on the surface of the ebullition results the unevenness of the inflections or refractions falling upon the wall, that is, the unevenness of the trembling shadow projected. By this experiment, therefore, it follows that the rays of light on the surface of the fiery substance however much they may be invisible are

Kepler points out the errors of Vitellio and Pena. Both had perceived the phenomenon of refraction but had been confused in their explanations of what they saw. Vitellio attributed rightly the cause of refraction to the influence of the air but erred in calculating this from the changing positions of the moon. Pena, on the other hand, while discrediting the region of fire, mistook the phenomenon of refraction for that of parallax. It was Tycho who first corrected Pena by proving that the refractions are not so much from the moon as from the fixed

---

sensibly broken. It may be concluded that there is no such fiery substance extending under the heavens, either fluctuating or tranquil, because the observers of the constellations notice no such thing, nor do they note this refraction (trembling) in individual stars. Nor do they observe either the change of place or the constancy that would be measurable in the figure of the fiery sphere. In truth, there is no other thing present than the surface of the air itself.

"Pena treats this very solid argument without caution. Though he challenges the walls of the fiery sphere, he is exceedingly perplexed by his own arguments. He thinks it pertains to the strength of his argument if he plainly admits no refractions in the stars, and thus does not feel any uncertainty in detracting from the faith in the observations of the astronomers, which Vitellio makes use of. Vitellio had said that the rays of light were broken and that this was observable in the moon whose latitude is seen to vary often as the tables of motion admit. But Pena declares that the cause of the breaking of the rays is not in refraction but in the phenomenon noted by astronomers, known as parallax. What confusion, this! For each doctrine has the truth and each proves this in a perverse way; meanwhile, it must be established in the errors it brings upon matters that are known. Truly Vitellio says that the curving of the sidereal rays results from the density of the air; he is also right, but accidentally so, in saying that this is to be observed in the moon. In presupposing the places of the moon to be set forth accurately by the calculations of his time and in formulating from these the rule for estimating observations and comprehending refractions, he was thoroughly deceived. In fact, I should say that it was not before Tycho Brahe that the refractions of the moon were discerned, not, however, because of the error in the ancient calculations, but because of the negligence of the early observers. Brahe discovered the refraction, not so much from the moon, because that would have been more difficult on account of the variety and quickness of its motions, as from the fixed stars themselves. However, in the moon alone, even if its calculation is not most certain, the refractions are easily discerned. But so much for the hallucination of Vitellio. Let us now look at the judgment of Pena. He is right in maintaining that no refractions are caused by a sphere of fire; but he adds falsely that there are no refractions at all, not even caused by the air. Ineptly he goes against the argument of Vitellio, and as stated, uselessly and to his own ruin in attributing to parallax what Vitellio attributed to refractions. Astronomers are aware of the fact that the effects of these two (parallax and refractions) are contradictory: refraction raises and enlarges the moon; parallax depresses it. This, Pena did not consider carefully. But, as I have said, there is no loss even if Pena does not avoid the refractions of Vitellio: they are indeed effected by the air and not by the fire. Therefore, as said, they establish the greater density of the upper part of the air; and as Pena intended, they shake inwardly and eliminate the more tenuous region of the fire. Thus, in every way the excellence of the above experiment of the principles of the optics helps as much to establish the distinction between the air and the ether as to bear out the fiction of the fiery sphere."—Frisch, II, 522-23.

stars. Kepler, however, disagrees erroneously with Tycho in not admitting a successive diminution in the density of the air as it rose from the environs of the earth to the highest ether.[30]

Though it cannot be established that Donne read the *Dioptrice*, its appearance in January, 1611,[31] together with its close association with Galileo's *Sidereus Nuncius*, would not conflict with the probability of his having made use of its information before composing *The first Anniversary*. However, even if Donne had not seen this particular work of Kepler, he could have been instructed adequately by the earlier treatise on the optics, *Ad Vitellionem*, and by the *De Stella Nova* itself. In the former, Kepler recalls the conclusion of Pena and Rothmann that the air extends from the earth to the confines of the moon, uninterrupted by the traditional region of fire, and takes note of Tycho's agreement with them that the "Aristotelian fire" does not exist.[32] In the *De Stella Nova*, in the course of his demonstration that the new star was generated in the highest ether, he makes use of Tycho's proof that as the ether succeeds directly upon our air, there are no solid orbs, as tradition teaches, and that if the new stars had existed under the moon, contrary to fact, they would have been borne around with the lunar orb as Aristotle supposed the fire to have been.[33]

In *The second Anniversary*, when the flight of Elizabeth Drury's soul to heaven is described, there is the same definite reference to the fiction of the fiery region. Here Donne expresses himself with an indifference to the existence of the element of fire that is not so much the product of disbelief as of his conviction that the matters of philosophical controversy are ridiculously unimportant in the consideration of one's final salvation. Donne, in *The second Anniversary*, is definitely trying to shake off a concern with the matter of doubtful sense experience and the things of reason in behalf of the primary claims of faith:

[30] Delambre, in calling attention to the dispute between Tycho and Rothmann, notes this error of Kepler as well as his faulty explanation of the cause of refraction.—*Histoire de l'astronomie moderne*, I, 363. Note Kepler's examination of the causes of refraction as set forth by Tycho, and the statement of his own opinion: "Denique apparuisset, superficiem quae frangit radios neque vaporem esse temere oberrantium neque corporis alicujus sublimis ad Lunae confinia, sed plane aëris ejus, in quo nos homines spiritum eum in modum trahimus, quo pisces trahunt aquam. Statuisset itaque Tycho non successioram attenuationem aëris in aetherem et obliterationem densitatis aëriae, sed manifestum et evidens discrimen, quod si quis supra consisteret, non minus ipsi in oculos esset in cursurum, ac jam superficies, quae aërem ab aqua separat, in oculos incurrit."— *Astronomiae pars optica*, Frisch, II, 177-78. See also §2, "Varii variorum modi metiendarum refractionum refutati," *ibid.*, p. 178.

[31] "Cal. Januariis anni undecimi de seculo septimo decimo." Dedication of *Dioptrice*, Frisch, II, 518.

[32] *Ibid.*, pp. 207-8. [33] *Ibid.*, pp. 694-95.

. . . This to thy Soule allow,
Thinke thy shell broke, thinke thy Soule hatch'd but now.
And think this slow-pac'd soule, which late did cleave
To'a body, and went but by the bodies leave,
Twenty, perchance, or thirty mile a day,
Dispatches in a minute all the way
Twixt heaven, and earth; she stayes not in the ayre,
To looke what Meteors there themselves prepare;
She carries no desire to know, nor sense,
Whether th'ayres middle region be intense;
For th'Element of fire, she doth not know,
Whether she past by such a place or no.[34]

The same poem contains an allusion to a controverted phase of the history of the elements that derives more generally from the arguments of natural philosophy and medicine than from mathematics and astronomy, revealing that Donne did recall passages in Cardan's book as well as those in Kepler's discourses, when he was thinking of the elements. The absurdities of learning shadowed by uncertainty and relativity involved the microcosm as well as the greater world; and consequently the befuddled notions of the physiologists contribute their share to the uncertainty of knowledge about a world from which Donne's soul turns aside in its search for the abiding solution of the problem of the truth about the nature of things:

Thou art too narrow, wretch, to comprehend
Even thy selfe: yea though thou wouldst but bend
To know thy body. Have not all soules thought
For many ages, that our body'is wrought
Of Ayre, and Fire, and other Elements?
And now they thinke of new ingredients,
And one Soule thinkes one, and another way
Another thinkes, and 'tis an even lay.[35]

It was Cardan who denied the elementary nature of fire and as a consequence rejected it as a constituent of the body. In brief, he declared that there are but three so-called elements, earth, air, and water, common to all things and possessed of definite properties that entitle them to the name of elements. These properties are the capacity to provide nourishment, to resist decay, to remain fixed in a certain place, and to assist generation. As fire has no quality other than heat (*caliditas*) it is not worthy of being known as an element.[36] Donne's

[34] Grierson, I, 256-57, ll. 183-94.
[35] *Ibid.*, pp. 258-59, ll. 261-68.
[36] *De Subtilitate*, quoted by Frisch, VIII, 598-99.

reference to the "new ingredients" doubtless pertains to the Paracelsian doctrine that the three principal constituents of the body are salt, sulphur, and mercury.[37]

The expulsion of fire from the sublunary region, did not mean, however, that the element was entirely discredited. Kepler went on believing that it was a real part of the original stuff upon which creation exercised itself. Despite Cardan's dogmatic pronouncement, it continued to hold its place with earth, air, and water as one of the ultimate constituents of matter. Nevertheless, Donne is treading upon the heels of irony when he affirms his constancy in terms that seem to mock the recent conclusions of the scientists:

> Nay, if I wax but cold in my desire,
> Think, heaven hath motion lost, and the world, fire.[38]

[37] Cf. Hakewell, op. cit., p. 230.

[38] Elegie XII. His parting from her, Grierson, I, 104, ll. 99-100. Though there is a stubborn crux in the problem of its chronology, I venture to include the poem from which the above lines are drawn among those of Donne's middle period. Of this elegy and the fifteenth, Grierson writes, "it is impossible to date [them], but it is not likely that they were written after his marriage."—Grierson, II, 62. The tone of the poem is serious and the style exalted, matters, of course, which prove very little concerning its date. However, its elegiac mood definitely linking it artistically with A Nocturnall upon S. Lucies day and Twicknam garden, poems very likely written after his marriage, suggests that the poem was the product of his maturer years. The crux appears in one of those passages with which Gosse played so freely when he conceived of the autobiographical significance of certain of Donne's elegies. The following lines, if taken with Gosse's literalness, certainly do not commend the fidelity of Anne Donne's husband:

> "Was't not enough that thou didst dart thy fires
> Into our blouds, inflaming our desires,
> And made'st us sigh and glow, and pant, and burn,
> And then thy self into our flame did'st turn?
> Was't not enough, that thou didst hazard us
> To paths in love so dark, so dangerous:
> And those so ambush'd round with houshold spies,
> And over all, thy husbands towring eyes
> That flam'd with oylie sweat of jealousie:
> Yet went we not still on with Constancie?"
>
> Ibid., ll. 35-44.

On the other hand, Elegie XIV, containing evidence of having been composed later than 1609 (ibid., II, 62, 83-85), pays no higher tribute to Donne's domestic gravity, if the poem is to be accepted as a personal record, the manner of which warrants the autobiographical approach. But such "comparisons are odious" and get us nothing in establishing the date of the authorship. There are several things in Elegie XII worth considering as probable evidence for ascribing its date to a later period in Donne's life than that usually accepted. The poem is especially rich in astronomical allusions (see ll. 6, 86-88, 90-100), and it is pretty certain that most of Donne's images based on astronomy appear in poems written after 1600. In the second line of the passage cited above in the text, namely, "Think, heaven hath motion lost, and the world, fire," the first figure reveals perhaps nothing more than such an image as, "The heavens re-

Nor is it in jest that he represents the source of honor in terms of one of the arguments raised by the philosophers against the existence of the fiery region:

> Honour is so sublime perfection,
> And so refinde; that when God was alone
> And creaturelesse at first, himselfe had none;
>
> But as of the elements, these which wee tread,
> Produce all things with which wee'are joy'd or fed,
> And, those are barren both above our head.[39]

In an age when scholars chanted the "even lay" of dissidence, and when what one thought seemed to be as valid as the speculations of another, contradictions were inevitable. Nevertheless, Donne knew that below the disturbed surface of the stream of controversy there was the deeper running current of a scientific opinion that was very apt to be telling rather more than less truth about the nature of things. It was not because the scientists were wrong, but because they appeared to be more nearly right than traditional popular sentiment, that he was able to testify so certainly to their capacity to provoke doubt. Among the glosses that they were penning in the book of knowledge was the one which spelled the end of the old fiction of the four elements, and Donne was thus aware that in the sphere of terrestrial things as well as in the higher heavens the new philosophy had begun the story of a new world order.

---

joyce in motion" (*Elegie XVII. Variety*, I, 113, l. 1), drawn from the turning of the spheres; but the adaptation of the idea—"Heaven hath motion lost"—may not be without significance. This conjecture is emphasized by the subsequent figure, "Think . . . the world [has lost] fire." That is, it is just plausible that the images would not have come to Donne's mind until after the validity of the doctrines on which they were based had been questioned. Though Donne frequently refers to the impairment of the sun in the new philosophy (see *ibid.*, p. 196, ll. 37-38; p. 224, ll. 3-4; p. 239, ll. 263-74), it is only because the figure is closely associated here with the much controverted subject of the element of fire, that one is led to surmise that he was thinking of something other than the obvious and undisputed fact that the heavenly bodies move. Moreover, Donne's declaration of devotion would not be sapped of its sincerity if it is assumed that the imagery in which it is expressed is derived from controversial scientific doctrine, not from established, unalterable fact.

[39] *To the Countesse of Bedford, ibid.*, p. 218, ll. 1-6. [1611–12.] Recall Cardan's argument that fire is not elementary because it is incapable of nourishing and has no capacity for generation.

IX

FIGURES OF SPACE

> And for the Heav'ns wide Circuit, let it speak
> The Makers high magnificence, who built
> So spacious, and his Line stretcht out so farr; [1]

wrote Milton, aware of one of the most significant contributions of the new philosophy—the conception of a vastly extended universe. Though the earth may have been shorn of some of its traditional dignity when it ceased to be regarded as the center of the world, and though man may have recoiled from the suggestion that his universe was so created, spacious,

> That [he] may know he dwells not in his own;

doomed to

> An Edifice too large for him to fill,
> Lodg'd in a small partition . . .[2]

as time has proved, the grasp of the meaning of space has been one of the most fertile achievements of the human intellect. Rightly, the Renaissance has been thought of as an age of expansion, both geographical and intellectual. Beyond the familiar reaches of the sea new continents invited the adventurer and explorer; and the imagination before which the horizons of experience had begun to recede, beholding the things of this world in new perspective, ventured upon the fascinating theme of the world beyond death, as

> The undiscover'd country, from whose bourn
> No traveller returns.

The astronomer, while he

> Let sea-discoverers to new worlds have gone,

and allowed the poets to contemplate the movements of a mind and body released from the "gothic night," turned to survey anew the universal sphere and disclosed measurements bewildering in comparison to the restricted conceptions of the older philosophers. Thus, Copernicus declares in recalculating the world order:

[1] *Paradise Lost*, VIII, ll. 100-02.　　　[2] *Ibid.*, ll. 103-5.

The size of the world is so great, that the distance of the earth from the sun, though appreciable in comparison to the orbits of the other planets, is as nothing when compared to the sphere of the fixed stars. And I hold it easier to concede this than to let the mind be distracted by an almost endless multitude of circles, which those are obliged to do who detain the earth in the centre of the world.[3]

"The distances of the firmament and of the fixed stars," Gilbert states, "seem to the best mathematicians inconceivable." [4]

It is to the telescope, however, that the imagination is greatly indebted for investing space with a kind of concrete reality by bringing the immensity of the heavens into proximity to human experience. Though, "with a telescope, they [the fixed stars]," as the *Sidereus Nuncius* reports, "appear of the same shape as when they are viewed by simply looking at them," but enlarged; the fact that other bodies "invisible to the naked eye" were made apparent gave a startling reality to the abstraction of mathematical calculation.[5] "Space," it is true, "is not a notion obtained by experience." [6] When we speak of the reality of space, it is the illusion of the modification of the properties of perceptible things—form, position, and magnitude—by the influence of space to which we refer. Though it defies sense perception, space is, nevertheless, an inseparable part of sense experience; in fact, it is a "form of perception" itself, "not a thing which affects our senses, but an idea to which we conform the impressions of sense." In brief, as Whewell concludes, "it is not only a form of sensation, but of *intuition*." [7] Thus, when it became possible for the eye to peer further into the invisible areas of space and to gain a close acquaintance with its inhabitants, both familiar and undreamed of, this element or "form of perception" took on a significance hitherto unknown. It inevitably became an intimate part of nature, and before Galileo's death Descartes had expressed the idea that "extension [space] is the essential property of that [the physical] world, just as thinking is the essential property of the mental world." [8]

The assimilation of this new concept into the creative mind, where it might be contemplated along with other "objects of science" and treated imaginatively, did not occur at once. For the appreciation of what the poet could make of this new experience one must await

[3] Quoted by Dreyer, *History of the Planetary Systems,* p. 327.
[4] *De Magnete,* p. 218.   [5] Page 40.
[6] William Whewell, *The Philosophy of the Inductive Sciences* (London, 1840), I, ii, "Of the Idea of Space," 82.
[7] *Ibid.,* p. 86.
[8] Descartes, *Selections,* ed. Ralph M. Eaton (New York, 1927), p. xxvi. Cf. Gibson, *op. cit.,* p. 217.

Milton's description of the fall of Mulciber, his conception of Satan's journey from hell to earth through the "spacious Empire" of chaos, and Pascal's meditation on the *disproportion de l'homme*, contemplated against the background of *la nature entière dans sa haute et pleine majesté*, where amid the *espaces imaginables, nous n'enfantons que des atomes*.[9]

The concept of space, though endowed with a new life by telescopic exploration of the heavens, was familiar enough to the pre-Galilean mind. Geometry, the purpose of which, according to Euclid, is to investigate the properties of space, experienced a revival among Renaissance philosophers, provoking an enthusiasm rivaling Plato's devotion to this science because the knowledge at which it aims is "knowledge of the eternal, and not of aught perishing and transient." [10] "Yet can no humayne Science saye thus, but I onely," declares Robert Recorde in praise of geometry, "that there is no sparke of untruthe in me; but all my doctrine and workes are without any blemishe of errour, that mans reason can discerne, . . . and what mervail," he continues, "if he [Plato] so much esteemed Geometrie, seying in his opinion, that God was alwaies workyng by Geometrie." It is the mathematical science in the "similitudes" of which the "faculties of mind" are expressed; [11] and as John Dee affirms in his "very fruitful" Preface to his translation of Euclid, geometry is "an arte . . . the knowledge whereof, to humaine state is necessayre." [12] The notion of space held by the Renaissance geometricians, like that of their ancestors, was that of the "actual space in which the universe is set," though its immensities were but vaguely comprehended. Moreover, in so far as astronomy, according to John Dee, demonstrates "the distance, magnitudes, and all natural motions, appearances, and passions propre to the Planets and fixed Starres: for any time past, present and to come; in respect of a certaine Horizon, or without respect of any Horizon," [13] astronomy was the *geometry* of the heavens.

An idea of how thoroughly Donne responded to the influence of the science of space can only be obtained by noting how frequently and effectively he calls upon "similitudes" to geometrical figures to express the "faculties of mind." Whether derived from its association with the practical "skilles" to whose service it was put by the navigator and map maker or from its association with the science of

[9] *Penseés, d' après l'édition de M. Brunschvigg* (Paris, 1913), pp. 24-25.
[10] *The Republic, The Dialogues of Plato,* trans. B. Jowett (New York, n.d.), II, 283.
[11] *The Pathway to Knowledg* (1602), sig. A ii and A iii.
[12] Sig. a iii.
[13] *Ibid.,* sig. b ii.

astronomy, so easily elevated to philosophy where it is concerned with
matters of the spirit and the greater world, the symbolism of geometry
was for Donne a source of imagery that was to be increasingly congenial to his intellectual temper.⌉The nature of the great realm of
intangible realities, like the perfection and greatness of God, matters
over which sense has no jurisdiction, could be suggested in terms of
this science, itself a system of symbols of a reality that cannot immediately be perceived. It could serve to elicit poetic value from such forms
of perception as the poet's intuition of the relation of reason and faith
and of the singleness of true lovers, as well as from his efforts to
comprehend the approaching end of life and the wonders of the
cosmos which no amount of visual contemplation could reveal.[14]

"One of the most convenient Hieroglyphicks of God, is a Circle,
and a Circle is endlesse," [15] he tells his listeners at St. Paul's. Though
the figure of the circle and the conception of circular motion had long
been associated with the idea of divine perfection and had even been
made by Nicholas of Cusa a structural part of his Christian mysticism,[16]
the figure here is irrelevant to any systematic mystical interpretation
of God; it remains exactly what it purports to be, a poet's symbol
whereby is borne in upon the imagination his simple conviction that
"Whom God loves, hee loves to the end." [17] "Convenient Hieroglyphicks" never wither under Donne's treatment into dry conventional
epithets. Within this figure of perfection and eternity, as he early
pointed out, lurks the paradoxical suggestion of fragility; there is

> Nothing more endlesse, nothing sooner broke.[18]

At another time it becomes the emblem of man's sinful career.[19] Circles
are but "poor types of God," [20] and beyond the "Symetrie Perfect as
circles" [21] is the perfection of Elizabeth Drury's soul, itself the symbol
of all goodness, truth, and beauty:

> To whose proportions if we would compare
> Cubes, th'are unstable; Circles, Angular.[22]

The figures of geometry appeal most richly to Donne's imagination
as they are employed in the maps of the heavens and the earth and

[14] Cf. Plato, *op. cit.*, pp. 287-88.   [15] *LXXX Sermons*, 2, fol. 13.
[16] See above p. 73 n. 27.   [17] *LXXX Sermons*, 2, fol. 13.
[18] *A Ieat Ring sent*, Grierson, I, 65, l. 4.
[19] See *LXXX Sermons*, 79, fol. 806.
[20] *To the Countesse of Bedford*, Grierson, I, 220, l. 46.
[21] *Satyre IIII, ibid.*, p. 166, ll. 207, 208.
[22] *The Second Anniversary, ibid.*, p. 255, ll. 141-42.

in the descriptions of the movements of the celestial bodies. The net "weav'd out" of the "Meridians, and Parallels" and "throwne Upon the Heavens" [23] to chart the positions of the stars, the wheels and eccentrics on which the planets run their courses, and the great circles of the tropics, of the zodiac, and of latitude and longitude have for him a fascination testifying not only to hours of poring over the charts of seamen and astronomers but also to a striving to read with intelligence the *"bookes of heaven* (. . . the Mathematiques)," [24] this side of divine revelation the most authentic key to the understanding of the secrets of the cosmos. Above, we have seen how the Copernican explanation of the motions of the earth, illustrated by the circles on which its diurnal and annual orbits are described, provided a device for studying the relations of faith and reason.[25] In Donne's *Obsequies to the Lord Harrington, brother to the Lady Lucy, Countesse of Bedford,*[26] he elaborates an amazingly intricate figure, showing to what ends of beauty and brilliance the poetic imagination can embrace the widely varied uses of an abstract science in an effort to capture one of the elusive mysteries of human experience:

> O Soule, O circle, why so quickly bee
> Thy ends, thy birth and death, clos'd up in thee?
> Since one foot of thy compasse still was plac'd
> In heav'n, the other might securely'have pac'd
> In the most large extent, through every path,
> Which the whole world, or man the abridgment hath.
> Thou knowst, that though the tropique circles have
> (Yea and those small ones which the Poles engrave,)
> All the same roundnesse, evennesse, and all
> The endlesnesse of the equinoctiall;
> Yet, when we come to measure distances,
> How here, how there, the Sunne affected is,
> When he doth faintly worke, and when prevaile,
> Onely great circles, than can be our scale:
> So, though thy circle to thy selfe expresse
> All, tending to thy endlesse happinesse,
> And wee, by our good use of it may trye,
> Both how to live well young, and how to die,
> Yet, since we must be old, and age endures
> His Torrid Zone at Court, and calentures
> Of hot ambitions, irrelegions ice,
> Zeales agues, and hydroptique avarice,

[23] *The first Anniversary, ibid.,* p. 239, ll. 278-80.   [24] *Fifty Sermons,* 31, fol. 273.
[25] See above, pp. 106 ff.   [26] Grierson, I, 271-79. Feb. 27, 1614.

Infirmities which need the scale of truth,
As well as lust, and ignorance of youth;
Why did'st thou not for these give medicines too,
And by thy doing tell us what to doe? [27]

Though death threatens the fair proportions of the world, in bringing to a close the virtuous life, it in some mysterious way presents us
with a pattern of "endlesse happinesse" prefigured in the lines and
circles sweeping their curves perfectly and evenly round the earthly
sphere. Three years earlier, however, we find Donne in a mood of
despair, attacking the geometer himself for breaking the "round proportion" in which he had conceived the universe after the design
existing in the mind of the Creator. This confession of gloom and
disillusionment appears in *The first Anniversary:*

For the worlds beauty is decai'd, or gone,
Beauty, that's colour, and proportion.
We thinke the heavens enjoy their Sphericall,
Their round proportion embracing all.
But yet their various and perplexed course,
Observ'd in divers ages, doth enforce
Men to finde out so many Eccentrique parts,
Such divers downe-right lines, such overthwarts,
As disproportion that pure forme: It teares
The Firmament in eight and forty sheires,
And in these Constellations then arise
New starres, and old doe vanish from our eyes:
As though heav'n suffered earthquakes, peace or war,
When new Towers rise, and old demolish't are.
They have impal'd within a Zodiake
The free-borne Sun, and keepe twelve Signes awake
To watch his steps; the Goat and Crab controule,
And fright him backe, who else to either Pole
(Did not these Tropiques fetter him) might runne:
For his course is not round; nor can the Sunne
Perfit a Circle, or maintaine his way
One inch direct; but where he rose to-day
He comes no more, but with a couzening line,
Steales by that point, and so is Serpentine:
And seeming weary with his reeling thus,
He meanes to sleepe, being now falne nearer us.

[27] *Ibid.,* pp. 274-75, ll. 105-30. Cf. "God hath made all things in a *Roundnesse,* from
the round superfices of this earth, which we tread here, to the round convexity of those
heavens, w^ch (as long as they shal have any being) shall be our footstool, when we
come to heaven, God hath wrapped up all things in Circles, and then a Circle hath no
Angles; there are no *Corners* in a Circle."—*Fifty Sermons,* 27, fol. 230.

So, of the Starres which boast that they doe runne
In Circle still, none ends where he begun.
All their proportion's lame, it sinkes, it swels.
For of Meridians, and Parallels,
Man hath weav'd out a net, and this net throwne
Upon the Heavens, and now they are his owne.
Loth to goe up the hill, or labour thus
To goe to heaven, we make heaven come to us,
We spur, we reine the starres, and in their race
They're diversly content t'obey our pace.[28]

The argument is extended still further to include an account of the disproportion in the earth itself, constituting what is at once one of the most curious and significant utterances that Donne ever made. Here is Donne working toward an appreciation of an idea fundamental in his religious philosophy, to be developed fully in his sermons, that spiritual happiness is independent of the conclusions of science. Earlier, a part of the above passage from *The first Anniversary* was noted to show that the skepticism aroused in Donne by the new philosophy calls in doubt the whole traditional conception of the universe.[29] With the sole exception of the allusions to the "new starres" arising in the constellations (1. 260), derived from the knowledge of the recent discoveries, all the matter referred to is that "observ'd in divers ages" of the past. The admission of traditional astronomy as the cause of skepticism marks the birth of an idea in Donne's mind that a critical study of the new philosophy was bound to produce, that all systems of natural philosophy, traditional and new, are subject to modification and revision, and, therefore, will not suffice as a foundation for a satisfactory religious faith. This idea of the relativity of natural knowledge is essential to an understanding of the poem; but no less fundamental is an appreciation of the rôle of the new philosophy in bringing Donne to this conclusion. Donne is not merely echoing the medieval poet's contempt for the world.

Moreover, Donne here senses the true end to which the accumulating efforts of science throughout the centuries were pointing, namely, to the control and domination of the natural world, an end which Bacon would ennoble by making its results contribute to "the glory of the Creator and the relief of man's estate." [30] In the past the "goal of the sciences" had been obscured by teleological implications; it remained for the Renaissance to awaken man's consciousness of his

[28] *Ibid.*, pp. 239-40, ll. 249-84.
[29] See above, pp. 134-35.
[30] *Of the Advancement of Learning, Works*, VI, 134.

power over matter, and with this awakening came the promise of fulfillment and success.

> Man hath weav'd out a net, and this net throwne
> Upon the Heavens, *and now they are his owne.* [Italics mine.]

Why this, however, should be anything but the cause for exuberant
optimism is not hard to answer. Traditionally, natural philosophy,
or science, and theology were intricately confused; the conclusions of
the one were neatly dovetailed into those of the other; the relation of
the world of matter to that of the spirit was capable of rational demonstration. Thus, salvation itself depended as much upon the construction
of the physical world as upon the pronouncements of Scripture and
the dictates of conscience. To cleave apart these twins of logic, theology
and natural philosophy, and to view their relations in a new light
were among the major achievements of the "great instauration." Inevitably the break-up of tradition is accompanied by uncertainty and
doubt, and, it is equally important to observe, by an inordinate confidence in the new. Thus, Donne, mindful that

> . . . On a huge hill,
> Cragged, and steep, Truth stands, and hee that will
> Reach her, about must, and about must goe,[31]

views with despair verging upon contempt the slackness of those who
are

> Loth to goe up the hill, or labour thus
> To goe to heaven,

thinking that natural knowledge can "make heaven come to us." [32]

The shattering of the old world order would not have proved so
calamitous for Donne had he not been temperamentally constrained
to recognize a subtle convergence of the worlds of spirit and matter
and their inherent interdependence. The old philosophy was a device
whereby this interrelationship could be illustrated; and the new philosophy confirmed what must have been a native intuition, that the
relationship of the two exists rather in the mysterious nature of things
themselves than in the elaborate rationalizations of philosophy and
theology. Donne, however, never reaches the "calm of mind" and
settled conviction of Milton whose simple faith triumphs over the
claims of natural learning:

> To ask or search I blame thee not, for Heav'n
> Is as the Book of God before thee set,

[31] *Satyre III,* Grierson, I, 157, ll. 79-81.
[32] For Donne's growing distrust in "natural knowledge," see below, ch. xv, *passim.*

Wherein to read his wondrous Works, and learne
His Seasons, Hours, or Days, or Months, or Yeares:
This to attain, whether Heav'n move or Earth,
Imports not, if thou reck'n right, the rest
From Man or Angel the great Architect
Did wisely to conceal, and not divulge
His secrets to be scann'd by them who ought
Rather admire; or if they list to try
Conjecture, he his Fabric of the Heav'ns
Hath left to thir disputes, perhaps to move
His laughter at thir quaint Opinions wide
Hereafter, when they come to model Heav'n
And calculate the Starrs, how they will weild
The mightie frame, how build, unbuild, contrive
To save appeerances, how gird the Sphear
With Centric and Eccentric scribl'd o're,
Cycle and Epicycle, Orb in Orb:

    . . .

Sollicit not thy thoughts with matters hid,
Leave them to God above, him serve and feare;

    . . .

. . . Heav'n is for thee too high
To know what passes there; be lowlie wise:
Think onely what concernes thee and thy being;
Dream not of other Worlds, what Creatures there
Live, in what state, condition or degree,
Contented that thus farr hath been reveal'd
Not of Earth onely but of highest Heav'n.[33]

Donne's mature position is suggested by the passage in a sermon of 1622 wherein he welcomes the lesson that natural learning teaches, in St. Paul's words, that "The invisible things of God are seen by things which are made," but does not allow, useful as the helps of learning are, that it is only the mathematician, the mariner, the statesman, and the chemist who see God. That privilege, in the Christian democracy which Donne envisages, is for all, regardless of learning and independent of it, in whom faith works. Indeed, it is one of the inevitabilities of human experience, for all men are "in Abraham's bosom" though they know it not.

To end this, you can place the sphaere in no position, in no station, in which the earth can eclipse the Sun; you can place this clod of earth, *man*, in no *ignorance*, in no *melancholy*, in no *oppression*, in no *sinne*, but that he *may*,

[33] *Paradise Lost*, VIII, ll. 66-84, 167-68, 172-78.

but that he *does* see God. The Marrigold opens to the sunne, though it have no tongue to say so; the Atheist does see God, though he have not grace to confesse it.[34]

The figures of space derived from geometry, upon which the above discussion turns, increasingly enrich the verse and prose of Donne's maturer years. Life is comprehended within the figure of the circle which death draws tangent to the circle "that hath no pieces." [35] All "religious tipes" to "the peeclesse centers flow" of the grand circle of Divinity.[36] A straight line marks the shortest distance between two points; all men have direct and immediate access to God who is perpendicularly above them.[37] There is a "new Mathematiques":

without change of Elevation, or parallax, I that live in this Climate, and stand under this Meridian, looke up and fixe my self upon God, And they that are under my feete, looke up to that place, which is above them, And as divers, as contrary as our places are, we all fixe at once upon one God, and meet in one Center; but we do not so upon one Sunne, nor upon one constellation, or configuration in the Heavens.[38]

Some "weake spirits" "prescribe a Fate" "unto the immaculate,"

> Measuring selfe-lifes infinity to'a span,
> Nay to an inch,[39]

and the approach of death is conceived as

> My spans last inch, my minutes latest point.[40]

Though efforts to visualize concretely the vast physical spaces revealed by the new astronomy are wanting in Donne, he nevertheless responds to the fascination of an ancient conjecture, revived in his own day as the result of the greatly extended universe and the encouragement of Galileo's discovery of the four new planets and the mountains on the moon. It is the old idea of the plurality of worlds like the earth, which recent estimates of the infinity of the universe seem to make credible.

In reckoning the size of the sphere of the fixed stars Copernicus allowed the idea of the infinity of space to pass through his mind, but he concluded, in the words of the translation of Thomas Digges, his enthusiastic English champion, "whether the worlde haue his boundes or bee in deede infinite and without boundes, let vs leaue that to be

---

[34] *Fifty Sermons*, 31, fol. 275.   [35] *LXXX Sermons*, 79, fol. 816.
[36] *To the Countesse of Bedford*, Grierson, I, 220, l. 47.
[37] *LXXX Sermons*, 67, fol. 677.   [38] *Ibid.*, 68, fol. 686.
[39] *Crvcifying*, Grierson, I, 320, ll. 8, 9.
[40] *Holy Sonnets, VI, ibid.*, p. 324, l. 4.

discussed of Philosophers." [41] Digges himself propounded the idea of an infinite universe in England as early as 1576, and Giordano Bruno preached it with heretical zeal in the latter years of his indiscreet and romantic career.[42] Closely connected with the idea of the world's infinity is the question of the inhabitability of planets other than the earth. If the heavens are subject to alterability, why not suppose that space should bring forth worlds like our own; in fact, why not conclude that those already known and those but recently revealed to the eye of man are similar to the earth? Today the whole subject bears the taint of amateurish scientific speculation, better stuff for fiction than for solid consideration. But the idea had appealed seriously to a number of ancient philosophers and poets.[43] Particularly was the moon, the planet nearest the earth and therefore considered to be most like it, thought apt to be inhabitable. Now something like vindication of this chimera had been established. Though Galileo does not touch upon the subject in *Sidereus Nuncius*, he does prove that the moon has certain terrestrial characteristics; furthermore, Kepler made no little capital of the idea in his dissertation on Galileo's book and repeatedly argued its plausibility with seriousness.[44] That Donne took notice of the speculations on the inhabitability of the moon in itself is of less importance than the fact that such notice evidences that he was busy reading the books of the astronomers and philosophers for whom the idea was one of vital importance. How legitimate the idea seemed to the seventeenth-century Englishman may be gained from noting the appear-

[41] *A Perfit Description of the Coelestiall Orbes*, sig. O₁ verso. In Digges's diagram of the universe, he describes the heaven of the fixed stars as the "orbe of starres fixed infinitely vp, etc." Fol. 43, sig. M 1.

[42] On Bruno, see Henry Osborn Taylor, *op. cit.*, II, 352 ff. See above p. 87 for Kepler on Bruno, and n. 67.

[43] See treatment of the history of the idea in John Wilkins, *The Discovery of a New World*, in *The Mathematical and Philosophical Works* (London, 1802), I, Prop. vi, "That there is a world in the Moon hath been the direct opinion of many ancient, with some modern mathematicians; and may probably be deduced from the tenets of others," 43-50.

[44] For example, in *Astronomiae pars optica* he cites the testimony of Plutarch and concludes, "claras in Luna partes materiam esse aqueam, quae vero caligant, continentes et insulas esse: totam vero Lunam, ut infra dicetur, aërea quadam essentia circumiri, quae omnium partium radios transmittat."—Frisch, II, 286-87. In the *Dissertatio cum Nuncio Sidereo*, with the confirmation of the idea of mountains, valleys, and seas on the moon effected by the telescope, Kepler becomes enthusiastic about the subject of other worlds. He refers to his own statement from the *Optics*: "His inquam argumentis plane satisfecisti: do, maculas esse maria, do, lucidas partes esse terram," and then remarks, "si sunt in Luna viventes creaturae [Plutarch is cited on the possibility of the moon's habitation], illas ingenium suae provinciae imitari, quae multo majores habet montes et valles quam nostra Tellus . . ."—*Ibid.*, p. 497.

ance in 1638 of Bishop Wilkins's popular treatise, *The Discovery of a New World,* wherein the Bishop's orthodoxy is hedged in and doubly safeguarded by anonymity and by one of the most beautifully evasive subtitles ever written: *a discourse tending to prove, that it is probable there may be another habitable world in the moon.*[45]

The idea may have been in Donne's mind when in one of his Holy Sonnets he calls upon those,

> . . . which beyond that heaven which was most high
> Have found new sphears, and of new lands can write,
> Powre new seas in mine eyes, that so I might
> Drowne my world with my weeping earnestly,
> Or wash it, if it must be drown'd no more.[46]

From time to time it is alluded to in the *Sermons,*[47] but never does it occupy his attention as a major controversial issue. However, in 1611, largely under the influence of the impetus given the idea of the plurality of worlds by Galileo's observation of the mountains of the moon and the four new planets of Jupiter, Donne enlists its service in the capacity to which it is best suited, as a device for satire. It is in this way that Lucian and one of the authors of the *Menippean Satire* had exploited its resources.[48] Donne's tract, *Ignatius his Conclave,* directed against the Jesuits, does not miss the opportunity of proposing a "Lunatique Hell" to which to consign the subjects of its satire. As this tract is replete with the influence of Galileo's *Sidereus Nuncius,* it calls for the fuller treatment that will be accorded it later.

The habitability of the moon is referred to, incidentally, without denial in *The second Anniversary.* The reference is embedded, however, in matter far more interesting, both for its recapitulation of the universal system and as an illustration of the way in which Donne treats extension, or spatiality. Describing the flight of Elizabeth Drury's soul to heaven, Donne writes:

> But thinke that Death hath now enfranchis'd thee,
> Thou hast thy'expansion now, and libertie;
> Thinke that a rustie Peece, discharg'd, is flowne
> In peeces, anⁿ the bullet is his owne,

---

[45] First published (Bk. I only), London, 1638. The same was reissued anonymously in 1640, "with a discourse concerning the possibility of a passage to the moon." The copy that I examined was marked, "third impression." The second book was first published (also anonymously) in 1640 and bound up with the third impression of the first book under the general title, *A Discourse Concerning a New World, and Another Planet, in Two Bookes.*

[46] *V,* Grierson, I, 324, ll. 5-9.

[47] See particularly, *Fifty Sermons,* 28, fol. 239.

[48] See below, pp. 197 ff.

And freely flies: This to thy Soule allow,
Thinke thy shell broke, thinke thy Soule hatch'd but now.
And think this slow-pac'd soule, which late did cleave
To'a body, and went but by the bodies leave,
Twenty, perchance, or thirty mile a day,
Dispatches in a minute all the way
Twixt heaven, and earth; she stayes not in the ayre,
To looke what Meteors there themselves prepare;
She carries no desire to know, nor sense,
Whether th'ayres middle region be intense;
For th'Element of fire, she doth not know,
Whether she past by such a place or no;
She baits not at the Moone, nor cares to trie
Whether in that new world, men live and die.
Venus retards her not, to'enquire, how shee
Can, (being one starre) *Hesper*, and *Vesper* bee;
Hee that charm'd *Argus* eyes, sweet *Mercury*,
Workes not on her, who now is growne all eye;
Who, if she meet the body of the Sunne,
Goes through, not staying till his course be runne;
Who findes in *Mars* his Campe no corps of Guard;
Nor is by *Iove*, nor by his father barr'd;
But ere she can consider how she went,
At once is at, and through the Firmament.
And as these starres were but so many beads
Strung on one string, speed undistinguish'd leads
Her through those Spheares, as through the beads, a string,
Whose quick succession makes it still one thing:
As doth the pith, which, lest our bodies slacke,
Strings fast the little bones of necke and backe;
So by the Soule doth death string Heaven and Earth;
For when our Soule enjoyes this her third birth,
(Creation gave her one, a second, grace,)
Heaven is as neare, and present to her face,
As colours are, and objects, in a roome
Where darknesse was before, when Tapers come.
This must, my Soule, thy long-short Progresse bee.[49]

In these lines, written after Donne could call the ˈmoon a "new
world," Professor Grierson says, "Donne summarizes . . . the old

[49] Grierson, I, 256-57, ll. 179-219. In line 198 Donne continues a curious error made
in his ninth *Problem*, "Why is Venus-Star Multinominous, Called both Hesperus and
Vesper?" To my knowledge there is no justification for Donne's confusion. Both
Clavius (*op. cit.*, p. 383) and Kepler (*Dissertatio cum Nuncio Sidereo*, Frisch, II,
502), assign the correct names to Venus in distinguishing between her morning and
evening appearances in the heavens.

concentric arrangement of the universe as we find it in Dante." [50]
This statement, apart from the fact that it errs slightly in making
Dante's arrangement precisely identical with Donne's, should not be
allowed to suggest that Donne and Dante use the "concentric arrangement" of the heavens in the same way.[51] To be noted first is the
almost entire insignificance for the meaning of the poem of the route
followed by Elizabeth's soul in its ascent to heaven. For Dante, on the
other hand, the spheres of the Ptolemaic universe, in their symbolic
implications, are the very rungs of the ladder on which the soul's
striving for its consummation is achieved. The route of the progress
of the soul is the concomitant of a system of thought on which Dante
depends, a metaphysic inseparable from the development of his interpretation of the grand question of the relation of the Many and the
One. In short, it is the skeleton which gives rigidity to the body of
disciplinary thought whereby salvation is attained.

In 1612 the Ptolemaic concentric system could not be for Donne,
who had seen it crumble under the influence of the new philosophy,
anything more than a convenient device, well enough understood and

[50] *Ibid.*, II, 198, note "l. 189 to page 257, l. 206."
[51] In placing Venus below Mercury Donne does not follow the order of the planets
given by Dante, who, accepting Ptolemy's arrangement, reverses the positions of the
two. In the ancient order of the planets determined upon by Anaxagoras, the Pythagoreans, Plato, Eudoxus, and Aristotle, Venus is below Mercury, but both are beyond
the Sun. "This arrangement was also first adopted by the Stoics, who afterwards
abandoned it for the following arrangement: Moon, Mercury, Venus, Sun, Mars,
Jupiter, Saturn, which fell in well with their notions about the dominant position of
the sun, as it placed the orbit of this body half-way between the earth and the fixed
stars, with three orbits of planets on either side." As this arrangement agreed with
Ptolemy's calculations, it was universally adopted down to Copernicus, who, beginning
with the sun as center of the universe, distributed the planets as follows: Mercury,
Venus, Earth, Mars, Jupiter, Saturn. See Dreyer, *History of the Planetary Systems*, pp.
168, 169, 339.
   Donne's account of the positions of the planets thus disagrees with the traditional
Ptolemaic scheme (as far as Venus and Mercury are concerned), and with that of
Copernicus. If we assume that Donne accepts the earth as the center of the sphere, it
is not uninteresting to make some conjecture as to the cause of his irregularity. A
glance at the orders given by Ptolemy and Copernicus may suggest at once what Donne
has done. Is it not likely that he has adapted an old device of the progress of the soul
through the heavens to the new order of the planets? In fact, Elizabeth Drury's soul
from the earth through Venus and Mercury follows the Copernican order exactly in
the order of their relation to the earth. As the universe cannot have two centers, however, and as the device demands that the soul begin its flight at the earth, Donne needs
must throw in the sun above Mercury, thus giving the illusion of having regarded the
earth as the center of the universe, though actually it appears that he grudgingly gave
the sun a place in order to complete the framework of his device, else, why the doubt
cast upon its position:

> "Who, *if* [italics mine] she meet the body of the Sunne,
> Goes through, not staying till his course be runne."

appreciated by his readers, whereby a purely spiritual experience might be invested with the semblance of concreteness. The metaphor does not become an intimate part of a metaphysical system into which may be infused the vitality and richness of the energy of his imagination. In short, Donne takes no advantage of the orthodox theology which related logically the old account of the physical world to a Christian ethic and metaphysics. In *The second Anniversary* it is the manner of the journey, not its geography, that receives the poet's first attention, for Donne conceives of a direct communication of the soul with God that renders its ascent by the arduous ladder of systematic discipline unnecessary. The planetary spheres are not ascending levels of spiritual growth on the upward course but a blur of merging mileposts suggesting the swiftness with which the soul cuts through the celestial landscape.[52] The immediacy of communion with and instantaneous approach

[52] In a recent illuminating account of the nature of metaphysical poetry by James Smith ("On Metaphysical Poetry," *Scrutiny*, December, 1933, pp. 222-39), the author, while pointing out the difference between poets who write "metaphysics in poetry rather than metaphysical poetry" (p. 237), draws an interesting contrast between Donne and Dante, which without qualification may seem to contradict what I have said, for the passage in *The second Anniversary* cited in the text above provides the basis for Smith's distinction. Smith writes: "Dante, speaking of his and Beatrice's instantaneous ascent from star to star, says:

> . . . del salire
> non m'accors'io, se non com' uom s'accorge,
> anzi il primo pensier, del suo venire.
> È Beatrice quella che sí scorge
> di bene in meglio, sí subitamente
> che l'atto suo per tempo non si sporge.
> [*Paradiso*, Canto X, ll. 34-39.]

Donne, on the other hand, says of the flight of Elizabeth Drury's soul to heaven:

> 'And as these stars were but so many beads
> Strung on one string, speed undistinguisht leads
> Her through those Spheres, as through the beads, a string,
> Whose quick succession makes it still one thing.'

Dante presents us with a *fait accompli:* he and Beatrice are at the end of their mystic journey, and it does not trouble him how. Donne, on the other hand, tries to follow Elizabeth Drury point by point: the problem of how the journey was possible interests him at least as much as the fact that it was made. In short, there is in Donne, there is not in Dante, the metaphysical conceit."—pp. 237-38.

Sound as I regard Smith's general conclusions concerning metaphysical poetry, I cannot think that his interpretation of the particular passages from Donne and Dante, in fairness to both poets, can be accepted. In the first place, in the tenth canto of the *Paradiso* Dante and Beatrice are not yet "at the end of their mystic journey." They have but reached the circle of the Sun and have still to traverse the spheres of Mars, Jupiter, Saturn, as well as the starry heaven and the Empyrean, before the journey ends. Moreover, the passage cited does not record Dante's impressions of his and his guide's "instantaneous ascent from star to star." The starry sphere is still far above them, and it is important in reading Dante to distinguish between stars and planets; Dante, transported by the wonder of the spirit-heavens revealed to him, simply pays tribute

to God are further emphasized by the sense of impatience and almost reckless speed imparted to the journey of the soul as it takes the most direct and shortest route to heaven. The solid spheres are disregarded entirely; a passing comment on the soul's indifference to the terrain through which it is moving is all the attention given to the elementary and planetary regions. "At once" it is through the firmament, and the *Primum Mobile* does not exist at all. Nevertheless, Donne's figure, though it is independent of association with the traditional metaphysics, does help to mark the poem with a genuinely metaphysical quality. This deeper meaning, implicit in the directness of the soul's flight, resulting in the immediate communication of earth and heaven, is best recorded in Donne's own words:

> And as these starres were but so many beads
> Strung on one string, speed undistinguish'd leads
> Her through those Spheares, as through the beads, a string,
> Whose quick succession makes it still one thing;
> . . .
> So by the Soule doth death string Heaven and Earth.

What exactly has Donne accomplished? With an emphasis on the cosmic value, it is the same thing that he attempted years before in *The Extasie* when he found the union of lovers prefigured in the relations of soul and body. In *The Extasie* his imagination is bent upon the analysis of the "subtile knot, which makes us man"; in *The second Anniversary* he extends his imagination to comprehend the more cosmic aspect of the same situation, the relation of the One and the Many, here assumed in the words "heaven" and "earth." This compelling yet perplexing theme is itself a mystery to be sensed intuitively rather than examined rationally; but, significantly, Donne does not regard it as a theme from which the intellectual faculty should withhold its energies.

---

to the miracle which brought him thither. Again, Smith has chosen a passage describing no more than a step in the long progress of Dante and Beatrice, the exposition of which occupies the space of the entire poem.

In contrast, for Donne, "the problem of how the journey was made" frankly does *not* hold the same interest as the fact that it was made, as I have pointed out above, unless Smith means the manner (as distinct from the geography of the route) in which Elizabeth's soul accomplishes its journey. The spheres are traversed with impetuous speed and with utter disregard for their respective values. There is no time wasted on wonder and admiration, no sense that when the soul has reached the sun it has been led *di bene in meglio*. The "beads" are not interesting except as they permit "stringing" on the thread of the flight. Donne is concerned primarily with the string that holds them together and how it holds them together, namely, by the swiftness with which it passes through them.

Whereas in *The Extasie* it is love, consummated in both flesh and spirit, that knits up the unity of "pure lovers soules," here it is death that releases the soul to achieve its communion with God, and thus to "string" heaven and earth. Donne has moved far away from the Aristotelian metaphysics with its eternal process of the realization of potentiality; nor is he following the Neoplatonic mystic way, whereby the soul, soaring on the wings of contemplation, perfects its union with the One. He has rather the Christian poet's simpler and more direct perception of the disparity between the material and the immaterial as more apparent than real, a shadow blurring the glass of human experience, which death removes. "For now we see through a glass, darkly; but then face to face." This conclusion is one from which Donne never seriously departs; and one to the formation of which the new philosophy made its contribution in so far as it helped to shatter his faith in the religious philosophy of the Middle Ages.

If Donne's survey of the heavens in the above passage is essentially Ptolemaic, and though the new conception of the world's immensity seems to have added little to his inspiration, he is not untouched by the implications of the transformation of the universe worked by the new philosophy. The very disregard that he shows for the old order in dismissing it, stripped of all astrological and philosophical import, almost with contempt, is an attitude hardly to be thought congenial to one afflicted with an undue reverence for tradition. Again, in the immediate and unimpeded access of the soul to God, revealing Donne's sincere religious feeling, one is aware that the poet's thought is reflected against a background of the new philosophy, which, in effecting the ruin of the old system, not only justified a direct personal approach to God, but also made it imperative. Finally, while Donne has followed roughly the description of the heavens given by the old philosophers, he has allowed to pass into his description certain remarks that are explicable only in the light of the scientific revolution. Thus, the soul of Elizabeth Drury in its upward journey finds some of the old signposts changed or illegible:

> She carries no desire to know, nor sense,
> Whether th'ayres middle region be intense;
> For th'Element of fire, she doth not know,
> Whether she past by such a place or no.

But more astounding still is the doubt cast upon the position of the sun:

> Who, if she meet the body of the Sunne,
> Goes through, not staying till his course be runne.

Only Donne's recognition of the Copernican philosophy can account for this disrespect for the major planet. It is almost as if Donne had made a concession to the old order out of a grudging courtesy alone, realizing, too, that the inclusion of the sun in the soul's itinerary is desirable if only to give a sense of completeness to the "long-short Progresse." As the starting point of the flight, the earth must necessarily appear as the center of the universe, but the uncertainty about the sun's position makes the question of whether Donne really regarded the earth as the center all the more pertinent.

The concepts of space and of the world's immensity are always emerging as intimate parts of Donne's imagination. Upon his ear there falls the sound of angels' trumpets blown from the "round earths imagin'd corners" calling the "numberlesse infinities Of soules" to the resurrection; [53] that "endlesse height which is Zenith" upon which he "durst not looke" is a mystery only less bewildering than the face of divinity itself; [54] and again and again he strives with futility to contemplate the greatness of God's benefits and the endlessness of eternity in terms of the vanity of Archimedes' effort to compute the number of grains of sand that would fill the vast concave of the firmament, an exercise which Clavius had revived.[55] How skillfully Donne accommodates the idea of the world's greatness to his religious thought appears in the passage from *The second Anniversary*, cited above, where the directness and immediacy of man's communion with God is emphasized by the great disparity of the human and divine, symbolized by the immensity of the heavens through which the soul must run its course. In like manner, the "long-short Progresse" of an angel's flight from heaven—"Our quick thought cannot keepe him company"—seems swifter still when the poet directs the attention to the vast distance traversed in his instant approach.[56] Thus, not only does the world's immensity of the new philosophy adapt itself to Donne's belief in the

[53] *Holy Sonnets, VII,* Grierson, I, 325, ll. 1, 3-4.
[54] *Good Friday, 1613. Riding Westward, ibid.;* p. 337, ll. 23, 29.
[55] See above, p. 88 n 2. See also *LXXX Sermons,* 26, fol. 266, and 75, fol. 765.
[56] See *Obsequies to the Lord Harrington, brother to the Lady Lucy, Countesse of Bedford,* Grierson, I, 273-74, ll. 79-86. Lord Harrington died on February 27, 1614. This passage should be compared with that above from *The second Anniversary* (ll. 179-219), as it contains a similar treatment of the planetary landscape. Here, even more definitely than in the *Anniversary,* Donne strives to achieve the illusion of the swift compass of great distance. The purpose of the figure, however, is different, being designed to exhibit how

". . . in few yeares [of a virtuous life] as much [is accomplished], As all the long breath'd Chronicles can touch."

Harrington's capacity to do so much in so brief a span is as miraculous as the swiftness of an angel's flight:

direct, personal communion of man and God (earth and heaven), but also it actually encourages this directness by removing the obstruction of the "impervious spheres" whose "intelligences" were wont to waylay the heaven-bent soul with improving discourse. But, above all, the concept of the greatness of the universal frame gifted Donne with a sense of wonder at the "inexplicable mystery" of his own mind. Dwarfed though he may be in the company of the great creatures of the earth, but a point in the vast expanse of created nature, and a "nothing" compared to God, his is the mind to comprehend this fact and to extend itself to the bounds of the universe in contemplation, even to transcend these contemplations:

It is too little to call Man a little World; Except God, Man is a diminutiue to nothing. Man consistes of more pieces, more parts, then the world; then the world doeth, nay then the world is. And if those pieces were extended, and stretched out in Man, as they are in the world, Man would bee the Gyant, and the world the Dwarfe, the world but the Map, and the Man the World. If all the Veines in our bodies, were extented to Riuers, and all the Sinewes, to vaines of Mines, and all the Muscles, that lye vpon one another, to Hilles, and all the Bones to Quarries of stones, and all the other pieces, to the proportion of those which correspond to them in the world, the aire would be too little for this Orbe of Man to moue in, the firmament would bee but enough for this star; for, as the whole world hath nothing, to which something in man doth not answere, so hath man many pieces, of which the whol world ha[t]h no representation. Inlarge this Meditation vpon this great world, Man, so farr, as to consider the immensitie of the creatures this world produces; our creatures are our thoughts, creatures that are borne Gyants: that reach from East to West, from earth to Heauen, that doe not onely bestride all the Sea, and Land, but span the Sunn and Firmament at once; My thoughts reach all, comprehend all. Inexplicable mistery; I their Creator am in a close prison, in a sicke bed, any where, and any one of my Creatures, my thoughts, is with the Sunne, and beyond the Sunne, ouertakes the Sunne, and ouergoes the Sunne in one pace, one steppe, euery where.[57]

A treatment of Donne's use of the concept of space should not overlook his significant statement that "our mortal eyes do not see bodies here; they see no substance, they see onely quantities, and dimen-

---

". . . when an Angell down from heav'n doth flye,
Our quick thought cannot keepe him company,
Wee cannot thinke, now hee is at the Sunne,
Now through the Moon, now he through th'aire doth run,
Yet when he's come, we know he did repaire
To all twixt Heav'n and Earth, Sunne, Moon, and Aire."

Note how Donne gives emphasis to the fact of distance and swiftness of flight by a reduction of the number of the planetary mileposts.

[57] Devotions, pp. 64-69.

sions." [58] Not only does this testify, as the foregoing illustrations make clear, to his intimate regard for the mathematics and those sciences dependent upon it, but it also serves to suggest the nature of the controlling principle of his art. Things seen by Donne, like Venus-star, have a double aspect: there is the shape of things as viewed by the physical eye, to which the "vision" of intellect imparts another quality. Experience, passing through a mind so richly stored with various learnings, emerges like rays of light passing from one medium into another, broken, to reveal alike, "the truth to flesh, and sense unknown." Whatever be its faults in the way of distortion or perversion of reality, it must be recognized that this mode of "vision" is in the main responsible for any quality in Donne's art that may be termed metaphysical. To make this vision acute Donne has drawn into use the science which devises "quantities and dimensions" to symbolize reality.

[58] *Fifty Sermons*, 31, fol. 274.

X

IGNATIUS HIS CONCLAVE

IN 1611 Donne went abroad with Sir Robert Drury. The visit to Paris, Amiens, Spa, and Brussels was not, however, the inspiration of any journal of continental travels. There are letters to friends at home, both in verse and prose, and, it would seem, *The second Anniversary* to the memory of Elizabeth Drury. Perhaps the most interesting personal experience of the nine-month sojourn [1] is that related by Walton—told him "by a Person of Honour"—of Donne's harrowing vision of his wife's painful labor and the birth of her dead child. Gosse laments that Donne leaves no report of having heard of the work of St. Francis de Sales, while in Paris, of having listened to the eloquence of Coëffeteau, or in any way of having fallen under the influence of the great evangelical movement within the Roman Church. "Donne has an exasperating way of being silent exactly when we wish him to speak. We are almost indignant that a great English theologian should be in Paris in 1612, and have nothing to tell us of the evolution of French theology." [2] Such a question must have been raised in retrospect of Donne's own career as an ecclesiastic and might well be answered by asking why he leaves no account of famous English preachers in these years before he took holy orders. In truth, by 1612 Donne could hardly have considered himself "a great English theologian." If anything, Donne is a sensitive observer of affairs of state while abroad, a fact betraying that his aspirations for diplomatic or court preferment are not yet dead. But a more intelligent reply to Gosse is to be found in the fact that while Donne was well enough acquainted with the Catholic reconstruction, his sympathies with this movement were anything but warm. Thus, though he is silent on the romantic side of early seventeenth-century French Catholicism and says nothing of "the picturesqueness and humour of St. François de Sales," [3] he does write of "our adversaries the Sorbonists," "the usurpations of the Roman Church," [4] and complains in *A Letter to the Lady Carey*,

[1] Donne was abroad from November, 1611 till August, 1612.
[2] *Op. cit.*, I, 299.
[3] *Ibid.*, p. 299.
[4] "To the Honourable Knight Sir H. Goodyer," April 9, 1612, *ibid.*, p. 298.

and Mrs. Essex Riche, From Amyens, of the low ebb of religion:

> Here where by All All Saints invoked are,
>   • • •
> Where, because Faith is in too low degree,
> I thought it some Apostleship in mee
> To speake things which by faith alone I see.[5]

This expresses but confirmation of an attitude that Donne had taken before he went abroad, an attitude that is clearly analyzed in *Pseudo-Martyr,* and sharpened by the wit of *Ignatius his Conclave* published early in the same year that Donne set out for the continent.[6] Again, if we assume that *The second Anniversary* was written in France,[7] we see that he was struggling to reach a spiritual point of view at variance with one of faith in "too low degree," one that more fully expressed the soul speaking of "things which by faith alone I see." As Donne's "Protestantism" had advanced pretty far by 1611, and as at this time he could have had little more than a vague thought of becoming a clergyman in the Church of England—hardly an ambition—there is no good reason why Gosse should be concerned that Donne did not take advantage of his visit to France to put himself under the tutelage of the homilists of the Congregatio Oratorii, whose founder he had but shortly before described as "stupid," and whose members he had reproached for "their incessant Sermons to the people, of the lives of *Saints* and other *Ecclesiastique Antiquities.*" [8]

[5] Grierson, I, 221, ll. 1, 10-12.

[6] There are three 1611 editions of *Ignatius his Conclave,* two Latin and one English. Which of the two Latin editions appeared first has not been determined. The Latin edition in duodecimo, without imprint, was entered in the Stationers' Register, January 24, 1610/11; the other, a quarto volume, Keynes conjectures (and I think rightly), was printed abroad at Hanau, because, as he remarks, "each of the only two copies known to me [both are at Cambridge in the University Library, Acton Collection] is bound up with other tracts which were printed at Hanau, *apud Thomam Villerianum* (possibly a fictitious imprint), and it is probable for typographical reasons that this edition of the *Conclaue Ignati* was issued from the same press."—*Op. cit.,* p. 12, n. My comparison of the typography of the quarto *Conclaue Ignati* bound up with the specified imprints of "Villerianus" thoroughly confirms Keynes's conjecture that the book was printed abroad. Moreover, there is reason to believe that Donne meant his tract to appear abroad as well as at home, for in "*The Printer* to the Reader" (Donne's own fiction) appears the statement, "At last he yeelded, and made mee owner of his booke, which I send to you to be delivered over to forraine nations, (a) farre from the father: and (as his desire is) (b) his last in this kinde."—p. 358. The nature of the subject matter would have made a foreign edition especially pertinent. The English edition was entered in the Stationers' Register to the publisher Richard Moore [More], May 18, 1611. See Simpson, *op. cit.,* pp. 180-83.

[7] So assumed by Grierson, II, 202, note on "ll. 511-18."

[8] "But *Nerius* [Philip Nerius, founder of the Oratory] was too stupid, to interprete them aright."—*Ignatius his Conclave,* p. 395. See also p. 394.

But our present concern is with *Ignatius his Conclave* and the new philosophy, not with the religious conditions in France at the beginning of the seventeenth century. However, in so far as Donne's satire seems to have derived its form and method in part from the *Satyre Ménippée* which came at the climax of the struggle between the League and the forces of Henry of Navarre,[9] and as it appears that Donne may have found in an early supplement to this famous piece the suggestion for using the new science to abet his attack on the Jesuits,[10] it is necessary to be alert to the historical conditions out of which the attack developed. Mrs. Simpson rightly says that "it is not, however, for these [the bitter attacks on the Jesuits which form so large a part of *Conclaue Ignati*] that the book now interests readers, but for its references to the 'new astronomy' and the discoveries of Galileo and Kepler." [11] Nevertheless, the purpose of the tract was to ventilate Donne's grievances against the Society of Jesus, and even if we are to derive interest or pleasure from a by-product of this purpose, a just consideration of the satire dare not disregard the claims of its principal motive.

The opposition of the Catholic party in England to the Oath of Allegiance, nourished mainly by Jesuit propaganda,[12] had led Donne

[9] *Satyre Ménippée de la vertu du Catholicon d'Espagne. Et de la tenue des estats de Paris. A laquelle es adiousté un discours sur l'interpretation du mot de Higviero d'inferno, & qui en est l'autheur. Plus le regret sur la mort de l'asne Ligueur d'une damoyselle, qui mourut durant le siège de Paris* (1593 [94]). This famous satire, "s'il faut en croire les contemporains . . . porta le coup fatal à la Ligue qu'elle tua sous le ridicule." *La Satire Ménippée,* ed. Paul Deny (London, 1911), p. 32. First published in Paris, 1594, it was frequently reprinted for a score of years, with variations and additions. An English translation appeared in 1595 under the title, *A Pleasant Satyre or Poesie: Wherein is discovered the Catholicon of Spayne, and the chiefe leaders of the League . . .* This same was reissued in 1602 with a new title, *Englandes bright Honour: Shining through the darke disgrace of Spaines Catholicon Serving as a cleare Lantherne, to give light to the whole world, to guide them by; and let them see, the darke and crooked packing, of Spaine, and Spanish practises . . .* For a treatment of the historical conditions giving rise to and surrounding the composition of the *Satyre Ménippée,* see Paul Deny, *op. cit.,* pp. 7-63.

[10] See below, pp. 201-2 and n. 22.

[11] Simpson, *op. cit.,* p. 180.

[12] See *ibid.,* pp. 165 ff. Cf. "When the Oath of Allegiance Anno. 3 Regis Iacobi was made and confirmed by Act of Parliament, it is probably supposed, that all the Recusants in England would willingly have taken it, as sundry of them began, had not the Iesuits opposed themselves, and procured the Pope to command the contrary."— J. B., *The Copie of a Late Decree of the Sorbone at Paris, for the condemning of that impious and haeretical opinion, touching the murthering of princes; generally maintained by the Iesuites, And amongst the rest, of late by Ioannis Mariana, a Spaniard: together with the Arrest of the Parliament for confirmation of that decree, and the condemning of the said Marianas booke, to be publiquely burnt by the executioner ¶ taken out of the register of the Parliament, and translated into English* (London, 1610), "The Preamble," sig. B,

to undertake the composition of *Pseudo-Martyr* for Thomas Morton, later Bishop of Durham. In this pamphlet, which appeared in 1610, Donne readily reduces the difference of opinion to its first principle, that of a conflict between the temporal power of pope and king. His argument against the recusants runs in this fashion: the power of the prince rests on divinely given authority; an affront to this power, such as the refusal to subscribe to the Oath, amounts to sedition, punishable by death—and death for sedition is not death for the glory of God but false martyrdom. The case is argued temperately and sympathetically, but with forceful logic.[13] He appeals directly to the patriotism and good sense of the English Catholics and attempts to set forth a right understanding of true religious faith on grounds respecting the claims of allegiance to both State and Church. As in *Ignatius his Conclave*, "*The Printer* to the Reader" remarks, Donne "chooses and desires that his other book [*Pseudo-Martyr*] should testifie his ingenuity, and candor, and his disposition to labour for the reconciling of all parts." [14]

In resolving the controversy into a question of the respective claims of the authority of prince and pope upon the loyalty of English Catholics, Donne suggests his awareness of the implications of an insidious phase of the Jesuit propaganda instigated against the Oath. Of late, particularly in France, the Jesuits, acting under the primary influence of one of the members of their Society, Juan de Mariana, a Spaniard, had sanctioned the use of force and violence to dispose of princes who were tyrants, namely, princes who resisted the temporal sovereignty of the papacy. The right to make use of this method of dealing with heretical kings Mariana had affirmed in the sixth chapter of his treatise, *De rege et regis institutione*, first published in Toledo in 1598.[15] As already France had suffered the loss of two kings by

[13] See W. H. Frere, *The English Church in the Reigns of Elizabeth and James I* (1558-1625) (London, 1911), p. 349.
[14] Page 358.
[15] Mariana's book also was issued at Mainz, 1605. Of this imprint, see I, v, "Discrimen regis & tyranni," 43-51, and I, vi, "An tyrannum opprimere fas sit," 51-63. Mariana's position, that the sovereignty of the monarch is not of divine origin but is derived from "a grant made by the community," and is therefore to be shared with the Estates of the realm, whose will must ultimately prevail, drew him to the conclusion that "if the Prince overstep the limits of his authority, he may rightfully be restrained by force, warred upon and deposed and killed." Though initiative lies with the Estates to establish the tyranny of the prince, once it is ascertained, "tyrannicide is justified in anyone by any means, except poison: and even poison may be used so long as the tyrant is not made to kill himself with it." It was this sanction of a common right to kill tyrants, really a detail of Mariana's political theory, that was seized upon and exploited by his disciples, and, at the same time, taken up by the enemies of the Jesuits to discredit his work generally. See J. W. Allen, *A History of Political Thought*

assassination and England had been frightened by the Gunpowder Plot, concern with the menacing proportions reached by the old quarrel between temporal and spiritual authorities can hardly be said to have been chimerical.[16]

On May 27, 1610, within a fortnight after the murder of Henry IV, the famous "Arrest" of the Parliament of Paris went forth, ordering the Dean of the Faculty of Divines of the University of Paris to convene the Faculty for the purpose of confirming an ancient decree of the Council of Constance, making it an offense to injure the person of the prince or to interfere against him with arms. The Faculty assembled on the fourth of June (1610), confirmed the decree, and proscribed Mariana's book, De Rege, which was generally agreed to have caused much of the seditious activity. Four days later the Parliament recognized the action of the Faculty, and passed a further censure

---

in the Sixteenth Century (London, 1928), pp. 360-63. How thoroughly the motives of the Jesuits in respect to tyrannicide were ascribed to the inspiration of Mariana may be appreciated upon noting the following from The Copie of a Late Decree, wherein the author writes of the disaffection caused by Jesuit books: "This second booke [he has just mentioned De iusta abdicatione Hen. 3.] is thus intituled, Ioannis Marianae Hispani e societate Iesu, De Rege . . . In this booke the murthering of Princes by private persons is in direct terms fully approved, and particularly the butcherous and traiterous slaughter of the French King, Henry the 3. by Iames Clement a Dominicane." The doctrine of "king killing" has been revived "by the Iesuites (the most industrious Purveyours for the Popes Court) and by their Lectures and bookes nourished and brought to those flames that now wee see: as it hath beene not seldome obiected unto them, but never yet by them wel denied; I am sure the doctrine never publikely condemned by any resolution of their schooles, as heretofore, and of late by the Colledge of Sorbone. So as whosoever put the knife into the villaines hand [Ravillac, the assassin of Henry I,V, and Jean Châtel, who attempted Henry's assassination], it is evident that the metall whereof it was made, (I meane the aforesaid doctrine) was tempered in their forge, and their bookes (as it is confessed) gave edge unto it."—Sig. B₂-B₃, and sig. E₃.

[16] That Donne was sensitive to the situation is clearly testified to in the following words from Ignatius his Conclave, spoken to Machiavelli and Lucifer by Ignatius: "For it is not our purpose, that the writings of our men should be so ratified, that they may not be changed, so that they bee of our Order which change them: so by the same liberty, which Daemon-Joannes hath taken in delivering the King of Britaine from the danger of Deposition; (because as yet no sentence is given against him) and also from many other Canons, which others thinke may justly bee discharged against him, it will be as lawfull for us, when that kingdome shall be inough stupified with this our Opium, to restore those Canons to their former vigor, and to awake that state out of her Lethargy, either with her owne heat, intestine warre, or by some Medicine drawne from other places: for Princes have all their securities from our indulgence, and from the slacke and gentle interpretation of the Canons: etc."—p. 383. Note also the very interesting report of Donne's personal experience while in Paris in a letter to Goodyer wherein is told how an "assignation" to meet Richer, "a doctor and syndic of the Sorbonists" who had written "against the Pope's jurisdiction," was frustrated when Richer heard "that the Jesuits had offered to corrupt men with rewards to kill him."—Gosse, op. cit., I, 296-97.

upon *De Rege* to the effect that it "shall be burnt by the Common Executioner before our Ladies Church in Paris." Provision was made for giving publicity to the confirmation of the decree and to the proscription and burning of Mariana's book.[17]

These legal activities were preceded, accompanied, and followed by a flurry of pamphlets both in France and in England,[18] most of which were aimed directly at the Jesuits, because from them emanated the pernicious doctrine that threatened the "peace of states" and the "Safetie of Kings and Princes." Among these, appearing early in 1611, was Donne's *Ignatius his Conclave*. To suggest that it was the direct result of what had happened in France would be to miss the significance of the local situation that had concerned Donne in *Pseudo-Martyr*. The assassination of the French king and the subsequent action of the Parliament and the university brought the case against the Jesuits to a climax, and while bringing further support to the Englishman's opposition to the Society of Jesus, exposed a weakness in the entire Catholic party which to the pamphleteering strategist invited attack. The confirmation of the decree of the Council of Constance by the Faculty of Divines definitely placed the "Colledge of Sorbon" in opposition to the Jesuits, and thus, for the time being, Catholicism was divided against itself, so that Donne might well take advantage of the situation to ridicule "The Two Tutelar Angels, Protectors of The Popes Consistory, and of the Colledge of Sorbon" to whom he dedi-

---

[17] *The Copie of a Late Decree*, Sig. D, D₂, D₃, E, E₂.

[18] The bibliography of this controversial literature is too extensive to be included here. However, attention may well be directed to one French tract and its English translation, because the sequel to the matter it undertakes to refute is alluded to by Donne in a letter from Amiens [February, 1612] to Sir Henry Wotton. The tract is the *Anticoton, ou réfutation de la lettre déclaratoire du Père Cotton . . .* (no place, 1610). The translation, with a supplement printed at London the following year, is from the hand of G[eorge] H[akewell] and carries the title, *Anti-Coton, or a Refutation of Cottons Letter Declaratorie: lately directed to the Queen Regent, for the Apologizing of the Jesuites Doctrine, touching the killing of Kings. A Booke, in which it is proved that the Jesuites are guiltie, and were the authors of the late execrable Parricide, committed upon the Person of the French King, Henry the fourth, of happie memorie. To which is added, A Supplication of the Universitie of Paris, for the preventing of the Jesuites opening their Schooles among them: in which their King-killing Doctrine is also notably discovered, and confuted.* Donne writes to his friend Wotton that, "Cotton, the great Court Jesuit, hath so importuned the Queen to give some modifications to the late interlocutory arrest against the Jesuits, that in his presence, the Count Soissons, who had been present in the court at the time of the arrest, and Servin, the King's Advocate, who urged it, and the Premier president, were sent for. They came so well provided with their books, out of which they assigned to the Queen so many, so evident places of seditious doctrine, that the Queen was well satisfied that it was fit by all means to provide against the teaching of the like doctrine in France."— Gosse, *op. cit.*, I, 292.

cates his satire.[19] If in *Pseudo-Martyr* he had labored "for the reconciling of all parts," recent events had made so sanguine a prospect as their reconciliation appear ironically remote. The inevitable response to his first "failure" was to write a book that "must teach what humane infirmity is," and, as Donne adds, fully aware that he is particularly equipped to pursue his satirical course, he must teach "how hard a matter it is for a man much conversant in the bookes and Acts of Jesuites, so throughly to cast off the *Jesuits,* as that he contract nothing of their naturall drosses, which are *Petulancy* and *Lightnesse.*"[20] Donne's assumption of the nature of a Jesuit marks a complete abandonment of the tolerant and benevolent tactics of *Pseudo-Martyr.* It is open warfare now, and the above quotation is a sample of the proper weapons of attack: scorn, ridicule, and innuendo mocking with an agile humor while it thrusts deep into the flesh of "humane infirmity." As first-hand knowledge of English landlords and Irish tenants prepared Swift to make his "Modest Proposal," early subjection to Jesuit instruction and steady attention to their activities and books gave Donne easy access to the vulnerable spots in his enemy's defense.

That he may more faithfully emulate the "petulancy" and "lightnesse" of Jesuit controversial acrobatics, he feels obliged to equip himself further with a certain amount of paraphernalia upon which his ready wit can exercise itself. Thus, two pieces of apparatus are called into use: the one is the method of the *Satyre Ménippée,* a piece to which had accrued, in its good service in behalf of kings and true religion, a bulk of Jesuit wrath;[21] the other, the new science which Galileo's recently published *Sidereus Nuncius* had brought to a dramatic climax. How Donne came to make use of the scientific learning in a satirical way may be appreciated by relating *Ignatius his Conclave* to an ingenious device used by the author of a supplement to the *Satyre Ménippée,* published in 1595. The supplement bears the following title: *Le Supplement du catholicon, ou nouvelles des regions*

---

[19] *Ignatius his Conclave,* p. 359. Cf. "two adversary angels, which are protectors of the Papall Consistory, and of the Colledge of Sorbon," in subtitle, p. 357. Cf. letter to Goodyer, "on the appearance of schism amongst our adversaries the Sorbonists."— Gosse, *op. cit.,* I, 298.

[20] *Ibid.,* pp. 358-59.

[21] Both *Ignatius his Conclave* and the *Satyre Ménippée* are anonymous; both have the letter of the "printer" to the reader (see *A Pleasant Satyre or Poesie,* the 1595 English translation of the *Satyre,* sig. A₂); both have bits of verse interspersed throughout; but most striking is the use of the "harangue" by the representatives of the Estates in the *Satyre Ménippée,* of which the "orations" in *Ignatius his Conclave* are the counterpart. The subject calls for careful investigation.

de la lune, ou se voyent depeints les beaux & genereux faicts d'armes de feu Iean de Lagny frère du Charlatan, sur aucunes bourgades de la France durant les Estats de Ligue.[22] The probability of Donne's acquaintance with this work is a subject for special inquiry; that it was the very sort of thing to make him aware of the possibilities of Galileo's discoveries, in fact, the doctrines of the new philosophy, for satire, cannot easily be discredited. Moreover, it is not likely that Donne without the stimulus of a fertile suggestion could have brought himself to treat the new philosophy with such levity at the same time that he was admitting his deepest concern for its disillusioning influence.

In detail *Le Supplement du Catholicon* has far greater affinity with Rabelais (whom the author recognizes as his inspiration) than with Donne. But it is like *Ignatius his Conclave* in enough ways to warrant the hypothesis that it provided the hint for Donne's ingenious and original attack upon the Jesuits. In the first place, the *Supplement,* like the *Satyre Ménippée* itself, and presumably Donne's pamphlet, comes from an anonymous hand. It is made public by a person into whose hand the manuscript has fallen by happy accident. This person, masking as a Jesuit or assuming the manner of a Jesuit, like Donne's "printer to the reader," explains the matter of the satire in a gracefully mocking letter. The dedicatory letter of the *Supplement* is addressed to the "Majesté Espagnole," *en memoire de tant de bienfaits que tout nostre Ordre en general a receu de vous,* of whom Donne's "adversary angels," regarded as patrons of the Society of Jesus, are the counterpart. This, however, is the only part of the *Supplement* devoted entirely to an attack upon Loyola's order. Again, in both there is an account of a visit to hell, hell being for the author of the *Supplement,* France itself, a veritable anarchy, wherein the devils, representing the various factions of the League, are in a continual uproar of contention for supremacy. In Donne's satire Lucifer is the monarch of hell, but there is a "secret place" "beside Lucifer himselfe," "to which, onely they had title, which had so attempted any innovation in this life, that they gave an affront to all antiquitie, and induced doubts, and anxieties, and scruples, and after, a libertie of beleeving what they would; at length established opinions, directly contrary to all established before." For the privilege of occupying this place, "heretics" not only such as "have innovated in matters, directly concerning the

---

[22] Bound up with the above-cited French edition of the *Satyre.* See n. 9. *Le Supplement* was reissued in 1612. The text of *Le Supplement* on which my comparison, following, is based is that included in the edition of the *Satyre Ménippée* printed at Ratisbon in 1709: *De la vertu du Catholicon . . . dernière édition divisée en trois tomes. . . .* See especially, I, 239-319.

soule, but they also which have done so, either in the Arts, or in conversation, or in any thing that exerciseth the faculties of the soule, and may so provoke to quarrelsome and brawling controversies," constantly besiege Lucifer.[23] So far, Boniface III has held this place as principal innovator, but he is always being pressed, until at last Ignatius Loyola, rushing up to the former Pope, succeeds in hurling him from the coveted seat. Lastly, in both there is an account of an empire in the moon. For the earlier satirist the moon is inhabited by the shadows of earthly men and events, an epitome of human frailties, revealed to the travelers by means of an altered perspective with which they are temporarily endowed. Donne, too, is provided with a set of marvelous spectacles, "the same, by which *Gregory* the great, and *Beda* did discerne so distinctly the soules of their friends, when they were discharged from their bodies, and sometimes the soules of such men as they knew not by sight and of some that were never in the world." For Donne, however, this device only enables him to see "all the channels in the bowels of the Earth; and all the inhabitants of all nations, and of all ages . . . made familiar." [24] It is Galileo's telescope that is to draw the moon near to the earth so that the Jesuits may thither be translated to their *Lunatique Church.* Thus, the parallels pointed out between the two satires help to strengthen the notion that it was *Le Supplement du Catholicon* that suggested the device which Donne could revise in terms of the new philosophy. It is this revision that Donne undertakes, though actually he does not go so far as to effect the transfer of the followers of Loyola to the moon. However, as it is by way of satire that he makes use of the doctrines and discoveries of the new science, it may be assumed that any judgment passed on its merits will represent pretty certainly his unprejudiced opinion at the time the pamphlet was written.

At this time the treatment of excursions to the moon and of the nature of its possible inhabitants is of no particular concern. It is worth noting only that Galileo's work strengthened the plausibility of old opinions and enriched its effectiveness as a conceit of the satirist, whereby, for example, the author of the *Supplement* might have hoped to give a greater degree of authenticity to the cosmic vantage point from which he surveyed the infirmities of a nation of people drawn and quartered by intrigue and faction, or, whereby Donne could anticipate a more eager welcome of the means he proposed to effect the banishment from society of an obnoxious party. Galileo put into the satirist's hands a new machine for making these celestial excursions. Hitherto

---

[23] *Ignatius his Conclave,* pp. 361, 362.   [24] *Ibid.,* p. 360.

he must needs call to his aid miraculous wings, mysterious winds to sweep the voyager up to heaven, or magical engines by which to traverse the interplanetary spaces. Now, it became much simpler and more convenient to call the moon hither with the telescope and thus with greater dispatch accomplish his journey or deport the victims of his ridicule.[25]

That Donne has in mind from the beginning to make use of the conceit of another habitable world to which to transfer the Jesuits is certain. Although most of the action of the piece takes place in hell, the author takes advantage of the "extasie" into which his

> . . . *little wandring sportful Soule,*
> *Ghest, and Companion of my body*

has fallen, before descending to the lower regions, first, to prospect among "the volumes of the heavens, and to comprehend the situation, the dimensions, the nature, the people, and the policy, both of the swimming Ilands, the *Planets,* and of all those which are fixed in the firmament." [26] In this preliminary survey, he "spies out the land" to which in anticipation of the urgent necessity of disposing of his enemies we may expect them to be dispatched. Even at the outset he is mindful of the fact that Galileo has explored these parts before him with the aid of some new machine. Having made this observation out of modesty and deference to a fellow pioneer, he refrains from saying more. His business demands that he get on quickly to hell where he will find the Jesuits, and, in a verse surpassing the powers of realistic observation of the past and subsequent skylark poets in English literature, he accomplishes his translation to the lower regions.[27]

If we accept the fact that Donne so carefully calculated the use of a trip-to-the-moon device, we must be prepared, too, to account for his neglect to make use of it in the end. Though raising the question at this time may be somewhat irrelevant to the progress of the treatment of the new philosophy in *Ignatius his Conclave,* the fact that we have been dealing with the device as a by-product of Donne's scientific as well as his literary learning makes a consideration of this failure not untimely. It is characteristic of Donne to provide the unexpected. His imagination works this way from the youthful *Song,* "Goe, and catche a falling starre," to his own funeral sermon. Thus in *Ignatius his Conclave* the stage is set for disposing of Loyola by transferring him to the moon where he is to become the head of a *Lunatique Church.* Lucifer has argued the case well with Ignatius, and the latter is virtu-

[25] *Ibid.,* p. 399.   [26] *Ibid.,* p. 359.   [27] See *ibid.,* p. 360.

ally persuaded to be "transferred from an Earthly *Hell,* to a *Lunatique Hell*." [28] But to have discharged his wrath upon Loyola in this fashion, despite the indignity implied in giving him power over an inferior planet with a reputation for vacillation and inconstancy, would have meant for Donne to reveal more faith than he really had in a device, which, after all, had done its turn in the promise of so ridiculous an end for Loyola. Moreover, it would have meant stopping just short of the "knock-out" blow. Donne thinks of a more diabolic fate. To make Ignatius supreme in an "Earthly *Hell,*" a place of far greater and more vivid reality in his mind than all the "swimming Ilands" lately discovered, or an empire in the moon, would give the *coup de grâce* to his antagonist. This, too, is certainly the proper end of his lesson on "humane infirmity," and the most impious confession of the perverse influence of the "bookes and Acts of Jesuites" upon his imagination. A savagely ingenious way opens for Donne's purpose. A hubbub in hell, noisily interrupting Ignatius's long speech of acceptance of his appointment to the lunatic dignity, ushers in a "certaine idle Gazettier" bringing news from Rome of Loyola's recent canonization.[29] The situation is dramatically intense. Sainthood is the hall-mark of heresy and at once legitimizes Loyola's claim to a seat on the right hand of Satan:

These things, as soone as *Lucifer* apprehended them, gave an end to the contention; for now hee thought he might no longer doubt nor dispute of *Ignatius* his admission, who, besides his former pretences, had now gotten a new right and title to the place, by his *Canonization;* and he feared that the *Pope* would take all delay ill at his handes, because *Canonization* is now growne a kinde of *Declaration,* by which all men may take knowledge, that such a one, to whom the Church of *Rome* is much beholden, is now made partaker of the principall dignities, and places in *Hell.*[30]

Lucifer graciously takes Loyola by the hand and leads him to the gate. Only Boniface III remains in the way of the consummation, with his centuries-old reputation as "principall Innovator." However, the one who "first chalenged the name of *Universall Bishop,*" is not long an obstacle, for Ignatius rudely thrusts him down from his seat. Just before Donne's soul takes its way back to his body, it catches sight of Lucifer going to Ignatius's help, "lest, if hee should forsake him, his owne seate might bee endangered." [31]

Apart from the idea of establishing a church in the moon, the suggestion made by the *Supplement* to the *Satyre Ménippée* gives

[28] *Ibid.,* p. 404.
[30] *Ibid.,* p. 405.
[29] See *ibid.,* pp. 407, 404.
[31] *Ibid.,* p. 407.

Donne further opportunity of exploiting his knowledge of the new philosophy. In the greater demands made by the framework adopted, of a cosmic journey ranging from earth to heaven, from heaven to hell, and back again to earth, Donne finds occasion to call attention to every one of the new discoveries announced by the *Siderial Messenger.* There are the moon, of whose "hills, woods, and Cities" *"Galilaeo* the *Florentine"* "hath thoroughly instructed himselfe," the planets, and "the other *starrs,* which are also thought to be worlds." [32] Furthermore, he takes advantage of the opportunity placed at his disposal by the cosmic wanderings to intrude his judgment upon the new philosophy in a way that may be thought to represent, at the time, his mature appraisal of its merits. The immediate condition making such a judgment possible derives from the very means he has chosen to motivate his contempt for the Jesuits. Heresy, conceived as innovation, a deliberate and malicious affront to antiquity, is made the prime qualification of anyone wishing to establish his right to sit at the right hand of Lucifer. Consequently, as all the principal innovators from Christopher Columbus to Copernicus participate in the "conclave," only to be foiled in their aspirations by the prior claims of Loyola himself, the chief innovator since Boniface III, it may be concluded that the ill success suffered by these at the expense of Loyola's diabolical supplications for favor implies an honest notion of Donne's attitude toward the Renaissance revolt against authority; and since Copernicus is one of the chief rebels, it implies Donne's particular opinion of the new astronomy. The matter, then, resolves itself into just this: when set alongside the "heresy" of the Jesuits, how will the innovations of Copernicus, of Machiavelli, of Paracelsus come off, or even of those "which had but invented new attire for woemen," or of those "whom *Pancirollo* hath recorded in his *Commentaries* for invention of *Porcellan dishes,* of *Spectacles,* of *Quintans,* of *stirrups,* and of *Caviari"?* [33]

The approach to an answer to the question must be made with Donne's definition of "innovation" in mind and continued through the application of this definition to his treatment of each of the innovators who sues for admission to the "sacred" precincts. Thus, to repeat the words quoted above with one addition:

Now to this place, not onely such endeavour to come, as have innovated in matters, directly concerning the soule, but they also which have done so,

---

[32] *Ibid.,* pp. 359, 399. Donne does not speak here of the Milky Way as made up of innumerable stars, but it is certainly included in "the other starrs."
[33] *Ibid.,* p. 391.

either in the Arts, or in conversation, or in any thing that exerciseth the faculties of the soule, and may so provoke to quarrelsome and brawling controversies: *For so the truth be lost, it is no matter how.* [Italics mine.] [34]

The last sentence is the important one and carries the full significance
of the definition. Innovation is a denial of truth, not simply established
and accepted opinion, but truth, and the methods of innovation are
congenial with its essentially undignified and disrespectful ends. This
is the test imposed upon all the participants in the *Conclave,* and according to their approximation to its standards are the "pretenders" to
be considered worthy successors to the seat of Boniface. Although here
we intend to deal only with the judgment passed upon the champions
of the new science who have challenged the world scheme of antiquity,
it is pertinent to note briefly how Donne handles the others. To each
Donne metes out his deserts as he has honored or dishonored the
truth. Thus, for every one of the innovators except Ignatius, Donne
has some degree of sympathy; Ignatius alone is subject to unremitting
abuse as a person who has utter disregard for truth and is possessed
of no quality on which even the frailest case for redemption might
be established. Even the giant sins of Aretino are mitigated so that
Donne may intensify his bitterness toward the Jesuits in the cruelest
passage of the book. Donne "was sory to see him [Ignatius] use
Peter Aretine so ill as he did," for whereas Aretino had confined his
obscenity to "his licentious pictures," the Jesuits will not content themselves with such "theoretical" wickedness, boasting rather

that when themselves had first tried, whether *Tiberius* his *Spintria* and *Mar-
tialis symplegma,* and others of that kinde, were not rather *Chimeraes,* and
speculations of luxuriant wits, than things certaine and constant, and such as
might bee reduced to an Art and methods in licentiousnes (for Jesuits never
content themselves with the *Theory* in anything, but straight proceed to
practise) they might after communicate them to their owne *Disciples* and
Novitiates.[35]

Philip Nerius, too, the founder of the Congregatio Oratorii, though
he had revived many superstitions about saints and had preached too
much and too enthusiastically about *"Ecclesiastique Antiquities,"* is let
off rather easily because of his stupidity and the fact that "either

---

[34] *Ibid.,* p. 362. Donne's appreciation of the greatness and the character of the age
in which he was living is well expressed in the lines immediately following: "But the
gates are seldome opened, nor scarce oftner than once in an Age. But my destiny
favoured mee so much, that I was present then, and saw all the pretenders, and all that
affected an entrance, and *Lucifer* himselfe, who then came out into the outward cham-
ber, to heare them pleade their owne Causes."—pp. 362-63.
[35] *Ibid.,* pp. 391-92.

he never knew, or had forgot that he had done those things which
they write of him." [36] With the little innovators Donne has no quarrel,
and he shows his tolerance for them by reproaching Loyola for treating
them so rudely: he "scattered all this cloud quickly, by commaunding,
by chiding, by deriding, and by force and violence." [37] As Machiavelli
is the only pretender whose wit approaches that of Ignatius, he comes
in for much longer treatment. Against his suit, tricked out in his best
Florentine diplomacy and barbed with "some venemous darts, out of
his *Italian Arsenal,* to cast against this worne souldier of *Pampelune,*
this *French-spanish* mungrell, *Ignatius,*" [38] Loyola, put on his mettle,
releases an interminable harangue, the longest and dullest passage in
the satire, which serves the useful purpose of allowing Donne to
reveal his genuine sense of the dramatic and his impeccable satiric
wit. At the close of the long-winded discourse Donne remarks with
a slyness akin to that which Chaucer intrudes into Host Baily's bore-
dom with the Monk's tragical omnibus that

truely I thought this Oration of *Ignatius* very long: and I began to thinke of
my body which I had so long abandoned, least it should putrifie, or grow
mouldy, or bee buried; yet I was loathe to leave the stage, till I saw the play
ended: And I was in hope, that if any such thing should befall my body, the
Jesuits, who work *Miracles* so familiarly, and whose reputation I was so careful of in this matter, would take compassion upon me, and restore me againe.[39]

The upshot of the "long Oration" is that Machiavelli's affinity with
some very worthy ancients, among them Plato, "and other fashioners
of Common-wealths," the Fathers of the Church, Origen, Chrysostom,
and Jerome, nullifies the force of his argument for admission into
hell, as well as his claim to have "brought in the liberty of dissembling,
and lying." Moreover, Machiavelli's politics are at odds with the
Jesuits, for, as Loyola declares,

all his bookes, and all his deedes, tend onely to this, that thereby a way may
be prepared to the ruine and destruction of that part of this Kingdome,
which is established at *Rome:* for what else doth hee endeavour or go about,
but to change the forme of common-wealth, and so to deprive the people (who
are a soft, a liquid and ductile mettall, and apter for our impressions) of all
their liberty: and having so destroyed all civility and re-publique, to reduce
all states to *Monarchies;* a name which in secular states, wee doe so much
abhor, (I cannot say it without teares,) but I must say it, that not any one
Monarch is to be found, which either hath not withdrawne himselfe wholy
from our kingdome, or wounded and endamadged in some weighty point.[40]

[36] *Ibid.,* pp. 394, 395.   [37] *Ibid.,* p. 391.   [38] *Ibid.,* p. 369.
[39] *Ibid.,* p. 390.   [40] *Ibid.,* pp. 385-86.

Thus, Machiavelli's sympathy with the strength of states, in opposition
to the policy of the Jesuits, is made one recommendation for Donne's
appreciation of his "innovation."

Perhaps the one person appearing before Lucifer who is potentially
the most susceptible butt of the satirist is Paracelsus. Nor is Donne
unaware of his opportunity, though it would be beside the point for
him to exercise himself for any length of time upon the Bombast and
his sect. In sharp contrast to the mild impression made by Copernicus,
who immediately precedes him, is the fright thrown into Lucifer by
Paracelsus's announcement of himself as *"Philippus Aureolus Theo-
phrastus Paracelsus Bombast of Hohenheim."* Lucifer recovers in time,
however, to ask him what he has to say to "the great *Emperour, Sathan,
Lucifer, Belzebub, Leviathan, Abaddon."* [41] This exchange of address
will serve to suggest the manner of Donne's treatment of the hocus-
pocus of Paracelsus. Nevertheless, it is significant that Donne allows
his satire to fall upon only the quackery of the doctor and his dissembling arts. The more serious and respectable champion of a new kind
of medicine remains unscathed, save for some disparaging remarks of
Loyola which may be interpreted as the author's inverted favor.

Though the rivals of Ignatius thus briefly alluded to are given a
share of praise and blame alike, it is not so with the astronomers. In
fact, Galileo, Kepler, and Tycho Brahe are too worthy to be used as
a means of satire, and their work too recent, perhaps, to have come
to Lucifer's attention. They are the abettors in the grand plan of
attack, and consequently are mentioned with respect that should not
be overlooked. It is not they, however, but Copernicus, the founder
of the new philosophy, who is chosen to battle with Lucifer and
Ignatius. It is important to note also that though Copernicus is an
"innovator" of the first order, he is not of the heretical stamp that
can pass successfully the perverse test imposed upon all who storm
the gates of hell.

While Donne's soul is still among the "swimming Ilands," he is
moved by the experience of seeing so much of the heavens to recall
Galileo and his fellow observers, Kepler and Tycho. The remark
following commits Donne to an attitude toward the new philosophy
which is confirmed by his ensuing treatment of Copernicus. Generally
speaking, it is an attitude that he continues to hold. Of the new heavens
revealed by the astronomers, he writes,

I thinke it an honester part as yet to be silent than to do *Galileo* wrong by
speaking of it, who of late hath summoned the other worlds, the Stars to

come neerer to him, and give him an account of themselves. Or to *Keppler,* who (as himselfe testifies of himselfe) *ever since* Tycho Braches *death hath received it into his care, that no new thing should be done in heaven without his knowledge.* For by the law, *Prevention* must take place; and therefore what they have found and discovered first, I am content they speake and utter first.[42]

This, in all probability, is the first specific reference, though it is accompanied by his recollection of a passage in Kepler's *De Stella in Cygno,*[43] that Donne makes to the *Sidereus Nuncius,* which he had read but shortly before composing *Ignatius.* His reluctance to comment further on the recent discoveries indicates an openness of mind and readiness to receive new learning and also that this is not the place for concerning himself with their more serious philosophical meaning. Having acknowledged his respect for the law, "Prevention," and having given Galileo and Kepler a chance "to speake and utter first," Donne is at liberty to speak for himself, and what he utters concerning the new philosophy, whether it be before Galileo's discoveries or afterward when it became a more accustomed part of his thought, is expressed with tolerance, even with sympathy. At no time does he ever flatly deny its truth; if the new philosophy helped to nourish a native skepticism, it is because he recognized that its approach to new truths made indifference toward it and complacency toward the old philosophy impossible. The definition of his conception of the relation of man to the universe, urged upon him by the new philosophy, gains much of its vitality and richness in the later chapters of his spiritual experience, because he went to the ends to which his fearless and honest curiosity led him rather than retreat into the doubtful sanctity of traditionalism.

With thoughts of Galileo still running through his mind, Donne drops "plummet-like" into hell, where Copernicus is seen as the first contender for the favor of Lucifer. As the entire scene is conceived in dramatic terms, it is necessary to follow the dialogue and action closely if a full understanding of the speakers is to be had. Thus, at first Donne does not recognize "a certaine Mathematitian" who comes up to the gates with "an erect countenance, and setled pace,"[44] quite unlike the succeeding candidates who approach with a great deal more impudence than dignity. Inconsistent with this dignity, Coper-

[42] *Ibid.,* p. 359.
[43] See above, p. 83 n. 49.
[44] The remaining quotations from *Ignatius his Conclave* in this chapter are found on pp. 363-66.

nicus batters the doors "with hands and feet"; but Donne parenthetically explains that his conduct is to be taken as a demonstration of his lack of respect for Lucifer and not a mark of crudeness. By this single gesture, both amusing and significant, Donne clearly anticipates Copernicus's failure to persuade either Lucifer or Ignatius, for, to no other suppliant does he admit a show of such spontaneous irreverence. Copernicus's successors plead, some with boldness designed to impress, some with obsequiousness that disguises guile and presumption, but none without a certain amount of awe and reverence for the presence of the ruler of hell.

Having made himself heard Copernicus announces his claims, and it is not until then that Donne realizes that the person before him is none other than the champion of the new philosophy. This revelation comes as a surprise to Donne who "had never heard ill of his life, and therefore might wonder to find him there." In the words that follow, Donne absolves the new philosophy from heresy and confesses his admiration for its doctrines, for it is a perversity ascribed to the papists rather than fate or merit that has brought Copernicus thither:

yet when I remembred, that the Papists have extended the name, and the punishment of Heresie, almost to every thing, and that as yet I used *Gregories* and *Bedes* spectacles, by which one saw *Origen*, who deserved so well of the *Christian Church, burning in Hell*, I doubted no longer, but assured my selfe that it was *Copernicus* which I saw.

In laying his case before Lucifer Copernicus saves himself from any charge of blasphemy by qualifying his work of remodeling the heavens as "almost" that of a "new Creator." Again, while pleading that he has thrust the sun, Lucifer's greatest enemy, "an officious spy, and betrayer of faults," into "the lowest part of the world," he is obliged to admit having carried the earth (Lucifer's prison) up into heaven, and one is inclined to regard the doubtful favor canceled by its ironical complement. Lucifer, throughout the satire a victim of gullibility, presenting a blunt foil to the sharper wit of Ignatius, is inclined to be favorably impressed by Copernicus and can think of but one argument "which he might have conveniently opposed, but he was loath to utter it, least he should confesse his feare." It is then that Ignatius, self-appointed advocate of Satan, steps forward to clear up his client's perplexity. In thus entrusting to Loyola the refutation of the astronomer and in courageously delivering up the new philosophy to rely on its own merits, Donne gives further proof of his respect for the new science and his openness of mind. At least, he feels safe in exposing his favorite to the bias and ignorance of one who, however subtle, is "utterly ignorant in all great learning," and knows not "so much as *Ptolomeys,* or *Copernicus* name, but might have beene perswaded, that the words *Almagest, Zenith,* and *Nadir* were Saints names, and fit to bee put into the *Litanie,* and *Ora pro nobis* joyned to them." Yet, since Loyola's time, the Jesuits have picked up considerable knowledge of the goings-on in the world, and from those who have trooped daily to hell he has obtained a great deal of popular information about the new astronomy. Thus equipped, "hee undertakes *Copernicus.*" The refutation following consists briefly in denying that "our *Lucifer*" has any relation with "that starre *Lucifer* [which is but Venus]," except to use her "aversly and preposterously," and in reciting an altogether favorable history of Copernicus's theory. First, he affirms that the report of the evil and devastating effects of Copernicus's theory upon the minds of men has been grossly exaggerated:

But for you, what new thing have you invented, by which our *Lucifer* gets anything? What cares hee whether the earth travell, or stand still? Hath your raising up of the earth into heaven, brought men to that confidence, that they build new towers or threaten God againe? Or do they out of this motion of the earth conclude, that there is no hell, or deny the punishment of sin? Do not men beleeve? do they not live just, as they did before?

Immediately upon this, Loyola scornfully speaks that which Lucifer "might have conveniently opposed," had it not been that he was afraid. The "argument" that Lucifer withheld is simply this: "Besides, this detracts from the dignity of your learning, and derogates from your right and title of comming to this place, that those opinions of yours may very well be true." This recalls Donne's conception of heresy and innovation, and the test to be applied to every candidate for Lucifer's favor—"so the truth be lost, it is no matter how." By implication Copernicus is another of the world's great patrons of the truth. For Ignatius it is "our *Clavius,*" rather, persisting as he does in fostering myth and superstition beyond their appointed time to possess men's minds, who is the more legitimate candidate of the two. Clavius is the "Author of all contentions, and schoole-combats in this cause"; and his merit is enhanced because he troubled "both the peace of the Church, and Civill businesses" with his Gregorian Calendar. "Nor," as Ignatius adds,

hath heaven it selfe escaped his violence, but hath ever since obeied his apointments: so that *S. Stephen, John Baptist,* and all the rest, which have bin commanded to worke miracles at certain appointed daies, where their Reliques are preserved, do not now attend till the day come, as they were accustomed, but are awaked ten daies sooner, and constrained by him to come downe from heaven to do that businesse.

Lastly, Ignatius calls attention to the worthy predecessors of Copernicus, the ancient *"Heraclides, Ecphantus,* and *Aristarchus,"* whom all the champions of the new philosophy from Recorde and Rheticus to Kepler had invoked to justify Copernicus's radical departure from the traditional world scheme of Ptolemy. In these final moments of the little drama between Ignatius and Copernicus Donne does not miss the opportunity to imply his sympathy for the latter. With a triumphant gesture Ignatius sarcastically throws out a morsel of hope to Copernicus, indirectly conveying Donne's complete exoneration of the "little *Mathematitian":*

And if hereafter the fathers of our Order can draw a *Cathedral Decree* from the Pope, by which it may be defined as a matter of faith: *That the earth doth not move;* and an *Anathema* inflicted upon all which hold the contrary: then perchance both the Pope which shall decree that, and *Copernicus* his followers, (if they be Papists) may have the dignity of this place.

Again, the only apposite comment is, "so the truth be lost, it is no matter how." Copernicus, now reduced to "this little *Mathematitian"* by Ignatius, withdraws; but Donne is deferent to his opinions to the last, for his retreat is made in silence, figured in the language of his great innovation—"and *Copernicus,* without muttering a word, was as quiet, as he thinks the sunne."

XI
GENTLE INTERPRETATIONS

THAT Donne's mind had absorbed much of the learning of the new philosophy by the time he had composed *The second Anniversary* is patent from the exhibition of facts that has been given. On the heels of this observation runs the question of just how it affected him. By this is meant something other than objective contact with a body of learning through which, when transformed into poetic imagery, may be expressed the poet's thoughts or feelings, such as we note in Spenser's use of the romantic epic of the Renaissance or in Milton's use of scriptural story. In short, is the new philosophy more than a "mythology" through which the poet may approach the subject of friendship, love, or the destinies of his soul? The craftsman's personality is disclosed in his choice of tools, and the tools themselves affect his work. It goes without saying that the new philosophy modified Donne's way of looking at life at the same time that it served as a vehicle to facilitate his expression.

Though the subject is difficult, it can be studied with a fair degree of concreteness by considering what there is in Donne that corresponds with the more general characteristics of the new philosophy. In his analysis of the "dominant intellectual movement of the later Renaissance" (of which "the Reformation and the scientific movement were two aspects"), Professor Whitehead characterizes the new philosophy as a revolt against scholastic authority—a revolt assuming an anti-intellectual trend in that it was directed upon the overthrow of medieval rationalism—and an effort to revise the conception of the nature of knowledge and to discover the ultimate grounds of truth. There is also a belief in the final order·of things and a revival of naturalism, a concern for the concrete fact as such. The belief in the final order of things implies the possibility of their correlation according to some principle understood as law or even as a fatalistic chain of cause and effect. The revival of naturalism means an attempt to get at the principles or causes believed to be inherent in the universe through the observation of facts by the senses closely checked by reason.[1]

[1] See *op. cit.*, ch. i, "The Origins of Modern Science," ch. ii, "Mathematics as an Element in the History of Thought," ch. iii, The Century of Genius," *passim*.

To affirm that one can readily identify these forces playing upon Donne's imagination is to simplify the matter to absurdity; to assert that there is anything more than a certain spiritual kinship between Donne and men like Bacon and Galileo is to distort the meaning of the facts. Donne was not a man of science but a poet; yet, he may share with the former certain qualities of mind. Whatever the correspondences may be, the ends to which poets and philosophers direct their minds are not identical nor the method of this direction the same; consequently, it is well to be cautious in observing the differences as well as the similarities in the manifestation of the above characteristics in men who, though they are of the same age and spiritually related in many ways, are geniuses of a different order. Bacon's *Novum Organum* was developed to help men win "the true and lawful goal of the sciences" which is "that human life be endowed with new discoveries and powers." [2] Galileo had a much less philosophical and humanitarian end in mind when he projected and composed his *Dialogues*. It was rather to record the discoveries of the new philosophy and to show how in the light of the new facts the old conception of the universe was no longer tenable. Donne has only the purpose of expressing the way in which one man of extraordinary sensitivity and learning responded to his world.

The fact that Donne and Bacon lived for different purposes does in no wise exclude the possibility that they were affected by the same intellectual environment. It is as obvious in Donne as in Bacon, or in any other man of the Renaissance alert to the spirit of the times, that acceptance of the authority of the medieval past is entirely unsatisfactory. By authority, here, is meant what Bacon described as "a blind custom of obedience" or "an absolute resignation or perpetual captivity" of the mind,[3] and what the historians of the Renaissance regard as an uncritical belief in the ideas of other men (usually, dead men, as if death made sages of us all), and an unquestioning adherence to all traditional modes of conduct and expression; in short, the notion that the past is the one sure repository of truth. Anyone conversant with Donne's work will readily appreciate how consistently his revolutionary temperament is implied and how frequently specific statement of his unorthodoxy is made. Nor is this remark inserted here with disregard of the fact that he like his learned contemporaries and successors persistently calls upon dead authors to confirm his opinions. This was the method of Renaissance scholarship, inherited from the past; but

[2] *Works*, VIII, 113.
[3] *Of the Advancement of Learning*, *Works*, VI, 104, 129. Cf. "an extreme admiration of antiquity," *Novum Organum*, *Works*, VIII, 85.

if one is to appreciate the difference between the Middle Ages and the Renaissance, he must look behind the formidable array of learned quotation and reference to antiquity to detect the spirit breathing through these later works. The consultation of a glossary to *Of the Laws of Ecclesiastical Polity* or *Biathanatos* may suggest a cabinet of antiquities. One must read critically to note that Hooker is defining Anglicanism as a religion thoroughly consonant with a broadly conceived human nature and that Donne, in a book of unparalleled audacity and originality, is using a scholastic method, "rather because scholastique and artificiall men use this way of instructing; and I made account that I was to deale with such." [4]

[Already we have given a short account of Donne's early predisposition to disregard authority; the spirit of his writings complementing this disregard is no less significant than an awareness of self as the supremely important and interesting fact of life and the instrument of our conceptions of divinity and truth.] Perhaps it is most easily sensed in *Songs and Sonets,* against which the charge has been laid so frequently that in more ways than one they respect authority all too little. They are free enough from an overt dependence upon tradition. But his other works, including the *Anniversaries* and particularly the essays and sermons, may seem to reflect an excessive reverence for the past. This may be said, however, only because marginal note, allusion, and reference make obvious Donne's familiarity with old writers (and new ones too, for that matter). Thus, in considering his various writings one must appreciate the varying demands imposed upon the author by different forms of discourse: a sonnet is not written according to the rules of tractarian controversy, nor should a sermon follow the outlines of a pamphlet. But in the face of the psychological facts one can hardly admit the notion of marked cleavage in personality between the poet who in a manner most perverse supplicates the goddess of love, and the "saint" who prolongs a rather unseemly doubt about his own salvation. Though it would be folly to announce that Donne "broke" with the medieval world and freed himself entirely from its influences, it would be no less absurd to hazard that a catalogue of his medieval doctrines could not be drawn up as conveniently from the heretical verses of his youth as from the copia of his later years wherein those "engines" of medieval learning worked so energetically. Early or late, it is imperative to note that the energy of the poet's own active soul is the one dominant, kinetic force, an energy that

[4] *Biathanatos,* p. 23.

was more abundantly released and given direction by the influence of the new philosophy.

With the recognition that this spirit controls Donne's writings, it may be said that it affected his attitude toward authority in a number of specific ways. It brought to his poems an amazing originality; it encouraged an attitude of tolerance and respect for all sound opinion gathered from his various learning and rich experience; it led him to practice discriminating and critical methods of scholarship; and finally, it caused him to seek in conscience, rather than in the varying opinions of men, the criteria of authentic religious experience.

As the astounding originality of Donne's poetic utterance is the one constant theme among Donne's critics, it would be presumption here to do more than take note of the fact. What is axiomatic needs no proof. That Ben Jonson told Drummond that Donne deserved to be hanged "for not keeping of accent" [5] receives its perennial attention from all who concern themselves with the criticism of Elizabethan verse. M. Legouis in recent times, however, has done good service in justifying his reiteration of the famous dictum by analyzing Donne's roughness of meter and complexity of stanzaic form into a "craftsmanship" that reflects no particular subtlety upon Jonson's judgment, nor, if we are to follow M. Legouis, pays any tribute to the sensitivity of his ear for the numbers of some of the early Elizabethans.[6] In addition to the fact that Donne is a proficient and original technician, he proves his originality in the treatment of the matter itself. Well aware of his heresy, he tabs himself "Rebell and Atheist" as he flaunts his contempt for the elegant triflers in verse who would trust to a profuse exhalation of wit to warm their stereotyped devices into the stuff of true love poetry. Like Shakespeare's, Donne's mistress "went on the ground." Authentic flesh and blood into which is infused a no less authentic soul awaken his muse. He pursues the mistress of his imagination through the shadows of genuine hate and distrust, through the sunlit moments of pure ecstasy, and into the realms of love which flourished "before the god of Love was borne" whose worship had become "sicklied o'er" with the unfeeling formalism of compliment and the celebration of spineless beauty. Dryden supposed that Donne in his love poems tormented the fair sex with an over-refined intellectualism, but this marks a misconception of Donne's purpose. It is doubtful whether many of his songs were ever meant for feminine eyes;

---

[5] *Conversations with William Drummond of Hawthornden,* in *op. cit.,* p. 133.
[6] *Op. cit.,* p. 12, and Appendix A, pp. 85 ff.

three women, however, to whom Donne does frequently address his verses, Anne Donne, Lady Herbert, and the Countess of Bedford, seem to have understood them pretty thoroughly. The fact is that Donne is tormenting the fair sex far less than he is vexing himself into the revelation of the electric condition of his own soul. Taken as a group, his love poems are the expression of his own personality; wayward, dialectical, and unorthodox as they may seem, they are written in a native vigorous English idiom, the language of John Heywood, Wyatt, the early Spenser, and Shakespeare, and give evidence that the poet appealed from the authority of a nice convention to something as fundamental as the heart of man.

As was the originality of his verse, so the catholicity of his learning has been the subject of frequent comment. Professor Grierson, Miss Ramsay, and Mrs. Simpson have well recorded the versatility of Donne's studies and the enthusiasm he evinces for experience, though it is well to note that even Donne's taste has its limitations—for instance, the great revival of classical learning is but sparingly reflected in his work. Without repeating what already has been adequately demonstrated, we wish here only to re-emphasize that Donne possesses the catholic mind in common with his Renaissance contemporaries and to make clear that amidst the multifarious learning in which he was accomplished he maintained a singular independence of mind, a tolerant spirit, and therefore cannot easily be classed as a disciple of any particular school of thought. In *Pseudo-Martyr*, the drought of which is watered with many significant autobiographical confessions, his anticipation of the attacks of his critics provides the key for an appreciation of the way in which he regards his own learning:

And if they will be content to impute to me all humane infirmities, they shall neede to faine nothing: I am, I confesse, obnoxious enough. My naturall impatience not to digge painefully in deepe, and stony, and sullen learnings: My Indulgence to my freedome and libertie, as in all other indifferent things, so in my studies also, not to betroth or enthral my selfe, to any one science, which should possesse or denominate me.[7]

Apart from the beautiful irony gracing this passage, immured within the rubble which his painful digging has brought to light for the construction of his argument against the recusants, there is to be noted the declaration of his intellectual independence and the admission of his patience. Nor should one overlook the statement that his studies are arduous and difficult, "stony, and sullen learnings." As Donne's writings witness, he does not search among old authors for pretty

[7] Sig. B₁ verso and B₂ recto, § 2.

shells of learning with which to adorn his thoughts nor for the flowers of rhetoric whose petals dropped here and there would impart to his language the pattern of some rich old damask. Though more than a gentleman's familiarity marks his acquaintance with the poets of antiquity, the grace and Arcadian beauty which enrich the lines of Spenser are notably lacking. His idiom is a homelier, more direct English idiom:

> Meet mee at London, then,
> Twenty dayes hence, and thou shalt see
> Mee fresher, and more fat, by being with men,[8]

and his eloquence is the product of his own ingenious and original phrasing:

> O strong and long-liv'd death, how cam'st thou in?
> And how without Creation didst begin?
> Thou hast, and shalt see dead, before thou dyest,
> All the foure Monarchies, and Antichrist.
> How could I thinke thee nothing, that see now
> In all this All, nothing else is, but thou,
> Our births and lives, vices, and vertues, bee
> Wastfull consumptions, and degrees of thee.
> For, wee to live, our bellowes weare, and breath,
> Nor are wee mortall, dying, dead, but death.[9]

Further, in an effort to characterize the quality of Donne's learning it is not amiss to remark that he does not indulge in a taste for purely antiquarian curiosities. True, he seems to have ranged widely and far afield among all sorts of books and men, but too much can easily be made of his indebtedness to recondite and exotic sources. The satiric ease with which he parodies the curious libertine authors in the *Catalogus Librorum* does reveal a native enjoyment in playing with erudition, but it likewise reveals an underlying contempt for it. One does find such mysteries of learning as "a hundred controversies of an Ant,"[10] and the romance of "a toyfull Ape" "with Adams fift daughter *Siphatecia*";[11] also, there is the story of Beza's attempt to drown himself "from the Millers bridge in *Paris*" because of the "anguish of a Scurffe, which over-ranne his head,"[12] and the anticipation that perchance he would starve himself who "would vow a fast, till he

[8] *The Blossome*, Grierson, I, 60, ll. 33-35.
[9] *Elegie on M^ris Boulstred, ibid.*, pp. 282-83, ll. 21-30.
[10] *The second Anniversary, ibid.*, p. 258, l. 282. I hope soon to publish a note on this interesting figure, suggesting one of St. Basil's epistles as its source.
[11] *The Progresse of the Soule, ibid.*, p. 313, l. 457.
[12] *Biathanatos*, p. 17.

had found in nature, whether the Egge, or the Hen were first in the world." [13] Though this list might be extended greatly, it would still be a meager catalogue beside Burton's hundreds of pages of curiosa, recorded with whimsical delight, to say nothing of credulity, and Browne's refutation of "vulgar errours" for which his lingering and careful indulgence betrays an infection with a more than moderate sympathy. But one should be gracious in allowing these worthies, Donne included, their freedom to exploit the absurdities of the past garnered from their studies, especially when one recalls that in all seriousness pigeons were laid on the Dean's feet during an illness, as late as 1623, "*to draw the vapors from the Head.*" [14]

Nevertheless, the statement holds that Donne does not inject into his works a multitude of curiosities for their own sake. Though the pages of books like *Biathanatos* and *Pseudo-Martyr* are tributes to an acquaintance with dozens of authors unknown to us, a Clapmarius, a Steuchius de Valla, or an Althmerus, they cannot have been entirely unfamiliar to his learned friends, for Donne, though he delights in learning, is not vainly pedantic. Such unfamiliar names as these and scores of others are among the subjects of his "naturall impatience not to digge painefully in deepe, and stony, and sullen learnings," but there is also the company of a more distinguished host of scholars. Whether it is in poem, pamphlet, or sermon, one observes that Donne most frequently keeps the society of the great philosophers, theologians, and scientists of both the past and present: Plato and Aristotle; Augustine, Aquinas, Calvin, and Luther; Galileo and Kepler. In his own confession that he was ever prone to an "hydroptique immoderate desire of humane learning," the word "humane" should be underscored. True, not all the authors whom he follows fall into the category of those who wrote *literas humaniores;* yet a technical phrase cannot rob an Augustine or a Galileo of his just contribution to the enrichment of human experience.

Cursory as this note has been, it may serve to emphasize the breadth and depth of Donne's learning and provide a preface to an inquiry into the truth of his declaration that he did not "betroth or enthral" himself to any one science or author. An intellectual independence and openness of mind, hidden from the superficial reader, is stamped deeply upon his work. From the mass of learned quotation and allusion emerges something that is peculiarly Donne's—not a synthesis of diversities into a new scholasticism, nor a new Platonism, nor any kind

[13] *XXVI Sermons* (1669), 24, fol. 322.   [14] *Devotions*, pp. 284 ff.

of revision of the old philosophy. Nor is there simply, as Dr. Johnson thought, a violent yoking of incongruities. Rather, there is revealed a complex though unified personality; and to this revelation the heterogeneous company of many authors is made to contribute their paradoxical services.

A mind of catholic interests and tastes is well-nigh certain to be a mind of tolerant inclinations and broad sympathies. However, as tolerance is a word frequently destined to become a name for a self-given permission to run the gamut of experience indiscriminately, it is essential to an understanding of our application of the term to Donne to make certain qualifications of its meaning. We shall understand tolerance here as a genuine sympathy for all sound learning and valid human experience. What is sound in learning and valid in experience may be perplexing because of the difficutly of finding any adequate objective test. But if we are convinced of the ultimate integrity of the person concerned, as it is reflected both in the sincerity of response to facts and to emotional stimuli and in the exercise of a critical and discriminating judgment in matters of the mind, the difficulty will be minimized sufficiently to allow the definition to stand as it is.

If there is anything in Donne that can be brought against his personal sincerity and soundness of judgment, in fairness it should be exposed at this time. We recall his vituperations against women; his superlatively refined compliments and tender addresses; his solicitations for patronage; the extravagance of his eulogy of Elizabeth Drury, fitter for the Virgin Mary than for a mere woman, according to Ben Jonson; [15] and his wavering between the world and the Church. Furthermore, it would be to praise Donne unjustly to suggest that he was a consistent model of discretion and a poet of impeccable tastes and fixed purposes. How serious these charges are may be known from a brief review of their relative significance to the whole of his career. His arraignment of women, to be noted in certain of the *Songs and Sonets, The Progresse of the Soule,* and in certain elegies, though it has associations in time, at least, with the prevalent Elizabethan and Jacobean outbursts against the sex, cannot be condoned or condemned simply as a mannerism of the times. Against such a construction argue the poet's earnestness and intensity of feeling. Whatever be the explanation—and in detail this may be left to the reader—it must be made with the thought in mind that Donne was inclined to look realistically at a subject ridden by convention and falsified by romantic

---

[15] *Conversations with William Drummond of Hawthornden,* in *op. cit.,* p. 133.

illusion, and that a cynical attitude did not allow him to violate the sanctity of true love, as when he says,

> T'were prophanation of our joyes
> To tell the layetie our love,[16]

or when he makes such confessions of supreme devotion as *Sweetest love, I do not goe,* and *A Valediction: of weeping.*

Again, to suggest that Donne toyed with friendship in the hyperbole of Petrarchian affectation is to credit the women whom he addressed with a susceptibility to a most perverse kind of flattery and a weakness for adulation that vitiates their tribute of genuine friendship for Donne. The subtlety with which he analyzes feminine virtue and the courtliness that chooses learning rather than grace as an ornament are not commonplace things. If he seems at times to drift into extravagance and flattery he is aware of it himself and apologizes by saying,

> If you can thinke these flatteries, they are,
>   For then your judgement is below my praise,
> If they were so, oft, flatteries worke as farre,
>   As Counsels, and as farre th'endeavour raise.
>   . . .
> And if I flatter any,'tis not you
>   But my owne judgement, who did long agoe
> Pronounce, that all these praises should be true,
>   And vertue should your beauty,'and birth outgrow.[17]

The charges that Donne sought preferment by trimming his sails to the wind and that when the wind blew fitfully from court and pulpit alike he wallowed indecisively can easily be pressed too far. That such a tacking about, common enough in Donne's time, should seem shocking today is rather strange. It is by regarding the extenuating circumstances of necessity to provide in some way for an ill-fed family warring with a natural restlessness encouraged by much learning and diverse tastes that a satisfactory explanation may be approached. Whatever may be said against Donne on this score, it should be remembered that the ends attained go far to justify the means and that the means involved no disloyalty to friends or self. His overtures to Sir Robert Drury resulted in Donne's greatest poem, if not in a proper encomium for Elizabeth or the Virgin Mary. Somerset was rewarded beyond his deserts by an Epithalamion prefaced by an "Ecclogue" attempting to teach him something of "heavens glory"

---

[16] *A Valediction: forbidding mourning,* Grierson, I, 50, ll. 7-8.
[17] *To the Countesse of Huntingdon, ibid.,* p. 203, ll. 49-52, 57-60. [1614-15.]

and "the heart of man." [18] Finally, the glory of his preaching proved ample vindication of his decision, albeit reluctant, to take holy orders. It is a fact, Donne did not always choose to make discretion the better part of valor. Presumably, youth inclined him toward an immoderate indulgence of the flesh and a disposition toward revolutionary and novel ideas. The notion, however, of a wild, insatiable rake indulging his passions at will is hard to believe, particularly as the evidence cited to confirm such a hypothesis—certain of his early poems—cannot be considered strictly autobiographical. Walton's apologies for Donne's youthful conduct are more certainly the outpourings of a man made nervous by his idol's own retrospective exaggeration of his early sins than the words of one thoroughly conversant with the facts. Again, there are several things that interfere with the acceptance of the traditional attitude toward Donne's marriage as one of the major errors of his life. He married the woman whom he loved and who in turn loved him. In the correspondence on the subject with his father-in-law, Sir George More, the "culprit," as Gosse dubs him,[19] not only employed considerable discretion, but also proved himself a man whose sense of honor and devotion could not be compromised by a stubborn and outraged father.[20] Writing from prison, while naturally unable to conceal his anxiety for his own well-being, he is unselfish in his concern for his bride, and temperate in his address. True, it appears that he had lost all of his means and had little prospect of gaining more, and for that reason it is to his credit that he did not resort to obsequious apology nor allow the occasion to provoke him to unseemly anger. He simply insisted that his love was honest and sincere. Whatever course might have been taken, the one Donne chose was not reprehensible.

The frailties of human nature exposed in the *Satyres* continue as the themes of many sermons; from this bundle of frailties afflicting humanity may be singled out a few especially pertinent to the revelation of his intellectual sanity and independence. Among them are servitude to devitalized convention; superstition; proneness of men to conceal their motives in learned sophistries; and the deliberate hurt that is done to truth by contentiousness and opinionated conceit. From his prose writings can be drawn abundant proof of his disposition to regard these as among the major vices of mankind. Just as Donne sees love become a sickly passion when dehumanized by the poet who observes its "laws" and codifies the elements of beauty, so he

[18] *Ibid.*, p. 133, ll. 48-52. See above, pp. 112 ff.
[19] *Op. cit.*, I, 100.   [20] See *ibid.*, pp. 100-7, 112-14.

sees divinity stifled by canonists and authors of decretals. No more striking evidence of the struggle of Donne's spirit to free itself from medievalism is to be found than in his biting and persistent effort to liberate the Church from ecclesiasticism and to free theology from the accretions of gloss and subtilized opinion that hide its great foundation in the Holy Scriptures, the plain statement of the Apostles' Creed, and the undistorted pronouncements of the first Fathers.

Even though we may, today regard many Renaissance ideas as still shadowed by the superstition of an unenlightened age, we should not fail to recognize that the Renaissance looked in the same way upon many of the ideas of the past. Of such were Bacon's "idols" and Browne's "vulgar errours." Donne, also, knowing that complete independence demands shaking off the illusions of antiquity, looks askance upon a great part of his medieval heritage as being nothing more than a bundle of superstitions fostered by popular credulity and not infrequently encouraged by intelligent persons who find it politic to keep the people in ignorance. It is deplorable, he thinks with Canus, that "men otherwise very graue, haue gathered vp rumours, and transmitted them to posterity, either too indulgent to themselues, or to the people: and that Noble Authors haue beene content to thinke, that that was the true law of History, to write those things which the common people thought to be true." [21]

How readily he could coerce with mild contempt and levity such old wives' tales into the service of art he had early demonstrated in his Song, Goe, and catche a falling starre, wherein woman's fidelity is made to keep company with such "strange sights, Things invisible to see," as the magic of mandrake roots, the cleft in the "Divels foot," and the songs of mermaids. But it is not always in jest that Donne opposes superstition. In the cause of truth the scholar joins the satirist, as when he exposes the popular errors deliberately encouraged in the Church of his birth at the expense of true religion. He condemns papal approval of "stories" like that of St. Brigid's Reuelation which gave rise to the ceremony of turning to the north "when the Gospell is song," "from whence all euill is deriued, and where the Diuels dwell," because Brigid was of "Swethland." [22] Repeatedly he challenges the legends of the saints with their preposterous miracles; those "infinite Miracles" reported by the Jesuits in the "propagation of Christian Religion in the new discoveries," fictions which even "the best amongst them ingenuously deny"; [23] and what is perhaps for him the most reprehensible error maintained by Rome, "this Comique-Tragicall doc-

---

[21] Pseudo-Martyr, p. 106.   [22] Ibid., p. 107.   [23] Essays in Divinity, p. 186.

trine of *Purgatory"* of which "all discourse . . . seemes . . . to bee but the *Mythologie* of the Romane Church, and a morall application of pious and vseful fables." [24]

In his effort to lay the ghost of popular error, and particularly that of Roman "superstition," Donne's sincerity and intelligence save him from narrow prejudice and petulant carping against antiquity. For instance, in the Roman Church itself Donne can find an exemplar of the free mind and the liberal spirit—Sir Thomas More, an illustrious member of his mother's family. The following is Donne's tribute to the sanity of the great Catholic humanist in regarding falsehood as heresy; also it is proof of Donne's own affinity with the emancipating influence of the Renaissance. He records that More

vndertooke to translate Lucianus Dialogue Philopseudes, to deliuer the world from superstition: which was crept in vnder Religion: For (saies he) superstitious lies haue beene tolde with so much authority, that a Cosoner was able to perswade S. Augustine, thogh a graue man, & a vehement enemy of lies, that a tale which Lucian had before derided in this Dialogue, was the[n] newly done in his daies. Some therfore thinke (saies he) that they haue made Christ beholden to them for euer, if they inuent a fable of some Saint, or some Tragedie of hell, to make an olde woman weepe or tremble. So that scarce the life of any Martyr or virgine hath escaped their lies, which makes me suspect, that a great part of those fables, hath beene inserted by Heretiques, by mingling therof to withdraw the credite due to Christian Histories.[25]

Truth suffers most, however, at the hands of those who conceal their motives in curious and subtle sophistries and disputations. In other words, dishonesty propagated by rationalization is the "letter" that truly kills the "spirit" of truth. In taking this stand Donne is at one with Bacon when he attacks the scholastic method in the following definition:

This same unprofitable subtlety or curiosity is of two sorts; either in the subject of itself that they [the schoolmen] handle, when it is a fruitless speculation or controversy . . . or in the manner or method of handling of a knowledge; which amongst them was this; upon every particular position or assertion to frame objections, and to those objections, solutions; which solutions were for the most part not confutations, but distinctions: . . . And such is their method, that rests not so much upon evidence of truth proved by arguments, authorities, similitudes, examples, as upon particular confutations and solutions of every scruple, cavillation, and objection; breeding for the most part one question as fast as it solveth another.[26]

[24] *Pseudo-Martyr*, p. 106.   [25] *Ibid.*, p. 108.
[26] *Of the Advancement of Learning, Works*, VI, 122-23.

Unconsciously the mind recalls Donne's indictment of the Jesuits in *Ignatius his Conclave,* "so the truth be lost, it is no matter how," and turns again to the satirical bequests made in *The Will:*

> Mine ingenuity and opennesse,
> To Jesuites;
>
> . . .
>
> To Schoolemen I bequeath my doubtfulnesse.[27]

In later years his attitude is well described by the axiomatic pronouncement, "It is the Text that saves us," and by the trenchant observation immediately following:

"the interlineary glosses, and the marginal notes, and the *variae lectiones,* controversies and perplexities, undo us; the Will, the Testament of God, enriches us; the Schedules, the Codicils of men, begger us: because the Serpent was subtiller then any, he would dispute and comment upon Gods Law, and so deceiv'd by his subtilty." [28]

If at times Donne falls into a contentious mood, as in *Biathanatos* or in parts of *Pseudo-Martyr* and *Ignatius his Conclave,* it is with the knowledge that he is dealing with "scholastique men" who best understand their own language, an idiom with which his youthful training fortunately made him familiar. Thus equipped, he is a whetted knife in the hands of the Reformed Church, able to cut through the casuistic verbiage of his opponents' arguments to the heart of a problem, as is illustrated in his reduction of the matter of the temporal sovereignty of the papacy: *"But as* Erasmus *said of that Church in his time,* Syllogismi nunc sustinent Ecclesiam, *wee may iustlie say, that this Doctrine of temporall Iurisdiction, is sustained but by Syllogismes,* and those weake, and impotent, and deceiueable." [29]

How odious the scholastic method of disputation was to Donne is recorded in a hundred places. For him truth lies in the study of the fact, whether it is the response of the pulse to new love, the intimations of the good life portrayed by some scriptural story, or the fate of the sinner brought home by the tragedy of disease and penury. The tenacity with which he adheres to this position imparts vitality to his poetry and humanizes his sermons. If today we should not approve his emphasis on the literal acceptance of the Scriptures, for he views them as an authentic record of experience, we should, nevertheless, not lose sight of the historical fact that for him as for the whole of the Reformed Church, the Holy Scriptures, reclaimed from the shadow of medieval theologizing, are as fresh as the newly discov-

---

[27] Grierson, I, 56, ll. 12-13; 57, l. 30.　　　[28] *XXVI Sermons,* 4, fol. 47.
[29] *Pseudo-Martyr,* Preface, sig. D₄ § 27.

ered facts of science. Moreover, the acceptance of the Bible with a certain literalness discouraged strained allegorical interpretation and tended to remove the mysteries of religion and the problem of salvation from the hands of controversy. Unfortunately, they were too soon returned to these hands; but for Donne, at least, the Bible read in the light diffused by the Christian Church was sufficient. This particular attitude will be dealt with again; at present, let us consider only how it encouraged his abhorrence of the kind of contentiousness and debate which, practiced by traditional theologians, threatened to dissipate the unifying influence of true religion.

The approach to a statement concerning Donne's tolerant spirit has been somewhat circuitous, leading to a consideration of what he was prone to condemn rather than to a consideration of those things toward which he was sympathetic. Nevertheless, to forestall any notion that Donne's desire for "humane learning" disposed him to like the taste of every fountain at which he drank, it was necessary to treat the grounds on which his discriminations were established. As stated above, toward all sound learning and valid experience he was sympathetically inclined. The meaning of these terms as restricted and qualified by Donne's temperament has been given. The actual measure of his open-mindedness can easily be taken by reference to a few places wherein it is notably expressed. Already we have noted his agreeableness toward the new philosophy, intelligently set forth in *Ignatius his Conclave*, in his desire to let Galileo and Kepler "speake and utter first" for themselves, rather than dismiss them with a gesture of contempt. The same spirit warms his sympathies for the "heathen," "that great successive Trinity of humane wisdom, *Socrates, Plato,* and *Aristotle*," [30] and it appears again in his lenient judgment on Nerius's "apparitions" when he recalls that he, unlike many of his fellows, was reluctant to name anything miracle that could be explained on natural grounds.[31] Perhaps, however, its most significant manifestation is to be seen in his attitude toward the Roman Church. Unlike many converts—if Donne really can be termed a convert—he had something more generous than scorn for the Church from which he turned. The explanation is to be found in his thoroughly catholic temperament which found a narrow sectarian spirit intolerable. Whether bred at Geneva, Rome, or London, he has no sympathy for those who *"thinke presently, that hee hath no Religion, which dares not call his Religion by some newer name then* Christian." [32]

Donne's idea of the Christian Church is that of a Church unified by

[30] *Biathanatos*, pp. 57-58. Donne frequently returns to this subject.
[31] See *Ignatius his Conclave*, p. 395.   [32] *Pseudo-Martyr*, Preface, sig. B₃ § 5.

the common acceptance by all its members of the authority of the Holy Scriptures as the revelation of God's will and of the Creed as a statement of one's allegiance to this authority. More was unnecessary, except a proper devotion and worship. These demands, Donne found, were met more satisfactorily by the Anglican Establishment than by any other church. Thus, he turned from Rome, but not, however, without humility and diffidence, nor before he had, as he confesses, "to the measure of my poore wit and iudgement, suruayed and digested the whole body of Diuinity, controuerted betweene ours and the Romane Church." [33] Though he considered the Anglican Church more nearly his ideal and the most likely instrument for the propagation of true religion, he did not lose that "easines" of which he writes, "to affoord a sweete and gentle Interpretation, to all professors of Christian Religion, if they shake not the Foundation." [34] Nor was he warped by pride or by any affectation of insular superiority into forgetting that it was through the cultivation of this very "easines, to affoord a sweete and gentle Interpretation" to all branches of the Christian Church, that the peace and unity which he so earnestly desired could be brought about in both Church and State. The purpose of his "other booke" (*Pseudo-Martyr*) was to "reconcile all parts." [35] The full statement of his consistent policy is to be found in the preface to that "other booke." While disclaiming any desire to enter a *"Booke-warre,"* he declares that

My principall and direct scope and purpose herein, is the vnity and peace of his Church. For as when the roofe of the Temple rent asunder, not long after followed the ruine of the foundation it selfe: So if these two principall beames and Toppe-rafters, the Prince and the Priest, rent assunder, the whole frame and Foundation of Christian Religion will be shaked. And if we distinguish not between Articles of faith & iurisdiction, but account all those super-edifications and furnitures, and ornaments which God hath affoorded to his Church, for exteriour gouernment, to be equally the Foundation it selfe, there can bee no Church; as there could be no body of a man, if it were all eye.[36]

Donne's sympathies never degenerate into sentimentality and false enthusiasm. When frankness is needed to shatter illusion, it is ready. Thus, on the question of false martyrdom, he affirms,

it is not the Catholicke faith, which you smart for, but an vniust vsurpation, . . . it is not the Lyon of Iuda, for whose seruice and honour your liues were well giuen, but it is for a Weasell, which crept in at a litle hole, and since

[33] *Ibid.* § 4.   [34] *Ibid.,* sig. B₂ § 2.
[35] See above p. 201.   [36] *Pseudo-Martyr,* sig. B₂ § 3.

is growne so full and pamperd, that men will rather die, then beleeue that he got in at so little an entrance.[37]

Again, when he realized that *Pseudo-Martyr* had fallen short of its end he did not hesitate to bring against the Jesuits the complete arsenal of his satiric wit. Nevertheless, for Donne satire maintains, as it should, an essentially constructive purpose. It is this constructive purpose, or perhaps better, a positive reaction toward experience and learning, that is the condition of Donne's liberalism. He stands in the midst of a new age, aware that it has brought the human mind one stage nearer its maturity and independence. As he wittily puts it:

Our stomachs are not now so tender, and queasie, after so long feeding upon solid Divinity, nor we so umbragious and startling, having been so long en- lightened in Gods path, that wee should thinke any truth strange to us, or relapse into that childish age, in which a Councell in *France* forbad *Aristotles Metaphysiques,* and punished with Excommunication the excribing, reading, or having that booke. . . . Contemplative and bookish men, must of neces- sitie be more quarrelsome then others, . . . But as long as they goe towards peace, that is Truth, it is no matter which way.[38]

[37] *Ibid.,* sig. D₂ § 22.   [38] *Biathanatos,* p. 20.

XII

THE TEXT SAVES US

The subject of Donne's attitude toward authority will be illuminated
by a consideration of the scholarly habits of his mind. That he had
such habits we are prone to take for granted, assuming that where
there is learning there is at work the mind of the scholar. Scholarship
is not the inevitable companion of learning. Though the former
requires the latter, learning alone may suffice no further than to produce
another "marginal Prynn." Scholarship is to learning what form is
to matter; it is a technique employed in the use of learning giving
a meaning to an otherwise amorphous body of information and making it contribute to the expression of truth. In Donne we detect the
operation of a mind that attempts to evaluate what it studies and to
give to it some purposeful direction. For these reasons we regard him
as a scholar.

Donne searches for ultimate sources; he compares texts to test their
validity and acknowledges freely and generously his indebtedness to
those who supply him with information. He has his "footnotes";
he understands a collation; and he knows how to cast a list of his
errata. Even so, though the intervention of three hundred years between
him and us is enough to make us cautious, we should be wary of drawing a picture of Donne decked out in all the paraphernalia of the
twentieth-century "scientific" scholar. One thing, and that of first
importance, distinguishes him from the scientific scholar: he was a
poet; and to a poet truth is something approached by a thrust of the
imagination and grasped by intuition. It may find expression in such
cryptic terms as "all divinity is love and wonder," or be announced
in lines like the following:

> To'our bodies turne wee then, that so
> Weake men on love reveal'd may looke;
> Loves mysteries in soules doe grow,
> But yet the body is his booke.

Even *Pseudo-Martyr,* a work wherein hard reasoning prevails and
"sullen learnings" abound, a glimmer of the light that illumines the
poetic mind is reflected from Donne's vision of the "unity and peace
of his Church," produced by intense desire and the conviction that

the end sought by the controversialist should comport with the greater truth of Christianity.

The above passage from *The Extasie* and the citation of "the principall and direct scope" of *Pseudo-Martyr* will suggest the way Donne manages to convey the idea that he is seeking to express something more general and comprehensive than is necessarily demanded by either the unrecorded occasion for writing a love poem or the desire to dissuade the English Catholics from refusing the Oath of Allegiance to the King. Too often, it is true, Donne's curiosity and subtle learning seem to stand in the way of clear and effective realization of his objective; but careful study will persuade one that Tillyard goes a bit too far when he says that Donne "does not really know what he wants: or rather he wants everything and cannot harmonize his wants." [1] Though Donne lacks Milton's genius for organization and his ability to subordinate "sensibility" to "power, order, stability," he does not blind us to his purpose by the "eagerness of his sensibility." It is not his failure to "harmonize his wants" that is frequently disturbing, but his failure to "harmonize" the means by which these wants might best be expressed.

What Donne "wants" is not to present an ordered picture of the universe, justifying the ways of God to man, but to explore the fundamental conditions of the human personality, as disclosed by self-analysis, upon which any systematic interpretation of man's relation to the greater universe must be predicated. To achieve the expression of such truth as he brings to the surface by the penetrating search within himself, scholarship and learning come to his assistance. Thus, a poem like *The Extasie* draws upon the resources of Plato, more particularly of Aristotle, and probably of Epicurus; the composition of *Pseudo-Martyr* required Donne's knowledge of the "whole body of Divinity." This learning is exhibited not for its own sake but as the instrument for analyzing, illustrating, and strengthening the truth that is begotten upon the poet's imagination through the combined activity of sense and intellect. For Donne, then, scholarship becomes auxiliary to the subjective process through which truth is evolved. It supplies the matter with which the poet associates experience in his effort to endow it with its particular value. Furthermore, because it demands the exercise of discrimination and critical understanding it sharpens the contours of his thought and gives rigidity to his interpretation of experience.

The technique of the scientific scholar, on the contrary, is not of this secondary importance, because the purpose controlling its use is

[1] *Milton* (London, 1930), pp. 357-58.

found not within the scholar himself but in the demand made by the matter upon which it is directed, namely, that it be described accurately. Such a distinction does not mean, however, that the poet is committed to a respect for arbitrary, *a priori* premises divorced from foundation in fact and real experience any more than it relieves the scientific scholar from an obligation to correlate his descriptions in anticipation of the discovery of generalizations that may be made about them.

The fact that Donne is a poet subordinating his learning to the expression of the truth that is within himself does not exclude him from the company of true scholars. From an accumulation of the statements made here and there of the principles controlling his use of learning and from a study of their application we can construct a definition of his idea of scholarship capable of refuting any hastily formed conclusion that he adheres blindly to the authority of the writers whom he read or expects his own works to be read and interpreted with an eye fixed on their literal statement.

Already we have taken into account how his openness of mind and tolerant spirit encouraged a charitable disposition toward all kinds of learning that "goe towards peace, that is Truth," but reserved a just contempt for "the torture and vexation of schoole-limbicks, which are exquisite and violent distinctions." [2] The liberal mind moves toward a peace, which, understood in its fullest implications, is for Donne the end of life and learning. How firmly this attitude is fixed in Donne may be seen in his warning to the critic of *Biathanatos:*

If any Divine shall thinke the cause, or persons injured herein, and esteeme me so much worth the reducing to the other opinion, as to apply an answer hereunto, with the same Charitie which provoked me, and which, I thanke God hath accompanied me from the beginning, I beseech him, to take thus much advantage from me and my instruction, that he will doe it without bitternesse. He shall see the way the better, and shew it the better, and faile through it the better, if he raise no stormes.[3]

In addition to "Charitie," there are at least four other characteristics of Donne's scholarly manner that should be considered. They are, first, insistence on the accuracy of any text used and the obligation of the scholar to make accurate use of this text as well as his obligation to consider the meaning of any part in its relations to the larger context and not to be contented with the meaning of isolated passages; second, the necessity of subordinating authors cited to the purpose of

---

[2] *Biathanatos*, p. 34.
[3] *Ibid.*, p. 156. In deciding whether or no Donne intended the book for the printers this passage should be kept in mind.

the writer; third, the importance of comparison, contrast, and correlation of opinions, in order to make a just evaluation of their worth;
and fourth, recognition of the relativity of all human knowledge and
its dependence upon its historical environment.

A no less significant achievement of the Renaissance than the exploration of new lands and the discoveries made in the heavens was
the development of philological study. With the awakened enthusiasm
for the study of Latin, Greek, Hebrew, and some of the oriental
languages came the desire of scholars to reclaim from error and neglect
the texts of the worthies of antiquity. To the more purely humanistic
trend of linguistic study was added the ardor of the religious reformers
to secure a more exact recension of the Holy Scriptures themselves.
With historical scholarship as we know it not yet born, results that
would satisfy the twentieth-century critic could not be expected. However, we can forgive these early scholars their pseudo-Aristotelian texts
and their disagreements regarding the scriptural canon. The important
thing was that henceforth the scholar could not look upon the printed
word with equanimity and certainty; he must needs be critical of the
text. This new obligation was strengthened, as it applies to the Scriptures, by the demands for accuracy in controversy made upon Roman
and Protestant alike, and it is to the credit of a hundred pamphleteers
upon whom we are now inclined to look with abhorrence that at least
their airing of a great many textual matters marked an enthusiasm
for correctness—though certainly often directed toward partisan ends
—that has not been without profit. Some of their own results were of
signal value and have proved, with the help of later criticism, to be
of lasting worth. The Clementine recension of the Vulgate (1592)
remains the "authorized" text of the Roman Church; and that generation of "learned and vnderstanding persons . . . such as were con-
uersant in the holy and originall languages," who "gaue the first
entrance and way to this Reformation" [4] begot a numerous family, some
of whose members produced as a lasting and eloquent tribute to their
scholarship the King James Bible.

Donne's conversancy "in the holy and originall languages" may not
have been sufficient to qualify him as a thoroughly competent textual
critic, but his aptness in linguistic study generally afforded his native
critical sense an opportunity to exercise itself with considerable effectiveness on the works of authors of which he had occasion to make use.
For instance, in *Pseudo-Martyr* he finds it necessary to undertake an
examination of the Canon Law to show that in both matter and treat-

[4] *Pseudo-Martyr*, sig. C, § 18, and D § 18.

ment its unreliability affords to the Roman Church "no warrant, to aduenture these dangers, for this refusall" [that is, the consequences contingent upon refusing to take the Oath of Allegiance to the King]. Thus, while respecting the "obligation which belongs to the ancient *Canons* and *Decrees* of the Church," he attempts "a briefe Consideration upon all the bookes thereof," and "a particular suruey of all those Canons, which are ordinarily cyted by those Authours, which maintaine this temporall Iurisdiction in the Pope." [5] The result is a careful criticism of the authority of the Canons, showing a familiarity with the material for which he apologizes by saying, "I may rather be ashamed of hauing read so much of this learning, then not to haue read all." [6]

The whole of the Canon Law, Donne accounts *"a Satyr, and Miscellany of diuers and ill digested Ingredients,"* the "straw" and "Feathers" thrown by the Roman Church into the breach made in her armor of authority "in this *spirituall* warre which the *Reformed Churches* vnder the conduct of the *Holy Ghost,* haue vndertaken against *Rome,"* not, he adds, "to destroy her, but to reduce her to that obedience, from which at first she vnaduisedly strayed, but now stubbornly rebels against it." [7] Turning then particularly to "the first part . . . the *Decretum,* compiled by *Gratian,"* he finds it "so diseased and corrupt a member thereof, that all the Medicines, which the learned *Archbishop Augustinus,* applied to it, and all that the seueral *Commissioners, . . .* haue practised vpon it, haue not brought it to any state of perfect health, nor any degree of conualescence." [8] Gratian, Donne remarks, deceives in matters of faith as well as fact; but it is the latter which concerns us primarily, for in exposing the errors of "fact," Donne shows how critically he has considered the text. In general, he observes, the text is completely enervated by gloss and comment that distinguish it as having no relation to the vital expression of a Scripture inspired by the Holy Ghost.[9] Though Gratian makes mistakes in *"Chronologies,"* as when he gives "Pope *Nicholas* a place in the Councell of *Carthage,* who was dead before," these errors are nothing compared to his deliberate "falsifications" in which Donne finds "malignitie and danger to our cause." Gratian misquotes Ambrose and plays free with other sources. His text as transmitted abounds in scribal errors.[10] Furthermore, the critics of the Canons have gone far to strip them of authority by refusing to recognize their uneven quality and the varying intelligence of their authors, as indicated in Bellarmine's declaration

[5] *Ibid.,* pp. 264-65.   [6] *Ibid.,* p. 321.   [7] *Ibid.,* pp. 267, 264.
[8] *Ibid.,* p. 267.   [9] *Ibid.,* p. 271.   [10] *Ibid.,* p. 268.

that any criticism of the Canons is a sin against the Holy Ghost; by exploiting them for partisan purposes; and by a generally careless regard for the text, resulting in misleading quotation and the omission of words on which great store is set.[11]

In refuting the pope's claim to temporal jurisdiction Donne, again, is moving on the grounds of the best Renaissance scholarship when he cites the forgery of the Donation of Constantine on which the papal prerogative in civil affairs was presumed to have been established. How well Donne appreciated Lorenzo Valla's significant piece of philological research is evidenced by his reference to the "barbarous language discording from that time" when the *Donation* was supposed to have been drafted; its "false Latine vnworthy of an Emperours Secretarie"; and its mention of the "Patriarchate of Constantinople, before it had either that *Dignity,* or that *Name.*" Donne thinks its spuriousness is also affirmed by the fact that "the *Emperour* had not power, to giue away halfe his Empire, and that that *Bishop* [the pope] had not capacitie to receiue it." Consequently, it may be read as any other fable, "to study what the Allegory thereof should be." [12]

It is the exactness of the scriptural text, however, that concerns Donne most. The authority of the Bible as the authentic voice of the Holy Ghost he never doubted. Thus, as he shared with the Reformation its regard for the Bible as the certain source of Christian doctrine, so he grasped the importance of establishing the most correct reading if the doctrine based thereon was to be considered sound. This subject involves a study of Donne's familiarity with numerous translations of the Scriptures into English and other tongues that appeared throughout the Reformation, as well as his acquaintance with the available texts in the ancient languages, to which he frequently alludes; [13] but here we can touch upon so large a subject only by noting typical passages in which Donne's scholarly interest in the Biblical text appears. The numerous situations illustrating Donne's high respect for textual accuracy usually center upon establishing the correctness of the text from

[11] *Ibid.,* pp. 267-77.   [12] *Ibid.,* p. 296.

[13] Without attempting to make critical comment, I wish to call attention to the following texts of the Scriptures that Donne makes use of: "the Arabique translation," "the Chaldee Paraphrase," "the Syriack Translation of S. *Matthew,*" the Vulgate (the "Roman translation"), Tremellius, "the Septuagint," "Pagnins translation," "Luther . . . in his German translation," "the Complutense Bible," "that collection . . . made upon this variation," "the great Bible," "the Bishops Bible," "the Geneva Bible," "the Kings Bible" ("the Kings version," or "the great translation"), the texts of "some translators" ["Symmachus," in Alford's note, *Works of John Donne* (London, 1839), V, 477].

which he is preaching. From these one may derive at least two important principles whereby he seeks to establish the soundness of the
accepted reading: a comparison of the text with other translations and
its final reference to the oldest text that he knows as the most authentic;
and, second, a comparison of the words of problematical meaning in
his text with their usage elsewhere. The following from a Lenten
sermon preached before the King as late as 1630, when Donne's
ability as a preacher was proved and his scholarship brought to as high
a state of excellence as it was to reach, will demonstrate both. The
text of the sermon is from one of his favorite books, Job, the sixteenth
chapter, verses seventeen to nineteen: *"Not for any injustice in my
hands; Also my prayer is pure. O earth cover not thou my blood; and
let my cry have no place. Also now behold, my Witnesse is in heaven,
and my Record is on high."* [14]

According to his accustomed practice, Donne partitions the text into
several divisions of thought briefly set forth in the opening paragraphs. Here the text is "digested" into three parts, the last one, with
which we are particularly concerned, being that

it [that is, *"Also now behold, my Witnesse is in heaven, and my Record is
on high"*] delivers us the foundation of his [Job's] confidence, and the re-
covery from this his infirmity, and from his excesse in the manner of expressing it, if he have beene over-bold therein, *My Witnesse is in heaven, and my
Record is on high;* God is his Witnesse, that that which they charge him
with, is false, That that which he saies in his own discharge (in that sense
that he saies it) is true.

In closing his summary, he says, "in these three branches, and in some
fruits, which, in passing, we shall gather from them, we shall determine all that appertaines to these words." Inviting his auditors to
accept his "humble petition . . . That you will be content to heare
plaine things plainly delivered," he develops the first two "branches"
carefully, and passes on to the third, where, "We must do in this last, as
we have done in our former two parts, crack a shell, to tast the kernell,
cleare the words, to gaine the Doctrine." The "shells" to be cracked are
the phrases, "my witness" and "my record"; the way he proceeds to
get at their meat may be left to Donne himself:

I am ever willing to assist that observation, That the books of Scripture are
the eloquentest books in the world, that every word in them hath his waight
and value, his taste and verdure. And therefore must not blame those Translators, nor those Expositors, who have, with a particular elegancy, varied the
words in this last clause of the Text, *my witnesse,* and *my record.* The oldest

[14] *LXXX Sermons,* 13, fols. 127-36.

Latine Translation received this variation, and the Latine, even *Tremellius* himselfe, (as close as he sticks to the Hebrew) retaines this variation, *Testis,* and *Conscius.* And that collection, which hath been made upon this variation, is not without use, that *conscius* may be spoken *de interno,* that God will beare witnesse to my inward conscience; and *testis, de externo,* that God will, in his time, testifie to the world in my behalfe. But other places of Scripture will more advance that observation of the elegancy thereof, than this; for in this, the two words signifie but one and the same thing, it is but *witnesse, and witnesse,* and no more. Not that it is easie to finde in Hebrew (nor, per-chance, in any language) two words so absolutely Synonymous, as to signifie the same thing, without any difference, but that the two words in our Text are not both of one language, not both Hebrew. For, the first word, *Gned,* is an Hebrew word, but the other, *Sahad,* is Syriaque; and both signifie alike, and equally, *testem, a witnesse. He that heares the voice of swearing, and is a witnesse,* says *Moses* (Levit. v. 1), in the first word of our text; and then the *Chalde* paraphrase, intending the same thing, expresses it in the other word, *Sahad.* So in the contract between Laban and Jacob, Laban calls that heap of stones, which he had erected, *Iegar-Schadutha* (Gen. xxxi. 47), by an extraction from the last word of our Text, *Sahad;* Jacob calls it, by the first word: and the reason is given in the body of the text it selfe, in the vulgat Edition, (though how it got thither, we know not, for, in the Originall it is not) *Vterq juxta proprietatem linguae suae;* Laban spake in his language, Syriaque, Jacob spake in his, Hebrew, and both called that heape of stones, *a witnesse.*

If such an exposition was inserted to flatter the royal ears, similar expositions were also lavished upon his ordinary hearers at St. Paul's and St. Dunstan's, and if they were mere flattery, we may assume that his auditory paid dearly enough for it in the hard coin of the unre-laxed attention which Donne insisted upon. True, this is not the angel preaching from the cloud, whom Walton loved to hear; nor is it the kind of exposition London thronged to St. Paul's to listen to; in fact, the "angel" never remained in the cloud throughout his discourse, but often descended to such levels of erudition as that laid out above, which Donne regarded as a plain way of delivering plain things. Even if it fed the pride of his hearers, that pride must soon have subsided before their awareness of being led on by the preacher's sincerity and the significance of his larger purpose. The end is the revelation of the nature of a genuine Christian experience, to whose validity the Scrip-tures give assent; it is not the exposition of a point of doctrine. Yet, the truth of the experience is not to be accepted until the words in which it is affirmed are established as the authentic and correct expression.

Against misleading and subversive interpretation of authors, secular and divine, Donne consistently takes his stand. An example is his criticism of the way Bellarmine construes the attacks of Dante, Boccaccio, and Petrarch upon the Court of Rome:

when *Bellarmine* vndertooke to aunswere all, which had beene obiected out of *Dante,* and *Bocace,* and *Petrarche,* against *Rome,* it was but a lasie escape, and a round and Summarie dispatch vpon wearinesse, to say, that all that was meant of the *Court of Rome,* not of the *Church;* and therefore it was a wise abstinence in him, not to repeate *Petrarchs* words, but to recompense them by citing other places of *Petrarch* in fauour of the *Romane Church.* For though *Petrarch* might meane the *Court,* by the name of *Babilon,* and by imputing to it *Couetousnesse* and *Licentiousnesse,* yet when he charges *Rome* with *Idolatrie,* and cals it the *Temple of Heresie,* can this be intended of the *Court of Rome?* [15]

One abusive use of authority Donne calls by the name "detorsion," or, in proverbial language, the practice of making the devil quote Scriptures for his own purpose. How vicious this practice is may be gathered from Pope Sixtus V's effort to prove the legitimacy of the formality of kissing the pope's feet out of isolated and irrelevant passages in Isaiah, St. Luke, and Deuteronomy wherein the words "kissing" and "feet" happen to appear. "This Bishoppe," Donne continues,

is so transported with this rage of detorting scriptures, that rather then not mis-applie them, hee will apply them to his owne Condemnation: For thus hee concludes his Epistle with the wordes of the Apostle: *Gaudeo siue per veritatem, siue per occasionem, Romanae Ecclesiae dignitatem extolli:* so that it is all one to him, whether scriptures bee faithfully applyed or no, so it be to the profit and aduantage of that Church.[16]

The persistent condemnation of a malicious wresting of word or sentence from the context of a book would seem to be derived from Donne's disposition to view no fact, thought, or experience as unrelated to some larger pattern of facts, ideas, or experiences. It becomes something more profound than a mere observance of logical relationships; it is rather an awareness that within the complex interior of the mind things are bound together as they depend upon one ultimately common source, or as they are associated through a highly individualized experience of sense or reflection. As applied to his learning, this principle takes the form of an insistence on the interpretation of the part as it is related to the whole—the word as it is an element of the sentence, the sentence as it is an ingredient of the larger text—and the subordination of detail to the controlling purpose.

Thus in *Biathanatos,* when weighing the authority of the three great

[15] *Pseudo-Martyr,* pp. 338-39.   [16] *Ibid.,* pp. 88-90.

THE TEXT SAVES US

sources of knowledge: the light of nature, reason, and the Scriptures, Donne protests against those who abuse the last by weaving whole webs of argument from one isolated text.

If any small place of Scripture, misappeare to them to bee of use for justifying any opinion of theirs; . . . they extend it so farre, and labour, and beat it, to such a thinnesse, as it is scarce any longer the Word of God, only to give their other reasons a little tincture and colour of gold, though they have lost all the waight and estimation.

Such "detorsion" is directly contrary to the scriptural injunction "That no Prophecie in the Scripture, is of private interpretation" (2 Pet. i. 20); consequently, "the whole Church may not be bound and concluded by the fancie of one, or of a few, who being content to enslumber themselves in an opinion, and lazy prejudice, dreame arguments to establish, and authorize that." [17]

Donne tells the reader that his justification for writing *Pseudo-Martyr* and the reason why he undertook a criticism of the false martyrdom encouraged by the Roman Church will be revealed only to him "who shall be pleased to read the whole worke." [18] In his sermons this principle is most frequently put to work in the treatment of his own Biblical texts and in his exposition of the validity of sacraments and religious ceremony. Invariably Donne places his text in its relation to the immediate context from which it is drawn and to other parts of the Scripture illustrating the theme which it implies. Though passages where he sets forth "the history which occasioned and induced these words" [19] (of the text) are too numerous to make citation practicable, it will not be amiss to call particular attention to one of his most successful efforts to correct the results of a literal interpretation of an isolated text. For his Prebend Sermon of May 8, 1625,[20] he chose the following text from the Psalms: *"Surely men of low degree are vanity, and men of high degree are a lie; To bee laid in the balance, they are altogether lighter than vanity."* Gloomy as the scriptural statement is, Donne affirms that measured against the standard of human excellence established by God himself "unconditionally we cannot annihilate man, not evacuate, not evaporate, not extenuate man to the levity, to the vanity, to the nullity of this Text." Its narrow, literal acceptance overlooks the fact that

man is not onely a contributary Creature, but a total Creature; He does not onely make one, but he is all; He is not a piece of the world, but the world it self; and next to the glory of God, the reason why there is a world. . . .

[17] Page 155.
[19] *LXXX Sermons*, 42, fol. 412.
[18] "An Advertisement to the Reader," sig. ¶.
[20] *Ibid.*, 65, fols. 643-62.

But [he goes on to say] we must not determine this consideration here, That
man is something, a great thing, a noble Creature, if we refer him to his end,
to his interest in God, to his reversion in heaven; But when we consider
man in his way, man amongst men, man is not nothing, not unable to assist
man, not unfit to be relyed upon by man; for, even in that respect also, God
hath made *Hominem homini Deum*, He hath made one man able to doe the
offices of God to another, in procuring his regeneration here, and advancing
his salvation hereafter. . . . Neither hath God determined that power of as-
sisting others, in the Character of Priesthood onely . . . but he hath also
made the Prince, and the secular Magistrate, a god, that is able to doe
the offices, and the works of God. . . . God sends man to the Priest, to the
Prince, to the Judge, to the Physitian, to the souldier, and so . . . to the
Merchant, and to cunning Artificers . . . that all that man needs might be
communicated to man by man.

With the conditions of man's greatness established and repeated,
Donne reaffirms in the spirit of a new age awakened to his god-like
felicity, paradoxical as it may be, that

still, simply, absolutely, unconditionally, we cannot say, Surely men, men altogether, high or low, or meane, all are less than vanity. And surely they that
pervert and detort such words as these, to such a use, and argue from thence,
Man is nothing, no more than a worme or a fly, and therefore what needs
this solemne consideration of mans actions, it is all one what he does, for all
his actions, and himselfe too are nothing; They doe this but to justifie or
excuse their own lazinesse in this world, in passing on their time, without
taking any Calling, embracing any profession, contributing any thing to the
spirituall edification, or temporall sustentation of other men.

It is only when we "take the words, as the Holy Ghost intends them
comparatively [italics mine], what man compared with God, or what
man considered without God, can doe any thing for others, or for
himself?" that they will yield their meaning. With man thus exalted
to the privilege of being compared with the infinite greatness of God,
the first part of the sermon is concluded, the preacher having avoided
the literalness that debases human value, and the presumption that
recognizes no existing standards of judgment. If the outcome is paradoxical, at least, it is not ironical, for Donne has made the one
comparison that is not odious. The nobility of man is not impugned
because it falls short of the divine glory, any more than human wisdom is debased by being called the "foolishness of God." Donne would
have appreciated fully that Milton meant more than a figurative allusion
to Edward King's drowning in "*Lycidas* sunk low, but mounted high."
Both appreciate how the thoughts which environ a word or phrase
substantially affect its meaning.

Further evidence of the stress Donne lays upon the consideration of a subject in relation to its surroundings is to be found in his attitude toward religious ceremony and the forms of worship. Faithfully and devoutly as Donne performed the offices of priest, he did not celebrate a service like a puppet responding to liturgical wire pulling; nor did he have Milton's lack of sympathy for all ritual and sacrament. There are, fundamental and necessary to all Christian Churches, certain forms of worship through which devotion to the Christian life is most properly and effectively expressed, such as the sacraments of the Lord's Supper and Baptism, and prayer. These forms of worship are not just beautiful symbols, any more than they are empty formulae perpetuated by a superstitious priesthood. They are authentic instruments of worship, avenues defining one's access to Deity, not, however, efficacious in themselves. If a service is to assist in the' work of regeneration, to it the worshipper must bring an active soul; he must be something more than a passive, unresponsive subject. Thus, the meaning of forms of worship is largely the product of Donne's own reflection, disciplined by the thought of great spirits like Augustine and Calvin and by the freshness and vitality of his spiritual life.

It is a Candlemas Day service that gives Donne the occasion to consider the subject of religious ceremony.[21] First, he notes that the celebration of "the day of lights" is an occasion taken over from the Gentiles, having affinities with the celebration among the pagans of the feast of *Februus* or *Pluto*. From this he is led to observe that "the Church of God, in the outward and ceremoniall part of his worship, did not disdain the ceremonies of the Gentiles."]Nor does Donne hesitate to state the shocking truth that the most sacred institutions of worship in the Church are derived from pagan ritual:

. . . Men who are so severe, as to condemne, and to remove from the Church, whatsoever was in use amongst the Gentiles before, may, before they are aware, become Surveyors, and Controllers upon Christ himself, in the institution of his greatest seales: for Baptisme, which is the Sacrament of purification by washing in water, and the very Sacrament of the Supper it self, religious eating, and drinking in the Temple, were in use amongst the Gentiles too.

Donne's conception of Christianity is too catholic to allow him to be greatly disturbed by these seeming perversities of history.]Though the ceremonies of which he speaks are to be found in use among the Gentiles and are abused by them, they are more likely to have been adopted and instituted by the Jews before Christ took them and re-

[21] *Ibid.*, 12, fols. 112-23.

stored them to good use. It is the use to which a thing is put rather than the thing itself that determines its value; therefore, as Christ "returned to a good use againe" what he found corrupted by pagans and Jews, so the Reformed Church is right in not giving up "some ceremonies which had been of use in the Primitive Church," just because they had been "depraved and corrupted in the Romane." Thus, carefully and learnedly Donne attempts to dispel the illusions and fears from minds becoming infected by a strong prejudice against all religious practices reminiscent of papistry. Any notion that he himself is tainted with Roman superstition is cleared away by his condemnation of the way "the people doe commit Idolatry, in their manner of adoring the Bread in the Sacrament." Donne complains that "they never preach against this error of the people, nor tell them wherein that Idolatry lies." At the same time, Donne teaches how a right use of ceremony, whatever its derivation, or however corrupted in the past, can be made to contribute to true worship by awakening the religious imagination, or by symbolizing a spiritual experience. Thus, the feast of lights is celebrated in the Church "because he who was the light of the world, was this day presented and brought into the Temple . . . The Church would signifie, that as we are to walk in the light, so we are to receive our light from the Church, and to receive Christ, and our knowledge of him, so as Christ hath notified himself to us."

Turning then to the text, as it is "a piece of a Sermon, of that blessed Sermon of our Saviours, which is called the Sermon of Beatitudes," he becomes involved in the treatment not only of the historical background of that sermon but also of the "sacrament" of preaching as instituted by Christ. In the course of the development of the latter theme he takes up the matter of how a sermon should be delivered, "in what manner, in what position of body Christ preached this Sermon." According to St. Matthew, "it seemes that Christ preached sitting," according to St. Luke, "he preached standing." Donne concludes from the scriptural evidence, that "for the most part, Christ did preach sitting." The fact that this fashion no longer prevails argues for the utter unimportance of following a rule of thumb in religious ceremony. This observation makes an easy transition to a comment on the disputed question of how the Holy Sacrament should be received and an affirmation of the utter folly of denouncing the common practice of the Church as a violation of the Scriptures, when the Scriptures themselves are vague and inconsistent on the subject:

Why then will such men, as in all actions of Divine Service, pretend to limit every thing precisely to the patterne of Christ himself, to doe just as he did, and no otherwise, why will they admit any other position of the body, in preaching, then sitting, since, *ut plurimum,* at least, for the most part, Christ did preach sitting? Or if Christ did both sit, and stand, why will they not acknowledge, that all positions of the body, that are reverent, are indifferent in themselves, in the service of God; and being so, why will they not admit that position of the body, which being indifferent in it selfe, is by the just command of lawfull authority, made necessary to them, that is, kneeling at the Sacrament? They who refuse it, pretend but two Reasons; First, because Christ at the institution thereof, did not use that position of kneeling, but sitting; Secondly, because they might scandalize others, or enter a false beleefe into others, who should see them kneele, that they kneeled in such adoration thereof, as the Papists doe.

By close searching among the bits of evidence afforded by the Scriptures and by secular history Donne is rewarded by the discovery that "it cannot be a cleare case, In what position of body Christ did institute this Sacrament." His argument runs thus: "There was at that time, a civill Supper, the ordinary houshold Supper, and there was a legall Supper, the eating of the Passeover, and then this Sacramentall Supper, of a new institution; And it is cleare, that Christ did not continue one position all this while, but he arose and did some actions between; Neither could that position of body, which they used at the Table, for their civill Supper, and naturall refection, be properly called a sitting, for it was rather a lying, a reclining, a leaning upon a bed." Immediately there follows a subtle stroke, one often practiced by Milton, showing that those who would discount the traditional form, themselves contradict their own scriptural authority:

. . . And let it be exactly a sitting, and let that sitting run through all the three Suppers, yet how will that position of sitting, justifie that Canon, which hath pased in a Synod amongst our neighbours, *Liberum est stando, sedendo, eundo, coenam celebrare, non autem geniculando?* How will standing, or walking, be any more maintainable than kneeling, by Christ's example? and yet they say, sitting, or walking, or standing, they may receive, but kneeling they must not; But this, I presume that particular Synod did not declare by way of Doctrine, to binde other Churches, but enjoyned a Discipline for their owne.

The second objection, that kneeling for the Sacrament betokens "the Adoration of the Romane Practise" is answered more directly, for the English Church attaches no superstitious meaning to the bread and wine as the catechism makes clear; only because kneeling is the position of greatest reverence should it be assumed at the reception of the Sacrament. Coming within a time soon to encounter Laud's high-handed compulsion of strict formulary conduct, as well as the crudities of dissenters throwing their hats upon the communion table, Donne's attitude seems thoroughly temperate and sane. Though his resolution of the matter accords with "the just command of lawfull authority," his reasons for accepting this authority appeal to the reverent spirit and are not demands made by any one bishop's sense of ecclesiastical decorum. Moreover, it is because of a painstaking and scholarly criticism of the problem that he is able to reach so commendable a conclusion, not because he has exercised an arbitrary power which a dogmatic person might well have considered his prerogative.

XIII

ENGRAFTING OLD AUTHORS

In our treatment of Donne's scholarship, it is pertinent also to take into account the principle governing his use of authors. Garnishing a discourse with quotation from many books was an accepted method common to pamphleteer and preacher—in fact, to all who wrote on learned subjects. In following an approved method, it may seem that Donne is simply keeping within a scholarly tradition inherited from the past, but within any tradition one may exercise considerable originality, and it is because Donne does not fall compactly into a stereotyped practice that the present subject is pressed upon our attention. Unconscious, instinctive adherence to traditional practices makes originality —sometimes, even earnestness—impossible, or, at least, seem unnecessary; on the other hand, awareness of the traditional mode of doing a thing marks the beginning of its decay, for it implies a deliberate use of method that results in lifeless imitation or encourages a critical attitude that sooner or later must transform the tradition into something that it was not in the beginning. That Donne has such a conscious appreciation of the use of authors is disclosed at the outset of his ambitious prose career, where it receives expression in a passage from *Biathanatos,* already cited in part:

Because I undertooke the declaration of such a proposition as was controverted by many, and therefore was drawne to the citation of many authorities, I was willing to goe all the way with company, and to take light from others, as well in the iourney as at the journeys end. If therefore in multiplicity of not necessary citations there appeare vanity, or ostentation, or digression my honesty must make my excuse and compensation, who acknowledg as *Pliny* doth [*That to chuse rather to be taken in a theft, then to give every man due, is* obnoxii animi, et infelicis ingenii.] I did it the rather because scholastique and artificiall men use this way of instructing; and I made account that I was to deale with such, because I presume that naturall men are at least enough inclinable of themselves to this doctrine.[1]

Apart from the Holy Scriptures, which are of paramount authority for Donne, his "sources" fall roughly into four groups of authors: the early Fathers of the Church, both Greek and Latin; the schoolmen; the "later" writers (theologians) of both the Roman and the

[1] Page 23.

Reformed Churches; and, finally, the great body of secular writers, the philosophers, historians, and scientists of ancient and modern times. Although an examination of Donne's use of all these sources cannot be made here, a generalization to be drawn from the study made of the influence of the latter group of authors in earlier chapters of this work can be safely applied to his use of authors of the first three groups. This generalization is that Donne does not allow authority to usurp the foreground of his particular purpose, that he successfully subordinates learning to his own ends. The achievement of such a subordination is literary as well as logical. Quotation, allusion, and figurative expression derived from learning, while directing the attention to their origins, tend always to become absorbed into his manner of expression. The literary method of subordination is supplemented by a logical approach to the use of learned materials that manifests itself in a critical attitude toward these materials. Evidence of this critical attitude particularly present in his prose writings appears in the form of a conscious use of the opinions of authors for analysis and argument; in an insistence on accurate and honest use of quotation; in an appreciation of the varying quality of men's thoughts; and last, in an attitude of caution toward singular and unconfirmed opinion.

In the Preface to *Biathanatos,* Donne's most elaborately documented writing, we find this confession: "Every branch which is excerpted from other authors, and engrafted here, is not written for the readers faith, but for illustration and comparision." [2] If not *for* the reader's faith, then certainly not *with* the writer's belief in their uniform value. Not only in this singular essay, but also in the sermons, Donne gives adequate evidence of his lavish use of quotation and allusion for "illustration." Illustration, however, is not for Donne an idle hanging of paper flowers upon blank walls of thought; it is not, in short, superficial and superfluous decoration. His own word "engrafted" is more descriptive of the effect he aims to produce. Unlike Burton's *Anatomy,* which gives the impression of being an elaborate macaronic, Donne's better prose presents the form of a unified discourse, with the learned matter gleaned from many books, thoroughly digested, and incorporated into the structure of the thought. The result, with its easy reference to Pliny, to those "engines of God," Augustine and Aquinas, or to Ptolemy's and Aristotle's outworn spectacles,[3] may seem to present a ragged and bizarre pattern to the eye and ear accustomed to the more direct statement and simpler rhythms of Swift and Defoe, or to the elegance of Gibbon's parallel and balanced structures; yet,

[2] Page 23.   [3] *LXXX Sermons,* 80, fol. 818.

the fact is that "all the Citations of places of Scriptures, . . . all the deducements, and inferences of the Schooles, . . . all the sentences of ornament produced out of the Fathers" [4] do not obtrude themselves harshly upon the reader. They fall naturally and smoothly enough into the fluent periods of his discourse, as if an intimate part of the corporate body of his thought, disposed with an art that makes learning appeal to the emotions as well as strengthen the exposition. The reason for such control of external materials, apart from the mastery of the thought contained therein, is partly the result of careful attention to the effect of the spoken word—an effect not absent in the reproductions of oral address, made often many years after its delivery. It is partly, too, the result of the way Donne is predisposed to regard all things as capable of being, in some way, related by the imagination.

To his insistence upon the honest use of authors considerable attention has already been paid. Between the practice of making learning minister to the establishment of such conscious and legitimate purposes as control Donne's efforts and the practice of a perverse use of information to sustain personal ambition, narrow prejudice, and intrigue, there are worlds of difference. It is to point this difference that Donne persistently derides the controversial methods of the schoolmen, involving, as they do, a careless and unfair use of authority. The *locus classicus* of Donne's statement of this principle of intellectual integrity is in *Pseudo-Martyr*, where he declares:

I haue no where made any Author, speake more or lesse, in sense, then hee intended, to that purpose, for which I cite him. If any of their owne fellowes from whom I cite them, haue dealt otherwise, I cannot be wounded but through their sides. So that I hope either mine Innocence, or their own fellowes guiltinesse, shall defend me, from the curious malice of those men, who in this sickly decay, and declining of their cause, can spy out falsifyings in euery citation: as in a iealous, and obnoxious state, a Decipherer can pick out Plots, and Treason, in any familiar letter which is intercepted.[5]

Perhaps in no way does Donne's use of authors commend itself more vigorously to our sympathies than in his recognition that the quality of books is by no means uniform. Even Homer nods, and Donne knows it—the Holy Scriptures themselves are not of uniform value for edification nor of equal beauty throughout. Aquinas and Augustine, though always treated with respect, are not always subject to approval. Donne departs from Aquinas whenever he considers his opinion unsound, as in his too enthusiastic approval of martyrdom,[6] his controversy with Scotus,[7] his doctrine of "works," and his too-great

---

[4] *Ibid.*, 12, fol. 114. [5] Sig. ¶₂. [6] *Ibid.*, p. 204.
[7] *LXXX Sermons*, 7\ fol. 66. Donne declines to enter the controversy.

emphasis on reason as a help to the knowledge of God.[8] Nor does he hesitate to express himself against Augustine when his too-narrow interpretation of the Scriptures warps their meaning.[9] Likewise, though the Venerable Bede has said many good things, his history suffers from the inclusion of too many fairy tales about early Britain.[10] On the contrary, his bitterest enemy, Bellarmine, may occasionally commend himself to Donne's favor, though it is feared that this concession is more damaging to Bellarmine's cause than ennobling to Donne's charity.[11]

Among his judgments passed upon authors there are anomalies such as his apparent reversal of opinion on Pico della Mirandola and Francis George; but more often they are straightforward criticisms, resulting from a demand for accuracy or from the estimation of their value according to a standard of liberality and soundness of doctrine which they approach or fall short of. Because his tribute to Francis George in the *Essays in Divinity*, as "that transcending Wit," [12] and his esteem for Pico, even to the extent of applying the method of exegesis of the *Heptaplus* in the *Essays in Divinity*,[13] stand at such odds with the way they are treated in the *Catalogus Librorum*, the question of what Donne actually thought of these writers is interesting. In the *Catalogus* Mirandola is described as that "super-seraphical John Picus," *"the Judaeo-Christian Pythagoras"* who has proved "the *Numbers 99 and 66 to be identical if you hold the leaf upside down"*; and George, as the author of a volume establishing "that the Book of Tobit is canonical; in which following the Rabbis and the more mystical of the Theologians, the hairs of the tail of his Dog are numbered, and from their various backward twists and intertwinings letters are formed which yield wonderful words." [14] Presumably a number of years separate these varying opinions; and a revision of opinion might well be expected and legitimate, but that the revision should be in favor of these mystical-cabalistic writers seems strange indeed.

Mrs. Simpson is doubtless right in concluding that "if the mystics and the occultists are satirized in the *Catalogus* and studied with fervent attention in the *Essays*, we have but one more proof of that curious

[8] *Essays in Divinity*, pp. 37-38.

[9] *LXXX Sermons*, 27, fol. 270. Donne also disagrees with Chrysostom and Ruffinus. Cf. *ibid.*, 50, fol. 506.

[10] *Pseudo-Martyr*, p. 106.

[11] *Ibid.*, pp. 110-11.

[12] Page 14.

[13] This subject needs further investigation. Donne refers to the *Heptaplus* in *Biathanatos*, pp. 49, 119, 174; and in *Essays in Divinity*, pp. 14, 21, 65.

[14] Pages 45, 44.

duality in Donne's nature which meets us in all his work." [15] But to leave Donne an inexplicable enigma, true or false as that conclusion may be, affords little satisfaction to the critic. There must be a way of untying the knot, and it would seem that by considering the divergent purposes of the two works referred to, together with the circumstances surrounding their composition, we may approach more nearly a satisfactory explanation. First, the *Catalogus* is in part a deliberate satire on the "high-brow" pretensions of Donne's intellectual compatriots and in part a revenge taken upon "spies and informers, like Topcliffe and Philips," and upon Bacon for his desertion of Essex. "The man who wrote it," Mrs. Simpson says, "had generous sympathies. He detested treachery and meanness, he hated pretence." [16] In short, the book expresses Donne's contempt for "humane infirmity" in a vigorous and amusing way. Thus, it is to be expected that such "occultists" as Pico and Francis George should be ridiculed for that which in their books is ridiculous, their hyper-enthusiasm for fantastic and mechanical methods of demonstrating the unity of all things and the validity of their mystical thought.

In the *Essays in Divinity* Donne's purpose and approach are vastly different. Whether or not we accept the younger Donne's statement that they were written for his father's own satisfaction on the threshold of his going into the ministry,[17] we must believe that they were "private" rather than public discourses, in which he wished to clear up in his mind certain fundamental religious problems. In this respect they are more fitting as a companion piece to the *Anniversaries* than as a prelude to his assumption of holy orders. Donne has been confronted, through a study of the new philosophy rendering the old conception of a unified world scheme entirely hopeless, with the necessity of discovering other means whereby the natural world may be significantly related to a new universal order. [In other words, with the machinery demolished by which the duality of physical and metaphysical were reconciled, a new way of resolving the contradiction has become imperative.] Donne looks to pagan and Christian alike, occultist and orthodox Christian, for means to help him; hence, the generous attitude toward Catholic and Protestant, cabalist and occult mystic, and Greek philosopher. In the cabalist a way was open for such a reconciliation; Professor Saurat thinks that the new world synthesis, incorporating the attitude of modern science, was formed upon this basis.[18] Donne, how-

---

[15] *Ibid.*, "Introduction," p. 21.   [16] *Ibid.*, p. 25.
[17] See title-page, "Before he entred into Holy Orders." See above p. 87 and n. 66.
[18] See *Milton, Man and Thinker* (New York, 1925).

ever, pledges no allegiance to the cabalists. Frequent as his references
are to Pico della Mirandola, Francis George, and Reuchlin in the
Essays in Divinity, he gives them finally but grudging support. In his
"private" exercises he might range freely among them; but even here,
despite the fact that he finds momentary pleasure in George's observation "that in the Decalogue there are just so many letters, as there are
precepts in the whole law," [19] there are passages of more significance
verifying his suspicion of this kind of arithmetical spiritualism. The
claims made upon his faith and reason by the Scriptures and by nature
and conscience he needs must resolve in a way more compatible with
his critical temperament; and the conclusions reached are far less
suspect than some of the authors selected to guide him to these ends.

Where there is little agreement among authors there can be no
uniform acceptance of their ideas. Donne finds that among the Fathers
within the Primitive Church itself there is dissension, as well as within
the ranks of the later expositors, the schoolmen, the reformers, and
the counter-reformers. The exercise of discrimination is imperative.
The rule that he follows, simple enough in its statement but susceptible
of abuse in its application, is that where there is agreement among
authors, there is significance in their thought.[20] In religious matters
agreement indicates accord with the Scriptures, which, correctly understood, provide the only sound basis for Donne's liberal conception of
Christianity. Donne appreciates fully, however, that error may be
perpetuated by agreement, just as truth cannot be extracted from petty
carping and contention. Hence, though he generally looks askance at
"singular" opinion, he unhesitatingly expresses opinions of his own
so long as he regards them as in accord with his conception of sound
doctrine. At one time he does Calvin the supreme honor of accepting
his opinion though it differs from that of all the Fathers and the
succeeding expositors and divines.[21] Donne's rule is conditioned by a
knowledge of history that reveals how infrequently agreement occurs
to which authoritative reference is possible. For instance, though he
generally approves the spirit of the ruling laid down by the Council
of Trent, "that no Scripture shall be expounded, but according to the
unanime consent of the Fathers," he concludes that this imperious
and arbitrary statement is not only repulsive to the free conscience,
but actually stupid. It is stupid, as he notes in a brilliant piece of his-

[19] *Essays in Divinity,* p. 211.
[20] For illustrations of this idea, see, for example, *Fifty Sermons,* 26, fols. 218 ff.;
LXXX Sermons, 21, fol. 200; *ibid.,* 69, fols. 695-96.
[21] *LXXX Sermons,* 24, fols. 234-35, on the interpretation of Job iv, 18.

torical criticism, because "it would trouble them to give many examples of that Rule" in their exposition of the authorship of the ninetieth Psalm, wherein there is no agreement whatsoever. Nor will he follow Bellarmine's advice, "which is indeed their most ordinary way amongst their Expositors," that "where the Fathers differ, to adhere to S. *Augustine.*" [22] So, thrust back upon the one point common to all expositors, that the book is canonical and that the words are therefore those of the Holy Ghost, Donne takes his text in hand and expounds it as he thinks best accords with the meaning that it contains.

In the citation made above from *Biathanatos,* along with the use of authors for "illustration," Donne includes "comparison." In declaring that the scholastic method does not result in "truth proved by arguments, authorities, similitudes," Bacon recognizes the usefulness of comparisons in analysis.[23] Only through the use of "similitudes," or comparisons, can the margin of truth existing among diversities be ascertained; or conversely, the degree of error common to like phenomena be determined. The emphasis Bacon lays on this method as a means of getting to the truth about nature makes it the most important instrument of his "novum organum," and, perhaps, its gravest defect, for it is too arbitrarily presumed upon in the absence of a well developed experimental technique. In the world of physical fact the comparative method depends for its success upon preliminary observation and description; in the realm of ideas it functions successfully only when charitably practiced and controlled by some principle or standard generally approved by the reason of all men. How difficult it is to find such a standard or how easy it is to abuse one is well illustrated by Voltaire's pronouncement upon the plays of Shakespeare, or Dr. Johnson's pedantic treatment of *Lycidas.* But Donne does have insight into the kind of principle that will suffice to control comparative statement. We shall repeat it:

Contemplative and bookish men, must of necessitie be more quarrelsome then others, because they contend not about matter of fact, nor can determine their controversies by any certaine witnesses, nor judges. But as long as they goe towards peace, that is Truth, it is no matter which way.[24]

It is this spirit which animates his comparative study of authors, old and new. It allows him to steer a straight course between the warring schools of Thomists and Scotists,[25] the Sestos and Abydos of the declining days of scholasticism; to see that it is more important to

[22] *Ibid.,* 79, fol. 803.
[24] *Biathanatos,* p. 20.
[23] *Of the Advancement of Learning, Works,* VI, 123.
[25] See particularly *Fifty Sermons,* 31, fol. 274.

direct the soul onward toward perfection than to wallow in the controversy of whether it came into the body by propagation or by infusion; and to take a rule from the Stoic Seneca [26] or to look with sympathetic eyes upon those "glimmerings" of true divinity which Plato and Trismegistus saw,[27] as well as to respect in full the teachings of Christ. In short, the principal force that Donne's "similitudes" communicates to his writings results from the fact that they tend to direct the reader's attention to the broad background of truth which Donne is expounding. This background may be enriched by supporting quotations, or it may be set in sharper outline by the differences exhibited between Donne's own thought and that of the author he is using.

In a great sermon from which quotation already has been drawn appear these words:

It hath been observed amongst Philosophers, that *Plato* speaks probably, and *Aristotle* positively; *Platoes* way is, It may be thus, and *Aristotles,* It must be thus. The like hath been noted amongst Divines, between *Calvin* and *Melanchthon; Calvin* will say, *Videtur,* It seemes to be thus, *Melanchthon,* It can be no otherwise but thus. But the best men are but Problematicall, Onely the Holy Ghost is Dogmaticall; Onely he subscribes this *surely,* and onely he seales with Infallibility.[28]

Apart from the acuteness of Donne's observation, there is here the expression of a great critical principle—the relativity of the best human learning. It is the expression of a conviction arising directly from Donne's cautious, skeptical temperament and a belief in the relative values of all human circumstance. Though strengthened by study and sharpened by the turmoil attendant upon the new philosophy, it is a way of thinking deeply rooted in his nature, as the early lines concluding *The Progresse of the Soule* gloomily reveal:

> Ther's nothing simply good, nor ill alone,
> Of every quality comparison,
> The onely measure is, and judge, opinion.[29]

According to where the emphasis falls in Donne's application of this principle, does it make clear the varying courses his skepticism is capable of taking. In *The second Anniversary,* where his "problematical" nature extends itself to answer the question,

> Poore soule, in this thy flesh, what dost thou know?[30]

it might seem that Donne's esteem for human knowledge has reached

[26] *XXVI Sermons,* 6, fol. 75.   [27] *Biathanatos,* p. 38.
[28] *LXXX Sermons,* 65, fol. 658.   [29] Grierson, I, 316, ll. 518-20.
[30] *Ibid.,* p. 258, l. 254.

its lowest pitch; but, in fact, neither here nor in the sermon referred to above does he cast bitter aspersions upon the potentialities of the human mind. It is rather the misdirection of man's intellectual energies that receives his criticism: the vain and imperious presumption of discovering truth—in the *Anniversary* truth amounts to an understanding of the will of God—by the same means used to explore the natural world from which only uncertain and precarious knowledge may be derived. Donne makes no unfair discrimination against the human intellect in declaring how far man's "yea, yea, and nay, nay" fall short of the wisdom of God, the "surely, verily" of the Holy Ghost. This realm of the *prima philosophia,* the unknowable kingdom of the divine will, if not to be entered, may be seen afar off only by the faculty of a simple and unquestioning faith in the divine Word. Thus, at one time Donne may emphasize the relativity of human knowledge to throw vanity and presumption into a stronger light; at another, he may strive to suggest the nature of the divine wisdom that the human mind may be ennobled by the inspiration of so sublime a contrast.

In the sum of its manifestations Donne's conception of the problematical nature of human learning comprises one of the most significant aspects of his scholarship. It includes not only an awareness of the relative value of knowledge but also an appreciation of the sanity of suspended judgment; it underscores, as stated earlier, the sense of the importance of historical circumstances in the interpretation of fact and idea; and, finally, it has a respect for tradition conceived not as an unchangeable description of life, but as an effort to generalize about human thought and conduct, and as a force continually being reshaped by the ever-changing condition of things. So closely related are these manifestations that an effort to classify the supporting evidence for their presence in Donne would be futile.

Perhaps it is in *Biathanatos* that Donne presents his most sustained argument for the consideration of traditional ideas and customs as subject to the influence of changing circumstances. Because suicide is generally assumed to be a violation of the three great currents of authority, understood as the law of God, the law of reason, and the law of nature, it is necessary for Donne to establish at the outset that obedience to these laws is not mandatory but contingent upon circumstances. "No law is so primary and simple, but it foreimagines a reason upon which it was founded: and scarce any reason is so constant, but that circumstances alter it." [31] Furthermore, Donne flees the ped-

[31] *Biathanatos,* p. 47.

antry of the schoolmen who distinguish between these primary laws. All are "so compos'd and elemented and complexion'd, that to distinguish and seperate them is a Chymick work: And either it doth only seeme to be done, or is done by the torture and vexation of schoole-limbicks, which are exquisite and violent distinctions. For that part of Gods Law which bindes alwayes, bound before it was written, and so it is but *dictamen rectae rationis* and that is the Law of Nature." [32] While stressing the unconventionality of this simplification, Donne warns the reader against falling into the current confusion of meanings given the term, law of nature, to which he has reduced all three laws.

This terme the law of Nature, is so variously and unconstantly deliver'd, as I confesse I read it a hundred times before I understand it once, or can conclude it to signifie that which the author should at that time meane. . . . if they will meane any thing, and speak to be understood, they must entend the law of rationall nature: which is that light which God hath afforded us of his eternall law; and which is usually call'd *recta ratio.*[33]

Again, " . . . the Christian law, and the law of nature, (for that is the law written in hearts) must be all one," as both are referred to their common source, man's "rationall nature." [34]

Not content with these abstract terms, Donne, as is his accustomed practice in dealing with moral and philosophical generalizations, translates them into the vernacular of the layman, where they come to life as something of vital human significance. Thus, "our safest assurance, that we be not mislead with the ambiguity of the word *Naturall Law,* and the perplex'd variety thereof in Authors, will be this, That all the precepts of Naturall Law, result in these, *Fly evill, seek good;* That is, doe according to Reason." With this catholic and charitable interpretation of the law of nature Donne can find no fault; it derives its authority from the "heart of man," and "our hearts shall ever not onely retaine, but acknowledge this Law." [35] However binding this law may be, it is binding only as it remains an expression of universal truth, not as it may be broken up into the pieces of law, the precepts deduced from it by overzealous philosophers and divines, for though these deductions may appear to follow logically from the controlling principle, "doe according to reason," they are not necessarily just and sound. At this point, Donne is at one with Aquinas who says, "The lower you goe towards particulars, the more you depart from the necessitie of being bound to it." Exactly what he means is made clear by his citation from Acacius:

[32] *Ibid.,* p. 34.
[34] *Ibid.,* p. 41.

[33] *Ibid.,* pp. 36, 39.
[35] *Ibid.,* p. 45.

It is naturall, and bindes all alwaies, to know there is a God. From this is deduced by necessary consequence, that God (if he be) must be worshipped; and after this, by likely consequence, that he must be worshipped in this or this manner. And so every Sect will a little corruptly and adulterately call their discipline *Naturall Law,* and enjoyn a necessary obedience to it.[36]

Having pointed out one of the major conditions respecting obedience to the law of nature, Donne is faced with the task of showing how his own thesis that self-homicide is not always a sin is compatible with the precept, "doe according to reason." The law of nature as it applies to his thesis is understood as the law of self-preservation; and it, too, is subject to corruption and adulteration by deductions suggested thereby which do not command universal obedience. In treating this delicate phase of his discourse he openly admits with Aeneas Sylvius that "though our substance of nature, (which is best understood of the foundations and principles, and first grounds of Naturall Law,) may not be changed, yet *functio natura,* (which is the exercise and application thereof,) and deduction from thence may, and must." Hence, there is not only justification for the violation of the law of self-preservation to be found in the lower order of nature (though it is unfortunate that Donne sought no more authentic a naturalist than St. Ambrose, "Philosophying divinely in a contemplation of Bees"), but also, there is stronger justification in "rectified reason" itself, which "instructs us often to preferre publique and necessary persons, by exposing our selves to unevitable destruction." In this heroical and unselfish extremity reason is acting in accordance with the supreme circumstance that alters it—the conscience, the final arbiter and judge in all matters of human conduct: "And he whose conscience well tempred and dispassion'd, assures him that reason of selfe-preservation ceases in him, may also presume that the law ceases too, and may doe that then which otherwise were against that law." [37]

With examples drawn from many sources to support and enrich his argument Donne concludes the first section of his discourse on how the light of nature may itself direct a man to the extremity of taking his own life. He then passes on to an exposition of the way "humane Lawes" may do the same. Here, he is among the concrete facts of human experience, liberated from a necessary indulgence in purely speculative concepts. His method of argument, however, remains very much the same. There are two branches of "humane Lawes," the civil and the canon, neither of which is so general that it "deserves the name of *Jus gentium,*" for if either could be so universally under-

[36] *Ibid.,* p. 46.   [37] *Ibid.,* pp. 46, 47.

stood it would be at one with the law of nature. The first branch, the civil law, "hath pronounced nothing against this *Selfe-homicide,* which we have now in disputation." The latter branch, the canon law, is so vast and so clumsily organized and so confused in its interpretation "as we know not in what books to seeke the limits thereof, nor by what rules to set the land-marks of her jurisdiction." Moreover, Donne can find "no tradition nor definition of the Church in the point at all [that is, that self-homicide is not always a sin], much lesse as of a matter of faith." [38]

[All law is subject to the control of two great forces, one external, the other internal: custom and conscience.] How the former, mutable from age to age, deprives precedent of its authority and renders "common opinion" the illusion of the short-sighted and biased historian, Donne illustrates by the citation of many historical events, all tending to confirm the pronouncement of Azorius that *"Controverters often say on both sides this is the common opinion; And certainely that is the common opinion in one Age which is not in another; yea, in one Kingdome at the same time, which is not in another, though both be Catholik."* [39] But even stronger than custom is the conscience of man, "which can in no case come to be so entangled and perplexed, that it can be forced to ch[u]se any thing naturally evill." So powerful are its claims that Donne discovers nowhere in his survey of the laws of both Church and State a single instance where its prerogative was justly or effectively impugned. [40]

Nor does Donne, in the third part of his argument, conclude from an examination of the divine law as laid down by the Scriptures that it is so absolutely and consistently binding as always to pronounce self-homicide a sin. With equal emphasis he argues that as all things on earth are mutable, so are the constructions placed upon the scriptural evidence which seems to oppose his thesis:

But since the Scripture it selfe teaches, [*That no Prophecie in the Scripture, is of private interpretation,*] the whole Church may not be bound and concluded by the fancie of one, or of a few, who being content to enslumber themselves in an opinion, and lazy prejudice, dreame arguments to establish, and authorize that. [41]

At the close comes the boldest effort of the entire book. That the expositors of the divine law are unreliable is assumed and proved; but even the law itself does not apply so generally as to make legitimate exception impossible. In the strictest of all Biblical canons, the

[38] *Ibid.*, pp. 78, 79, 82, 84.
[40] *Ibid.*, p. 124.
[39] *Ibid.*, pp. 84, 85.
[41] *Ibid.*, p. 155.

Decalogue, Donne finds that "there are naturally included and incorporated some exceptions," and "this case may fall within those exceptions." [42] The sanction for such freedom with the literal statement of the Biblical text lies in Donne's conception of evil as finally dependent upon the flexible standard of circumstance and thought, which in turn are amenable to the influence of the fluctuating conditions implicit in the passage of time. The idea is compactly summarized in his declaration that

to mee there appeares no other interpretation safe, but this, That there is no externall act naturally evill; and that circumstances condition them, and give them their nature; as scandall makes an indifferent thing hainous at that time; which, if some person go out of the roome, or winke, is not so.[43]

To have accepted as evidence for Donne's scholarship a book so generally regarded as one of the curiosities of literature and as little more than an ingenious rationalization of a morbid disposition may appear to some to be a suspect kind of criticism. Donne himself foresaw that *Biathanatos* was destined to wholesale condemnation if it ever came to light, but his reluctance to destroy it indicates that he believed a charitable examination of the arguments supporting his "misinterpretable subject" [44] would reveal the weakness of such censure. Revolting as the book may be upon hasty reading, it is, in fact, notably free from morbidity and the outward signs of perverted taste. The fascination of death for Donne, so frequently leading him to meditation on dust, and worms, and the decomposition of the body in the grave, suffers a singular suppression in this treatise. Even the prolonged recital of famous suicides is anecdotal rather than gruesome.[45] There is nothing like Hamlet's brooding or the deep moodiness of Montaigne's *That to Philosophize, Is to Learne How to Die*, to suggest that Donne is half in love with easeful death. To go no further than to regard *Biathanatos* as "an exercise in casuistry" [46] is to miss the fact that the method of exposition used was chosen deliberately as the best means of countering traditional criticism, not because Donne was incapable of treating the theme in any other manner. In fine, it appears that Donne had in mind to do something entirely different from that which he is commonly thought to have done, namely, to have submitted a clever, yet wholly dubious, case for suicide. And, as

[42] *Ibid.*, p. 176.
[43] *Ibid.*, pp. 173-74.
[44] See "To Sir Robert Ker with my book 'Biathanatos' at my going into Germany," Gosse, *op. cit.*, II, 124. [April, 1619.]
[45] *Biathanatos*, pp. 50 ff.
[46] *Simpson, op. cit.*, p. 156.

we shall see, his purpose was in truth much less perverse than this. His temperament may have dictated the particular subject through which to elaborate this purpose or it may be that his inclination to come to grips with serious and difficult matters persuaded him to choose among many this most stubborn obstacle to normal human sense. The title plainly states that *Biathanatos* is *A Declaration of that Paradoxe, or Thesis, that Selfe-homicide, is not so Naturally Sinne, that it may never be otherwise,* and in the Preface it is declared that my end is to remove scandall. For certainly God often punisheth a sinner much more severely, because others have taken occasion of sinning by his fact. If therefore wee did correct in ourselves this easines of being scandalized, how much easier and lighter might we make the punishment of many transgressers? for God in his judgements hath almost made us his assistants, and counsellors, how far he shall punish; and our interpretation of anothers sinne doth often give the measure of Gods Justice or Mercy.[47]

Certainly, neither the title nor the fuller statement of the purpose in the Preface can be construed to mean that Donne is trying to justify suicide; and only a deliberate effort to make the author say more than he intends can warrant the conclusion that these words are a guise to cover up his inclination to take his own life. The truth of this may be tested by noting that the only condition on which suicide is ever permissible is that "wherein the party is dis-interested, and only or primarily the glory of God is respected and advanced." [48] Neither at the time of the book's composition nor later was Donne ever so presumptuous or so much devoted to martyrdom as to think the wanton act of killing himself would go far to advance the glory of God. Thus, the "dangerous doctrine" is not that we may at times, under certain conditions, take our own lives but that the common opinion of self-homicide as a sin is contrary to historical evidence and a rational understanding of the true nature of sin.

Therefore, it is one of the grand illusions of the race that Donne wishes to dissipate, namely, that there are in nature certain practices that are fundamentally and naturally evil. Only through his grasp of the sense of the dependence of all things upon conditions imposed by time, place, and the human will, does his argument become convincing. In this respect *Biathanatos* is no mere casuistical exercise but an expression of the author's awareness that in a mutable world nothing can be held so constant as inflexibly to bind all men and every generation to its authority. The grandeur and philosophic breadth of this principle are obscured, it is true, by copious references to un-

---

[47] Pages 23-24.   [48] Page 99.

familiar authors, by the use of a terminology already becoming decadent in Donne's time, and by the application of a logical method aimed to convince "scholastique men" rather than twentieth-century critics. Nevertheless, the spirit of a new age lurks amidst the copia of illustration, syllogism, and obsolete conception of the "laws" assumed to be the controlling forces of life. The presence of this spirit triumphs over pedantry to give to the book any vitality that it has for us today. That Donne was aware of having put something more than learning into it, some share of himself, his sincerity and imagination, can alone account for the fact that he cherished it throughout his life and laid upon his friend, to whom he entrusted one of the manuscripts, the perplexing obligation of saving it from both the press and the flames —"and between those, do what you will with it." [49]

Shortly after the composition of *Biathanatos* followed *Pseudo-Martyr,* wherein Donne again illustrates the ultimate relativity of the influences assumed to control human destiny. In this respect *Pseudo-Martyr,* coming so shortly upon the heels of *Biathanatos,* presents a difficult problem to both Donne's conscience and his argumentative genius, in superficially demanding a complete reversal of the position taken in the earlier book. In *Biathanatos* he had argued that no act is naturally a sin simply because it seems to violate certain accepted laws. In *Pseudo-Martyr* it is required that he give evidence to show that martyrdom— one of the palliating conditions considered in *Biathanatos*—may at times be wrong, and particularly so when achieved in violation of the Oath of Allegiance to the King. There is no real contradiction in Donne's position, however, for in the earlier essay he has laid down the strictest sanction for martyrdom, the enlightened conscience directing itself upon the glory of God. The refusal to subscribe to a civil oath is entirely irrelevant to true martyrdom because it is encouraged by selfish and prejudiced ecclesiastical powers and entirely misunderstands the origin and scope of regal authority. The power of the king is as surely from God as that of the priest, and its purpose, for Donne, as for Dante, is the preservation of the peace and tranquility of human society.

The refutation of the claims of the "pseudo-martyrs" may thus be reduced to a consideration of the interrelations of temporal and ecclesiastical power. In their effort to justify false martyrdom the Roman party, Donne thinks, have misconstrued the evidence of history in that they formulate from isolated and doubtful examples of the encroachment of Church upon State a sweeping generalization that the

⁴⁹ "To Sir Robert Ker . . ."—Gosse, *op. cit.,* II, 124.

pope's authority extends to his power over the prince. Not only is
there abundant evidence that the current of history up to Gregory's
time consistently favors the unimpaired jurisdiction of the prince but
also that all arguments to the contrary are the concoction of men
ignorant of the historical facts. One example is the erroneous conception of the power of bishops, which Donne clears up by examining
the "derivation" of the word:

Bishop hath a metaphoricall, and similitudinarie deriuation, and being before
Christianitie applied to Officers, which had the ouerseeing of others, but yet
with relation to Superiours, to whom they were to giue an account, deuolu'd
conueniently vpon such Prelates, as had the ouerseeing of the inferiour
Clergie, but yet gaue them no acquitance and discharge of their dueties to the
Prince.[50]

But laying aside the testimony of history and following his usual
independence of mind Donne affirms that reasons of the past cannot
be adduced to support present conditions, for even if they have grown
out of the past they have assumed forms different from those in which
they originally were known.

There follows an exposition of the roots of temporal power, but
it is a "cloudie and muddie search, to offer to trace to the first roote of
Iurisdiction." One attributes it to the family, another to the "double
Iurisdiction of the soule ouer the body, and of the reason ouer the appetite"; but these explanations are "examples and illustrations, not Rootes
and Fountaines, from which Regall power doth essentially proceede,"
"since it growes not in man." [51] His conclusion favoring the theory of
the divine origin of temporal power, especially at the very time the
sovereignty of kings was being threatened, even transgressed, by the
disciples of Mariana, is expected, diplomatic, and even necessary if
the prince is to challenge effectively the theory of papal supremacy.
"Certainely all power is from God"; he writes, "And as if a companie
of Sauages, should consent and concurre to a ciuill maner of liuing,
Magistracie, & Superioritie, would necessarily, and naturally, and Di-
uinely grow out of this consent." [52]

Donne is not so completely bound to a theory that he is blind to
the contingencies which encompass it. He does not deny that other
influences may concur to help establish the power of kings nor that
it is immutable against all circumstances. His purpose demands, however, that he emphasize the fact that secular authority springs from
as legitimate and noble a source as spiritual authority:

[50] Pseudo-Martyr, pp. 33-34.   [51] Ibid., pp. 169-70.   [52] Ibid., p. 83.

Ecclesiastique authority is not so *immediate* from God, that he hath appointed any such certaine *Hierarchy,* which may vpon no occasion suffer any alteration or interuption; Nor is secular authority so *mediate,* or dependant vpon men, as that it may at any time be extinguished, but must euer reside in some forme or other.[53]

The qualification "in some forme or other" definitely lifts Donne's argument above mere academic disputation confined to the support of some particular conception of government. If he finds it possible to cast his lot with the Stuarts as far as the "forme" of secular government is concerned, he remains sensitive to the larger issues at stake, namely, that *any kind* of secular power has claims upon man equally as valid as those of the Church, and the corollary, that the Church has no priority in the imposition of obligation.

In the fairness characteristic of the discourse throughout, Donne lays down further conditions to flank his conception of the power of kings which lead him to the bold conclusion that "these circumstances giue it all the life it hath, so that to make it obligatory, or not so, depends vpon them." What are the circumstances? Simply, they are those which—in striking anticipation of Milton—would affect a king so that he "may growe to be no King." If we assume that a king must be obeyed,

It followes, Therfore they must be able to commaund iustly; therfore they must haue some to enable and instruct them; therefore they must doe according to their instruction; therefore if they doe not, they are subiect to their corrections; therefore if they be incorrigible, they are no longer Kings; and therefore no subiect can sweare perpetuall Obedience, to his person, who by his owne fault, and his superiours Declaration, may growe to be no King.

Thus, he has opened a breach in his argument through which his opponents might hope to enter; but he at once closes it against them:

yet it is impossible to discerne those circumstances, or vnentangle our consciences by any of those Rules, which their *Casuists* vse to giue, who to st[r]engthen the possession of the *Romane* Church, haue bestowed more paines, to teach how strongly a conscience is bound to doe according to a *Scruple,* or a *Doubt,* or an *Opinion,* or an *Errour,* which it hath conceiued, then how it might depose that *Scruple,* or cleare that *Doubt,* or better that *Opinion,* or rectifie that *Errour.*[54]

This passage makes eminently clear exactly where Donne's thought is leading him, namely, back again to the conclusion reached in *Biathanatos,* that no generalization, no arbitrary rule can hold the conscience.

[53] *Ibid.,* p. 81.   [54] *Ibid.,* pp. 225-27.

What at a glance seems like a restraint upon the freedom of the mind is essentially a declaration of independence, though here, because the circumstances do not require him to speak, Donne is silent upon the grounds whereon the conscience may even resist civil authority. That there are such grounds he has declared in *Biathanatos*. What Donne has done is to relieve the conscience of any obligation to "blind counsels" and to return it again to itself, where alone it can enjoy its most perfect freedom, secure in the precept dictated by right reason and confirmed by nature and the Holy Scriptures, that *"we must obay such a power, as can preserve us in Peace and Religion."* [55]

Upon matters of the spirit alone Donne's predisposition to regard all knowledge as relative does not encroach. They are referred ultimately to the dictates of an enlightened conscience. In doing this he is wielding his most powerful weapon against blind rule and arbitrary reason. Of the conscience he once wrote, "that's the Sphere I move in, and no higher." [56] But lest it be thought that he moved with an undisciplined course in this sphere of inmost privacy, it is well to recall his mature statement of the principle to which this conscience must submit. Though it is implied in many of his later utterances, nowhere does it receive more dramatic form than in the great Prebend Sermon of 1625:

It is in doctrines and opinions, as it is in designes and purposes; *Goe to*, (says the Prophet, by way of reprehension) *Goe to, you that say, we will goe to such a City, and trade thus and thus there, &c.* So, goe to, you that pronounce upon every invention, and Tradition of your own, a *Quicunque vult salvus esse*, Whosoever will be saved, must beleeve this, and clogge every problematicall proposition with an *Anathema,* Cursed be he, Excommunicated he that thinks the contrary to this: Goe to, you, that make matters of faith of the passions of men. So also, goe to you that proceed and continue in your sinnes, and say, Surely I shall have time enough to repent hereafter. Goe to you that in a spirituall and irreligious melancholy and diffidence in Gods mercy, say, Surely the Lord hath locked up his mercy from me, surely I shall never see that Sunne more, never receive, never feele beame of his mercy more, but passe through this darknesse into a worse. This word, *surely,* in such cases, in such senses, is not your mothers tongue, not the language of the Christian Church. She teaches you, to condition all in Christ; In him you are enabled to doe all things, and without him nothing. But absolutely, unconditionally, this *surely* is appropriated to the propositions, to the assertions of God himself. [57]

As in the great love poems a conception of love in its sincerity and earnestness outreaching the trivial conventions of feigned passion

[55] *Ibid.,* p. 225.   [56] *XXVI Sermons,* 5, fol. 67.   [57] *LXXX Sermons,* 65, fol. 658.

"conditions" his emotion, so here, in the maturity of many years and much experience, Christ conditions all his thinking. It is a confession of his submission to "a new control," but one that embraces rather than excludes the old. Nor is it wrapped up in any doctrine or opinion that makes it less effective for being "the language of the Christian Church." Some may argue that this contracts experience into too narrow a scope; that it definitely abrogates most of Donne's poetical ventures. It would be idle to say that Donne's love poems are within the range of doctrinally conceived orthodoxy; yet it is hard to dissociate the element of spirit from honest outrage, sincere passion, and fidelity to self. Certainly the experiences of flesh and spirit are not so distinctly unrelated in Donne that what is true for one is false for the other. The vigor and passion of the youthful rebel still live in the voice that inveighs against dogma and the "surelies" of the careless tongue and the thoughtless mind. But the correlation of the young Donne with the old is not our present purpose. It is sufficient to take account of the end toward which he was moving and to note that learning and scholarly habits of mind brought him nearer to that end. If its actual realization was thwarted by the extension even to himself of the problematical conception of things, it must be observed that he knew moments in which he approached an understanding of life not unworthy of Dante's sage description of complete spiritual happiness.

XIV

A SENSIBLE DECAY OF THE WORLD

MUCH has been said about Donne's skepticism, both in this study and elsewhere. No better theme can be selected to unify the conclusion of our analysis of Donne's affinities with the intellectual temper of the Renaissance.

In his important study of Donne's thought, Professor Bredvold points out that Donne's skepticism has relations with certain currents of Renaissance philosophy represented in Montaigne and Sextus Empiricus.[1] Though the study of these authors indicates Donne's early drift toward libertinism, this was not the course of his later thought, matured by the sobering influences of true love, adversity, and deep study. As we have pointed out, the exultation in defiance of convention and the diabolical cynicism tend to subside, and in their place develops a kind of "philosophic doubt," directed not upon the construction of a systematic world view but upon a better understanding of the experiences in which the soul and body are entangled. To this the new philosophy made its contribution.

In the first place, Donne is inclined to regard the new thought as responsible for a general confusion and uncertainty which seemingly support the current notion that the world is in its senescence, approaching its final dissolution. Second, it raises in his mind so great a distrust of reason that he turns to faith as the final sanction of spiritual truth. The former response may appear to be mainly destructive, a misapprehension of facts, and a blind wandering amidst illusion and misunderstanding. The latter, on the contrary, definitely promises to be of a more positive character. The two are inseparable and, when their relationship is understood, constitute a revolt against medieval rationalism and an effort to gain the complete emancipation of the spirit on which any genuinely convincing spiritual experience finally must be founded.

In considering the first phase of Donne's skeptical response it is necessary to have some appreciation of the contemporary conditions which encouraged the Elizabethan inclination to reassert the claims of the ancient doctrine of the world's decay. Going back to the Stoics and

[1] *Op. cit.,* pp. 198-201.

continuing through the Middle Ages, this doctrine offered to the Elizabethan mind a particularly valid means of describing the low estate of the present times as compared with the golden days of remote antiquity. Great as the age of the Renaissance in England was, so vigorous and lavish in the inspiration of genius and so rich in the discovery of new lands and the extension of the bounds of human knowledge, it carried with it, like every period of exceptional enthusiasm, the seeds of reaction and disillusionment. The glory of the beginning of the rebirth gave way to the somberness of the later Elizabethan days, and the passing of the Queen seemed to mark some "great climacteric" in human destiny. It was as if the assurance and confidence following the defeat of the Armada, the praise of England's greatness in early drama, and the selfconscious and magnificent vigor of Marlowe had been but the dreams of men awakening at last to the sober, even repulsive, realities of life, such as Marston depicted in *The Malcontent* and Jonson, in *Volpone*. It is not without significance that tragic themes came to appeal more strongly to Shakespeare than such fanciful and romantic subjects as those of *Midsummer Night's Dream* and other comedies of love, and that Spenser suspended the elaboration of his grand conception of the place virtue should have in the education of a gentleman with the Blatant Beast again abroad in the land. Because Donne anticipates the disillusionment of the later Renaissance, he is less spiritually akin to the early Elizabethans than to the writers of the early decades of the new century. Thus, it is not surprising to find him, about 1598, addressing his friend Wotton with melancholy reminiscence of better days that are past:

> . . . wretched wee
> Are beasts in all, but white integritie.
> I thinke if men, which in these places live
> Durst looke for themselves, and themselves retrive,
> They would like strangers greet themselves, seeing than
> Utopian youth, growne old Italian.[2]

To whatever source this gloominess may be traced, its frequent iteration is fair indication that it is not solely the expression of the personal misfortunes of poets. What was happening in the individual seemed to be repeated in the larger world. Youth had dreamed dreams beyond the capacity of age to fulfill; its enthusiasm had accumulated experience that would require generations to assimilate; and, as the Elizabethan was conscious of his vigor and ambition at the dawn, he was

[2] Grierson, I, 182, ll. 41-46. See above, p. 164.

aware of his shortcomings at the close of the day, or at least, aware of the vanities of the world in which his greatest conquests had been made. It was inevitable that this pessimism should be expressed and natural that the expression should assume a reactionary form.

As the balm which assuages the modern disconsolate soul, the ideas of progress and the perfectibility of the human race, had not yet been fully concocted to ease the melancholia of the later Elizabethan, he was inclined to heed the voice of those traditions which echoed his uncertainties. The destruction of the universe was taught by the Scriptures, and its likelihood was so firmly believed that it was held not only a natural inevitability, but an event to be awaited. Moreover, philosophy gave a kind of support to the idea in Plato's doctrine of the phoenix-like cycle of universal decay and regeneration, an idea closely related to the Stoic doctrine of the periodical destruction and restoration of all things in the world.[3] In 1604 Thomas Wright added a supplement to his book *The Passions of the Mind* wherein he hoped to prove by ingenious arithmetical calculations based on the birth year of Elizabeth, the length of her reign, and the date of her death, that the world had reached its "Clymatericall yeare" when the Queen died.[4] The Aristotelian doctrine that as the world had no beginning in time it could have no end in time went counter to the notion of the world's dissolution; but Christians did not follow Aristotle at this point. Henry Cuffe, for instance, in setting forth the symptoms of universal mortality in *The Differences of the Ages of Man* (1600), affirmed the Christian belief as refutation of the Peripatetics.[5]

For Donne the closing years of the sixteenth century are not simply an age of iron but "O Age of rusty iron!"[6] from which to turn with hope of some poor comfort to contemplate the good old days when men lived longer, grew to greater stature, were not caught in the toils of enslaving conventions, and dwelt at peace with one another according to the law of nature. Again and again echoes of this way of thinking are heard in Donne's poems: he longs "to talke with some old lovers ghost, Who dyed before the god of Love was borne";[7] he pretends that he would exult in the libertinism of free love and

[3] R. D. Hicks, *Stoic and Epicurean* (New York, 1910), pp. 32 ff.

[4] *The Passions of the Mind in Generall. Corrected, and Enlarged, and with sundry new discourses augmented. With a treatise thereto adioyning of the Clymatericall yeare, occasioned by the death of Queen Elizabeth.*

[5] See pp. 20 ff. I refer to the edition of 1607, a copy of which was in Donne's library.

[6] *Satyre V*, Grierson, I, 169, l. 35.

[7] *Loves Deitie, ibid.*, p. 54, ll. 1-2.

persistently complains of the restraining influence of custom.[8] In later years his mind returns to the happiness of Eden and, more frequently, to the hardihood of the Biblical patriarchs and to the strength and unity of the Primitive Church.[9] George Hakewell, who analyzes the whole problem in detail, attributes the cause of this disesteem for the present to the weak grounds upon which it rests: the *"fictions* of Poets," the complaints of the morose, and "an excessiue admiration of *Antiquity*.[10] The second-named is as much an effect as a cause and has no particular historical significance; but the others, if they may be accepted as causes, were sown by the energies of the Renaissance itself. They are responsible for the discovery and the emphasis of the tradition on which rests the idea of the world's decay. In time, as well as in the realm of physical fact or nature, the Renaissance, as Professor Whitehead points out, sought the causes of things; [11] consequently, the revelations of the golden age as figured forth in the ancient poets, in the stories of the youthful vigor of the scriptural heroes, and in the accounts of the purity of the first Church were assimilated by the imagination of poet and divine as completely as the behavior of natural phenomena was impressed upon the mind of the scientific observer. It is paradoxical that an age holding out such high hopes for the future should, likewise, look with a longing eye upon the past. The divergent views were not necessarily contradictory; but unless one were to regard tradition as a source of strength on which to advance into the future, conflict was inevitable; and on the particular issue under consideration the conflict was drawn, a conflict intensified by the scientific element of the Renaissance which seemed to contribute directly to the justification of a pessimistic view of life.

Before treating Donne's use of the opinion of the world's decay to illustrate his skeptical mood it should be noted that such a gloomy construction as we have described was not placed upon the intellectual benefits of the Renaissance by all minds. Bacon, though he had a doubtful understanding of, and a more doubtful sympathy for, Copernicanism,[12] nevertheless, was himself a champion of the scientific revolution and regarded the extension of the bounds of human empire as

[8] See *Communitie, ibid.,* pp. 32-33; *Loves diet, ibid.,* pp. 55-56; *Farewell to love, ibid.,* pp. 70-71; *Elegie III. Change, ibid.,* pp. 82-83; *Elegie XVII. Variety, ibid.,* pp. 113-16.

[9] Cf. *LXXX Sermons,* 12, fol. 112; *ibid.,* 45, fols. 450, 451; *ibid.,* 69, fols. 698, 699; *Fifty Sermons,* 11, fols. 85-86; *ibid.,* 24, *passim.*

[10] *Op. cit.,* p. 22.

[11] *Op. cit.,* p. 12.

[12] De Morgan, *op. cit.,* in *Companion to the Almanac* (1855), pp. 10-11.

the reasonable grounds for a universal optimism. Under the great formula, "knowledge is power," is comprehended his new system of inductive inquiry, whereby the conception of human progress appeared to be translated from the category of utopian hopes to that of realizable ambitions, the possibilities of which are glimpsed in his projection of life in *The New Atlantis*. Consequently, though Bacon had early looked pessimistically through the eyes of the ancient poet upon the world as a "bubble" and "the life of man Less than a span," when he came to the composition of his *Advancement of Learning* he urged the mind to free itself from the illusion that the golden age lay within antiquity, declaring that the concrete evidence for the advancement of human learning affirmed the present time to be the authentic ancient time of the world's history—*antiquitas saeculi juventus mundi*. The world has not fallen into a sickly decline, for it is capable of a "progression" toward the advantages of a maturing intelligence.[13]

As early as 1594 Robert Ashley had translated into English Loys Le Roy's book *Of the Interchangeable Course, or Variety of Things in the Whole World,* a treatise written to demonstrate the triumphant march of human history from antiquity to the present.[14] Inasmuch as this book is primarily a product of the more hopeful years of the Renaissance, it can hardly be cited as evidence of the challenge thrown down to the pessimists of the new age. Rather, to men like Bacon and Harvey and Gilbert belongs the honor of vindicating the Renaissance. Not only by encouraging declarations but also by actual accomplishment they helped to subdue the fears of those who saw the present as but through a glass darkly. Nevertheless, that the notion of the world's decay was a prolonged and prevalent opinion is witnessed by such literary forebodings as we have alluded to, by the reappearance of Henry Cuffe's book in 1607 and again in 1633, and perhaps most emphatically by the necessity which moved George Hakewell in 1627 to compose *An Apologie of the Power and Providence of God in the Governement of the World,* wherein he undertook an *Examination and Censvre of the Common Errovr Tovching Natvres Perpetvall and Vniversall Decay.*[15] How far the "common errovr" had penetrated the seventeenth-century mind may be gained from a statement in Hakewell's epistle dedicatory "to my venerable mother the famovs and flovrishing vniversitie of Oxford," that "in confidence heereof I haue to thy *censure* submitted this ensuing *Apologie,* which perchaunce to

---

[13] *Works,* VI, 130.
[14] Le Roy's work was published first in 1568. Editions followed in 1570, 1574.
[15] Hakewell's book (third edition) appeared in 1635 "much enlarged." Two more books had been added, and the text throughout "augmented by the Authour."

the *Vulgar* may seeme somewhat strange, because their eares haue bin so long inured vnto, and consequently their fancies fore-stalled with the contrary opinion." [16]

At the back of the whole question stands obviously enough a natural human inclination to regard the acquisition of knowledge with suspicion. In the early seventeenth century this suspicion was aggravated —as it still is—by the narrow interpretation of the Genesis story, in which knowledge was accounted one of the prime causes for the fall of man. Even sophisticated pens may give intimations of the vanity of human knowledge, as we know well enough from the bitter-sweet of Bertrand Russell's *A Freeman's Worship* and from the doubtful glory of our "much science" in Joseph Wood Krutch's *The Modern Temper*. As for Donne, it is quite clear that his intellectual energies, his predilection for study, and his keen sensitivity to new experience of the mind as well as of the body betray no distaste for knowledge in any form. The absence of distaste, however, does not exclude the presence of distrust. Both nature and study had nourished in Donne the "suspicious boldnesse" to "perplex security with doubt," [17] and consequently, to regard rational knowledge, if critically apprehended, of use in the natural world, yet inadequate to lead men to the *summum bonum* of spiritual happiness, an end for which faith is the primary instrument, even though its function is made clear by reason's help.[18] In brief, though Donne has no inclination to disregard the learning of the new philosophy, he is disposed to look upon it with the same doubtfulness that he entertains toward all experience. Moreover, as the new philosophy definitely challenged the rationalism of the old

[16] Sig. b₂ verso.

[17] *To the Countesse of Bedford,* Grierson, I, 200, l. 38.

[18] The relation of faith and reason is admirably set forth in another verse letter to the Countess of Bedford [1607–8], of which note the following lines:

> "Reason is our Soules left hand, Faith her right,
> By these wee reach divinity, that's you;
> Their loves, who have the blessings of your light,
> Grew from their reason, mine from faire faith grew.
> But as, although a squint lefthandednesse
> Be'ungracious, yet we cannot want that hand,
> So would I, not to encrease, but to expresse
> My faith, as I beleeve, so understand.
> Therefore I study you first in your Saints,
>
> . . .
>
> But soone, the reasons why you'are lov'd by all,
> Grow infinite, and so passe reasons reach,
> Then backe againe to'implicite faith I fall,
> And rest on what the Catholique voice doth teach."

Ibid., p. 189, ll. 1-9, 13-16.

philosophy, it sharpened his suspicions of all rational experience, and these suspicions he chose at times to express in terms of the popular conception of the world's decline.

In a way earlier demonstrated, the advancement in scientific thought and discovery struck vigorously at a salient and vulnerable point of the old philosophy: the doctrine of the incorruptibility of the heavens. With the explosion of this doctrine was destroyed the entire harmonious arrangement of the universe, systematically graduated from lowest matter to the pure form of God himself, with man occupying a pivotal position in the scheme, as one participating both in the elementary or temporal world and in the higher realm of immutability from which rained upon him the influence of angels and the celestial spheres.

For Donne the unity is broken and the world fallen into its decline. In *The first Anniversary* this pessimistic attitude is expressed in terms of the lost beauty of the world. [With Augustine, Donne regards the elements of beauty as harmony and color.[19] Harmony denotes particularly the formal beauty of the universe, the structure and arrangement of its materials, and is comprehended less by sense than by intellect. Color embraces all beauty discernible by sense; color is the property of things chosen to represent this beauty because it is the primary stimulus of the "noblest sense," vision:]

> Sight is the noblest sense of any one,
> Yet sight hath only colour to feed on.[20]

But "colour is decai'd" and the structural harmony destroyed because Elizabeth Drury is dead. As Elizabeth Drury is understood as the world soul, the unifying principle imparting beauty to all things, her departure is Donne's means of objectifying the extent to which he is becoming aware of the illusory character of the old "truths." Unless understood symbolically, as a way of expressing this disillusionment, the manifestations of the decay of physical beauty vigorously recorded in the poem, on the whole, are without meaning. Interpreted as forms of poetical expression, however, their implication is far-reaching, signifying that doubt has gone so far as to include the complete distrust of the senses. Although we must await *The second Anniversary* for the specific statement to this effect,[21] the implication is here clear enough. The particular significance attached to this misgiving derives from the prominent place given to sense in the scholastic conception of the nature of knowledge, a subject to be noted more fully in the chapter·

[19] See *ibid.*, p. 239, ll. 248-50; p. 240, ll. 312 ff.; p. 241, ll. 339-40. Cf. Bernard Bosanquet, *A History of Aesthetic* (London, 1892), pp. 134-35.
[20] *Ibid.*, p. 242, ll. 353-54.   [21] See below, ch. xv.

following. Moreover, the new science, while respecting above all the testimony of the senses, disclosed the fallacy of medieval empiricism by pointing out how sense experience uncritically considered injures the truth by presenting illusions rather than facts to the eye. Galileo's discoveries of such phenomena as the multitude of little stars in the Milky Way and the illumination of the moon by reflected light particularly revealed the inadequacy of this "noblest sense" unless aided, not only by the telescope, but also by a critical mind capable of interpreting sensation. Such a process of thought is not summarized by Donne in *The first Anniversary,* but that it is secretly at work in his mind is without question. The poem is a reflection of the full conflict of the old and the new philosophies.

On the subject of the destruction of the world's harmony Donne is more copious than on the decay of color, the first of beauty's elements. Inseparably joined with the lack of harmony is the idea of corruption; corruption is the evidence of the lack of harmony; conversely, immutability is dependent upon the symmetry and agreement of the world's parts. As frequently iterated, the beauty of the old cosmology lay in the systematic completeness into which all that was known about the world was harmoniously regimented. But this beauty of logical structure, for it was essentially logical, not physical, was its greatest weakness, for it made no allowance for change except those mutations appearing to the unaided eye within the elementary sphere, such as birth, growth, and death. Being complete and systematically organized, nothing could be added unless a new organization were to be effected, and nothing could be taken away without upsetting the fragile balance preserving the harmony. Moreover, it was assumed that God had created the world as thus described and that it served His end, the advancement of His glory, in the fulfillment of which the celestial sphere, because of its proximity to the Maker, remained pure and incorruptible, the instrument by which His benign influence was shed upon the sphere of mutability. How thoroughly the derangement of this "fair" scheme was accomplished by the introduction of a moving earth and a fixed sun, the disposal of the element of fire, and the discovery of new stars and planets; and how sensitive Donne was to the fact, have already been observed with considerable care. At this time we may simply recall how, as in the passage about the new philosophy calling all in doubt, these matters turn his mind to the idea of a decaying world. Assuming that

    . . . did the world from the first houre decay,[22]

[22] Grierson, I, 237, l. 201.

Donne finds the present manifestation of this decay in the new astronomical phenomena:

> And freely men confesse that this world's spent,
> When in the Planets, and the Firmament
> They seeke so many new; they see that this
> Is crumbled out againe to his Atomies.
> 'Tis all in peeces, all cohaerence gone;
> All just supply, and all Relation.[23]

In the same poem, enmeshed in a long exposition on the "disformity
of parts" of the world appears the figure of the sun, "being now falne
nearer us." [24] In a letter to the Countess of Huntingdon, written in
1614,[25] having many things in common with the argument of *The
first Anniversary,* the figure reappears, specifically adjoined to the idea
of the world's decay:

> If the worlds age, and death be argued well
> By the Sunnes fall, which now towards earth doth bend,
> Then we might feare that vertue, since she fell
> So low as woman, should be neare her end.[26]

Whether the case "be argued well" is of no present moment; but
we should note that Hakewell speaks of this as "an opinion of very
many," which "touches neerer to the quick, & strikes indeed at the very
throat of the cause," and thinks it of sufficient importance to· persuade
him to consult "both the learned *Professours* in the *Mathematickes* at
Oxford." [27] All, however, that Donne could have meant by the sun's
fall has been adequately discussed; it is necessary only to add in passing
that in these lines there doubtless lingers Donne's recollection of
Cardan's popular association of the fiction of the sun's decline with
the aging of the world.[28]

It is important to emphasize what already has been intimated,
that Donne simply took the popular opinion of the world's decay,
ready-made, as a device whereby he could express the skeptical mood
into which he had fallen. To affirm that he did not believe in the
ultimate dissolution of the physical world would be to impeach his
honestly expressed acceptance of this part of the Biblical teaching; at
the same time, to declare that he believed literally in the opinion as
defined above, when he wrote the *Anniversaries,* is to overlook the fact
that in his sermons where it might safely be presumed that he would

---

[23] *Ibid.,* p. 237, ll. 209-14.   [24] *Ibid.,* p. 239, l. 274.
[25] *Ibid.,* pp. 201-3 [1614–15]. On date of letter, see *ibid.,* II, 132, 163. See above,
pp. 142 ff.
[26] *Ibid.,* p. 201, ll. 17-20.   [27] *Op. cit.,* pp. 93 ff.
[28] *De Subtilitate* (Basil, 1560), III, 256-59.

have found occasion to justify his belief in this pessimistic view, no such justification appears. Rather, we find its antidote prescribed, *"Man is a future Creature,"* [29] even though futurity here is measured by eternity and not by the "rags of time" which number the periods of his mortal progress. Furthermore, to insist on literalness in this matter, especially in the *Anniversaries,* is to allow a secondary consideration to frustrate the fundamental purpose of the poems, namely, to discover amidst the wreckage of philosophy the secure grounds of spiritual happiness. Because the theme of the world's decay is capable of being linked with the new philosophy, it contributes an effective device for the exhibition of the doubts provoked by the new science, which in turn point to the futility of trusting in the methods of the old philosophy to provide a satisfactory justification of the ways of God to man. In brief, the symbol must not be confused with the purpose for which it is used. As is Donne's common practice in analyzing a state of mind, he makes use of materials the literal truth of which he may or may not accept. The symbol, however, as here, is often associated with the facts that have produced the state of mind. A passage in one of Donne's sermons, while illustrating one of the phases of Donne's expository method, also throws a clear light on the immediate problem:

As the world is the whole frame of the world, God hath put into it a reproofe, a rebuke, lest it should seem eternall, which is, a sensible decay and age in the whole frame of the world, and every piece thereof. The seasons of the yeare irregular and distempered; the Sun fainter, and languishing; men lesse in stature, and shorter-lived. No addition, but only every yeare, new sorts, new species of wormes, and flies, and sicknesses, which argue more and more putrefaction of which they are engendred. And the Angels of heaven, which did so familiarly converse with men in the beginning of the world, though they may not be doubted to perform to us still their ministeriall assistances, yet they seem so far to have deserted this world, as that they do not appeare to us, as they did to those our Fathers. S. *Cyprian* observed this in his time, when writing to *Demetrianus,* who imputed all those calamities which afflicted the world then, to the impiety of the Christians who would not joyne with them in the worship of their gods, *Cyprian* went no farther for the cause of these calamities, but *Ad senescentem mundum,* To the age and impotency of the whole world; And therefore, sayes he, *Imputent senes Christianis, quod minus valeant in senectutem;* Old men were best accuse Christians, that they are more sickly in their age, then they were in their youth; Is the fault in our religion, or in their decay? *Canos in pueris videmus,*

---

[29] *A Sermon of Commemoration of The Lady Dāuers, late Wife of Sr Iohn Dāuers . . . by* Iohn Donne, *D. of St Pauls* (London, 1627), p. 71: "Creatures of an inferiour nature are possest with the *present;* Man is a *future Creature.*"

nec aetas in senectute definit, sed incipit a senectute; We see gray haires in children, and we do not die old, and yet we are borne old. Lest the world (as the world signifies the whole frame of the world) should glorify it selfe, or flatter, and abuse us with an opinion of eternity, we may admit usefully (though we do not conclude peremptorily) this observation to be true, that there is a reproof, a rebuke borne in it, a sensible decay and mortality of the whole world.[30]

Here again, as is commonly true with Donne, the condition laid down in the concluding sentence gives the statement what significance it has, "we may admit usefully (though we do not conclude peremptorily)." Thus, there is express declaration that the description of the "mortality of the whole world" is for obvious reasons of edification; and in *The first Anniversary,* the purpose is no less explicit in the lines,

> But though it be too late to succour thee,
> Sicke World, yea, dead, yea putrified, since shee
> Thy'intrinsique balme, and thy preservative,
> Can never be renew'd thou never live,
> *I* (since no man can make thee live) *will try,*
> *What wee may gaine by thy Anatomy.* [Italics mine.] [31]

To regard the former as a mere illustration of a conventional way of explaining Scripture by allegorical methods and the latter as the introduction to the elaboration of a vulgar error is to miss a psychological truth lying behind both, namely, the attempt of a personality to realize concretely its own awareness of the mortality overshadowing all human experience. Though wanting the consummate grace of Shakespeare's "Full fathom five, thy father lies," wherein the oscillations between universal decay and the vision of regeneration are purely and clearly realized, unmixed with the intellectual and almost academic doctrinary quality of Donne's "anatomy," Donne comprehends the matter as a poet in his own way, and at the same time allows the reader to follow the analysis whereby he reaches not unlike conclusions. In Donne the imagination does not spring to the wonder of "something rich and strange" but climbs arduously through the study of the decay and corruption of physical things to the comprehension of eternity, and we touch with him every rung in the ladder of his thought.

Into the two *Anniversaries* Donne has poured the confusion of much learning, so that if we were of a mind to do so we could extract and isolate the strands of many opinions besides that of the decay of the world. Moreover, we could take note of the impact of experience encountered outside the covers of books, in the world of fluctuating hopes and despairs, of intense passions that have acquainted Donne with the triumphs and the scorn of the world of the flesh. For example, Professor Grierson, inclining to view the poems with a backward glance upon the medieval past, gathers up their purpose in the following generalization that has much in common with the idea of the decay of the world: "The burden of the whole is an impassioned and exalted *meditatio mortis* based on two themes common enough in medieval devotional literature—a *De Contemptu Mundi*, and a contemplation of the Glories of Paradise." [32] The "brief analysis of the two poems" following this statement reveals justification for making this consideration of the theme. Nevertheless, we should regard the interpretation with considerable caution, because it tends to incline the mind away from the intensely personal quality of the poems to a notion that they are a kind of formal religious or devotional exercise, and because it does not sufficiently suggest the fact that for Donne, the *contemptus mundi* arises not from an asceticism encouraged by theological discipline or a desire to flee the world of the flesh and the devil but from a mind that scorns the world for having lost its beauty through human infirmity, in the violation of God's "safe precontract," [33] and in submitting to "this Pedantery" of "being taught by sense, and Fantasie." [34]

Though only the former of the two *Anniversaries* is called an "anatomy," both are alike analytical. Even an anatomy must have something to work upon, and as the purpose of the anatomist is to lay bare the various structures of the body, we are apt to conclude that the framework or skeleton of the thought disclosed at length is the consummation of the poetic dissection. This, however, is giving too much credence to a false analogy, for the poet of the *Anniversaries* reverses the method of the scientist. Under the name of "an anatomy of the world," he gives us an anatomy of himself—the little world or the microcosm. At the outset he must be provided with a skeleton on which to hang the nerves and muscles of the man conceived by the imagination to be himself. From the beginning of *The first Anniversary* to the end of the *second,* the chief business of the poet is the analysis of his own consciousness. A third of the way through the latter poem Donne recalls our attention to this fact—"Thinke further on thy selfe, my Soule." [35] What results is something like the incarnation of a ghost—a living ghost, however, having its tangible existence from the skeleton which enables it to walk, but its true life from the par-

[32] *Ibid.,* II, 188.
[34] *Ibid.,* p. 259, ll. 291-92.
[33] *The second Anniversary, ibid.,* I, 264, l. 460.
[35] *Ibid.,* p. 255, l. 157.

ticular conceptions with which the imagination clothes the skeleton.

One of the very significant products of Donne's self-contemplation, or self-anatomy, is the revelation of the striking reality of the two primary entities of which the self is comprised: the body and the soul. As spiritual happiness depends upon the appreciation of the proper relations of both, it is upon a study of this relationship that the poet directs most of his energy. To give the subject its proper setting, in order that it may be observed more clearly and that its universal significance may be sensed, he projects the study of himself upon a cosmic background, whereon the relations of body and soul—the problem of the individual—are reflected in the great drama of spirit and matter. This is the heavy burden of religion and philosophy shouldered upon the fragile story of the life and death of Elizabeth Drury. Unless we recognize in her brief encounter with human experience the lofty parallel to the incarnation of Christ himself, Donne's attempt is hopeless— and for many this will but emphasize the doubtfulness of his taste.

In the elaboration of the soul and body theme, it is interesting to note the absence of anything like the medieval conception of the *psychomachia*—a conflict of the soul with the body. For Donne the two are not at war with each other, though their harmony is frustrated by the illusory and false efforts of mankind to appreciate the grounds on which their true and happy adjustment should be made. That Donne succeeds in giving the final "point and period" to the question may be disallowed; but that he draws out his answer, to be confirmed by death only (because death consummates *human* experience, restoring again to man's sight the pattern of true unity of soul and body in Christ) on lines indicating that the relations of body and soul are mutual, may be adduced from his contemplation of the perfect pattern of their relations:

> Shee, who left such a bodie, as even shee
> Only in Heaven could learne, how it can bee
> Made better; for shee rather was two soules,
> Or like to full on both sides written Rols,
> Where eyes might reade upon the outward skin,
> As strong Records for God, as mindes within;
> Shee, who by making full perfection grow,
> Peeces a Circle, and still keepes it so,
> Long'd for, and longing for it, to heaven is gone,
> Where shee receives, and gives addition.[36]

The perfect pattern for Donne, as for St. Augustine, is a concrete fact presented by history in the personality of Christ; and though Christ

[36] *Ibid.*, pp. 265-66, ll. 501-10.

is not named in either of the *Anniversaries,* He is definitely figured forth as Elizabeth Drury. The resolution of the apparent duality of man into the perfection of the unified personality is something divine, to be achieved only by death—

> Death must usher, and unlocke the doore; [37]

yet death does not deny that an advance toward this end may be made on earth; in fact, life commands it;

> (For they're in heaven on earth who heavens workes do).[38]

The expression "heavens workes" carries no connotation of the struggle going on between Catholic and Protestant on the doctrine of justification by works or by faith. Donne is far above that now; he is upholding the ideal of the active Christian life as an indication of his temperamental and doctrinal antipathy to the idea that spiritual experience may be perfected through mystical vision. In that conception the body is impugned as an obstacle to spiritual happiness, but for Donne "heavens workes" receives a broader interpretation as the full and complete direction of all the faculties of soul and body toward the ends agreeable to the good life.

The relation of the body and soul constitutes the fundamental problem of Donne's life, early, middle, and late. By the time *The second Anniversary* was completed it had received a definite Christian coloring, though a disposition to regard the matter in a way that would not allow originality to be misconstrued as doctrinal orthodoxy causes Donne to avoid specific mention of Christianity and its formal doctrines. The acknowledgment of Christian influence, however, does not necessarily alter radically his solution of the problem. The physical and the metaphysical, of which body and soul are the respective representations in human nature, are really aspects of one and the same thing. However, Donne never goes the full way with the Platonist in regarding the latter as the real and the former but a shadow of this reality; nor can he find himself congenial with a purely materialistic conception of things. At times it would almost seem as if he regarded the duality as pure illusion, having its authority in a deep-rooted tradition of so regarding the complexity of the human personality. But he himself is too fully caught in this tradition to escape its influence. Again, the idea of the one as the implement of the other, matter always tending to realize its formal potentiality, appeals to him; but with the conception of a pure form, apart from matter, to which the dialect of this Aristotelianism leads him, he has no final sympathy. God himself

[37] *Ibid.,* p. 255, l. 156.   [38] *Ibid.,* p. 255, l. 154.

for Donne must in some way share the qualities of both or is both in their perfect harmony. Donne wisely withholds a final dogmatic answer. That the body and soul exist and are inseparable, is enough; this is the great mystery and the great fact of life. As both body and soul are present in man, his completeness requires their mutual expression. In *The Extasie*, the exclamation,

> But O alas, so long, so farre
> Our bodies why doe wee forbeare? [39]

is no invitation to another mistress to become his lover. Such an interpretation belittles Donne, but not so much as it does the critic who so construes their meaning. It is the invitation to know the completeness that is the life of the unified activity of both body and soul. In this fact is the link that draws *The Extasie* into the company of the *Anniversaries*, where with a different emphasis the problem is expanded to its most general proportions.

As described above, the vigor of the *Anniversaries* comes from the amazing vitality of the consciousness of the poet presented by the self-anatomy, and the scope of their interest derives from Donne's discovery within himself of the pattern of a universal theme—the relation of the body and the soul, matter and spirit. Obviously Donne does not fit compactly into the formula set for the devotional poet. The "impassioned *meditatio mortis*" based on the themes of a contempt for the world and the contemplation of heavenly beatitude, into which Professor Grierson resolves the poems, is apt to be misleading unless the qualifications set out at some length above are thoroughly recognized. One cannot too strongly emphasize the fact that Donne's scorn for the world does not annihilate his passion to live:

> Yet in this deluge, grosse and generall,
> Thou seest me strive for life; [40]

and that the "vision"—if it may be called vision at all—of the beatific state has no kinship with the true visions of blessedness beheld by mystics like St. John, Crashaw, or Dante. For these the divine fervor informs the common language of men with strange and unearthly meaning, and sensuous impressions merge into the spiritual to create the wonder of pure apocalyptic vision. For Donne the vision is crossed continually by earthly shadows. The "essentiall joy" of heaven for which he yearns is quite unrealized, and the reason is simply stated:

[39] *Ibid.*, p. 53, ll. 49-50.
[40] *The second Anniversary, ibid.*, p. 252, ll. 30-31.

Only in Heaven joyes strength is never spent;
And accidentall things are permanent.[41]

On earth it is not man's destiny to enjoy the full heavenly bliss of his contemplations nor to regain the peace and freedom of the golden age of his dreams.

To return to an earlier theme, it is no less dangerous to regard Donne as an apostle of the doctrine of the world's decay. Donne's scorn for the world is the expected product of his intense skepticism; and, in the manner demonstrated, it assumes the pattern of this time-old doctrine which the conditions confronting the Elizabethan mind made generally acceptable. To affirm that Donne's reiterated "rebuke" of the mortality of all material things is evidence of his literal belief in the world's decay, is to "conclude peremptorily" on a subject which he "admits" as a useful means of measuring the depths of his disillusionment and doubt.

[41] *Ibid.*, p. 265, ll. 487-88.

XV

THE TWO LIGHTS

A PHASE of Donne's skepticism likely to be overlooked is one paradoxically destined to serve a constructive end. It results from the early self-exhortation to "doubt wisely" and receives the poet's tribute in *The first Anniversary*, where he is

> succour'd then with a perplexed doubt.[1]

That doubt, leading even to disillusionment, may be one of the ways of getting toward the truth can hardly be denied. In fact, such a questioning attitude was one of the freshest impulses released by the Renaissance. When exerted against the shams of antiquity it strengthened the grounds for a true "advancement of learning"; when put to use in the search for philosophical truth, it led to the evolution of a *Discourse on Method* whereby the truth might be found; again, when it infected the poet's imagination it threw into their right perspective the obvious, and therefore easily neglected or conventionalized, experiences of flesh and spirit.

Though this subject defies easy analysis, it does have several manifestations capable of isolation and concrete treatment. One of these is Donne's questioning attitude toward the scholastic conception of the nature and object of knowledge. "It is said often in Philosophy," Donne declares in departing upon an original exposition of the difference between philosophy and divinity, *"Nihil in intellectu, quod non prius in sensu."* [2] Years earlier, in a moment of ascendant faith and spiritual insight, under the immediate influence of the new philosophy and aware of the vanity of disputation, he had stripped this doctrine of the schools of all its latent significance as a definition of the way we come to a knowledge of the truth:

> When wilt thou shake off this Pedantery,
> Of being taught by sense, and Fantasie?
> Thou look'st through spectacles; small things seeme great
> Below; But up unto the watch-towere get,
> And see all things despoyl'd of fallacies.[3]

The condemnation of sense experience would appear to be a contradiction of the basis of all modern scientific thinking, for sense experi-

[1] Grierson, I, 231, l. 14.   [2] *Fifty Sermons*, 8, fol. 63.
[3] *The second Anniversary*, Grierson, I, 259, ll. 291-95.

ence is the very foundation of that naturalism, the rise of which "in the later Middle Ages" Professor Whitehead regards as "the final ingredient necessary for the rise of science." [4] The validity given to the use of the senses in the modern world, however, is something vastly different from the scholastic application of the dictum that there is nothing in the intelligence which was not first perceived by the senses. Further quotation from Professor Whitehead's book will make clear exactly what is meant by the naturalism of which he speaks:

It was the rise of interest in natural objects and in natural occurrences, for their own sakes. The natural foliage of a district was sculptured in out-of-the-way spots of the later buildings, merely as exhibiting delight in those familiar objects. The whole atmosphere of every art exhibited a direct joy in the apprehension of the things which lie around us. The craftsman who executed the late medieval decorative sculpture, Giotto, Chaucer, Wordsworth, Walt Whitman, and, at the present day, the New England poet Robert Frost, are all akin to each other in this respect. The simple immediate facts are the topics of interest, and these reappear in the thought of science as the "irreducible stubborn facts." [5]

This, in brief, is a vindication of the use of the senses as a means of discovering the truth about the natural world. For the poet it means that the expression of what he sees, feels, and hears, as organized and controlled by his imagination, is a representation of factual experience and a proper subject of art. For the scientist it means that knowledge of the natural world begins with observation, the direct perception of facts, such as Vesalius's examination of the human body and Galileo's exploration of the heavens. It should be recalled that Bacon's new method requires first a description of the things of nature. But, as the poet's record, or the sculptor's production is something different from nature itself, having, as stated, been subjected to the influence of the imagination, so the knowledge reported by the man of science does not end with a literal description of the sensory experience. Rather, as Galileo so ably and dramatically illustrates in his *Dialogues on the Two Great Systems of the World*, the experience must be reviewed by the reason and translated into common terms into which all other experience, likewise, may be translated. Thus, mathematical symbolism comes into use; as the observed facts are capable of quantitative description, this description must be given in mathematical terms if the relation of these particular facts to all other natural facts is finally to be established. As Galileo teaches at the expense of Simplicius the Peripatetic, whose inordinate faith in his eyes leads

[4] *Op. cit.*, p. 23.   [5] *Ibid.*, p. 23.

him to the absurdity of denying, in effect, that all that glitters is not gold, sense experience, as such, is unreliable and not to be trusted before it has been thoroughly criticized.[6]

The exercise of any privilege to make use of the sense given to the medieval mind by the sanction cited above or the sensitiveness to external nature shared by the medievalist with human beings of any other time, except with such isolated persons as Roger Bacon, did not lead to anything that may rightly be termed scientific knowledge. The inventions proceeding from the Middle Ages, for example, the mariner's compass, were the products of pure empiricism, not of a conscious application of law or principle induced from a deliberate study of the behavior of natural facts. The reasons why scientific knowledge is not one of the achievements of the medievalists are not far to seek. Reason was the accredited instrument of knowledge, and the schoolmen were primarily addicted to an *a priori* method of thinking, incapable in itself of serving the ends of science and at the same time concentrated on the solution of the eternal "why" of things in terms of an Aristotelianized Christianity. Observation and experimentation were not encouraged because they offered a direct "empirical challenge to the supremacy of reason." How persistent was this rationalistic method, inspired by teleological purpose, is clearly indicated by Urban VIII's declaration that "the tides cannot be adduced as a necessary proof of the double motion of the earth without limiting God's omnipotence." [7]

Having once accepted the description of the natural world as given by antiquity, particularly as presented by Aristotle, the Middle Ages expected nothing new, in fact, needed nothing new, and were satisfied with the deductions which their subtlety could elaborate from the original data. As the primary attribute of matter was thought to be quality rather than the measurable "unitary basis of quantity" considered by the scientist, a reduction of nature to a uniform system of quantitative relations was impossible. Moreover, under the influence of the Aristotelian doctrine of form and matter, as earlier pointed out, the entire universe of created matter was perceived as a unified system of things, with each manifestation of matter exhibiting its peculiar and underlying formal character or "essence," graduated from indeterminate matter to the pure form of God himself. In this conception there is no place, nor any need, for the explanation of the behavior of any phenomenon in terms of "an universal system of mechanical

[6] *Ed. cit.*, pp. 52 ff. Cf. pp. 223-24, 230-31.
[7] See Gibson, *op. cit.*, p. 7.

relations to which it belongs." [8] Briefly surveyed, this was the medieval attitude toward nature, and though it may have been assumed that there is nothing in the understanding which was not first in sense perception, the conditions to which sense perception was subjected produced the fantastic system of essences and ends which Descartes regarded as a mere "hypostatization of sensuous experience," irreconcilable with the new conception of natural law.[9]

To fix Donne in the naturalistic tradition of the Renaissance is a difficult task. The pure delight in the return of spring which animates the Prologue of *The Canterbury Tales,* and the clean, perfect translation of sensory experience into poetry to be found in Keats's *To Autumn* are quite absent from Donne. There are, however, intimations here and there of sensitiveness to the world of nature: the vivid report of the sea in storm and in calm, the flight of the lark, and the turning of the marigold toward the sun; but, for the most part his eyes look within rather than without. He walks on a primrose hill only to be led into musing upon the mysterious significance of the number of petals of the primrose; and in *The Extasie* his lovers recline upon a bed of violets, partly because of the traditional association of these flowers with pastoral amours, partly because of the lush sensual atmosphere which their mention provokes. Donne had no Stratford boyhood to remind him of green fields and the "bare ruin'd choirs" of a winter woodland; in his life there was no self-imposed retreat to some Horton where he could learn the "Flourets of a thousand hues" or delight in the nightingale singing amidst the blossoming may. Donne is primarily a man of the city, and circumstance never thrust upon him the necessity, as it did upon Herrick, of falling in love with the "stupid" country. The manners of men interest him, and their thoughts; but more still, his own self.

Nor is it as the man of science that Donne looks upon his world. Much as maps, the geometer's instruments, anatomical dissections, and telescopes betray the fascination scientific learning had for him, it is hard to imagine Donne ever trying to pack a hen in snow in an effort to discover the principles of refrigeration. Nevertheless, Donne appreciates the scientist's excursions into the new world of fact. He recognizes that as the "spectacles" of Bede and Gregory thrust fantastic shapes and superstitious visions before the eye, so those of Ptolemy and Aristotle becloud the sight of the new and changing face of nature; [10] otherwise, he could not have written of those followers of Aristotle who "stubbornly maintain his Proposition still, though by

[8] *Ibid,* p. 8.   [9] *Ibid.,* p. 177.   [10] *LXXX Sermons,* 80, fol. 818.

THE TWO LIGHTS

many experiences of new Stars, the reason which moved *Aristotle* [that is, to affirm the inalterability of the heavens] seems now to be utterly defeated." And it is just because Donne does appreciate that the arguments which "moved" Kepler and Galileo were based on the "irreducible and stubborn facts" of nature, not on the old premises of the schools, that for him the new philosophy calls all in doubt. A less sensitive or discerning mind would not have been so seriously troubled.

[If we are to accept Miss Ramsay's thesis, first expressed in *Les doctrines médiévales chez Donne* in 1917, and repeated in 1931,[11] based upon an impressive accumulation of materials, we must be disposed to find Donne more thoroughly at home with the medievalists than with his Renaissance contemporaries. But what Miss Ramsay does is to overlook the fact that the historical meaning of words is subject to change and that though the verbal reminders of an ancient tradition may be gathered from Donne's writings, their spiritual connotation betokens the influence of a later time. For instance, the naturalism of the Renaissance in its appeal from reason to the critical perception of natural facts, involving an alteration of the conception of the nature of knowledge and the activities of the knowing mind, though not argued philosophically, is, nevertheless, reflected in Donne as it implies the freedom of the mind to seek in fact and experience the ultimate basis for the truth about the nature of things.]

Whereas the schoolmen, "who have abandoned experience altogether," allowed the shadow of logic to be drawn between their eyes and the facts of experience, the men of the new philosophy, believing that experience is "the best demonstration by far,"[12] were encouraged to go in search of the final causes of things in the reality presented to them by experience. Though Donne does not aspire with the scientist to wipe away the cloudiness of rationalization and logical subtleties bedimming the vision of the senses, nor even to find inspiration in the world of external nature, he does, nevertheless, seek to find in experience itself some ultimate reality that does not need the support of logic and at the same time can withstand its powers to destroy.

The adjustment that Donne makes, or attempts to make—perhaps more aptly termed, simply his reaction to the changed conditions— is determined by two sets of facts, the one external, the other internal, the former acting primarily as stimuli to arouse the latter to expression. Though for purposes of analysis they may be separated, in reality, they

[11] "Donne's Relation to Philosophy," in *A Garland for John Donne*, pp. 101-20.
[12] *Novum Organum, Works,* VIII, pp. 92, 100.

are interdependent and reciprocally influential. Briefly stated, the external conditions begin with a familiarity, derived from early training and family tradition, with the scholastic synthesis wherein physical fact and metaphysical theory—nature and religion, broadly speaking—were wrought into a systematic harmony by a rationalistic method. In this system natural philosophy, under which is understood the matter of science, was not divorced from theology but rather subordinated to it. Conversely, religion was not isolated from philosophy; it was the *divina philosophia* for which natural philosophy existed. To this knowledge came the new philosophy, teaching Donne that the old synthesis was broken and that for the time being, at least, one could not acknowledge the validity of new facts without also acknowledging that these facts made a cleavage between the realms of the physical and metaphysical, as formerly understood. No matter how much one might admire the world of created nature as the example of the divine handiwork, it most certainly no longer enjoyed the same logical intimacy with the divine world that it had enjoyed in medieval thought. If, as Donne expresses it in *The second Anniversary*, the pure form which gave to the world—even to its accidental joys—the "essentiall touch" has departed and we are left with a welter of facts and experiences over which men wield their dissecting knives and measuring sticks and at which they look through their optic glasses, then certainly the old correspondence of heaven and earth is broken, and beauty's elements, harmony and color, are spent. There is no longer one law for each of the great orders of created nature, harmonized by the infusion of the influence of the great One through all the Many; rather, all creation is reduced to a dead level of existence. Inasmuch as Donne's vision hardly extends that far, he leaves the world in a state of perplexing lawlessness. But even more baffling than the state of the world is that of man, standing somewhere between heaven and earth, by virtue of his soul and body akin to both, yet for the same reason torn from each.

The internal conditions are the particular personal characteristics of Donne which must finally determine for him the way he is to meet the situation. First and by no means the least important is the exercise of an intense love for real experience combined with an ardent belief in the reality of the spiritual. In the greater world these two spheres exist as matter and spirit; in the lesser world, in man, where they are conjoined as body and soul, they may best be illustrated and observed. Here they are known to exist, each as a distinct kind of thing, separable, as death proves, yet in some way joined and mutually dependent.

How this union is effected is for Donne beyond rational analysis. Though death severs the knot, it is restored in the resurrection. Thus, life itself is the product of a unity in difference, whether it be life on this or the other side of the grave. This conception, not of the oneness of all things, but of the interpenetration and interdependency of all things, resulting from an intuition reinforced by deep learning and much experience, manifests itself not only in those incongruities of metaphysical poetry that were distasteful to Dr. Johnson, but also in the subtle language of *The Extasie;* in such figures as the "naked thinking heart"; [13] and in his description of Elizabeth Drury:

> . . . wee understood
> Her by her sight; her pure, and eloquent blood
> Spoke in her cheekes, and so distinctly wrought,
> That one might almost say, her body thought.[14]

Consequently, the difference between fact and idea is often obscured, so closely do the two realms impinge upon one another. To isolate pure sensory images in Donne is practically impossible; and to isolate thoughts or ideas and string them together as the expression of a system of thinking is downright futility. It is no exaggeration to say that for Donne sensory fact, the experience of the body, is ideated, and that thought, as such, exists as concretely for him as experiences of sight, taste, or touch.

Added to the above internal conditions is a native skepticism, one of the most forceful traits of his personality. Contrary to conventional opinion that doubt is a devastating and demoralizing influence, for Donne, though it does become the source of perplexity and melancholy, its effects, on the whole, are constructive—if it may be said that purging away the illusions of sense and spirit is constructive. At least, doubt was so regarded by Bacon and Descartes. It is the way we arrive at disillusionment rather than the condition itself that is painful, and it must be admitted that Donne took the painful route. He was unlike Shakespeare, whose vision seems always to have illuminated uncertainty, or Milton, whose serenity allows him to make Adam and Eve quit Paradise, reflecting that "The World was all before them, where to choose." By his fidelity to deep and sullen learning, to the demands of flesh and the promptings of a sensitive conscience, all presenting truths appearing to contradict one another, he was led into a troubled state of mind from which he never realized complete freedom.

[13] *The Blossome,* Grierson, I, 60, l. 27.
[14] *The second Anniversary, ibid.,* p. 258, ll. 243-46.

One thing, however, Donne is certain of, and that is the reality of his own experience and the sensitive machine of self which has this experience. As he early says of himself,

> . . . that I were one [a man],
> I needs must know.[15]

When skepticism has reduced all other things to the confusion of uncertain and even unknowable truths, he is thrown back upon the one constant fact of self, disturbed, nevertheless, as it may be by the awareness of the chaos without to which the inner man is unceasingly sensitive. If one dominant fact emerges from the confusion of suggestion with which Donne's writings infect the reader, it is this very thing. Consequently, when faced with the problems raised by the new philosophy, the attitude he takes is largely, if not finally, determined by this fact. "The ancient world takes its stand upon the drama of the Universe, the modern world upon the inward drama of the Soul," says Professor Whitehead in a criticism of Descartes.[16] Donne, with Descartes, is in the modern world, for it is in his own soul, the bundle of complexities compounded of the facts of sense and spirit, that the drama of his response to the new philosophy is acted. For him, it means that the self comes to life, not through an appreciation of laws such as science derives from an observation of the natural world nor of deductions such as the scholastic philosopher elaborates from his traditionally accredited premises, but from a realization of its own fullest potentialities through contact with stimuli which awaken these potentialities. What these stimuli are is determined by this self, not by a philosophical system or by scientific method, and the primary stimulus will be that which the self conceives to be essentially true. For Donne truth derives not from the separate experiences of body and soul but from the experience of both conjointly, and as demonstrated above, the spheres of matter and spirit in which they have their respective functions can no longer be harmonized under the old rationalism. Each must be known by the faculty which is best suited to know it; for the former, it is sense and reason; for the latter, faith.

No more perplexing problem than the relation of faith and reason troubled the schools, for it involved the important questions of how and to what extent man may know God, and the nature of the relation of divinity and philosophy. "Scholasticism, as perfected by Aquinas, implies the harmony of reason and faith, in the sense that both teach

---

[15] *A nocturnall upon S. Lucies day, ibid.*, p. 45, ll. 30, 31.   [16] *Op. cit.*, p. 202.

the same truths." [17] But Duns Scotus and William of Occam disturbed this harmony; reason and faith do not necessarily teach the same truths, as they function in different spheres of human activity. The intricacies of argument by which the respective claims and scope of reason and faith, intelligence and will, were elaborated by the schoolmen need not be summarized here. Nor is it necessary to detail Donne's response to this subject of disputation, for that work has been done by Professor Bredvold, who convincingly associates Donne with the less orthodox tradition.[18] At this time it is important for us to observe that the new philosophy confirmed Donne's separation of the functions of these faculties and to take note of the conditions which the Holy Scriptures imposed upon his exercise of faith and reason.

After his study of the new philosophy Donne recognizes that reason operates primarily in the realm of natural things and that faith operates in the realm of divine, for the new philosophy demonstrated that reason teaches truths that have nothing to do with divinity. In a passage cited earlier this distinction is made clear:

> Looke to mee faith, and looke to my faith, God;
> For both my centers feele this period.
> Of waight one center, one of greatnesse is;
> And Reason is that center, Faith is this;
> For into'our reason flow, and there do end
> All, that this naturall world doth comprehend:
> Quotidian things, and equidistant hence,
> Shut in, for man, in one circumference.
> But for th'enormous greatnesses, which are
> So disproportion'd, and so angulare,
> As is Gods essence, place, and providence,
> Where, how, when, what soules do, departed hence,
> These things (eccentrique else) on faith do strike;
> Yet neither all, nor upon all, alike.

But, it must be admitted,

> . . . reason, put to'her best extension,
> Almost meetes faith, and makes both centers one.[19]

If in *Biathanatos* Donne reduces the "three Lawes, of Nature, of Reason, and of God" to one, the law of nature, and makes it one with the "Christian law," it should be remembered that the subject

---

[17] Art. "Scholasticism," *Encyclopaedia Britannica* (13th ed.).
[18] *Op. cit.,* pp. 204 ff.
[19] *Elegie upon the Untimely Death of* . . . *Prince Henry,* Grierson, I, 267, ll. 1-14, 15-16. See above, pp. 104 ff.; p. 269 n. 18.

treated is a matter of conduct, not the "enormous greatnesses" of God, and that the law of God relative to human conduct is "written in our hearts," and therefore cannot be contradictory to nature and reason; [20] in fact, it is by reason that we comprehend what this law is, so inscribed within every man. Moreover, Donne's reduction is a simplification of scholastic diffuseness and intricacy, and represents a position which deep immersion in the study of the Holy Scriptures and the new philosophy does not permit him to accept in matters of pure divinity. By the time of the composition of the *Essays in Divinity* Donne is fully appreciative of the cleavage between natural philosophy and divinity and the particular limitations of the power of reason:

Men which seek God by reason, and naturall strength, (though we do not deny common notions and generall impressions of a soveraign power) are like Mariners which voyaged before the invention of the Compass, which were but Costers, and unwillingly left the sight of the land. Such are they which would arrive at God by this world, and contemplate him onely in his Creatures, and seeming Demonstration. Certainly, every Creature shewes God, as a glass, but glimeringly and transitiorily, by the frailty both of the receiver, and beholder: Our selves have his Image, as Medals, permanently and preciously delivered. But by these meditations we get no further, then to know what he *doth,* not what he *is.* But as by the use of the Compass, men safely dispatch *Vlysses* dangerous ten years travell in so many dayes, and have found out a new world richer then the old; so doth Faith, as soon as our hearts are touched with it, direct and inform it in that great search of the discovery of Gods Essence, and the new *Hierusalem,* which Reason durst not attempt. And though the faithfullest heart is not ever directly, & constantly upon God, but that it somtimes descends also to Reason; yet it is [not] thereby so departed from him, but that it still looks towards him, though not fully to him: as the Compass is ever Northward, though it decline, and have often variations towards East, and West. By this faith, as by reason, I know, that God is all that which all men can say of all Good; I beleeve he is somewhat which no man can say nor know. For, *si scirem quid Deus esset, Deus essem.* For all acquired knowledg is by degrees, and successive; but God is impartible, and only faith which can receive it all at once, can comprehend him.[21]

Donne was not, as the years proved, to swing toward extreme Protestantism, which permitted sudden impulse and wayward, unguided revelation to illuminate spiritual truth. Reason, as part of human nature, is valid and not to be denied the place wherein it can function effectively. It can give knowledge of the physical universe, thereby establishing the truth that there is a Creator and teaching what "he *doth.*"

[20] See above, p. 254.   [21] *Essays in Divinity,* pp. 37-39.

Moreover, reason makes known its own inadequacy to comprehend the greatness toward which the enlightened imagination reaches. But once the inadequacy is known, there is no plunging into the mists of fantasy; faith is no leap into the dark of spiritual illusion, for there are controls directing faith and illuminating its way until all the "cloudiness of earth" is dissolved. These directing influences are the Holy Scriptures themselves, and the historical record of the purity of the Primitive Christian Church.

In the *Essays in Divinity* Donne speaks of three books, the "eternall Decrees and Rolls of God," the book of creatures, and the Bible. The first is "impossible," being "onely insinuated and whisper'd to our hearts, *Ad informandum conscientiam Judicis,* which is the Conscience it selfe"; the second is "difficult," and though containing enough, as St. Paul says, *"to make us inexcusable,"* is not to be trusted so far as Sebund's "too abundant" credulity leads him; the third is "the book of life," "the common pasture" of all mankind. Though "even the ignorant are bid to read" this book, "the Church hath wisely hedged us in so farr, that all men may know, and cultivate, and manure their own part, and not adventure upon great reserv'd mysteries, nor trespass upon this book, without inward humility, and outward interpretations. For it is not enough to have *objects,* and *eyes* to see, but you must have *light* too." [22] As if in compensation for what reason lost in the breakdown of the old philosophy, the Holy Scriptures are given to human kind, like the freshness of revelation itself. Herein both reason and faith may operate. Reason makes clear their meaning, but only faith assures their acceptance.

The subjection of reason to these new controls, amounting to a definition of the sphere of its proper activity as far as divinity is concerned and to a criticism of medieval rationalism, places Donne in sympathy with the anti-intellectualism of the historical revolt from authority, which Professor Whitehead terms "the dominant intellectual movement of the later Renaissance." For the Reformation it meant an appeal to the purity and strength of the Primitive Church and to the authority of the Scriptures; for science it meant turning to the "brute facts" of nature as the source from which truth about the external world must proceed. For both it meant discarding accepted methods and sources and an avowal that in other circumstances will be found the true authority. It may be considered as a definite search for fundamental sources, the causes and grounds of truth, and in this respect the Ref-

---

[22] *Ibid.,* pp. 6-8. In the text Donne mentions the "book of creatures" last.

ormation and the scientific movement are aspects of the same mentality, as Professor Whitehead states in a terse summarizing remark: "The appeal to the origins of Christianity, and Francis Bacon's appeal to efficient causes as against final causes, were two sides of one movement of thought." [23]

Precisely what this anti-rationalistic movement is like may be illustrated by an episode in the Council of Trent, an episode also revealing that by the time of the Counter Reformation Catholic as well as reformed Christian had moved far enough away from the medieval ideal to perceive that authority could be determined by something other than the rationalistic method. In the year 1551 the Papal Legates presiding over the Council issued the order, "That the Divines ought to confirm their opinions with the holy Scripture, Traditions of the Apostles, sacred and approved Councells, and the Constitutions and Authorities of the Holy Fathers; that they ought to use brevitie, and avoid superfluous and unprofitable questions, and perverse contentions." Sarpi reports that "this order did not please the Italian Divines; who said it was a novitie, and a condemning of School-Divinity, which, in all difficulties, *useth reason,* & because it was not lawful [i.e., by this decree] to treat as St. Thomas [Aquinas], St. Bonaventure, and other famous men did." [24]

Though the liberal Catholic divines could go no further than to disclaim the medieval tradition and refer to what they considered the proper grounds for religious belief, the Protestant reformer could retreat still further from the practices of the schoolmen by finding in the Primitive Church the model of organization for the Christian Church, and in the Holy Scripture alone, the "efficient cause" and the "brute facts" of Christian faith. Thus Donne writes, " . . . we cannot err, if we keep with the Scriptures, and in the way that leads to Gods glory." [25] He praises "the purest and most *innocent* times, even the *infancy* of the Primitive Church," [26] cautious, however, to set the limits as close to the time of Christ and the Apostles as possible, for he was under no illusion, as he frequently makes clear, concerning the error that early crept into that "ideal" state of Christianity. Donne's disposition to regard the Scriptures as the basis for religious faith and the Reformed Church as the restoration of the model of pure antiquity has been emphasized sufficiently to remove doubt of his affinities with the phase of the Renaissance which sought to get nearer something

[23] *Op. cit.,* p. 12.
[25] *XXVI Sermons,* 14, fol. 192.
[24] *The Historie of the Councel of Trent,* p. 323.
[26] *Fifty Sermons,* 11, fol. 85.

fundamental that had been obscured by medieval traditionalism. Though such a belief may be explained as the phantom of the romantic imagination, the significance of its historical value remains.

The importance of Donne's consideration of the whole problem of reason and faith is that like Descartes he recognizes and admits the limitations of both and tries to define their respective spheres of operation. Scorning ignorance as the most degrading state of human kind, he would agree in full with Hooker's attack on those who deny any place to reason in divinity, "as if the way to be ripe in faith were to be raw in wit and judgment; as if reason were an enemy unto religion, childish simplicity the mother of ghostly and divine wisdom." [27] Because Donne lived on into the new world beyond Hooker and was familiar with the new philosophy, he came to know in a way denied to his illustrious predecessor that reason may be abused by "natural men" as well as by schoolmen and Puritans. While the new science stripped reason of many of its uses in divinity, it greatly strengthened its powers in the realm of natural philosophy. Certainly it is because Donne perceives, perhaps dimly. the dawn of an "age of reason," threatening to destroy pure religion as completely as Hooker thought Puritanism would, and to substitute for Christianity a religion of nature, that he is persuaded increasingly, without, however, impugning reason, to emphasize the necessity of faith for salvation, and to point to the vanities of the knowledge of "natural men." On Christmas day, 1621, he spoke the following memorable words:

Knowledge cannot save us, but we cannot be saved without Knowledge; Faith is not on this side Knowledge, but beyond it; we must necessarily come to Knowledge first, though we must not stay at it, when. we are come thither. For, a regenerate Christian, being now a new Creature, hath also a new facultie of Reason: and so believeth the Mysteries of Religion, out of another Reason, then as a meere naturall Man, he believed naturall and morall things. He believeth them for their own sake, by Faith, though he take Knowledge of them before, by that common Reason, and by those humane Arguments, which worke upon other men, in naturall or morall things. Divers men may walke by the Sea side, and the same beames of the Sunne giving light to them all, one gathereth by the benefit of that light pebles, or speckled shells, for curious vanitie, and another gathers precious Pearle, or medicinall Ambar, by the same light. So the common light of reason illumins us all; but one imployes this light upon the searching of impertinent vanities, another by a better use of the same light, finds out the Mysteries of Religion; and when he hath found them, loves them, not for the lights sake, but for the naturall and true worth of the thing it self. Some men by the benefit of this light of

[27] Of the Laws of Ecclesiastical Polity (7th ed.; Oxford, 1888), III, viii, § 4, p. 366.

Reason, have found out things profitable and usefull to the whole world;
. . . Others, by the benefit of this light, have searched and found the secret
corners of gaine, and profit, wheresoever they lie. . . . All the wayes, both
of *Wisdome*, and of *Craft* lie open to this light, this light of naturall reason:
But when they have gone all these wayes by the benefit of this light, they
have got no further, then to have walked by a tempestuous Sea, and to have
gathered pebles, and speckled cockle shells. Their light seems to be great out
of the same reason, that a Torch in a misty night, seemeth greater then in a
clear, because it hath kindled and inflamed much thicke and grosse Ayre
round about it. . . .

But, if thou canst take this light of reason that is in thee (. . . and cherish
that, and exalt that, so that that bring thee to a *love of the Scriptures,* and
that *love to a beleefe* of the truth thereof, and that *historicall faith* to a *faith
of application, of appropriation,* that as all those things were certainly done,
so they were certainly done *for thee*) thou shalt never envy the lustre and
glory of the great lights of worldly men, which are great by the infirmity of
others, or by their own opinion, great because others think them great, or
because they think themselves so, but thou shalt finde, that howsoever they
magnifie their lights, their wit, their learning, their industry, their fortune,
their favour, and *sacrifice to their owne nets,* yet thou shalt see, that thou by
thy small light hast gathered *Pearle* and *Amber,* and they by their great
lights nothing but shels and pebles; they have determined the light of nature,
upon the booke of nature, this world, and thou hast carried the light of
nature higher, thy naturall reason, and even *humane arguments,* have brought
thee to read the Scriptures, and to that *love,* God hath set to the seale of
faith. Their light shall set at noone, . . . and thy light shall grow up, from
a *faire hope,* to a modest assurance and *infallibility,* that that light shall never
go out, nor the *works of darknesse,* nor the *Prince of darknesse* ever prevaile
upon thee, but as thy light of *reason* is exalted by *faith* here, so thy light of
faith shall be exalted into the light *of glory,* and fruition in the Kingdome
of heaven.[28]

Thus, though reason may become the instrument of faith, in itself it
cannot lead to faith; paradoxically, it leads but to the recognition of
its own limitation, the appreciation that the mind is in the presence
of something greater than itself; this is the state of "wonder," the
"first step to faith." What proceeds beyond, if reason is bent upon
things divine, must be left to the poetic imagination to describe, for
it is as the poet that Donne speaks of "admiration," "wonder," standing in the midst "Betweene knowledge and faith":

The first step to faith, is to wonder, to stand, and consider with a holy
admiration, the waies and proceedings of God with man: for Admiration,
wonder, stands in the midst, betweene knowledge and faith, and hath an eye

[28] *Fifty Sermons,* 36, fols. 325, 326, 327.

towards both. If I know a thing, or beleeve a thing, I do no longer wonder: but when I finde that I have reason to stop upon the consideration of a thing, so, as that I see enough to induce admiration, to make me wonder, I come by that step, and God leads me by that hand, to a knowledge, if it be of a naturall or civill thing, or to a faith, if it be a supernaturall, and spirituall thing.[29]

A striking thing to note about the phase of Donne's thinking that we have been considering—or about any other for that matter—is that we cannot treat it dogmatically. Donne does not fit into classifications, and so personal is his attitude toward any subject that we cannot associate him with specific and well-defined currents of opinion or schools of thought. He is neither a Galileo, consciously and exultantly clearing a way over which the advancement of learning may proceed beyond the past; nor is he a reactionary, like Clavius, declaring that the new discoveries and the new ideas of his age are but hallucinations and illusions. He can cast a sympathetic eye upon the past without allowing his eagerness for the present to relax. Under the influence of a native love for all human experience, combined with an equally strong distrust for the permanent significance of these experiences, he finds his world extremely interesting, if not thoroughly satisfactory. If at times he seems to veer with the traditional winds of doctrine and at others to swing into the current of contemporary influences, it is not because he is wanting in the critical acumen to make a choice between the two. But any inclination to make such a choice is firmly subordinated to a higher wisdom, which, respecting the Self above the external conditions of the world, dictates the sense of the relative value of these conditions. This wisdom causes him to move, neither indifferent to, nor above, but among the divergent opinions and contradictory facts of life.

Thus, for Donne mortal life is kaleidoscopic. Turned as it may be by reason or by the free play of emotion or by the unified activity of both, it produces daily from the manifold appearances of the world a various and changing pattern of things. The figures formed by man's ways of regarding friends, love, enemies, books, and the daily bread— the common facts of life—and also by his ways of regarding the greater world and God are resolved continually into new shapes. Throughout the shifting patterns but one thing is fixed and constant, and that is the light revealing and illuminating these patterns. The source of this light is the vividness and intensity of the poet's consistently sensitive personality.

[29] *LXXX Sermons,* 20, fol. 194.

INDEX